Trump
Is a
Four Letter Word

Trump
Is a
Four Letter Word

Gateways Books and Tapes
Nevada City, California

Distributed by Gateways Books and Tapes
P.O. Box 370
Nevada City, CA 95959
1-800-869-0658

www.idhhb.com
www.gatewaysbooksandtapes.com
ISBNs:
Trade Paperback 978-0-89556-144-2
Pdf   978-0-89556-622-5
Epub   978-0-89556-635-5
Kindle   978-0-89556-623-2
Mobi   978-0-89556-624-9

Library of Congress Cataloging-in-Publication Data

Names: Gold, E.J., author.
Title: Trump is a 4-letter Word / E.J. Gold.
Other titles: Trump is a four-letter word
Description: Nevada City, CA : Gateways Books and Tapes, 2018.
Identifiers: LCCN (print) | LCCN 2018001151 (ebook) | ISBN 9780895566225 (pdf) | ISBN 9780895561442 (pbk.)
Subjects: LCSH: Trump, Donald, 1946- | United States--Politics and government--2017-
Classification: LCC E912 (ebook) | LCC E912 .G65 2018 (print) | DDC 973.933092--dc23
LC record available at https://lccn.loc.gov/2018000840

Trump Is a Four Letter Word

Table of Contents

INTRODUCTION
More Science High School Yearbook
June 14, 2017

On a lunch break at More Science High. Party On, Dudes!!!
Rufus Lives!!!

As you probably already know from the CNN, FOX and CNBC news media, I'm a visitor on "Guest" status with the U.S. Government, from the 37th century.

Oh, not your 37th century. You live in a SIM — a World-Simulation — and SIMS don't have time, not in the sense you're thinking of it.

Here in the 37th century, I'm enrolled as a sophomore in high school — More Science High — and I have a small grade problem. I'm presently carrying a D-Minus, slightly lower than a plain D Minus.

My classroom participation rated me an A+ and I have my hand in the air all the time at a pop quiz, don't you?

I get A and A+ test scores all the time, but that's dragged down slightly by an "F" in homework — I've yet to crack a textbook or do a homework assignment, because when I get home, I have a responsibility to my online clan to defend the base until dinner time.

Okay, so how does this affect YOU?

Well, technically, I AM you, and this is just another letter to yourself reminding yourself to wake up and live.

Waking up is hard to do.

Cindy 5-0 sports a new pair of sunglasses from Rigel IV.

If you can Remember Yourself, you can at least get a grip on it. In order to Self-Study or gain Self-Knowledge, you need to have some idea of what and where the "Self" actually is, because dollars to donuts, it isn't "in your body".

I'll explain in detail.

Here in the 37th century, I'm at my desk writing this blog, but inside the quantumized SIM machine in the History Lab at More Science High, I'm at my desk writing this blog. Can you see the difference?

Okay, let's go through the steps, until you remember THE KEY, and regain your presence here in the 37th century.

When you get THE KEY, you will immediately transfer your identity back to the PRESENT TIME, which is 4:08 Thursday here at

More Science High, but of course it's ALWAYS 4:08 Thursday here in the 37th century, but you knew that.

So let's review the situation:

You're sitting at what looks to you like a computer somewhere in the 21st century of Earth History, but you KNOW that actually your forehead is stuck to the SIM MACHINE here in the 37th century, and that the 21st century is constructed from a compound collection of historical data gleaned from the wreckage of the human race.

Fact is, we don't really know much about the 21st century. We're just beginning to learn a little, and we're probably not going to like it, from what I've seen.

Voncha Segdellia arrived back in the 37th century to tell us about Donald Trump.

War, hunger, pestilence.

Here in the 37th century at the History Lab, we have similar angst — Life-Pain. For instance, this morning, just after the class-change bell, I arrived here to discover that the Glarg Machine is out of order, so there goes MY lunch break.

I gulped down several cups of scalding hot Joke-a-Macha, logged on to 21st century Earth, and here I am to tell the tale.

Took rebirth somewhere around Pearl Harbor and the New York World's Fair, my double target for destination, and I've been at it ever since, collecting data for Professor Wasserman's "21st Century History" Term Report.

While here, I happened one day to watch one of your movies, entitled "Bill and Ted's Excellent Adventure", in which they persuade or capture several historical figures and bring them back to their time-frame to explain themselves.

Socrates does a marvelous job, and Billy the Kid is an obvious choice — he turned out to be much less cooperative when I tried to convince him to sign on to our high school project than in the film.

It wouldn't be so lonely here if we had one of those 56 position History SIMS.

Of course, not everyone you meet in the SIM is a student. Almost all of the 8 BILLION HUMAN-STYLE CHAT-BOTS that inhabit the Earth are empty, devoid of content, driverless cars.

You'll note a few taxicabs in the swarm of humanity — those will be the monitors, also known as "aliens" or "extraterrestrials".

When Georgio pronounces the word "extraterrestrials", it comes out "Extratesticles". It's hard not to laugh out loud.

So here at More Science High, we have a first-class high-tech History Lab, inside which is a 36-position HISTORY SIM.

It's not your ordinary High School History Sim, either. It's a Zeiss Hybrid World Projector, the kind with the 360-degree full-immersion and The Tingle, which allows you to actually feel and sense everything that's happening to your Avatar inside the world-SIM.

If you're able to Remember Yourself, you ought to be able to control your passage through the SIM. If not, you'll identify with the local lifeforms and you'll actually BECOME your History SIM personality, haw, haw.

It happens to the best of us.

Every teenager in the 37th century learns to live with those mistakes. I once thought I was actually a human being living on Planet Earth in the 29th century, where there's plenty of sex, drugs and rock-and-roll, in which anyone could get easily lost, and I'll bet you've had that experience at least once.

As if it's not bad enough to hang out in the organic world, we gotta hang on on Planet Earth — talk about pain, and then add in Donald Trump and you get nothing but insult added to injury.

Doctor tells patient: "You're sick." Patient replies, "I want to get a second opinion." Doctor says, "Okay. You're ugly, too.".

The only remedy I know of for identification is Transcendence, and the only way to achieve that is to take the World Sim Course at your local Blue Line Academy inside the SIM.

The first time you walk out onto a busy commercial street and the "Sea of Robots" Vision is granted to you, you will work hard to find your fellow students among the faceless mob.

We all bring bag lunches to school — we don't have government here.

Faceless mobs are what it's all about. The History SIM is very limited in resources, as you can well imagine.

You can see from the screen graphics behind your eyes that there's not a lot of pixels to go around, hence the SIM offers closeup views or wide-angle views, but they both contain the same number of attention-points, get it?

Okay, so it's easy to dis-identify when you're Blue-Lining, because you step outside the SIM for a while when working a map in the GODD® Engine, which hooks up to the History SIM by reason of identity — it's a quantum-connected double of the SIM.

Well, it's a SIM of a SIM, as it were.

When you "die", you merely withdraw through the crown of the cranium, flying backwards ever more rapidly toward the PRESENT TIME, until you snap back into your forehead — into your "Third Eye" — and wham, there you are, back home, safe and sound.

NOTHING BAD can happen to you in the History SIM, and even if you get killed or die of some disease or whatever, you'll just snap back to PRESENT TIME when you separate out of the organic body.

Yes, it's organic. The whole universe is alive — the strings of galaxies are the nervous system of the History SIM, to which humans of Planet Earth refer as "God". How quaint is that???

How many fellow students can you locate inside the SIM? Well, there are a total of 36 positions around the History SIM, so do the math — which I failed totally, along with chemistry.

In Physics, I got an "A". I usually do. It's History, Math and Chemistry that brings me down.

If you're feeling lonely inside the SIM, don't depend on the Chat-Bots to reduce that Sad Effect that comes from feeling alone, because it's no consolation to have the pity of human biological robots, nor the approbation of monkeys, although between the two, I'll take the monkeys.

The History SIM is a friendly place and as much fun as Disneyland, if you know the Rules and can SEE where you are.

It also helps to Know Thyself, so get your "Thy" there, and fast. There isn't much time left on the History SIM, and I'm running out of Quarters.

If you need a Proctor, they're called "Angels" inside the History SIM, just press the "HELP" button at the SIM Interface.

If you can't push the button, you're in worse shape than I thought. Better get your ass to a HISTORY SIM WORKSHOP or CLINIC to straighten out your relationship with the SIM before it's too late and you end up getting your own ass handed to you in a plastic cup.

Don't wait until it's too late.

The History SIM is set to explode at midnight.

It's not our fault — some senior grade practical jokers came in during the night and planted a stink bomb in the SIM.

They were kind enough to warn us lower classmembers beforehand, so we could hold our noses while the BIG FART went off.

We're not sure exactly when it's due to CUT THE CHEESE — nobody, including me, thought to ask them, so we're all holding our noses all the time, until it happens.

Already it's starting to stink, starting with Washington, D.C.. When the congress people start throwing bullshit, catshit, horseshit and dogshit around in congressional sessions, you'll know that the End is Near.

Who knew the 21st century was going to be such fun???

How Can I Create a Trump-Free Zone in my Home or Office?

January 27, 2017

This has all happened before. Can you remember? Try your PLS — Past Life Survey — to see how it all played out before, and how it will play out again!!!

Don't want to hear about Trump's latest outrage? Don't really give a shit whether he's insane or not? Want a little peace of mind and privacy? Don't give up the ghost, there's hope. I bring the TRUMP-FREE ZONE effects modules. BLOCK TRUMPISM with my TFZ — Trump-Free Zone — devices.

I don't hate Trump, although I have every reason to. He's about to destroy my personal freedoms, my healthcare benefits, my retirement, my real estate values, my stocks and bonds, and my family's freedom from fear and oppression, but that's HIS problem, not mine. I can live with it, but most folks will find domination by the rich to be unbearably oppressive. What's more, by his own personal example, he's made Nazi Propaganda a national sport, so what can you DO about it?

I know it's a shock to suddenly find yourself living in an upside-down world in which America is OFFICIALLY racist, but there IS something you CAN DO about it right now, and none of it involves getting rid of Trump — that will happen on its own. It will fall off all by itself after a while.

Up until now, Trump has just been a somewhat shady public figure, but now he's out in the open, and he's in charge, which means that BILLIONS of people will soon learn to FEAR Trump, if they don't actually hate him.

He doesn't care what you think about him, just so long as every waking moment of your life is consumed with TRUMP.

Americans have aligned themselves with the ideals espoused by Donald Trump, and therefore expose themselves and America in general as a racist state, and according to all the shootings and beatings, they like it there.

Like it or not, you're now lumped in with a bunch of white supremacists and upper class bastards who care nothing for the misery they cause on the poor and disenfranchised, and have especial dislike for those unable to defend themselves, always the mark of a coward, and understandably, you're ashamed to admit that you're an American.

Americans voted Trump into power, so clearly he embodies their American Ideal of White Supremacy and Isolationism. You're an American. Try going overseas now, and see what that buys you.

Totally dispassionately, in full objective professional assessment, he's a ravenous beast who needs to be fed with human flesh, but as politicians go, he's pretty much the average political shuck, but with a difference — he's a walloping, raging NPD — Narcissistic Personality Disorder.

That means he needs a LOT of attention, praise and respect, none of which he'll get, in the end.

He's a bully with a BIG stick, the U.S. Military and the Intelligence Community, neither of which he trusts. Trust Issues are a big thing with NPDs, and eventually that's what will trip him up — he doesn't trust his closest advisers.

Trump doesn't actually have a plan. It's always a new day, always a new idea. He can't sit still, doesn't know the meaning of the word "serenity" and has no respite from the hell of his own personal Angst.

He works on the fly, improvising at all times, trusting no one's judgment but his own, using every opening, every advantage, to create action of any kind. It doesn't much matter what happens, as long as he's at the center of it. He gets results through the lavish use of Overwhelm and Rage, as you've seen.

His primary weapon is to turn others against others, engendering fear and distrust, his own personal symptoms of his terrible need to satisfy the lusts of his NPD brain.

NPDs need lots of attention, which they didn't get from Mommy and Daddy when they were young.

He hates Mexicans, this we already know, and now the Mexicans know it, too. When he reads this blog — and he will, because he's not only an NPD, but an OCD — suffering from an Obsessive Compulsive Disorder — I'll be top on his revenge list, and like every NPD, you can be sure he has one, and if your name appears on the Impeachment Referendum list, he'll say you're an Illegal, which in his mind is the same as saying you're Hispanic.

He aligns himself perfectly with the Neo-Nazis in his views of other races and religions, and plays the HATE card pretty much all the time. The NPD's favorite game is to divide others and watch them fight it out, then he wades in and takes the victory, the glory and, of course, the money, and most importantly, the ATTENTION — and that's the key right there.

NPDs are all about getting attention, and they'll use any means at their disposal to get it, too. You just happen to be one of those "disposables" that might have to be dumped in the process of making him feel better about himself.

The history books will be re-written after the Trump family's total domination, but for a while, it will appear that he has beaten down the liberals forever, and gotten rid of a lot of the troublesome lower classes. We were scum anyway, right?

Greed is another not so nice feature of T-Rump's psycho makeup. He needs a LOT of money, a LOT of power and a LOT of people jumping at his command. His howling rage is evident on his face ALL the time — although it was impossible not to photographically compare George Bush to a chimpanzee, which was a popular sweatshirt back in the day — and it's not likely to get any better, because another charming trait of the NPD is PARANOIA, and Trump exhibits that in massive quantities.

Your entire personal net worth and personal freedoms, plus your sense of personal safety and freedom from fear, is now being targeted by his administration, and you need to take some action to prevent them from taking absolutely everything, including your home, your children and your savings, and that means some MAGICAL umbrella of protection, because the police, the army, the navy, the air force, the marines, the coast guard and the IRS are all on his side, and as of now, they're all against YOU and your children.

Yes, your children. Workers are needed for road repair. If you're an inmate, you can be forced to work at a menial task for no pay.

The American Infrastructure is collapsing due to a serious lack of free workers, such as slaves or prison inmates — which works out the same, experientially. You look to them like a candidate for a chain gang, my friend, and that's what you could well end up in, if you don't walk the Party Line, as Russian, Chinese and North Korean workers learned to do, or die.

Then there's your Freedom of Speech. He has issues with that.

Everyone, especially YOU, represented by the LIBERAL PRESS, is out to get him, and if they aren't now, he makes damn sure they are by the time he gets through with them.

If he weren't actually the President of the United States, he'd probably still be convinced that the CIA had a chopper parked over his house, the IRS had secret agents infiltrating his financial empire, and that the aliens are out to abduct him.

I'm in touch with the Greys and Orion Group, and they assure me that they want nothing to do with him. They're afraid that if they hold him for ransom, they'd end up having to pay us plenty, to get us to take him back.

I can't take credit for the gag in the above paragraph. It's based on a 1910 short story by O. Henry, first published in The *Saturday Evening Post*, about two kidnappers who capture a spoiled brat and end up having to pay the father to take the kid back.

Flag-Waving and Religious Fervor wins the crowd over every time.

This idea has grown into an iconical theme for many children's television shows and plays, which enjoy the concept of the captive actually enjoying captivity and liking his captors, who end up having the tables turned on them.

FEAR is another great driver of the NPD. His mommy probably turned out the light too early, and refused him a drink of water, and didn't leave the hall light on, and the monsters must have crowded around his bed and scared him plenty.

He has a serious problem being alone at night, which is not a terrific tendency in a U.S. President — indeed, a leader, doctor or priest is going to live a very public life. In those professions, you're "on call" all the time.

Trump gets bored VERY easily; we see this in his public appearances over a period of more than a few minutes, and this will eventually lead to his playing with the army — every boy his age loves to have his own private army, and Blackthorn is built to order for the wannabe dictator.

I assured you right at the beginning that I have no feelings toward or about Trump whatever, and that's completely true.

I regard him as a sign of bad times. People want the problem to just go away, and they'll pay anything to some pied piper who says he can lead the rats out of town. Every dictator starts out that way, and he's no exception.

Will he succeed?

Hell, no. In Future History, I can guarantee that Trump is the most vilified and contemptible creature amongst all the U.S. Presidents, but that's no compensation to the poor, to American women, to gays, to workers of all races, creeds and colors, for all the harm he causes to the American Ideal, freedom and equality for all.

Still, it's not my problem. I'm here to observe, and this is NOT my planet, nor is it yours. I prefer to live in a Trump-Free Zone, meaning minus the media frenzy that he's compelled by his illness to stir up.

What's wanted is not a "Trump Go Away" prayer. In my opinion, anyone in that office should be subject to humiliation — it's good deflation practice for anyone in the public trust.

What's needed is a SHIELD against TRUMPISM — which means the media impact on your life every day is somewhat reduced or vanishes altogether. We're talking about how he impinges on your daily life, and that's what needs reduction.

You'll also want a shield against Trump's programs that cause you pain, such as loss of medical coverage of any kind, loss of social security benefits, loss of personal freedoms, all of which is just down the road from here.

Is there any refuge?

No, there's nowhere to which you can run. He has plans for Canada, plans for Mexico, and he has friends out there who have their own private armies, control world banking, and the stock market, the real estate market and every other market you can name including drugs and prostitution.

It's all out there on the table. Oppressive Bullies gang up on the peaceful folks, and they take it, and take it, and take it, until it boils over, at which point, the bullies wonder why they end up having to confront an enraged and uncontrollable mob, like Mussolini and his mistress.

By the way, there are a LOT of comparisons of Trump to Hitler, but those my age remember Mussolini's postures and tone, and THAT's what Trump is imitating, more or less. Watch a little footage of Mussolini, and you'll see what I mean.

It's a feature of NPDs that they like a LOT of controversy, a LOT of conversation about them — they missed it when they were little, and they have to make up for lost time now.

If you want a real rundown on NPD, read "My Life as a Boy" Volumes 1 and 2. If you haven't read those books AND "SlimeWars", you have no clue what you're in for over the next six centuries.

It's all in the books, including this period of the U.S. Presidency. I made predictions back in the 1970s that are coming true today. Check it out, then take the necessary steps to protect yourself — the best way is to remove yourself from the trouble area.

If you're an intellectual, a scientist, a teacher or a liberal politician, you'll find yourself living in a different country or you won't be alive at all. It isn't the government there, it's the people, driven to mob action.

It's suddenly okay to beat up an old person, because one of our leaders hates seniors, or Jews, or blacks or whatever the current scapegoat turns out to be, and they do change. If you're name's not on the hate list now, it soon will be, depend on it.

If you stand by silently and watch people being taken away for speaking their mind, you'll soon find yourself being taken away your own self.

NPDs need reinforcement, agreement and acknowledgment to make them feel better.

I'm not suggesting action. I'm suggesting you put a shielding blanket over yourself, your family and your home, to protect yourself against the coming storm.

I'm now 75 years out of port, heading for home. I would have retired ten years ago at the age of 65, but nobody I know can afford to do that these days.

I figure that I'm going to lose all my medicare benefits and social security, upon which I depend mightily, so I better raise some money to pay my medical bills and personal items, such as soap and toothpaste, so here goes:

TFZ ITEMS FOR SALE —

Note: These items are priced to sell, to encourage as many folks as possible to protect themselves from personal impact. They may work for you, to keep your peaceful space both peaceful and serene, but don't look to me for an example of how well these things work — don't forget that, if not before, then certainly as of today, I'm the top name on Trump's shit list.

SILVER and GOLD TFZ EMBOSSED RING — SALE PRICE: $225. Stunning handmade embossed ring, very fancy and very fine piece of personal adornment, but the main idea is protection from impact and impingement on your personal life, and this will do the trick. It IS a Ring of Power. Keep it safe, keep it secret.

EMBOSSED COPPER DOLLAR-SIZED TFZ MEDALLION — SALE PRICE: $225. Encased in a Red-Velvet Lined Acrylic Capsule. Can be carried in pocket or purse, used bedside, as home or door protection, placed in safe deposit, great in combinations of four or eight for home feng-shui, for a completely Trump-Free Home.

EMBOSSED COPPER DOLLAR-SIZED TFZ EARRINGS — SALE PRICE: $225. These are simple copper disks on blackcore mounting boards, with standard French style ear-wires. They are light and easy to wear. If you lose one, I replace it free — once, but you pay postage — no problem.

EMBOSSED SILVER-RIMMED DOLLAR SIZED TFZ EARRINGS — SALE PRICE $375. It seems like a lot of money for a pair of earrings, until you translate that into candy bars and gas tank fillings. These use coin-edged bezels and I can't bring the price down any further, sorry.

GEMSTONE COPPER TFZ SPELLCASTER RING — $225. I can't get the price down any further than this, because of the unusual nature of the stone and the amount of sheer painful labor needed to make one of these puppies. It uses three elements of magic — Contagion, Similarity and Name — to create its effect, and what an effect! The stone is ancient and carries a very powerful contact with some of my Angelic friends. This is the best Ring of Power for a TFZ, in my opinion, and is the hand-held unit that I'd personally opt to wear on a daily basis. Comes in all sizes, including quarter-size, because each one is handmade to your personal order.

EMBOSSED COPPER PENNY-SIZED FANCY SILVER BEZEL TFZ AMULET — $225. Just try making one of these tiny things with all that embossing in there, making the right moves at the right time, crowding all the info into the copper field — and it all has to be in there, just right, to make it work.

EMBOSSED COPPER DIME-SIZED FANCY SILVER BEZEL TFZ AMULET — $225. If you think a copper disk the size of a penny is hard to emboss, just try a dime-sized piece to really throw your eyeballs into a frenzy.

EMBOSSED COPPER PENNY SIZED COIN-EDGE BEZEL EARRINGS — $375. I make two very tiny embossed copper disk pieces, then fit them into sterling silver coin-edged bezels, and affix ear wires to those, and there you have it, total personal protection from the Trump Vibe.

16"x20" FRAMED TFZ THANGKA — $450. This is a high-grade, very high-quality thangka of protection against the Trump Vibrations, and can be used in any home or office setting.

EMBOSSED 24K GOLD TFZ DISK IN ACRYLIC CAPSULE — $850. Pure, solid 24K gold disk, hand-embossed with prayers to keep your TFZ intact and unviolated. Keep this with any valuables, or in your safe deposit box, to prevent Trump from taking that, too, along with all the rest. Beware — during the Great Depression, banks prevented customers from accessing their safety deposit boxes, so many people lost their homes and farms. Yes, this has all happened before. Those who don't know their history are doomed to repeat it, just like you did with your personal relationships.

ALL-HERBAL TFZ INCENSE — $9.95 PER PACK. Seven-Day Supply of special handmade Tibetan TFZ Incense.

SPECIAL TFZ AROMATIC ESSENTIAL OIL — $35 PER 2 DRAM VIAL. Wear it, use it to dress a beeswax candle, burn it on charcoal or in an essential oil heater. This is compounded to SHEILD the space from unwanted influences.

TFZ AMULET — $375. Radio CQR Amulet formulated to create a personal TMZ around yourself. Peace, Freedom, Serenity and Easy Breathing. DON'T LET TRUMPISM BRING YOU DOWN!!! Stay High, Stay Calm, with TFZ!!!

TFZ SUPERBEACON DEFLECTOR — $225. Copper disk in an acrylic capsule for your Cloud Chamber. Use it with your SuperBeacon to create a TFZ in a larger space, such as an apartment building or an ashram, or a church, synagogue, temple or holy place. Make certain that your sacred spaces are not invaded by Trump's Minions.

I'll be producing more products along these lines, unless they come to take me away, which in these times is more likely than not, so stay tuned for developments, especially after having written this potentially easily misunderstood blog.

I remind you that neither the dinosaurs nor Neanderthals have died out. There are plenty of Neanderthals out there, and most of them have little or no restraint. Remember that the object is not to get rid of Trump — there are worse bastards than him, waiting in the wings — but to get the kerfuffle — the misery — out of your face.

NPDs need a LOT of attention, and will do just about anything to get it, which makes them dangerous. This can easily include off-hand remarks or actions that infuriate or enrage people, which to an NPD mind, certainly counts as "getting attention".

The whole goal of the NPD is to get attention. Keep this in mind as you helplessly watch the inevitable result of this illness being magnified by personal power — he is the most powerful single person in the world today and is enjoying every moment of it — poised menacingly and mockingly, with one finger on the nuclear trigger at all times.

Do you recall ever having been as impacted by a presidential campaign or presidency before? That's because they didn't need the attention the way Trump does. This is a little boy with a dangerous toy, the United States of America, and you're not gonna like how this kid plays the game — he cheats on his taxes, cheats on his Constitutional constraints, and he definitely cheats on his wife, and who could blame him?

An NPD will tell you anything, make up any story, tell any lie, to get attention.

As I've said many times before, I have no axe to grind — this is not my planet and even if it were, I would normally not give a shit who's running it. For the past 75 years, I've been barely aware of the President of the United States and his opinions, actions and attitudes, but all of a sudden, that's all there is on the news, that's all the conversation you hear:

"Do you believe what that asshole did TODAY???" You'll hear that on the street, and there's only one person to whom that could possibly relate in these times of trouble and tribulation.

In my opinion, Carrol O'Connor is to blame for the whole thing — he made Archie Bunker seem lovable, but on examination, you can see in a minute that he isn't. The show "All in the Family" was just another of those 20th century television shows that exploited the latest news stories, fads and fashions, as did its primary intellectual competitor, "Gilligan's Island".

Do you really want your children to imitate the President of the United States? They now think that being a bigot is okay, because the President is openly a bigot, a woman-hater who despises the poor, degrades his many mistresses and counts his score against his enemies, of whom he creates more every day.

I don't want to be a part of that scene, and I don't want that Nazi style influence on my family, so I want to establish a beach-head in my home, my office and my den, that is a TRUMP-FREE ZONE.

Get all the attention you want, Mr. Trump — just keep me out of it.

I guess most people would call this blog "Trump Bashing", but back in the not-so-distant past, we used to refer to it as "Free Speech".

You have every right to disagree, but not the right — and surely not the power — to shut me up.

Enjoy the next few miserable, stinking, befouled years of the same crap. Sooner or later, you'll want one of my TFZ items, unless you've waited too long, and it's too late to protect yourself.

Think of these TFZ items sort of like ear-plugs. They don't actually stop the drumming, they just stop the noise.

The Word-Processor is Mightier Than the Particle Accelerator
January 29, 2017

I got one vote in the recent election, but there was massive voter fraud.

I remember Woodie Guthrie's guitar. It was emblazoned with a clumsy hand painted scrawl that said "this guitar kills fascists". There's a video, "Power of Song", in which Pete Seeger shows how to bring about change, real change, by empowering the people.

I can't say whether there was voter fraud in the last election — I think it might very well be the last — but I can say with certainty that no one has even considered counting the VOODOO VOTE. Voodoo practitioners are uncounted — just try to take a survey and see what happens to you.

By my rough estimate, there are approximately 259 MILLION people out there who have their backs up against the wall, facing forced exile from friends, family and supportive jobs, which means, there goes the rest of the family right with them.

Have you ever found yourself wondering what to do in order to protect yourself, your family, your home, your business, your social security, your medical benefits and coverage and your personal freedoms FROM YOUR OWN FUCKING PRESIDENT???

Okay, so what's that got to do with anything?

Well, I'll tell you. People feel helpless. Just helpless. They're faced with the biggest, richest bully they've ever seen in their lives, and he has banker friends who can help him finance his own "Blackwater" private army if he takes it into his mangled head to overthrow himself, as Nero and Caligula did Back in The Day.

Magic, both black and white, is always popular among the poor and disenfranchised, because what else have you got, to give you enough hope to carry on? All ordinary avenues of expression and family and home and job protection is unavailable to you — you're just a working stiff, with no real voice. There is no popular vote, just the machine.

The thing is, there are some highly experienced voodoo queens out there, along with a large number of wannabe Harry Potters with the Official Harry Potter Magic Wand and Sorcery Kit — which really does exist, you can find it on eBay — not to mention all the spellcasters from a wide variety of cultures and backgrounds, even off-world in a few cases.

There are sorcerers, wizards, shamans, all sorts of magic-users in this world, and there's no reason to suppose that they won't use it, when deprived of a voting voice by the Electoral College, whatever the fuck THAT'S supposed to be.

My point is that they are threatened by the Trump Administration.

Every weirdo in America is under direct threat from the Fourth Reich.

So, if I were the kind of magic-user that took offense and felt aggrieved and under attack from the New Washington (see "SlimeWars" for what this really means, forecast with names, dates and places over 45 years ago at its first publication), I'd probably use my most bizarre magical spells to protect myself and my family and friends and lifestyle and freedoms.

I wouldn't want to see things like these on the Psychic Wizard Market:

TRUMPLESTILSKIN MENTAL ITCHING POWDER — This works intermittently, in sporadic randomly timed unguessable and indeterminate time patterns, to make any Trump itch uncontrollably, for just a few seconds at a time.

TRUMPLESTILSKIN MENTAL WHOOPEE CUSHION — Whenever you activate this spell, all Trumps will emit an odorless, harmless fart sound from their rear end.

TRUMPLESTILSKIN MENTAL HOT-FOOT — Gives any and all Trumps the definite mental sensation of having a hot-foot administered to them. Great for parties and other public gatherings.

TRUMPLESTILSKIN MENTAL JOY-BUZZER — When activated, this paranormal quantum effect gives Trumps the sensation of having their right palm tickled for just a second or two.

TRUMPLESTILSKIN MENTAL FLY-IN-PLASTIC-ICECUBE — Not a copy, this is the original mental fly in the plastic ice cube, made even funnier by the fact that it's strictly mental, and no one else in the room can see it.

TRUMPLESTILSKIN FAKE VOMIT — I've been asked politely to please not describe this effect in detail.

TRUMPLESTILSKIN DOGGIE-DOO — A Plastic Poo Pyramid that emits a foul odor and a smoky, greenish haze that will fool your friends.

TRUMPLESTILSKIN HAIRPIECE — Not a copy, this is the Real Thing. Not only is it wearable, it's alive!

TRUMPLESTILSKIN GORILLA MASK — Don't just bust your seams. Now you can LOOK exactly like the Raging Gorilla that's inside you, just bursting to get out! Have your way every time! Overwhelm! Break their shit!

TRUMPLESTILSKIN BRAIN TEASER — Just joking —

there's no sign of a brain.

THE PLAN

Gosh, I wouldn't even bring the situation up about all those Wizards and Warlocks and other magic-users out there just itching to get hold of some of that powder, but you don't really want the karma of the Dark Side magic stuff, right?

I hope not, because the result is never what you expect or want. To avoid bad karma, do NONE of the above. Instead, I propose the following remedies for the politically helpless:

TRUMPLESTILSKIN COMEDY ROUTINE — $9.95 — What better way to handle Trump and Trumpism than rough-and-tumble Trumplestilskin comedy? Gags written just for you, by Leslie Ann, personally pointed and barbed to hit home, all constructed for your personal delivery, and don't worry about the content of the act. She concentrates on his weak points, like his mind.

TRUMPLESTILSKIN VENTRILOQUIST DOLL — $350 — Professional vent dolls can run into the tens of thousands of dollars. I charge what I have to in order to pay folks to do some mechanicals on the doll. You can use mine, or you can make your own Trumplestilskin Vent Doll, with a used suit filled with dacron, a small ordinary volleyball, and a used mop.

TRUMPLESTILSKIN MAGIC ACT — $350 — I've created a complete magic act using a Trumplestilskin Doll as a prop. You send him into a different dimension, change him into a pig, make him vanish, reappear and perform a card trick. Your crowd will roar with belly-laughs at his shenanigans.

THE TRUMPLES COMIC BOOK — P.O.R. — Includes my template and designs for the Trumpies At Home, and other comic book fantasies.

THE TRUMPLES SATURDAY MORNING CARTOON SHOW — P.O.R. — Lin Larsen and I design the characters and the environment for the show. We produce the final result and guarantee a new show every week for a 26-week run. You are responsible for the broadcast costs, but on the other hand, you get the income from the advertising.

ELVIS TRUMPLEY IMPERSONATOR ACT — P.O.R. — You get the entire Claude Needham Elvis Trumpley Costume, an Original

16

Customized Weird Hand-painted Guitar with Full Cast Signed pickguard, the iconic black-and-white checkered Land's End wool shirt, and much, much more. We'll even help you make a video for YouTube with you as Elvis Trumpley, of course.

SEVEN NO-TRUMP, A BROADWAY MUSICAL REVUE — P.O.R. — Impress your friends and family when you tell them that you're backing a Broadway Musical Revue! Wow, will they be surprised, and you will be too, when they call the men in white coats — but wait! They'd be making a mistake. This show will be bigger than "Springtime for Hitler"!

TRUMPLESTILSKIN EFFIGY — P.O.R. — I provide the original and the mold to make this incredible crushable talking doll that looks like it came right out of the pages of the Brothers Grimm, you manufacture and market it worldwide. You will be thrilled at my incredible marketing plan for these little Point-of-Purchase Countertop Register Items that are just perfect for those family picnics and barbecues. These little puppies are CUTE as a PUSSY, and we have the offshore people to manufacture them cheap as dirt.

TRUMPLESTILSKIN CHEAP GARDEN PRODUCE — Picked by Unpaid Workers Living in Paper Shacks and eating out of paper plates — I predict that this is gonna be my hottest product. Talk to my people about rights and marketing plans for this incredible, cheap-like-dirt product, which comes directly from The Wall. Hey, remember the Berlin Wall? The Great Wall of China? The Pink Floyd album? Get your lettuce before it wilts.

TRUMPLESTILSKIN "NO MAKEE CHINA" WEBSITE — Special price! Inquire Within! Includes complete website creation and all that this entails. If seriously interested, contact Claude.

TRUMPLESTILSKIN "NO TRUMP VIBES HERE, PLEASE" INCENSE — This incense is the kind that Donald Trump HATES, along with Mexicans and all the rest of those Un-American non-white guys. Dispels ALL Trump vibes, and drives away any vestigial Trump supporters that remain in a mixed or integrated neighborhood or building project.

TRUMPLESTILSKIN ATHLETIC SUPPORTER — P.O.R. — I create the design for the product, package it and ship it. YOU supply the wherewithal to do that.

TRUMPLESTILSKIN FART MACHINE — I know, I know. I said "no whoopie cushions", and I meant it. This is different. It's a fart machine, not an inflatable cushion. It's a device that YOU control, YOU set it off whenever you like, and make the fart sound seem to come from anywhere you choose, just like our illustrious President does at home!

TRUMPLESTILSKIN TAX-EVASION METHOD WORKS EVERY TIME — In order to get away with this amazing self-help scheme to own everything in the entire world and to dominate every bitch in the area, all you need do is get yourself elected President, then have your dozens of lawyers stall any inquiry into your tax returns until you're out of office, if ever.

TRUMPLESTILSKIN TYRANT KIT — This is the Tyrant Kit of choice, the king of the hill, top of the heap! It's the Tyrant Kit that put Julius Caesar into Power just by crossing the Rubicon with his private mercenaries! You can be the Tyrant Ruler Forever with this amazing Tyrant Kit. It has everything! A silent and bitterly complacent mate, children who can't wait for the reading of your Last Will and Testimony, and a squadron of zombied-out goons who are prepared to carry out your slightest whim, should they survive your temper tantrums, for which you will someday be famous.

TRUMPLESTILSKIN RUDE AWAKENING FACE CREAM — Transforms your face into that of a rude, belligerent, chaotic and thoroughly scared and angry orangutan, thus creating many terrific photo opportunities for all the selfies you'll want to post when you get this amazing new product.

TRUMPLESTILSKIN CERTIFICATE OF SANITY — Haw, haw, fat chance!

TRUMPLESTILSKIN SWASTIKA ARMBAND — If you can't beat them, join them! This will make anyone overlook your thick Jewish accent, hooked nose and dark complexion, but it might not help much if you're Mexican or Middle-Eastern.

TRUMPLESTILSKIN THOROUGHLY VETTED ALIEN CERTIFICATE — You can't be just ANY alien to deserve and get this certificate and award. You have to be a Certified Orion or a Grey to get one, so if you're a Nordic or a Pleiadian, just fuck off, okay?

TRUMPLESTILSKIN PROTEST SIGNS — Might as well get them now, while they're still cheap, and there are still some people unoffended and unattacked for the moment, standing around, wondering what the fuck just happened...???

18

TRUMPLESTILSKIN "YOU'RE FIRED" SIGN FOR AMERICAN WORKERS — Sure, NOW you're hired, but soon you'll be fired, so we can get our roads built and our sewers draining properly, and you look like just the dummy to do it, too!!!

TRUMPLESTILSKIN iPHONE APP — $9.95 — Download the TRUMPLESTILSKIN APP today, and get into line, which forms at the right. Hysterical? You bet. Wild? More than merely wild. Over-The-Top Awesome on Steroids!

There, I believe that's all of them. I have even more ideas for a variety of applications, such as a 7-No-Trump Orb, that keeps the INFLUENCE of Trumpism from your door, although not from your neighborhood. You can't extend this over someone else's domain, just your own, although you can turn a neighbor on to The Plan.

I just happened to look to see if "Trumplestilskin" has been used by anyone. Gosh, it sure has. It's taken on a sort of "meme" meaning, "to scream senselessly and insanely on a meaningless topic".

How To Practice Psychic Self-Defense in a World Gone Mad
January 30, 2017

Psychic Self-Defense has three distinct meanings:

It's the only means for escape from suffering or expression of pain that you have left to you as a peasant.

It deals with spiritual energies only, well outside the realm of the physical world.

It's the only revenge you will ever have.

As Inigo Montoya so eloquently said: "There's no money in revenge." Revenge is stupid, pointless and empty, because you're fighting against a mechanical machine with no heart, no mind, no soul. What's wanted is not revenge, but protection. Are you scared to death to bring up the Trump subject for fear of violence??? Okay, let's talk, and listen up good, pilgrim:

I swear by all that's Holy that I have no personal interest in Trump.

He's a handy in-your-face-right-now character that readily serves as an example of a psycho-emotional organic world irritant that could intrude on your inner world and peaceful home, on a psychic or spiritual level, and my intent here is to demonstrate how to set up a line of Psychic Self-Defense for yourself, your family, your home, your business and your personal freedoms. About your stocks and bonds I can do nothing.

I'll be sharing secrets that have never been revealed in modern times. These are the Methods and Secrets of the Ancients, and in spite of the fact that I'll undoubtedly be sparking off the morons who voted for Trump, I'm NOT against Trump — as a matter of fact, he's doing me a favor, and I'll gladly explain why, as we go through this little exercise.

By the way, Trump is horrifically superstitious, which will probably come as no surprise to anyone. Besides being an NPD, he's also a hyper-charged up OCD, which has to get really sticky for anyone unfortunate enough to serve on his staff or be on his payroll in any capacity.

Even David Lo Pan had to make a living somehow. He had his Wing Kong, I have my angelic hordes, so just leave Jack Burton alone, okay?

Because the Toupee of the Year is SO in our faces, I'll be using The Trump Avatar as an example of someone who initiates and sets off psychic-level attacks, whether upon you intentionally and personally or as a member of a whole class of folks under said psychic attack.

It's probably too late to mention it to the bots who rage-quit on the previous paragraphs, but I want to point out that, had Hillary won the election, I'd be after her as well, if the media frenzy were as great, this far away from the election results. Christ almighty, the problem with Trump is not his politics, although they are nutty and will soon be reversed or erased — don't forget, I've seen it all a million times before.

Like I said, it's not Trump's politics, it's his Narcissistic Personality Disorder — a matter of public record — that creates an incessant need for attention, and a willingness to use shock and rage to get it.

That's why he negotiates with foreign powers ON TWITTER in full public view — he needs the attention and craves acceptance — and yes, he is a Twitter Addict, among other mental ailments and weaknesses, some of which have already been exploited by his playmate, Vladimir Potemkin, some of which haven't shown up in the public radar yet, but they will, Frodo, they will.

I treated myself in the above paragraph to what amounts to a 100 year old joke, so old a chestnut that you've probably heard it a thousand times before.

Putin — Potemkin, get it???

Potemkin was the name of a Russian battleship. See, it was during the Russian Revolution — the first one, I mean — or was it the second??? Oh, forget it — it is all so complicated.

All I remember from my lessons back in the 37th century is that there were a LOT of wars back in this time period, a LOT of wars. As a gamer and game programmer, I can't help but feel just a little responsible for all the wars, since I wrote the Back Story on this level.

Would a sincere "I'm sorry" be any compensation for all the misery and suffering of humanity throughout those wars? Well, the Great Mother sends her best, which is, of course, YOU.

Whether you like Trump, hate Trump, or are completely indifferent to the whole scene, as I am, you're inundated on an hourly basis, even minute-to-minute, with Trump's latest outrages and wild zany antics in the media and elsewhere, meaning supermarkets, restrooms and Born-Again Frozen Yogurt Youth Centers, where the conversation reflects little else.

He's restless and anxious, and he needs YOUR attention, and one way to get that is to make you angry, and that's easy to arrange, and it's something he does very well indeed — he has almost complete control of the media in a sort of knee-jerk reflex way.

If you don't care about the politics — as I surely don't, having seen all this go down a million times before — you still suffer the media effects on the general population, which currently includes you, like it or not, and he's aroused a very dangerous and violent segment of the population to help him get to power.

Problem there is, that segment of the population now has the authority and "right" to seek YOU out, and destroy you and your family, should you question Trump or his policies, or be an unfortunate member of the race, religion or political affiliations he has decided to set his dogs — that'd be you, if you're a Pro-Lifer – on you and your family and friends.

He will NEVER take responsibility for this, although he set them barking and howling for your blood. YOU are the enemy, YOU are why the country is so screwed up, YOU are the one blocking them from being GREAT again.

In short, if you're Jewish, you'll recognize the scapegoat, the Big Lie, and you already know what's coming next. The work-camps at first, and then, eventually, openly they become death-camps, with wholesale extermination sheds, and I have just the right company for the job.

You can get a really nicely made "Tuff Shed", and rig it up with gas, then place a cremation system right behind it. The original Nazi plans drawn up by Heinrich Himmler are still available, along with some stunningly ordinary original watercolors of the projected death camps signed by Adolph Hitler — some of which have already been built — and secret executive orders are being issued now for the rest of them.

You'll find the original Nazi documents somewhere in the Oval Office, probably the top item in the lap-drawer at the front of Trump's new desk — the one with the red telephone and the nuclear missile button.

Am I kidding? No, unfortunately, I'm not. He studied films of Hitler and Mussolini, to see what body language and facial expressions and tones and modulations they used to mind-fuck and control the crowds, and by golly, he got at least that one thing right!

Look at the cheering crowds around Hitler and Mussolini. They loved them, adored them, imitated them and wanted to be just like them!

Of course, when you're an Evil Avatar who's won four Academy Awards — one for Best Emotional Outburst — you can do any fucking thing you want. I can't take credit for that line — it's Charles Pierce at her best.

Trump craves attention, and he'll do anything — ANYTHING — to get it, which is more than proven in his public appearances which, by the way, have furnished enough evidence of Psychotic Personality Disorders to satisfy HUNDREDS of psychiatrists who otherwise are sworn to say nothing without a personal interview, but he's put his little dick right out there on the table, folks, and keep in mind that in public, HE'S ON HIS BEST BEHAVIOR!!!

What must he be like in private?

If you just want the Trump Daily Vomit out of your face completely, or at least reduced to a dull roar, you need do no more than carry, hang, place or wear a "TFZ" amuletic charm on or about your person, home, office or den.

If you want some Spiritual Merit, you might consider making efforts to get these to people who need and want them, but are understandably afraid to ask.

That, in a nutshell, is my sticking point, the place where I turn and fucking fight.

See, I no longer feel freedom from fear, one of the guarantees of a free America, and you surely don't, either, unless you're a Pro-Lifer Trump Supporter, in which case, you're safe.

Freedom From Fear is no longer possible in America. Only in a Trump-Free Zone can you feel some relief from the heavy oppression which is now coming from everywhere, not just Washington, because Trump has invoked and set in motion his very own "Brown Shirts", the Pro-Lifers.

I want to mention here that not all Born-Agains are fanatical, but all Pro-Lifers are both fanatical and violent, just like their Mr. Christ was, intolerant and violent, right?

Christian Fanatics (and there are Jewish Fanatics just as crazy) will ask themselves, "What Would Jesus Do?". Besides the "Axis of Awesome" answer to that stupid question, there is another answer — he would kill, maim, throw stones, destroy in anger, hate and misery.

Clearly, that IS what Jesus would do, or his followers, espousing the ideal of imitating Jesus, wouldn't kill, maim, destroy, tear down, smash and smear into the mud, am I right?

Okay, so they don't EXACTLY follow Jesus precepts. They break, in fact, several of the Ten Commandments in the name of Jesus, and this they do as a message of peace, mercy, brotherly love and forgiveness.

Nobody ever said it made sense. It's not a rational thing, not something with which you can reason. It's a robot with a mind-set that is unforgiving, holding YOU to blame for all its miseries. Why you? Because you got in the way.

A machine has a machine mind, a machine heart, a machine brain and a machine attitude, and you can't expect more.

What you really want is to be left alone, just left the fuck alone, that's all. What THEY want is to intrude, invade your privacy, your home, your office, your bedroom, your bathroom ... although why anyone would want to invade a bathroom??? ...just plain "Do whatever the fuck you want, just leave me and my family and friends alone, okay???".

Tell the truth, do you feel safe speaking your mind right now? Would you openly say any of the things I'm saying here? If you do speak out, you'd better be prepared for the bullies, because REAL free speech, the freedom to say whatever's on your mind without fear of instant deadly reprisal, SCARES them!

They're all for equality, freedom, free speech and freedom from fear, but they don't want that shit to end up in the wrong hands.

YOU REMEMBER WHAT IT WAS LIKE IN SCHOOL WHEN A BULLY BEAT YOU UP OR SCARED YOU???

My Dad taught me that there's only one way to stop a bully, and the longer you wait, the meaner and more aggressive and more openly nasty he'll be. Don't wait until you're actually on the stretching rack to pack your bags and get outta town.

Watch the brain-drain. Anyone with an ounce of sense and a few extra dollars is looking for a country of refuge right about now, and the pressure will get stronger, going forward. Going backward, things can only get better.

Some of the victimizers come in packs, like wolves, and are proud of the fact that they can overwhelm old, helpless people, beat them up and leave them lying there on the ground. Sometimes, however, they might not walk away from it.

They respect no woman — a woman is a sex object, like our President likes to feel up whether they want it or not.

They certainly don't respect you, your freedoms, your home, your life, and they will terminate any and all of that if they feel that they can get away with it.

It's your job to make sure that they don't. Right now, the only thing you can hope to do is avoid the mob, avoid some crazy fanatic who wants some headlines and momentary fame, although the very next generation will not remember anyone's name, even the big guys, the ones who put up buildings and statues to themselves — especially not them.

And THAT'S the America you're leaving for your grandchildren to inherit.

Like I said, leave me out of this particular ruckus. I'm only using the Trump issue to teach you a little psychic self-defense, and that's my whole purpose. The Trump Circus is funny to watch, even though it IS deadly, and the Great Mom and Lucifer both say "thanks" to everyone who voted for Trump, and I do, too, because for me, it's a great time for spiritual marketing, and especially for femme comedy!!!

Wow, will Leslie Ann take this schmuck to town!!! I've seen some of her comedy material on Trump, and it will send you into another dimension! Come to think of it, that might be a good plan.

"TFZ" stands for "Trump-Free Zone" and is **100% GUARANTEED to reduce the psychic influence of Trump and Trumpism to a radius distance of about nine feet,** a circle or bubble of "NO-TRUMP STUFF HERE, PLEASE" protection on a quantum level.

So if you merely want a little FREEDOM, to breathe a little fear-free air, you want to establish a beachhead of personal freedom and freedom from fear, which of course, would be a TRUMP-FREE ZONE.

NO-TRUMP ZONES, SEVEN-NO-TRUMPS and FUCK UP TRUMP quantum devices are in the planning and design stage, to the amusement and general hoo-raw of the design crew that's taking my designs to the world marketplace, there to exhibit for one and all the rump of Trump!

"WOW! These TFZ Medallions are really great!" — Your Name Here.

BUY A HUNDRED! Sell them! Give them away! You can send for the handmade super-charged quantum-force "TFZ" Medallion, which I sell for a lousy $10 bucks for the cardboard core, and only $149.95 for one that's made with a really nice U.S. Silver dollar!

Or you can make your own TFZ medallions and charms from my UNCOPYRIGHTED DESIGN, which I give away free to the world.

Why so cheap???

If you have to ask that question, you haven't suffered enough under the Trump Regime, but you will, and when you've had more than enough of the Fourth Reich, you'll ask for mercy, but to answer the question, "Why so cheap?" more directly, I don't need any more money than I have now, and it pleases me to work with almost nothing.

When you finally do beg for help, don't forget to enclose the ten bucks, plus 3 bucks for packing, handling and shipping. The only help I can offer you now is to BLOCK TRUMP from your personal life and home.

Until he takes further steps against his people — which all tyrants do, ho-hum, tell me a different story — I can't reveal more, but at the right time, I will.

Don't forget that THERE'S SOMETHING LIVING INSIDE TRUMP, and that "something" thrives on tension, apprehension and dissension, and they have begun. Hear that, Presteign?

I don't own an entire fleet of drones, nor do I own a world-wide fleet of delivery trucks, so I can't compete with Trump on the "No Shipping" level — another injustice with which we'll all have to live, so you'll need to cover the shipping. Overseas shipping may cost more, don't know, don't really care.

Psychic Self-Defense doesn't come naturally to someone who lives peacefully and in harmony.

Peaceful folks don't tend to defend themselves on the psychic level, because the educational system has taught us that we don't have any threat on the psychic level, since there is nothing outside the body and brain.

This, of course, is untrue, but most of what you learned in school is false, and just about everything you read or hear over the air is false as well, sometimes deliberately, as in the case of that equally crazy destructive asshole, Julian Assange, and his crony, Gavin MacFadyen, who seems to have lost interest since he passed to MY side of the curtain.

I sent him over to the Afterlife Motel as an assistant sanitation engineer.

Listen, these "people" don't have your best interests at heart. They don't listen to reason or to anything else. They are spiritually and emotionally unable to stop at a gas station and ask directions, which is how come they invented the Magellan Road Mate auto navigator.

The key word is "auto". Robots can't think, aren't paid to think. Go onto the street with a camera and ask people "How much is 100 times 200?", or "What is the Moon?"

The people working with Trump know how to create dissension, which is what he wants — to divide the people, send them to the streets, so he can call in the National Guard to wipe them out.

He wants to destroy any possible resistance, and one way to do that is to have the army do the job for you.

I personally don't go directly AFTER anyone, especially when I helped the Arabs win back their country, back in the day during World War I.

I ALWAYS prefer to go after the SUPPLY LINES and COMMUNICATION LINES and leave the troops to wander about looking for a fight. That way, you never have to use a weapon.

Oh, I wonder if it has occurred to you that you could easily and peacefully oppose the Trump Establishment — which is bankers, brokers, politicians and actual crime bosses, with whom they make deals, as if you didn't know — by strictly buying only those products that are actually made in China???

It's hard not to be cynical, in this environment, isn't it??? Go ahead and BE cynical — you've every right to distrust the whole gang.

You're absolutely right to love your country, but fear your government.

The politicians do NOT have your best interests at heart or in mind. They exploit whatever movement or emotional fad is happening at the moment, espousing whatever they need to espouse, in order to get into power and stay in power — and while they're in power, they'll be occupied most of the time with raping and pillaging, which they do best behind your back with you knocked unconscious.

Simply put, when you're dealing with men who define Chloral Hydrate as "foreplay", you're gonna end up at the shit end of the stick.

I'm doing more than dealing with them — I'm taking them on, on a psychic level. They can lock me up, but they can't invade my mind.

Properly and responsibly used, quantum effects, often called "Shamanic Magic", can be applied for some relief to the poor and oppressed, which is the idea behind the "TFZ" medallions.

One of my specialties as a game designer is Improvised Magical Weapons, and they work just as well in the so-called "Real World" as in the electronic quantum world of video gaming.

I'm going to outline a number of Secret Magical Formulae, Ritual and Scribing, using the quantum techniques of EMBOSSED PRAYER.

Prayer doesn't mean what you think it means.

Prayer is a kind of energy, that can be built and heaped up and combined and interwoven to create a wide variety of quantum effects, some of which happen to spill over into the realm of the organic world from time to time.

You DO have some power, but not in the organic world. Your power is in the spiritual realm, where Donald Trump CANNOT and WILL NOT go.

He's afraid of the dark, and when he DOES go to Hell, he'll be well rewarded. It's nice and light where he's going, with plenty of company, if you like demons with pitchforks.

You can COPY the design of my Trump-Free Zone Medallions,

teach it to others, give the Teaching with the medallion, keeping in mind that these are strictly protective measures, not aggressive in any way, shape or form.

Psychic Self-Defense is not inappropriate. The Washington Bullies will tell you that you have no right to defend yourself or to resist the will of Washington, but you don't have to believe them. They've never told you the truth before — why would they now?

Pass it on, spread the word about the TFZ Medallions, help to widen the gap between us and the evils of Trump and Trumpism.

You should act now, because you'll need a good head-start at the time when he orders the roundups of you and me and everyone we know, and he WILL do this when he thinks he can get away with it, and sadly, he CAN and WILL get away with every scam he's running, and every outrage he orders committed against you and your loved ones.

Why? Because he and the Religious Right have given themselves permission to be violent in the name of Christ, that's why, and this is the Second Inquisition, starting as of right now.

The rich bankers and stock merchants and defense contractors and most of all, the Silent Ones — those who actually run the world economy — hold all the cards, that's why.

What were you, born yesterday? You really haven't been paying attention, these past few millennia. This has all happened before, right here, on Earth, about 8,000 years ago, 24,000 years ago and 32,000 years ago, and each time, it ended with a bang, not a whimper.

Whenever they want to do it, Trump and his banker friends can, within a single day, raise a private army of millions of mercenaries, put you and your family into protective custody work compounds, put you on road repair for the rest of your shortened life, and that's part of the plan, which any Remote Viewer or Remote Reader can verify — the paper trail exists and can be followed easily, if you know where to look.

Don't want to be under that heavy load? Isn't LIFE already miserable enough without Trump and Trumpism adding insult to injury?

Use the "TFZ" Medallion, and make them, buy them, give them as gifts — if you dare. They come to you in a plain brown wrapper, and they don't ACTUALLY SAY ANYTHING, just "TFZ", and it's very, very discreet.

You can sell them on the street, but you'd better beware. The Trumpists are very, very violent. They're very likely to attack you physically, and you'd do well to avoid them as much as possible. If you're in a highly exposed Religious Right neighborhood, this might be the time to sell and move to someplace a little safer and less violent, if such a place can be found.

Jesus Christ was apparently some sort of gang leader who invited his followers to eat his body and drink his blood, which they enthusiastically still do today.

Radical Extremists of all kinds are always violent, always upset, always angry and always afraid. If possible, make them afraid of you, because if they're not, they'll make you another of their victims.

Problem is, it's not just Trump, it's his equally insane friends and playmates who are likely to react to his wild ravings and taunts, and boom, it's all over, including their reign of terror. At that point, you'll be glad to have hunting, fishing and gathering skills and opportunities for survival.

Do those guys in Power actually care?

The problem is, they DON'T care. They're totally suicidal, or they wouldn't be playing the Crazy Game, but they are, and you're the cannon-fodder that they intend to chew up in their frenzies — if you wonder what it is they really want, it's to take YOU with them, down, down, down, into the fire and brimstone of the Hell-World, which is where they already are, just waiting for your soul to hit the pavement.

Never mind about all that. Put all that aside, and concentrate on the actual lesson — Psychic Self-Defense. Let's look at your options.

You'll need a setting — that'd be the medallion, which is an acrylic capsule that contains a coin-sized medallion. What size coin? Well, there are a few choices here, each one of which creates a different "footprint" in terms of size, so they run from small to large, with different reasons for each size.

WORLD'S BEST "TRUMP-FREE ZONE" MEDALLIONS

PENNY-SIZED "TFZ" MEDALLION — $39.95 — This is the smallest of the hand-crafted "TFZ" Medallions. It comes in a 26mm wide acrylic capsule — easy to carry in pocket or purse. Uses Thorns as its main device — It's a simple "Reflect Back To You" blocker, made with a guaranteed authentic antique "Wheatie" copper penny, to give it some whammy power — the U.S. penny is preserved intact.

SILVER HALF-DOLLAR-SIZED "TFZ" MEDALLION — $99.95 — POWERED BY A GENUINE U.S. SILVER HALF DOLLAR! This will be the most popular medallion I make, and I have a large number of them on hand for fast shipping of large orders. Many social groups give these as Party Favors, depending on what kind of party it is. Made with an actual solid silver U.S. Half-Dollar.

DOLLAR-SIZED CARDBOARD CORE "TFZ" MEDALLION — $9.95 — The least expensive of the TFZ medallions, this is a great device for an Altar or for HOME protection against unwanted psychic nose-hairs like Trump.

GENUINE U.S. SILVER DOLLAR CORE "TFZ" MEDALLION — $149.95 — This power-packed whammy does the trick, no matter what the provocation. Made with a FINE GRADE OR BETTER genuine U.S. Silver Dollar, usable as a trade item in a severe emergency.

Okay, so much for the PASSIVE RESISTANCE devices, but what would you do for an ACTIVE RESISTANCE against Trump and his policies, for instance???

PRAYER CRAFTING FOR FUN and PROFIT

You'll need a powerful prayer-crafting, and keep in mind that, although the Christian Right uses prayer, they have no clue what prayer power is and what it can do, although they already think they know everything.

The Bible is a collection of stories that is just about as accurate and as personal and ax-grinding as any example out of Wikipedia, with about as much authority and truth.

The Religious Right, whether Christian, Moslem, Jewish or Zoroastrian, are by their nature upset and anxious, full of fear, which makes them violent, aggressive, self-righteous, unforgiving and savage, therefore highly dangerous, and moreover, they will not leave you alone to live your life as you wish.

And that's where I wade in with fists flying and feet kicking.

Here are some magical visual effects you can build into an EMBOSSED PSYCHIC SELF-DEFENSE MEDALLION, that has NO KARMIC BACKLASH, such as the ones I make here, and teach to my jewelry students and fellow videogamers who want something for their games a little stronger. Well, stronger they be, and here they are, each one a visual element in the embossed design, as you'd find on any magical shield or raiment:

THORNS — Return Spell, Mirror Incoming Spell, Reflect Influence or Attack.

SPIKES — Spear incoming — stab, spike and poke at incoming influences.

TRAPS — Little Black Holes for any incoming trash or harmful waves.

DEMONIC TRAPS — Cheese-baited traps for Demonic Avatar Thought-Forms.

QUICKSAND — Sucking Down traps for incoming Negative Thought-Forms.

GARGOYLE — Perfect Reflection of any harmful or negative incoming spell.

FLAME — Cleanses and Purifies any harmful or negative incoming spell.

ICE — Freezes the incoming spell and sends a chill to the sender.

DARK — Throws the incoming into the Darkness along with the sender.

VOIDNESS — Puts up a PASSAGE SHIELD between the incoming and you.

MOAT — Surrounds you with an impassable barrier against negativity.

SCATTER — Throws the incoming into ANGULAR MOMENTUM.

PIT — Tiger Pit with Spikes traps incoming negativity and harassment.

SPARK — Tesla Coil RETURNS the SHOCK to the sender.

ANKH — Magnetic Wave RETURNS the GRIEF to the sender.

There are more, hundreds more, but these few will give you an indication of how various symbols can be used in an amuletic form to create a psychic self-defense device that will work to keep you and your family safe and free from Trump and his devilish minions.

Keep in mind that Minions are Minions — they have no more soul or spirit than a can of beans, and that they are actually out to get you, and they will, if they feel they can get away with it — generally, a mob gives some idea of anonymity, or it did, until they put the cameras in all the streets, and that'll get worse.

Problem is, it's not for YOUR protection that those cameras are out there, but for the protection of the — I'm going to say it — unlawful government.

You have to wonder if anyone noticed that the election WAS rigged, by Trump — and YOU are the target, not the beneficiary, of all the mechanics going on in Washington at this time. Fact is, nobody cares, and Trump knew that the people would lie down and die, like they always do.

Myself, I don't give a shit. I'm 75 years out of Port, headed for home. I'm kind of in the "fuck off, you idiots" category of elder seniority.

I'm a Short-Timer. You guys will have to live with this schmuck for a while, and with his children, and their children, and their children's children. It's going to be a long, long time before YOU will ever feel freedom from fear, and you might never feel that freedom from fear ever again, at least not in The New All-Christian All-White Amerika.

If that's the case, it will be the religious fanatics that make it happen. They do get theirs, and really soon, but that's no compensation for the loss of all your freedoms if you happen to be non-white, non-Pro Lifer, or just not a card-carrying Party Member.

Don't forget to wear your swastika armband when you go out in public — they'll leave you alone if you're wearing one of those, you know?

Send for your TFZ Medallions today. Multiple orders accepted! Make your own! Teach others to make them! Spread the word, spread the energy, and spread the power!

Stop the World, I Want to Get Off??? NO!!!
Bust the Heads of the Bullies, and Stick Around!!!
January 31, 2017

BACKSTORY FOR "EXECUTIVE ORDER #1", a comedic satire film parody.

By now our femme superhero Waxonn Waxoff realizes that Trumplestilskin the Conqueror cannot be stopped, that his policies will surely lead not only to war with other nations, but to war within the boundaries of her native land, Annunakkia, and it's not just a single war, with a single purpose and two adversaries face-to-face, but a multiplicity of wars all going on at the same time, like World War I and the Russian Revolution and The Jewish Problem.

Waxoff finds herself in the midst of a race war, a religious war, a war of territory, a war of attrition and a war of total revenge, when the population finally catches up with the surviving leaders, and then, to top it all off, the Ancient Alien Invaders destroy what's left of human cities and centers of commerce and industry.

In short, they lay waste to the land, but after the Evil Avatar Trumplestilskin gets through with it, there's little left to crush into rubble.

Trumplestilskin himself is never personally at risk. His minions take care of everything. They defend him and destroy his enemies, for which they are well-paid.

Photo of Phil Bruns by E.J. Gold, circa 1967 "MacBird" political protest play by Barbara Garson — everyone in this play was harassed by Police Chief Parker's minions.

His only concerns are a fear of the dark, a fear of being alone, and a deep, insatiable craving for attention by any means necessary.

ACT ONE — scene one

TRUMPLESTILSKIN enters stage LEFT, goes to table, center stage, stands a moment, scowls, then says in a rage: "I CAN'T BELIEVE THEY SHUT DOWN TWITTER!"

[BLACKOUT]

I'll continue the script in a moment, but first, MORE BACKSTORY about the ideas examined, and the political, social and religious origins of this recently rediscovered ancient 21st century Pre-Revolutionary satirical play...

There is an amazingly enormous surfeit of Donald Trump satire and parody songs, dances, plays and movies, and for far longer than he deserves, he'll be the topic of conversation for decades yet to come. People are pissed at their rights and freedoms being taken away overnight without benefit of counsel.

Fact is, millions of people risk arrest at the hands of the New Amerika. Fascism is your future, if you manage to live through the first few weeks and months of the New Order.

The Illuminati are having their way with us, and the least we can do is resist rape and make the rapist pay.

Millions of people are surreptitiously and anonymously viewing these parodies and protests, for whatever good it does anyone, which is, frankly, none.

These hurt and angry video makers garner millions of views, while placing the progenitor — that means the producer of the video — in serious mortal danger, not from the government, but from the Christian Mob, as controlled and manipulated by Donald Trump, a master baiter.

He uses Hitler's tricks to keep himself above the law and above the ethics outrages. I can enumerate them for you, but hell, so can any World War II scholar or tabletop gamer.

YOU have no voice, and from now on, Trump's voice is the only one loud enough to be heard in this commotion and din, this dull, smoky atmosphere of hatred and distrust, which he created as a smokescreen for his evil acts.

If you're thinking to do something that will change the situation, do whatever you like, but he'll still be in power at the end of the day, and you might end up dead or in prison for your views — just your VIEWS, not your ACTIONS.

Although he will soon have his Secret Police in place to take YOU away for resisting his will, frankly, it's not the government any more that's doing this to you. It's his supporters.

He has given his CULT followers FORMAL PRESIDENTIAL PERMISSION TO HATE, permission to destroy, to riot against Jews, Moslems, Indians, Native Americans, Oriental peoples, just about everyone in the world, all of which is now the enemy of Trump Amerika, and YOU are the cannon-fodder, the sacrificial offering, that Trump is offering to his twisted Inner Gods.

It's not in some dim future that this is all going to happen. It's RIGHT NOW, and guess what? He has a plan to put together — hold onto your hats, folks — Trump has WRITTEN PLANS for a Fifth Crusade to free the Holy Land and return it to the Christian Right.

Think I'm going over the top here, eh? Haw, haw, I have the advantage. I'm not guessing, I'm remembering.

PRESENT DAY AMERIKA is NOW a hate-filled environment into which you cannot venture if you are dark-skinned, female, foreign-born, non-Christian, gay, overly intellectual, intelligent, smart or a smartass.

I tend to fall into the latter category, and derive some minor satisfaction from the quips I throw out with my last breaths.

Lot of good THAT does. At least get a drop of blood from them, so the Crime Scene won't be a total loss for the CSIs, but remember how O.J. Simpson got away with it? That can happen again. And again. And again.

RIGHT NOW, THIS WEEK, should be about the time the mobs start lynching the teachers, the scholars, the unlamented masses of educators and physicians, the rocket scientists and the engineers, just before they destroy their own factories and homes.

The stupid always destroy the works of the smart.

Did you know that the mob in Iraq destroyed ALL their ancient historical treasures and looted their museums, toppled ancient statues??? Reminds you of the purges in China, you say, by the Gang of Four? You'd be right, but not as right as the Far Right — nobody can take it as far as a fanatic, and the dumber they are, the more fanatical and frenzied they become.

And guess what? Within a few weeks or months, it's possible that YOU will be refused any and all medical treatment if you don't happen to be a Christian. I guarantee that, as outrageous as it seems now, this

WILL HAPPEN SOON, and it WILL HAPPEN HERE.

Christians will soon be hated and feared all over the globe.

Frankly, you haven't the chance of a snowball in Hell of surviving the mob action and the betrayal of your neighbors and former friends. Everyone's your enemy, to be treated with suspicion, under the Rule of Trump, which is:

"Do Unto Thy Neighbor Before He Has a Chance to Do Unto You."

Nuclear War is Trump's way of going out with a bang. He wants company when he goes, doesn't want to die alone, and by golly, with his very own nuclear war, he won't have to.

You no longer dare to speak up.

Thanks to Trumplestilskin and his minions, YOU NO LONGER HAVE YOUR FIRST AMENDMENT FREEDOMS. You lost the war before it even started. You won't get that freedom from fear back ever again until you are FREE FROM DONALD TRUMP!

TRUMP-FREE ZONE DOLLAR-SIZED MEDALLION — $9.95 —

Send for your very own TFZ today, and experience the thrill of being UNAWARE OF DONALD TRUMP for sometimes minutes and even hours at a time. At this price, you can afford to give them away!

Find out who your real friends are! Hand them out at parties!

Live dangerously! Wear your TFZ in public!

Risk Death at the Hands of a Mob! Set up a sales booth at a local street fair!

You will FEEL THE FREEDOM while wearing or carrying the TFZ Medallion, but what else will it do for you?

FREEDOM FROM THE TRUMP EFFECT — Be temporarily HATE-FREE.

EXPERIENCE THE JOY OF 7 NO-TRUMP — His voice is, for the moment, silenced.

THE BAD SMELL IS GONE — Temporarily, the fart-smell of the New Amerika is gone.

ENLIGHTENMENT — A sense of feeling a LOT lighter.

AWARENESS — The ability to appreciate others returns somewhat.

SENSITIVITY — The feelings of love and brotherhood return to the outer limbs.

HEART and SOUL — The sensation of being surrounded by thousands of robots is gone.

MENTAL ACUITY — A return of mentation with the absence of Mental Murkiness.

ONE-NESS — A Feeling of acceptance at being alone in the dark, thus blocking Trumpness.

SERENITY — A definite absence of worry and fear about what Trump will say or do next.

PEACEFUL VALLEY — A sense of being in a Place of Refuge against Trump and his minions.

ANOINTING OF THE INNOCENT — You will feel a definite sensation as if being anointed by a sweet, scented essential oil.

EXPANSION — A profound feeling of expansion and extension into the Boundless Realm of Cosmic Consciousness.

CALM — A reflection of the One.

LAUGHTER — Remembering always that those who laugh last, have the last laugh.

FREEDOM FROM FEAR — As long as you're alone in your room and say nothing out loud, you'll be okay.

RIDICULE OF THE TORMENTOR — A profound thrill as ridicule of the naked Emperor with the funny toupee spreads throughout the crowd. Ridicule is Trump's darkest fear, and by putting himself in the public spotlight on an hourly basis, he assures that his darkest fear WILL be realized, and he's right, it will. He becomes known as the "Crazy President" and is the most reviled of all U.S. Presidents.

REVENGE ON YOUR TORMENTORS — The Perfect Revenge — you do nothing. They suffer INVISIBLY and UNKNOWINGLY. Their punishment is to BE THEM!!!

Unfortunately, your **LEGAL RIGHT** to speak your mind has been overwhelmed by **THE FEAR** of being torn apart limb from limb for speaking honestly about your real thoughts and feelings.

The fact is, you're afraid to bring up ANY subject, for fear that the listener will be of the Unforgiving and Intolerant Religious Right, so the **ACTUAL FUNCTIONAL ABILITY** to speak your mind casually without fear has been terminated by Trump.

It isn't he who will take action against you; he's as clever as Hitler. He's made sure that whoever offends him is mentioned in the news or on Twitter, and the mob "takes care of them", the people to whom

Trump has given OFFICIAL PRESIDENTIAL PERMISSION to commit violent acts in the name of Christ, and then he denies any responsibility for their actions.

The well-known phrase comes up here. "Will no one rid me of this troublesome priest?" which resulted in assassination of Thomas Becket.

I have it on good authority that Donald was the kind of kid who rang people's doorbells and then ran and hid in the bushes.

You can find the footage where he says **"Maybe some Second Amendment supporter will "take care" of Hillary".** That sounds to me like a death threat if ever I heard one, but he GOT AWAY WITH IT, and had something happened, he'd be scot-free.

Charles Manson didn't get away with ordering people to participate in something in which he took no actual part, but Trump has BILLIONS of dollars and HUNDREDS of lawyers, more than enough clout to get away with everything, absolutely everything, and he will, I can forecast that for you WITHOUT prior knowledge or Remote Reading skills.

His supporters ARE OFFICIALLY LICENSED BY THE STATE TO USE VIOLENCE to enforce their Christian views on others and, by the way, it's a very small segment of the Christian population that's doing this to you.

This is a religious war, most of all, and the players are the Super-Christians vs. Everyone Else. The Christians are bound to lose in the end, because they're outnumbered billions to millions, but they'll make quite a stink in this latest Great Mother Population Reduction Plan which will eliminate billions of uselessly violent hairless ape descendants.

Sure, I know that humans aren't directly descended from apes, but they sure don't act it.

In this atmosphere of distrust and hate, you don't know whom you can trust, who your friends are. You DON'T DARE share your most private thoughts. Your neighbors might be Trumpists, and they by nature are intolerant, like their Mr. Jesus.

You don't know to whom you can SAFELY talk to, unburden yourself to, be honest with. You don't know who your friends or enemies are, but all of a sudden, you HAVE enemies, where before you just had friends.

People you've known for years and liked and gotten along with are suddenly in "THE OTHER CAMP" and you're their sworn enemy. They now look at you with evil in their eyes, intent on conversion to their camp or crushing destruction if you don't join them or at least offer temporary verbal agreement.

Gosh, now you're sharing Trumplestilskin's world. He lives there ALL THE TIME, not knowing who his friends are, making new enemies every day, and he definitely wants company in his own private hell.

But who or what IS Trump? How can he get so far, be so successful and yet so obviously, blatantly in violation of the law, the rules and the ethics of the land, the laws he has sworn on a stack of Bibles to protect?

First of all, he's a trickster — he has no soul. The fact is, he's not an ordinary human. He's what is called an Evil Avatar. He stirs up feelings of hate, revenge, fear, distrust, suspicion and terror, and in the 37th century, Trump is known as "The Father of American Terror" as well as being famous for starting World War III, which suits his ego just fine.

He doesn't much care WHAT he's famous for, just so long as he's famous.

What he doesn't know is that his name is soon folded in with the billions of other people who die in his nuclear holocaust, and within a few years, none of the 400 or so surviving humans remember him at all.

ACT ONE scene 2

We find Trumplestilskin in his Ovaltine Office, with a buxom underdressed girl taking notes.

TRUMPLESTILSKIN: "How could they let Twitter die? They are enemies of the State! I'll have them drawn and quartered! I'll have them roasted on a spit!"

SECRETARY: "Sir, your purging staffers have used up all the spits."

TRUMPLESTILSKIN: "Can I feel your pussy?"

Let's take a break from the script for a moment — I'm tired from all that thinking.

Just a wee bit more Backstory:

All this has happened before. If you can recover your Atlantean Self, you'll have the memories available, including what works and what doesn't, in reaction to this dire state of affairs for the weak and helpless. The people causing the ruckus are strong and naturally aggressive and territorial in nature. They have no qualms about destroying property or taking life, although they claim to be Pro-Life followers of the Man of Peace, Jesus Christ, whose message was of tolerance and peace.

Well, facts are facts. At first, the military keep the peace, according to my slight knowledge of human history, but then, eventually, when they can't be paid or fed, they are forced to take what they need from the civilian population.

Hopefully, that will be the population of folks who are NOT like them, so if they're Christian, they can easily justify taking food and shelter and clothing and sex from "other" religious groups.

It's a matter of record that every culture refers to itself as "The People", and all others "animals", thus de-humanizing them and making them ready victims for aggression. For example "Democrats aren't even people."

This dissertation is running along the lines of a scholarly work at this point, and I don't mean it to be. I've already given a blow-by-blow account of the coming wars in "SlimeWars", and I'm damned if I'll write it all over again in my blog just because you didn't happen to order the book from gatewaysbooksandtapes.com.

Frankly, there will soon come a time when you won't be able to order it. You won't be allowed to buy it, and we won't be allowed to sell it.

That goes for the ABD, the Koran, the Bhagavad Gita, the Talmud, and any religious text that isn't a specific edition of the King James Bible — no correct translation will do, no otherness will do, because they've memorized their rantings by page and paragraph.

Oy, if Jehovah could only get hold of those bastards!

But, like the rest of us, He can only stand and watch, or sit and watch, or pace around nervously and watch, as his bets are threatened by the events of the moment. He's still convinced the humans are going to somehow survive all this, and I can't wait to take his money — him and all the other idiots who bet on the humans.

My bets are ALWAYS on the side of the goonies, because they have no restraints, no ethics, no boundaries and above all, no respect for the spiritual nature of others outside their small realm of reality.

Okay, fair enough. Like I said, I'm 75 years out of port, and bound for Home. It ain't my problem anymore, and in fact, never was. I'm here to observe and to collect my bets after the very first of several upheavals, which is the Big Riot.

You'll note, if you bothered to read "SlimeWars", that the predictions made in that book 45 years ago are starting now to come true. You'll see that more and more as each stage of the disintegration of human society proceeds, and it's all laid out there for you to follow.

Want the instructions on how to handle it?

Since I've gone to the trouble to put that stuff down over a period of a number of years that I invested in the project, I'm surely not going to repeat that material here for those who haven't bothered to find out about or read my previous volumes.

Books about the joys of candle burning and meditation are NOT going to help you deal with the mob that's out there just waiting for a victim like YOU to accidentally cross its path. Take a look at a video I made I made back in the sixties about television westerns.

Think it can't happen here?

Wake Up, Schmuck! It already IS happening here! Don't you FEEL the oppression? Don't you FEEL the fear? Don't you FEEL the cramping sensation of being bound up and surrounded by suspicion and isolation?

This is how Trump feels all the time, and he wants company in his private hell, and YOU are tagged IT!!!

How to get out from under?

Physically, it's impossible. You are now officially a member of a Fascist State, and as such, you either toe the line or do as I do, and risk the result.

Spiritually, you CAN make a difference, and HERE'S HOW:

GET OUT FROM UNDER — Use as many **TFZ medallions, charms and amulets** as necessary to **UTTERLY REMOVE** any trace of Trumpist influence or thought-forms.

GET TRUMP OUT OF YOUR FACE — Erase any and all traces of Trump in your life, at least temporarily.

TAKE IMMEDIATE COVER — Don't go out anywhere you don't need to go, for a while, at least.

DRAW A BREATH OF FREEDOM — FEEL the absence of fear and apprehension.

LAY IN SOME EMERGENCY SUPPLIES — Include a RadBlock radiation blocker salt to replace radiated materials with safe materials in bone and bloodstream. Consult a health care professional for help in this regard. Otherwise, keep a four-week supply of food AND WATER available, along with a way to get rid of trash and waste.

FIND SOME FRIENDS — You'll need help in the coming emergency. You need to arrange things with a descending order of circumstances or social triggers.

KEEP THE FAITH — Do your spiritual practices every day, regardless of the threat.

BRING GOLIATH DOWN — Do your part to restore American freedoms, dignity and national honor as the Home of Tolerance and Freedom, the Land of Brotherly Love, by finding love and acceptance for those of a different faith, color or place of origin, and that includes extraterrestrials, too.

TRANSCEND THE WHOLE MESS — There are a variety of ways to do this, one of which is to perform aloud the script of "Norton Street" or "Redfin". Both plays will propel you neat and clean out of the Einsteinian Universe and into the world of Quantum.

RIDICULE and SCORN — Insure an Absence of Trump Shit with ridicule and scorn. Have you ever noticed how ape-like and downright UGLY and CRUDE he is and looks? Exploit that automatic revulsion! Give yourself permission to PITY this poor gorilla in a suit and tie!

ENJOY VOGON POETRY — Have your revenge in the form of poetry and song.

REVEL IN THE HISTORIC VIEW — In the future, Trump will be only slightly known, and then, merely as an asshole wannabe world-dictator, just another mass-murdering billionaire fuckhead with the intelligence of a moron. Want a second opinion? He's ugly, too.

YOU ARE HIS BOSS — Technically, he's a public servant, working for you, but we all know what his real agenda is — getting more attention — and his methods include ignoring his public service obligations.

TAKE THE HIGH ROAD — Fact is, he's how old now??? Haw, haw, 70 years old, eh??? Do the math — how much longer can he possibly live? And in the end, guess what? He shares the same fate as all kings, queens, emperors, popes, holy men, everyone dies, in the end, and it's right there that YOU will see him fall apart, crack up, to lose everything, all the STUFF he's built up and amassed in a giant personal pyramid, all this without the benefit of a SOUL, no less. YOU take the High Road, the spiritual path, and let him go to Hell his own damn way, along with his violent followers and the horse he rode in on.

RESIST HIM — Just because the President issues an order doesn't mean it's legal or binding — it must be tested in the courts, tested in the houses of congress, tested by THE PEOPLE. Of course, things are different now that the Constitution is being openly violated by the President himself, and so I wouldn't count on the Right to Free Assembly for much longer than a few weeks more.

CREATE YOUR OWN TRUMP-FREE ZONE — Make your own Trump-Free Zone for yourself and your family.

TRY TO KEEP YOUR FAMILY SAFE FROM TRUMP — Do what you have to do to avoid contact with Trump Zombies and rabid dogs. Best not to go to open places, malls, shopping centers, temples, SYNAGOGUES for SURE, anything with crowds where you might be cornered by a mob of hysterical stone-throwing Christians. It's quite possible, so don't dismiss it as ridiculous or outside the bounds of probability.

HAVE AN ESCAPE PLAN — You should never get yourself into a public space in which there is no second way out. You never know when a mob might ignite and form and swarm over you, even though you're an innocent bystander. There is no escape from mob swarming except to run. Don't bother to hide — a cave is a grave.

MAKE OUT A LAST WILL and TESTAMENT — Don't put it off.

PLAN TO LIVE WITHOUT MEDICAL CARE — It's likely you won't be able to get medical help, pharmaceuticals or even dietary supplements in a state of panic and emergency, which, I remind you, IS HIS PLAN, to use the National Guard to achieve total control of the nation.

FIND A SAFE HIDING PLACE FOR YOUR RELIGIOUS DOCUMENTS — All non-Christian books, audio and video recordings and artifacts other than crosses will be CONFISCATED AND DESTROYED by mob action AND by government Executive Order. When will this happen? Real Soon.

There are a few more steps toward SOME measure of personal freedom in a created Trump-Free Zone, but it will never be quite the same as it was "BT," Before Trump — a phrase I remember from my 37th century history textbook on the wars of the 21st century, because at some point, ALL TRUMP-FREE ZONES WILL BE DECLARED ILLEGAL.

You think I exaggerate, yes? I exaggerate, no! Believe it or not, you won't be allowed to have even a sign that says "Trump-Free Zone" IN YOUR OWN HOME!!! If you violate that, your neighbors might turn you in for the reward.

This is the kind of world into which your children and grandkids are heading. You might be able to prepare them for it, but they'll never again know the freedom you had before the world of Trump!

Again, specific steps and reactions to events as they unfold are given in specific detail in "SlimeWars", which predicted this specific chain of events, first published and read in groups over 45 years ago.

I'm so glad I decided to do a paper on "Heroes of the Second American Revolution" back in the 37th century! As a result, I'm able to name the names, give times, places, dates and circumstances, and lay out a plan of response for YOU to successfully avoid the panic, destruction and hysteria of the next few decades on your poor, suffering mudball.

There are a number of goddesses standing in the wings, waiting for their revenge for the misuse of their sacred names, but in the meantime, you've trouble enough with your own President, the highest leader in the land, the one with the highest ethics, the highest ideals and the highest concern for THE PEOPLE — at least, that's the job description.

It's clear that the present occupant of the White House knows nothing of any of these matters, and besides, it's all a fabrication of the Liberal Press.

He wasn't even a Republican until he decided to run, and said at that time, openly and in public, that he would run as a Republican "Because the Republicans are so stupid."

How could he make such a blunder? He knows that the public will stand for anything and would rather have a lie than face an uncomfortable truth, so he does what all powerful rich folks do — he ignores the rules, they're not made for aristocrats like him.

Thing is, he's NOT an aristocrat. He's a crude, mean creature with a brain the size of a walnut, and I'm being generous there, far too generous. Make that walnut a peanut.

It's already too late for me — I'll be happy to just watch it all come down. A loss of your world to you, but the gain of a Federation Dollar for me!

It must sound terrible to you that all we do is bet on the outcome of our historical simulations, but try to see our point of view — Eternity is SO boring without a game.

And what's the point of a game if you can't make a side bet?

And why bother to play a game you CAN'T LOSE??? What fun is THAT???

Send for a hundred TFZ medallions today and get them out there, if you want to have any effect at all!!! GET THEM OUT THERE!!! They WILL and DO have a powerful magical effect! GET THEM OUT THERE!!! Better hurry, before they impound the TFZ medallions in the name of Sith-Lord Trump!

If you get caught in this crunch, it will only be because you can't bring yourself to believe that your government was taken over by someone who got into office on hate and violence, racism, sexism and more violence.

He won't do a thing to you. All he need do is mention your name on Twitter, and you can kiss your ass goodbye.

His followers form the FIRST WAVE OF THE ZOMBIE APOCALYPSE for which we've all been waiting. They won't admit it, but zombies seldom achieve Self Awareness, much less higher intelligence. A zombie is a zombie.

WAKE THE FUCK UP. You no longer live in a Free Country. Shut your mouth and at least APPEAR TO walk the line, or be crushed into the gravel of the new reality.

BE CAREFUL when establishing a Trump-Free Zone, and remember that the Thought Police can come in anytime and find TFZ products in your home. They're not illegal to own ... yet.

HEAL TRUMP, DON'T DUMP TRUMP!
Compassion is the Key! Read On!!!
February 1, 2017

Compassion is my game. Brotherhood is why I came.

"Ray Guns Blasting, Johnny Jett burst through the door and sprayed the place with plasma." Not my gaming style at all, and I hope it isn't yours. I tend to play Trap Assassins, Druids or Necromancers, not Barbarians, Paladins or Sorceresses. Once in a while, I like to play Amazon, just to see the feathers fly.

How about a full-blown magical "White-Ops" that is intended to convert Donald Trump from a Man of War to a Man of Peace, from a Man of Rage and Hate to a Man of Love and Understanding, from a White Man to a Rainbow Man?

As you know, I'm not allowed by our Higher Law to interfere in local politics, not that I care enough to do that, anyway, and besides, as the Avatar of the Western Realm, it's in my goddam job-description.

So, like it or not, I can't interfere.

I didn't ask for the job. I got it because I'm good at it and I'm willing to wade in there and get all grimy from the human contact. Like I said, I didn't ask for the job.

What I CAN do, however, is act as an Adviser, at least until they come to take me away for speaking up about Trump.

The object is a conversion play, and I'll be only too happy to explain in some detail exactly what this means, what it means to you, and what YOU can do about it.

You feel helpless, eh? Not anymore, you aren't. Read on.

Even the Canadians, Europeans and Asians to whom I've spoken over the past few days have echoed the fears of those persons of color among my circle of friends, and that means about half, because I have a LOT of friends who are NOT WHITE, NOT CHRISTIAN and NOT AMERICAN, all over this planet, among other planets in the vicinity.

My non-white, non-Christian non-American friends are now in trouble.

I am allowed to give a hint now and then, but by my nature, I can't take direct action. What I propose is entirely consistent with good karmic practices.

All my Tibetan friends are taking part in this action, and they will, if asked, endorse the plan — why not obtain a few of my "HEAL TRUMP" Medallions to give to them???

Tell them Groucho sent you.

WHAT IS THE "CONVERSION HACK"???

CONVERSION is a SIMPLE "BACK DOOR" HACK into the human mind. It resources the fact that there is no defense set up there, because there has never been a perceived threat to the ego from that direction.

I reference here Lawrence's attack on Akaba in 1917, attacking unexpectedly from the desert side. All the guns were pointed out to sea — same basic effect as the Maginot Line had on the Germans. They merely walked around it.

I'm not talking about attack here, except in the psycho-emotional side, entirely through the aethers, having NO physical effect whatever.

This enables the prayer enchantment to penetrate the barriers as if it were a neutron, then at the moment it contacts the ego sphere, it explodes into tiny fishhooks that eat into the ego, bringing it into the Awakening Light of Enlightenment.

Simple game logic, simple application of an age-old secret, that is built into the universe, and is accessible on any and every level from anywhere in the level — not a bad feature, eh? All my games have that built in, so One can edit on the fly, from right within the game world.

When I videogame, I prefer a small, weak character to a strong one. Everyone who follows my gaming videos is familiar with my explanation on YouTube of why I deleted my Level 99 Character in Diablo II — a video that to date has captured a walloping 86,000 views from folks who had similar experiences.

Why did I take out a character that took a whole three months at an average time commitment of 16 hours a day every day of the week, to build up, and what's more, I did that three times in a row!!!

My character won the race to 99 in its class — Assassin — three seasons in a row. I would never take an Assassin to 99 in overall competition. Only a Sorc could do that.

So, why did I do it? To demonstrate that I could, that anyone dedicated enough could do it, that's why, and the simple fact is, I prefer a small, weak character — no armor, no magic, no weapon, no helm, no shield, no boots, no dagger, no assigned points, just the character as it first lands in the game world.

I like to do the same on all levels of gaming, even Life Gaming, which seems so vital and important to you right now.

Frankly, I have to handicap myself SOMEHOW, or the game's too easy. Don't forget, I design games, weapons, levels, characters and the occasional image. I'm frighteningly, lightning fast and tend to finish a game from front to back at about the fastest speed the game will allow in forward movement along the plot-line.

When you win every game, even those you didn't make or design, not even when you start playing on the Hell Level, you tend to stop playing, or you find some way to cripple your character in some imaginative way, to make yourself weaker, slower, dumber, easier to take down, easier to stop — in this particular case, I came out with a strong dice roll and it's too late, it's already a movement and cannot now be stopped by any human agency.

Echhh, about non-human agencies, I say nothing. Naw, even my dear, sweet brother, Numsi, can't stop it at this point, because my HEAL TRUMP COMPASSIONATE PRAYER will soon be manifested by my Tibetan friends, and then it will go viral, worldwide.

I maintain my interest in the life game by crimping my own style rather deeply and, as a result, I tend to come up with compassionate and friendly solutions to blockages in the Path, Obstructions in the Sacred Soil, as it were, such as "Uncle" Donald Trump Duck, rather than solutions that offend me spiritually, such as dumping him — that's never a solution. In the end, all parties must come to the peace table.

Have you noticed that he sometimes ACTUALLY SOUNDS LIKE DONALD DUCK??? That can't be mere coincidence. It's probably some gimmick installed on the microphones by the Liberal Media and the Leftest Press!

My COMPASSIONATE BUDDHA solution to obstructions on the Path is to walk around them, over them, under them or avoid them completely, but when the signs read:

"DEAD END", "NO U-TURN", "NO LEFT TURN", "NO RIGHT TURN", "NO EXIT", that's when I get out my little magic kit and start working the other side of the curtain as Avatar of the Western Realm, equivalent to the job of "janitor" at the Steam Bath in the Sky.

The idea is that you can eliminate blockages to the spiritual path by **converting them to your side,** and that's what I want to talk to you about.

Enough talk about dumping Trump, what a rump, what a grump, hump, bump, lump, stump, shlump. Useless. Resistance is futile. He has the Storm Troopers coming AFTER YOU, and they are brutes emanating from the Brute World.

The Gates of the Hell World and Brute World have been opened by the Avatar inside Donald Trump. That Avatar must be cast out like the demon he is, but don't let that get you uptight. It's just part of the shadow-show that is the Universal Cosmos, and the basis, the framework of which is the Quantum World and Zero Grid.

YES, EXORCISM IS PART OF THE HEALING.

The Demon inside Donald Trump has stacked everything on his side. His cronies are WORSE and even SICKER and more Nazi and

White Supremacist than he is, and he's PLENTY Nazi enough already, but you DON'T dump Trump, get him impeached or committed to a mental institution, because his replacements are FAR WORSE THAN TRUMP!!!

Donald became subject to the demonic possession because of his illness. Without that infamous PACT he signed, he'd have NOTHING, not a PENNY to his name. You don't become a billionaire like he did without signing SOMETHING.

An exorcism of the Demon inside Trump is part of the plan. The Demon will resist exorcism, if he becomes aware of it, but he can't stop it now — he's doomed to be cast out soon, when YOU take action!!!

If you were wondering who is pulling his chain, it's obvious, if you know how to look.

WAKE UP, SLEEPY HEAD!!!

You are TODAY living in Nazi White Amerika. You might never wake up to that fact, and you certainly won't wake up to it IN TIME!!!

When you're actually standing around in the mud of the barbed-wire stockade after the Big Roundup of Jews, African-Americans, Asian-Americans, Native Americans, Euro-Americans and Arab-Americans and other Problem People, it will then be too late for you to do anything other than wait for a swift death rather than endure years in the labor camps.

Yes, Labor Camps. You schmuck! You think I'm making this up? Exaggerating? Hitting the panic button too early? Wake up and hear the bugle call, Maggot!!!

The Internment Camps of World War II are very clearly remembered by Japanese-Americans, whose families were imprisoned there, having done NOTHING WRONG other than being Japanese or Japanese-American.

German-Americans are not obvious — they don't have different color skin than Amerikan whites, so they weren't rounded up, nor were Italian-Americans, invisible among all the other folks in the crowd, although Germany and Italy were belligerents back then, not our closest allies, as they were until Trump ruined NATO, which he has sworn to do.

The new Internment Camps are in the same places as the old ones, with a few new sites added on. Although they are super-secret, some photos have leaked out.

The Civilian Internment Camps for YOU and YOUR FAMILY are already built — have been thrown together in just a few weeks of secret stealth work by Army engineer corps.

Your Future Prison Camp Home is already in place, and your job breaking rocks is waiting for you to arrive, whenever they come to take you and your loved ones away.

They call them "Labor Camps", and they are characterized as places for workers, intended to bring workers closer to the work sites, which are infrastructure areas. The roads and highways and bridges in Amerika are crumbling, have you noticed that?

There isn't anyone else to fix it other than YOU.

There won't be any Christians in those Labor Camps, unless they're Catholic, Lutheran or some other unapproved form of Christian. That's not Donald Trump's plan — he's being used by the Christian Far Right, their return for putting him in power.

"ARBEITEN MACHT FREI" —

"Work Makes You Free" the World War II Death Camps proclaimed in signs at the entrance. The promise was, work hard and you will earn your freedom, but the freedom promised was a path that led through a gas chamber into a crematorium, and that's what's waiting for you at the end of the rainbow in this hellish scenario.

"So what are you gonna DO about it?" the big bully sneers.

"ME AND THIS ARMY," is the correct response, but make it an Army of Prayer and Compassion, not one of violence. Never meet violence with violence. It does no good, and makes the armpits itch.

Donald Trump does not understand Compassion, and has no idea what it's good for, so he will of course react badly if he comes to understand that this compassionate prayer force is being directed at him.

He may outlaw the prayer medallions.

WHAT IS HIS PLAN FOR YOU?

You are being targeted as a worker, a drone of the human kind, to be removed from the blue collar and white collar work force, to be imprisoned and offered food and survival in return for which, you're expected to do your part to help restore the bridges and roads to nice freshness and newness, so the tanks can roll over them, just as the Autobahn was intended by Hitler when he had them built.

The Autobahn did not carry civilian traffic during the war.

It's never for the good of the people. Will you ever learn? Probably not. You're too honest to get the picture.

The big politicians are CHEATING. They are out to skin you alive, to rape you, to destroy you and take your goods and chuck you down the drain.

No government has ever been beneficent or truly enlightened, even in Tibet. Government is always corrupt, some are more corrupt than others, like the administrations of Taft, Reagan and the most corrupt President to date other than Donald Trump, Dickless Nixon.

Politicians play a dirty game and love it.

They are not there for your welfare. As a matter of fact, if you're on Welfare, they don't need the gas chambers. What better way to get rid of you than to cut off your food supply?

Come to think of it, that's exactly MY strategy in war gaming. Go after the food supply, the ammo dumps, the resources, the factories, the warehouses, the shipping and rail system, the cargo ships — all the backbone, none of the meat, meaning don't get into a direct fight.

I use this exact strategy when fighting Baal in Hell in Diablo II — I don't play Diablo III because it's a piece of shit, and PoE is too visually disturbing to my old eyes, and badly designed anyway, but enough about videogames for the moment. I'll return to the subject in a few minutes.

The experts all agree that Donald Trump is a Narcissistic Personality Disorder, which drives him to say and do crazy things, things that are likely to get White Amerika blown out of the water, and us along with it.

You may also have noticed that he cheats on his income tax — hasn't paid any for decades — and has ordered U.S. troops to take actions against the Native Americans who are trying to stop his oil pipeline from crossing sacred Indian Burial sites.

He's also cooking up a scheme with Putin that will leave us in Putin's hands and force China into a nuclear exchange.

Something else he's after, is another Christian Crusade, to end the Moslem Menace forever. This guy is serious, and he's counting on YOU not waking up to that fact until it's too late and you're marching to the gas chambers along with the rest of us, and if you still believe that YOU are not on his "kill" list, you're dead wrong.

Donald controls Congress, the Supreme Court, the Justice Department, the IRS, the State Department, Department of Defense, CIA, FBI and a host of other Federal agencies both public and secret, and

YOU are his target.

He has "stacked" his administration with known self-professed Nazis and White Supremacists, and in a sense, has declared war against the American population. He regards us as hamburger to be chewed up for his personal satisfaction.

He is mean-hearted, spiteful, vengeful, aggressive, downright belligerent with everyone around him, always in conflict, AND HE'S NEVER WRONG.

Let me direct you to "My Life as a Boy" Volumes 1 and 2, to remind you of all the characteristics of the NPD, the Narcissistic Personality Disorder which, up until a few years ago, had been undiagnosed for centuries as "Megalomania", but it's not. It's NPD, and the outcome of NPD is VERY VERY specific.

Right now, I'd like to remind you of just a few simple details of the illness, which should serve to demonstrate the fact that he suffers deeply from it. Keep in mind that under ordinary circumstances, with ordinary medical treatment, THIS CONDITION HAS NO CURE.

My friends and I all agree on this point: Compassion is always your best answer.

WHAT CAN I DO???

Through the judicious use of SHAMANIC MAGIC, otherwise known as Quantum Mechanics, we will undertake to HEAL DONALD TRUMP of his Narcissistic Personality Disorder, plus the side-effects brought about by the legally prescribed, FDA-approved pharmaceuticals he's taking by the fistful to help him sleep, wake up, eat and take a dump.

As a former official U.S. Remote Viewer, I can tell you that he's basically in the same condition as Michael Jackson had been. Some people can't sleep without medication, and some can't sleep BECAUSE of medication. In Remote Viewing Mode, I am easily able to scan his medicine cabinet, and because of a little pharmaceutical skill and an ability to read and write Latin medical scrip, I can read his pill boxes like a map.

Any psychic sensitive will agree with me on what's wrong with Donald Trump.

Edgar Cayce would have spelled out both the cause AND the cure, but he would never have taken it. The CORE OF THE ILLNESS is that it doesn't exist.

The cure is simple and, although impossible with ordinary mental and psychological methods, it is quite possible, using special UNSEEN and UNDETECTED magical methods.

PURE COMPASSIONATE PRAYER POWER is what's used here. Nothing more. It is the most powerful magic in the universe. Nothing can withstand the power of prayer, and the most potent of prayers is that which leans on quantum energy to empower it.

The Christians also have prayer, but think a moment. What would they pray in order to counteract the Healing??? Make Trump even crazier?

His psychosis enables his supporters to control him. His needs are all the engine they need to fire him up and get him doing things to PEACEFUL and INNOCENT people, things that are the equivalent of ripping the wings off a butterfly, which he apparently did, as a child.

IT IS STRICTLY WHITE MAGIC

It is "WHITE MAGIC" in the sense that it intends healing, not harm, quite the opposite of the super-popular $10 Donald Trump Voodoo Doll that you see all over eBay and Amazon these days. Voodoo will do you no good. Removing Trump from power will not help.

I don't believe in killing, destruction, mayhem. It's just not my nature. I don't live life to survive or to dominate or to win. There are much higher goals in a game than winning.

Left photo, Tarthang Tulku, Rinpoche, at right, E.J. Gold, Temple Procession at the International Buddhist Meditation Center in Los Angeles, 1972.

Even in a video game "3-D shooter" style, I minimize or eliminate the weapons and concentrate on strategy, which is why I like this approach so much more.

In VIDEO GAMING terminology, this MAGICAL ACTION is called "CONVERSION".

You remember the Conversion of St. Paul? That was one of my gags back in the day. What "Conversion" means is that you take an occult — that just means "unseen" — action in the quantum world, altering the internals of someone who was your enemy.

They then become your friend.

If you've ever played a Trap Assassin in Diablo II, you'll be familiar with the Conversion Spell. It really works, and thanks to Dan for reminding me about it.

If we can MAGICALLY HEAL DONALD TRUMP, he WILL change. He will calm down. He might even remove his Nazi friends from cabinet positions, but he might not be able to do that — this thing has gotten out of his control already, but a calmer President would certainly help.

As it is now, he's so compulsive that he gives away State Secrets in his Twitter chats — of course unconsciously. He doesn't understand that he's giving out signals ALL THE TIME, powered by his deep and serious psychological illness.

As I said, ordinary medical means don't work in the case of an NPD, but magic does. We CAN DO THIS, if enough people work together to bring it about.

A MASS MAGICAL ACTION such as this requires MASSIVE PARTICIPATION to arouse the TOTAL PRAYER POWER to bring about the magical change in Donald Trump, who likes to be referred to as "THE Donald", kind of like "THE Craigus", eh?

If you missed the above "Craigus" reference, you have decided to ignore my help and warnings, by NOT watching "Creation of the Humanoids", as I strongly recommended.

You also need to look at "Big Trouble in Little China" to help you understand that this happens all the time, and to understand that the best approach is not a frontal battle, I would recommend "Lawrence of Arabia".

Why fight when you can bring them down by attacking the supply and communication lines without firing a shot?

So what can small, helpless YOU do to survive the wrath of the violent mobs?

Simple solution. Don't go after the mobs, go after the source of the cancer, Donald Trump. Help him to sanity, heal him, make him calm, patient, tolerant, kind, courteous, gentle, sensitive, humanitarian, even spiritual, if such a thing is possible.

A gentler, kinder President.

Can it be done?

Yes, it can. It's been done before. We'll talk about the previous times it has worked, when we go into workshop mode, so you can ask questions in the chat.

KEEP IN MIND THAT I HAVE NO PERSONAL AXE TO GRIND WITH DONALD TRUMP. I am simply listing the SYMPTOMS of his illness, so if you have any success in healing him, you'll be able to SEE THE EFFECT right there IN THE MEDIA.

It's easy to see his illness just from viewing the news media. An ABSENCE of those symptoms will be VERY OBVIOUS. First off, he'll apologize and ask forgiveness, then he'll act to reverse the damage.

You should be able to SEE the effects of your HEALING PRAYERS if enough people get behind the movement and actually DO IT.

John Lilly, Antonietta Lilly, and E.J. Gold at International Conference, 1973.

The main VISIBLE factors that you should watch for signs that the HEALING PRAYER is working are:

1. A very exaggerated sense of one's talents, skills and importance in the world at large. Donald Trump has extreme trust issues, probably stemming from early childhood. His mother was known to be a terrible bitch, and his father evidently ignored him. The reason Trump considers himself tax-exempt is because his Dad called him "a complete write-off".

2. An obvious and obsessive need for attention, lots of it, and admiration, if available. This guy can get admiration, but it has to be from someone who wants or needs something from him, like a Christian who belongs to the "right" Christian group in his LIST of friends and enemies, and he has one, believe it, and I'm on it already. How about you?

3. Fantasies of Great Romance. I don't have to spell this one out for you. Trump spent some news interview time defending the length of his dick. Do you know ANY public personality that has done the same?

4. Fantasies of Great Insight, Great Ideas, Personal Greatness in general. Trump imagines himself to be the Hero, the Greatest U.S. President in history, but in the end, he'll go down as just another schmuck, unless YOU help to HEAL DONALD TRUMP!

5. An NPD sees other people as objects or "dolls", as in "My dolls came to help me give a party!", or "Hey, bitch, how about a blowjob?". This personality trait was displayed in the now-famous helicopter landing video that went viral just before the election. It made no difference, the popular vote was thrown out.

6. Easily offended, and when offended, crushed beyond hope, until he or she gets his or her way with you. For the NPD, everything, even the most harmless and exalted thing, is a weapon to be used to keep you under control. Donald Trump ALWAYS goes on the attack after a slight or some perfectly harmless dig at his over-exposed ego.

7. Self-criticism and NPD do not mix well. NPDs who are confronted with any issues or problems will go immediately into a tailspin of rage and/or paranoiac accusations in every direction. This serves to create some of the more interesting — medically speaking — videos in the news coverage media.

8. Totally Unbelievably Powerful Sense of Righteousness. Even the most evil of acts can be easily rationalized by the NPD, because lying comes easier than telling the simple truth. Trump lies easily and gets away with it because he knows he can, and will. People will accept lies more easily than any truth.

9. An NPD's feelings are easily hurt. This is the first and sometimes last line of defense for the NPD who hasn't yet crushed you down all the way to the ground. As a last resort, the NPD will cry, but those are strictly crocodile tears, cold-bloodedly created just for the effect.

10. Seems very sympathetic and empathetic, but has a heart of stone, no feelings for other whatever, totally sociopathic in every respect, and a potential candidate for doing harm to others without a single drop of remorse. Wait until you see the NUMBERS of dead as a result of Trump's policies — he'll be held personally responsible in the Afterlife for all that he does to others.

11. Has no respect for others, yet demands respect from others, and has a temper tantrum when that doesn't happen to his or her expectations. Hey, I didn't write this about Trump — it's a dispassionate description of the medical condition known as NPD.

12. Is able to easily rationalize and justify the most barbaric and

animalistic acts, thinks of them as completely ordinary and in every respect totally normal. Doesn't everyone do what I do??? Of course they do! He wants around himself only those who mirror his views and fears.

13. Bad things tend to happen around an NPD. They get hurt easily and others get hurt just by being near them, either physically or emotionally or both.

14. Sense of Personal Entitlement. The world owes them a living, and they tend to let their totally disrupted partner carry the weight of earning the living for both of them. How many billions of dollars do YOU need to take care of and feed your family? He has most of what everyone else needs. Billions of dollars to one dollar of yours. HEAL DONALD TRUMP and maybe he'll stop stealing YOUR money and building oil pipelines through YOUR sacred soil.

Another VERY important factor in the NPD is his hatred of anything that allows people to be creative. That's why Trump closed the National Endowment for the Arts, National Public Radio and more, to eliminate possible areas of protest and resistance.

The restoration of public radio and art programs will signal a new, HEALED Donald Trump.

Those items listed above are just a FEW of the characteristics by which you can recognize an NPD. Why do I put them up there? To embarrass Donald Trump?

Not at all. I have no feelings toward Donald Trump whatever. He is merely a gaming problem to be solved, and he leaves us no options other than magic. All other options, including political, legal and ethical moves, are unavailable to us.

These symptoms are listed only as a guidepost that indicates that the HEALING is working!!!

CONVERSION is the Play of Choice.

MAKE OR BUY A BUNCH OF "HEAL DONALD TRUMP" MEDALLIONS OR EARRINGS.

GET THEM OUT THERE to as many people as possible. WEARING or CARRYING the HEAL DONALD TRUMP medallions or earrings ACTIVATES them!

SPREAD THE TEACHING — Spiritual Healing is the Best Medicine. Help others learn how to make the healing medallions by the millions.

E.J. Gold and Claudio Naranjo in private discussion, 1974.

I did say back at the beginning of the chapter that I would give some indications regarding video games and Donald Trump.

Before I go into detail here, I want to remind you that Shamanic Quantum Actions — commonly called "magic" by the uninitiated and uninformed — is an unstoppable force in the Quantum World.

It has no limits in space or time, and can be applied anywhere and anywhen. The rules of Quantum Magic are simple and easy to understand, the first of which is "Do No Harm".

You already have one strategy in the Struggle Against Trumpism — the HEAL TRUMP Prayer Medallion, but you can ADD TO THE MIX the action of using the HEAL TRUMP ORB!!!

I am working tonight, designing a "HEAL TRUMP" Orb which will be available as a public download as soon as it's complete. The magical action cannot at this time be duplicated in an iPhone app. It would take about $350,000 to develop the software needed, but the guys are standing ready if anyone wants to cover the costs.

I will take nothing for this personally except a "thank you". Actually, as Avatar of the Western Realm, it's my fucking job.

Frankly, I like a head-to-head MELEE with my opponent, which is why gamers call me "The Hatchet Man". I get in close and personal, see? You can watch how I fight by viewing my videos on gorebagdotcom and gorebagg channels on YouTube.

Sure, I'm aware that I could easily put hot links in there. I'm very skilled at HTML. So why didn't I do that?

Because if you're going to get anything out of this, YOU have to push the buttons, take the steps, make the moves, empower yourself, get out of your armchair.

You won't do a fucking thing until you're convinced that **YOU and YOUR FAMILY are the TARGET of Donald Trump.**

I can't and won't convince you of that, and you're well-trained to take it on the chin and roll over and die.

Trump can lie, and lie, and lie, and you won't react, won't do anything, and why is that? Because you can't believe that this can happen here, that the United States can be overthrown by a single man — he isn't acting alone, he has the backing of the Illuminati, the Secret Societies that put him in power.

E.J. Gold and Robert Anton Wilson at Writer's Conference, 1980.

When you finally SEE that THE TIME HAS COME, and that YOU ARE REALLY THE TARGET, you'll take action. I only hope for your sake, it won't be too late. For my own sake, it's already far too late. I'm high on the radar screen and frankly, I never care.

One of my primary strategies in Team Fortress 2 is to die and reappear at spawn just in time to deprive the enemy of our Intel. This thoroughly professional spiritual strategy is outlined in my gaming song, "You Can Make It If You Die", which again, you'll find on YouTube.

When your enemy attacks you, don't fight with fists or weapons of mass destruction. Don't form a mob, and storm the palace. BE SMART, work BEHIND THE LINES, like Lawrence of Arabia — attack the supply lines, the communication lines, the food and water, the rails, and leave the enemy soldiers alone to march wherever they may.

You don't yet know that you are at war. We've been at war for quite some time, and now it has expanded so that Amerikans will be fighting Americans, which you can easily avoid if you know how.

"These are not the droids you're looking for."

Use Quantum Magic — what is called in Star Wars "The Force" — to bring your enemy to his knees — IN PRAYER of THANKS for your spiritual HEALING intervention!

I don't mean the phony prayer that Trump mocks up for his Christian Brown Shirt civilian army, or his Christian posings for the media which are so reminiscent of the spiritual strivings of Saddam Hussein and Nicolae Ceausecu, the insane leader of Rumania who was deposed and tried for rape and murder.

Most folks won't remember these things, but I'm a professional Life Gamer, so of course, I do. If you plan to be a Bodhisattva, you'll need good information before you can take Right Action, as in this case.

I don't mean media prayer, but Real Prayer, in thanks for his Miracle Cure from NPD, a cure which YOU helped bring about through the use of the Heal Trump Orb and the Heal Trump Medallions!

He will CHANGE when he is HEALED, and he will feel the impulse of gratitude for the first time in his sad life!!!

Make this happen! You have the Power of Compassion, Forgiveness and Spirit!

USE THE FORCE, LUKE!!!

Send for your **"HEAL TRUMP"** MEDALLIONS and DOWNLOAD THE **"HEAL TRUMP"** ORB right now, this very moment! I can ship as many **"HEAL TRUMP"** medallions and earrings as you want, at only $10 apiece!!! At the moment, I make ALL of the medallions, but when the orders start pouring in, I'll need help.

"If you want them, come and get them, but you'd better hurry, 'coz they're going fast!"

"Alas, when wandering in the Bardo, overcome by fear and

65

loathing, let COMPASSION be your guide, forgiveness be your wisdom, enlightenment be your path", and you can quote me on that.

Frank Herbert and E.J. Gold, Los Angeles, circa 1975.

Never let anger rule you. Turn the Dark Side to the Light. Once Trump is HEALED, we can work to bring him to **ENLIGHTEN-MENT.**

With compassion, all things are possible.

NAZI OCCUPIED ALL-WHITE, ALL-CHRISTIAN AMERIKA "TRUMP BLOCKERS" FOR SALE
February 2, 2017

Zombie Girl Saved Millions in Ancient Atlantis.

"HELP US, ZOMBIE GIRL! DONALD TRUMP IS NUTS!"

He not only IS nuts, he HAS nuts, according to the reports from his female employees, and thanks to Shamanic Magic, YOU can kick him in the nuts, on the Astral Plane!

Fuckin' Hell, I warned you that RONALD MCDONALD T-RUMP WAS NUTS, FOUR FUCKING DECADES ago, when I predicted all this in "SlimeWars", which you probably haven't read, if you're still surprised by the daily outrages and attacks on YOUR personal freedoms.

Oh, but he's much more than merely nuts. He's an actual, real live Nazi Dictator, a tyrant, a slob and yes, he is actually possessed by an Evil Avatar, and he's ugly, too. Hard to watch on the news just because he's so ugly and strange looking.

He wants YOU to feel fear, just as he does, all day, every day, all night, every night.

All his closest advisers, cabinet members and social friends are actual card-carrying Party Member Neo-Nazis, except his bedmate and fellow wannabe mass-murdering fuckhead, Count Vlad Putin, who is the Father of Expediency and a former Communist. He's a member of whatever keeps him in power.

Is there something between them? Sure, there is, and it's not just another of those springtime romances. They've been plotting this all along, and Putin gets half the booty when all Trump's enemies lie dead, like an old chestnut Shakespeare play, eh?

He and his Nazi friends hate Mexicans, Jews, Italians, South Africans, Dutch, Poles, Iranians, Iraquis, Afghanis, Pakshis, Africans of all kinds, Arabs of any description, Blacks, Reds, Purples, Browns, Tans, Catholics, Buddhists, Shintoists, Hindus, and YOU and ME.

If they weren't doing his dirty work for him, he'd hate the Born Again mobs, too. Actually, he does, and if he follows true to form, he'll eventually kill them all, just as Hitler purged his S.A. troops to ensure that they didn't overthrow him after they put him in power.

RACE WAR, RELIGIOUS WAR, CIVIL WAR, NUCLEAR WAR.

That's TRUMP's agenda. Actually, he has no plan, just uncontrollable rage and hate.

He distrusts absolutely everyone, and thinks that everyone including Einstein is stupid. When it comes to war, he's smarter than any of his generals. He's smarter than any of his security advisers. He's smarter than any of his lawyers.

His smartness will eventually bring him down, but in the meantime, YOU and YOUR FAMILY will have suffered and perhaps died under his intolerant rule.

He's a legend in his own mind, the only smart monkey on the planet, and the only one willing to use his smarts to outwit the other monkeys, which are mostly Republicans, by actual count.

The reason he thinks that he is smarter than anyone else is because intelligent people can't believe that anyone that savage and soulless can possibly exist and interact with them, imprison them in a wall of fear, AND GET AWAY WITH IT.

This, in his twisted and tortured mind, is equivalent to "smart, real smart". Most monkeys think they're amazingly intelligent. There's more brainpower in the average grey than there is in the entire human race taken as a whole, just like comparing an iPhone with an adding machine.

"GO NUCLEAR!" SAYS DONALD.

Good advice, Donald!!! In the news yesterday, TRUMP told his Republican Congressional Thugs, "GO NUCLEAR!" his own words, and he apparently said and shouted it several times. It certainly won't bother me to see it all go up in smoke.

An NPD gives away his inner thoughts without realizing it. HE INTENDS TO GO NUCLEAR any day, now. He has the idea that HE will survive a nuclear exchange, and he's right. He'll be in his bunker, nice and safe and sound, while the rest of us watch the blooming mushroom clouds.

You'll spend the next few weeks after that bombardment from the heavens, trying to dodge the weather and fallout from more than 20,000 nuclear airbursts. Good luck on that. I have a way out of that scenario, but you can't afford it. The plan involves building a very expensive particle accelerator, which Claude and I both have the skills and math to do, but we'd need environmental impact reports filed first, of course, and I wouldn't build it here.

Accelerators are very likely to spawn radiation, but not nearly as much as 20,000 airbursts with an average yield of 50 megatons per weapon. That's a LOT of radiation, and a LOT of blast damage and guess what? The Earth is knocked 17 degrees off its present axis, bringing the most amazingly brilliant Eastern Lights you've never seen!

I never liked Polaris, anyway, the Pole star that always points North, until the nuclear weapon activated Global Polar Axis Shift, that is. I've had to study that event in school, and I wish I could remember the outcome, but it wasn't great, that much I recollect from my 37th century "21st century history" lessons, one of which is this experience in the Regression Simulator, with which you're all-too-familiar, I guess.

One of TRUMPIE-DUMPIE's plans is to find some excuse to lay waste to ISRAEL and take Jerusalem for the Christians. He already has a battery of Nukes AIMED DIRECTLY AT ISRAEL! Any Remote Viewer can find and identify them. I can read the serial numbers on the weapon casings.

I'LL BET THAT YOU CAN'T WALK ON THE STREETS NOW, AND FEEL SAFE FROM YOUR FELLOW AMERICANS!

Only when YOU face the death camp and the crematorium HERE IN NAZI OCCUPIED AMERIKA will you realize that this is really happening, and that it's happening HERE and that it's happening TODAY and that this is not some fantasy science fiction story, it's real and YOU are in it up to your eyeballs, like it or not, know it or not.

The chances are that, like everyone else, you'll choose to do nothing.

"Wait. Things will get better," you say.

Ask the Jews of Germany who said that same exact thing, right up until their very last breath of life.

They didn't live to regret those words. Most of them died. Six MILLION Jews died in those "nonexistent" death camps, and the death camps in Amerika don't exist, either. 55 million people died as a direct result of Hitler's actions.

Wouldn't Trump be proud of numbers ten times that size? That's how many will die in the first wave, and then there are five more nuclear wars to follow, if Trump manages to carry out his aggression and anger.

There is still a chance to stop him, but only through magic — no other options are open. He has already stolen your "safe" world, your "free" world and your "freedom from fear" world, and they will NEVER return while he and his ambitious and powerful family are still in power. Wait until you get into the future, where you'll discover to your utter consternation that YOU and YOUR FAMILY NEVER EXISTED, according to the "Second Holocaust Conspiracy Theorists" so popular with the High School Sophomores of the 33rd century. According to them, there was no Second Holocaust, just as there are schmucks who prefer to believe that it never happened, it was just a figment of imagination, the six million graves are NOTHING, nothing at all.

Don't give in to the Dark Side. The Force IS with you, I promise! Stay on the Light Side!

I'm not here to convince them. They're alien-dominated zombies. You can't reason with an alien-dominated zombie, especially in a world of hate and fear, distrust and betrayal.

Everyone's your enemy now.

I'm seriously prepared to have to physically defend some of my less white friends if I'm out in public with them and they happen to be attacked. I have no choice there, and I can't let the attacker continue the attack, or repeat the attack, ever again.

That's a really miserable position to find yourself in, having to defend one or more of your non-white or non-Christian friends, maybe to the death.

The only way you can prove there was a TRUMPish Second Holocaust is that YOU WERE THERE, so you'll just have to wait until you can reincarnate and find some evidence, and set the story straight, but by that time, there will be no one left to care, as if anyone ever did.

As a matter of fact, anyone who doesn't FEEL TARGETED BY TRUMP will tend to disbelieve that this could happen, right up until they die in the gas chamber or at the hands of the Blackwater Mercenaries or the civilian Born-Again Storm-Troopers and the mob hatred and the public stonings and lynchings and drive-by shootings and general mayhem.

Oh, if you think it's gonna be just the Jews, you got another think coming.

We're ALL on his "ROUND UP and DESTROY" list, and the list is getting longer every day. I want to point out that his biggest fear is RIDICULE, and now that he's in public life, he's going to get plenty of it, and he doesn't take it on the chin too well.

Trumpie Poo attacks anything and anyone who even suggests that his dick might be tiny.

Someone just said to me, "Our Native American friends in L.A. wanted a few TFZ (Trump-Free Zone) Earrings and Medallions for their friends."

Of course they do. It suddenly occurred to me that they know a LOT of people who aren't Christian, and aren't white. So do I, and if you read my blog, you probably have a lot of friends who would appreciate a Trump-Blocker of SOME sort.

I'm making new quantum devices tonight, one of which will be a SUPER TRUMP BLOCKER for the home, and yet another, for those who are past outrage, which will be a very powerful "BLOCK

TRUMP" device, using all the quantum effects you'd expect from an Atlantean or Hyperborean rig.

"Have you heard the latest outrage?" folks are saying every single HOUR of every single DAY.

FEELING HOPELESS, DEFENSELESS AND HELPLESS?

"I don't want to go to work anymore," I hear people saying, and "What's the point of living if it's going to be like this from now on?"

Jesus, who wants to live in a world like that? Myself, I have ways out of it, ways to block it, but maybe YOU don't, and would just like some goddam peace and quiet without having to look through your window curtains to see if there's a TANK parked outside your house, with its big gun pointed right at YOU and YOUR FAMILY!

DOUBT IT WILL HAPPEN?

I guarantee that that is EXACTLY what is going to happen, until Donald Trump is forcibly dragged off to the looney bin — which is his fate, eventually. He's crazier than you think he is, way off the deep end, driven even further by his apparent success in manipulating the masses and the media.

I predict that there will be national strikes, walkouts, sit-ins and marches, but that won't do any good, and Trump WANTS AN EXCUSE to send in the National Guard.

He's calculating that his troops will pull the trigger on American civilians, and that the resultant slaughter will reduce AND SILENCE the opposition, like the Kent State murders, which left four UNARMED student protesters dead on the ground, five more horribly wounded and paralyzed for life, on May 4, 1970.

28 National Guard soldiers fired on student protesters from a distance of several dozen yards. That wasn't the only time this happened.

My guess is that after the handcuffing, detainment and possible beating, of a lone, very scared five-year old Iranian boy at Dulles International Airport (Dulles must be turning in his grave right now) yesterday, everyone who isn't Lily-White and Pro-Life Christian will want some protection from their Insane President and his goonie hordes.

He's started rambling about bombs being planted in the buildings on 9/11, and he's been known to throw around speculation that the Moon might be hollow.

"WE NEED A TRUMP BLOCKER!"

I couldn't agree more, and that's why I'm working on some magical solutions. Nothing else will work. He's got his people in place, and he can't be knocked out except by two psychiatrists and a judge.

I can tell you which medical facility he lands in for treatment of psychosis, but I can't do that until just before it happens — my gaming constraints again.

I can tell you this much — at some point, Trump is removed from office, but I can't tell you the circumstances at this time, until more things happen, because, by my own playing rules, I'm not permitted to prognosticate in public.

(I timed the laugh on that one — it's a two-count.)

Okay, enough backstory, let's get to the products that are available at this time and keep in mind that I wouldn't put any of these on the market, but I need to raise some money for my medical coverage when Medicare is withdrawn, in a week or so. I have no other coverage, and will be unable to get any coverage, so like most folks I know, I haven't long under those circumstances, which puts me — and probably you, too — well into the "fuck it" category of senior citizens.

I have no patience for a Donald Trump, and I hope you don't, either. He's too sick, too psychotic and too racist to qualify for public office, and he WILL be removed from office, but not in time to help YOU and YOUR FAMILY escape his hate and rage, fueled all the more by his ability to get away with it.

All my TRUMP-BLOCKERS are absolutely GUARANTEED 100% EFFECTIVE against the VIBES, but I can't guarantee anything against the STORM TROOPERS. Watch as our military gets changed into STORM TROOPERS just like Star Wars and World War II Germany!

How fun is that???

SHAMAN MAGIC TRUMP-BLOCKERS
Hand-Crafted in California

TRUMP-FREE ZONE ITEMS:

TRUMP-FREE ZONE earrings:
TFZ PENNY-SIZED BRASS EARRINGS — $9.95 pair
TFZ DOLLAR-SIZED COPPER BOARD-BACKED EARRINGS — $35.00 pair

TFZ DOLLAR-SIZED COPPER STERLING SILVER EARRINGS — $139.95 pair

TRUMP-FREE ZONE medallions:
TFZ BASIC DOLLAR-SIZED BOARD-BACKED BLOCKER MEDALLION — $9.95
TFZ U.S. SILVER DOLLAR BACKED COPPER POWER MEDALLION — $149.95

TRUMP-FREE ZONE Handmade Tibetan Incense:
TFZ PROTECTION HOME DEFENSE Handmade Tibetan Incense — $9.95

TRUMP-FREE ZONE ATLANTEAN CRYSTALS:
TFZ PROTECTION HOME DEFENSE ATLANTEAN CRYSTAL — $9.95
TFZ COPPER-COIL ATLANTEAN CRYSTAL PENDANT — $19.95
TFZ COPPER-COIL ATLANTEAN POWER CRYSTAL PENDANT — $49.95

TRUMP-FREE ZONE METEORITES:

TFZ PROTECTION HOME DEFENSE CHARGED METEORITE — $9.95
TFZ COPPER-COIL CHARGED METEORITE PENDANT — $19.95
TFZ COPPER-COIL LARGE METEORITE PENDANT — $49.95
TFZ HOME PROTECTION LARGE IRON METEORITE — $350.00
TFZ SUPER PROTECTION NWA X-LARGE METEORITE — $2250.00
The extra-large North-West Africa Stony Meteorites are anywhere from 3/4 kilo to just over a kilo in weight, and are super-powerful allies against TRUMP'S ALL-WHITE CHRISTIAN AMERIKA.

TRUMP-FREE ZONE ACCESSORIES and SUPPLIES:

TFZ HOME OR PERSONAL PROTECTION ESSENTIAL OIL — $49.95

TFZ HOME OR ALTAR PROTECTION CANDLE — $19.95

TFZ HOME OR ALTAR PROTECTION SMUDGE STICK — $9.95

TFZ FREEDOM FROM FEAR ESSENTIAL OIL — $49.95

TFZ PILLOW DREAMING CHARM — $49.95

TFZ MAGNETIC BACK "KITCHEN WITCH" FRIDGE GUARDIAN — $49.95

TFZ KOSHER FLAKE "PROTECTION" BATH SALTS — $49.95

TFZ "FUCK YOU, DONALD" PROTEST SONGBOOK (Pre-Publication) — $24.95

TFZ TRUMP-FREE ZONE WALL-HANGING THANGKA — $149.95

TFZ TRUMP-FREE-ZONE MANTRA — FREE WITH ANY ORDER!

Personally, what I'd do is put up a Thangka Barrier (dare I say "wall"???) on the North, South, East and West outer walls, with a central Demon Trap and a Kitchen Witch to catch anything that gets past the first line of defense, then use candles, smudge stick and incense to keep it cleansed, perhaps every day, maybe once a week.

HEAL TRUMP ITEMS — WORK AUTOMATICALLY JUST BY WEARING:

HEAL TRUMP earrings:

HEAL TRUMP PENNY-SIZED BRASS EARRINGS — $9.95 pair

HEAL TRUMP DOLLAR-SIZED COPPER BOARD-BACKED EARRINGS — $35.00 pair

HEAL TRUMP DOLLAR-SIZED COPPER STERLING SILVER EARRINGS — $139.95

HEAL TRUMP medallions:

HEAL TRUMP BASIC DOLLAR-SIZED BOARD-BACKED MEDALLION — $9.95

HEAL TRUMP U.S. SILVER DOLLAR BACKED COPPER MEDALLION — $149.95

HEAL TRUMP Handmade Tibetan Incense works by usage, keeps your home, office or den Trump-Free:

HEAL TRUMP Handmade Tibetan Incense — $9.95

HEAL TRUMP ATLANTEAN CRYSTALS:

HEAL TRUMP ACTIVE PRAYER ATLANTEAN CRYSTAL — $9.95

HEAL TRUMP COPPER-COIL ATLANTEAN CRYSTAL PENDANT — $19.95

HEAL TRUMP COPPER-COIL ATLANTEAN POWER CRYSTAL PENDANT — $49.95

BLOCK TRUMP ITEMS:

BLOCK TRUMP earrings:

BLOCK TRUMP PENNY-SIZED BRASS EARRINGS — $9.95 pair

BLOCK TRUMP DOLLAR-SIZED COPPER BOARD-BACKED EARRINGS — $35.00 pair

BLOCK TRUMP DOLLAR-SIZED COPPER STERLING SILVER EARRINGS — $139.95

BLOCK TRUMP medallions:

BLOCK TRUMP BASIC DOLLAR-SIZED BOARD-BACKED MEDALLION — $9.95

BLOCK TRUMP U.S. SILVER DOLLAR BACKED COPPER MEDALLION — $149.95

BLOCK TRUMP Handmade Tibetan Incense:

BLOCK TRUMP Handmade Tibetan Incense — $9.95

BLOCK TRUMP ATLANTEAN CRYSTALS:

BLOCK TRUMP ACTIVE PRAYER ATLANTEAN CRYSTAL — $9.95

BLOCK TRUMP COPPER-COIL ATLANTEAN CRYSTAL PENDANT — $19.95

BLOCK TRUMP COPPER-COIL ATLANTEAN POWER CRYSTAL PENDANT — $49.95

TRUMP-B-GONE ITEMS:
These automatically seek a parallel universe where there is no Donald Trump. Believe me, it's a LOT better where he isn't.

TRUMP-B-GONE earrings:
TRUMP-B-GONE PENNY-SIZED BRASS EARRINGS — $9.95 pair
TRUMP-B-GONE DOLLAR-SIZED COPPER BOARD-BACKED EARRINGS — $35.00
TRUMP-B-GONE DOLLAR-SIZED COPPER STERLING SILVER EARRINGS — $139.95

TRUMP-B-GONE medallions:
TRUMP-B-GONE BASIC DOLLAR-SIZED BOARD-BACKED MEDALLION — $9.95
TRUMP-B-GONE U.S. SILVER DOLLAR BACKED COPPER MEDALLION — $149.95

TRUMP-B-GONE Handmade Tibetan Incense:
TRUMP-B-GONE Handmade Tibetan Incense — $9.95

TRUMP-B-GONE ATLANTEAN CRYSTALS:
TRUMP-B-GONE ACTIVE PRAYER ATLANTEAN CRYSTAL — $9.95
TRUMP-B-GONE COPPER-COIL ATLANTEAN CRYSTAL PENDANT — $19.95
TRUMP-B-GONE COPPER-COIL ATLANTEAN POWER CRYSTAL PENDANT — $49.95
FEELING ESPECIALLY THREATENED BY TRUMP and HIS STORM-TROOPERS?

If you're feeling really SINGLED OUT, cramped and slammed up against the wall, and you feel yourself to be under personal attack, you probably want something a bit stronger. I present for your consideration these products:

BEST TRUMP-BLOCKER, PERSONAL CQR AMULET — $375
Comes in a handcrafted in Amerika solid sterling silver heavy woven wire bezel and German crystals, with an extra-large wide bail loop for hanging from a chain — chain is not included. Created with the most powerful resistors, special front-end diode and black

tourmaline demon traps, a bit larger than the size of a U.S. Dollar.

TOTAL TRUMP-BLOCKER FOR HOME OR OFFICE — $2850

I've loaded this CQR RADIO WAVE POWERED BOX for BEAR!!!

It should keep even TRUMP'S STORM TROOPERS from your front door.

My TRUMP-BLOCKER BOX has the most powerful ANTI-DEMON QUANTUM MAGIC PROTECTION SPELL I'm permitted to make here on Earth.

Ask about the special discount for multiple units for home AND office.

Unfortunately, I can't help you block your home or office from ordinary civilian level "social media" eavesdropping equipment.

Time was, we didn't have little silent radio-controlled video drones suspended outside our windows, taking home movies in our bedrooms and bathrooms, eh?

The conventional wisdom will tell you to say or do nothing you don't want to see up on Facebook tomorrow, even in the privacy of your own home. No space is safe from TRUMP WITHOUT A TRUMP-BLOCKER! With all the micro surveillance gear out there available to civilians, you can't say anything without fear, and in fact, even in public, you DON'T DARE BRING UP THE SUBJECT OF TRUMP, either positive OR negative, for fear of getting punched in the face or lynched or stoned by a hysterical and frenzied mob lusting for YOUR blood. I'm not exaggerating. This story is becoming more true here in Amerika every single day that TRUMP remains in power:

Three guys in a prison cell in Lubyanka, Russia's most famous political prison. First guy says, "I was in favor of Comrade Radek."

The second prison inmate says, "I was AGAINST Comrade Radek."

The third prisoner sadly says, "I'm Radek".

It's no longer Russia that engenders that sort of humor. We are now in it up to our eyeballs, and it won't go away just by itself. If you want a world in which TRUMP is out of power, you'll have to wait until he's gone, or do it with pro-active white magic. You have no other choice.

POPULAR WISDOM SAYS "There's nowhere to run to, nowhere to hide. Take a stand now, and hold your ground while you can. Take as many of them with you as you can."

That's nonsense. Take them all out NOW, with my WEAK END SPECIAL:

SHAMANIC PORTAL TO A REFUGE DIMENSION —
$3,000,000.00

Am I kidding? Come up with the money, and see for yourself.

AFTERLIFE ACCOMMODATIONS:

I have tons of room in either one, and I expect a LARGE crowd from Planet Earth, any day now. We're all very amused at this, and have a large office pool here in the Between Lives State.

I have a dollar on a nuclear holocaust within two weeks, and I expect to win. It pays 36 to 1, and I'm ready to collect my bet from Saint Mike. He's got fifty bucks riding on the Raiders, so I guess it won't hurt him to take a loss in my direction.

Always cover your bets, strategize your betting, never mind the cards — the outcome of the game itself is of no concern.

HEAVENLY HAVEN HOTEL

Room Rates from $9.95, suites from $39.95 per night, includes a ticket booklet to HolyLand. You only pay for nights. Days are free. Poolside Food Service, Close to shopping, malls and sights of interest.

HELL'S BREADBASKET MOTEL

Rooms FREE, day or night. Social media is excluded from Hell, so you might enjoy it. As Avatar of the Western Realm, I can hardly refuse even TRUMP MAGGOTS a room, but I can and DO turn away White Christians from HELL. I gotta protect the neighborhood.

Christians in general prefer the climate of Heaven to the company of Hell, anyway. Myself, I don't favor spending ETERNITY with Billy Graham and Elvis Presley. Maybe YOU can hang there, but it's not my bag. Give me URTHGAME every damn time, and make it the HELL LEVEL to make it interesting.

POST-HOLOCAUST REINCARNATION INSURANCE

Worried about your next incarnation? Why not get GORBY'S GUARANTEED REINCARNATION INSURANCE now, while you still can? If you don't like your next rebirth, just present your REINCARNATION INSURANCE CERTIFICATE for a full refund. Save your receipt.

Keep in mind that, as a decade-long student of Pete Seeger, from 1950 to 1959, I keep the faith; there is power in song. Watch for my slashingly funny "People's Protest Songbook", with every protest song I can muster up, along with any contributions that fit the concept.

WATCH THE NEWS, DON'T BE IN THE NEWS
February 3, 2017

You're looking at one of my TFZ Ammies, which I'm designing and testing right now. I'll soon have them on the table, and you can be wearing one to protect yourself from your own President!!!

Haw, haw, haw!!! I can't stop laughing.

I'm posting some images and text for the **Trump-Free Zone** re-sellers and distributors. I didn't use photos of models' faces, because it's dangerous to speak out now, in the New Trump Amerika, and I'm afraid for their safety if they're associated with this product.

Most of the models I'd like to use are in serious danger, because they're not white, not particularly Christian or nominally Christian — sort of being Christian isn't enough to buy you safety from the rabid bloodthirsty Christian Mob that's out there just waiting to eat you alive.

They are now empowered to demand fanaticism and unswerving mindless loyalty to their particular brand of religious rightness, and thanks to their fearful leader, they have the RIGHT to kick you out, refuse you service or let you die outside a hospital, if you're not a white Christian.

Think I'm exaggerating? Check out the latest outrage, and you'll see the Congressional Bill Allowing Religious Discrimination READY FOR SIGNING!!!

It's more dangerous than that. You never know where the next attack will come from. Enemies are EVERYWHERE!

If you're not scared of the Violent Pro-Lifers, you might consider hiding away from all the UNION people, Trump's major blue-collar supporters. They think he's their buddy, but HISTORY SHOWS that they will soon be rounded up along with the Muslims, Jews, Buddhists, Hindus and skin-color variations that they hate AND FEAR so much.

In this atmosphere of hatred, fear and distrust, you have to have SOME PROTECTION, and the TFZ is about the best you can do, short of arming yourself and wearing a bulletproof vest and cap, which buys you nothing, when facing a mob.

There are just too many of them. You can take out one or two, but there are just too goddam many of them, and they are zombied-out, thirsting for SOMEBODY'S blood.

This is nothing new. Public stonings, public hangings, lynchings are all too common, and the people who profess Christianity are the most likely to commit such all-too-human atrocities.

WATCH the news, don't be IN the news!

If you're anything but lily white and super-Christian of the right kind, you MIGHT survive a few more years, but by the time people are turning each other in for Judaism or Islamic practices, it's gone too far, and it's far too late to do anything about it at that point.

If you can get a million of these TFZ earrings and medallions out there, you have SOME chance of stopping Trump from killing off more than half a billion innocent people.

I seriously doubt that you could put these TRUMP-FREE ZONE items up in public without risking death and disfiguration.

It's NOT SAFE anymore to talk to anyone, even someone you thought you knew well, proof enough that your liberties are under attack, if you needed proof.

You might get lucky with online listings, but you might attract some unwanted attention from the Neanderthals. It's best to keep your distance from wild animals, and those who live in captivity are even more savage and unpredictable.

We're backsliding into the Old West, where everybody packed a .45 Colt Peacemaker, my personal favorite for fast-draw. I kinda LIKED it back then, so I wouldn't be at all put out to strap on my Boise Fast-Draw on my next shopping trip to Raley's.

Of course, I wouldn't do that NOW, but when EVERYONE is packing a gun, I don't want to be left out of the fun, so I'm registering my personal preference now, for a REINCARNATION SPECIAL, a single Boise hip holster and a Colt .45 tucked away in there ready for fast-draw, just like the Old Days back in the 1800s.

Of course, we died back then, too, but that's the price you pay for reincarnation.

These days, I'm limited to bare hand knuckle-fighting only — and, even at the age of 75, I can still deliver a powerful hand-strike, and my kicking power and balance are undiminished with age. I strongly recommend a fast course in self-defense, and I'm willing to host such a class if wanted.

I used to teach an ancient form of self-defense that doesn't rely on strength, and that's probably what I'd choose now. I'm thinking of an incident a few months back:

I had just gotten out of the hospital and was walking around town to to try and get a little air and exercise, when three very large hoodlums stepped out of the shadows. One of them said he was going to kill me, just for fun.

I'm only 5'8" now, and I'm 65 pounds thinner. I used to be two inches taller when I was young. I didn't have the strength, the reach, the weight, the size or the advantage, nor the inclination to fight, so I merely smiled, and waited.

He never carried out his threat, nor would he have done well had he tried to deliver a killing blow, but he and his friends were AFRAID of me, although I made NO move, NO sound, and gave no indication of a willingness to fight right up to the last breath, to defend myself on the public street, against sudden unwarranted attack from an unknown source.

Secret Society Conference with E.J. Gold and Robert Anton Wilson, 1980.

They would have paid a terrible price, because although I would surely have been seriously hurt or killed, they would have been put into prison. What a shame, because they were youngsters, with a whole lifetime ahead of them, but they came very close, and what if I had panicked, or if I had been suffering from PTSD, Post-Traumatic Stress Disorder — which I could easily have come back home with from the war — just WAITING for ANOTHER chance to kill someone, JUST LIKE VIETNAM???

This is the New Amerika, and it takes some getting used to.

I'm sure that the mobs out there would not like to run into someone like me. I am capable of taking and DOING a LOT of damage before I go down, and I have friends in High Places.

Like I said, at 75, I'm a SHORT-TIMER here on Earth, and couldn't care less what happens to me or to the planet at large. I've amassed over $300 in what's left of my savings after the Big Boys got through with my retirement portfolio, so there's not a lot I can accomplish against a multi-billionaire with thousands of billionaire friends.

I'm not real good at fighting huge organizations such as the Freemasons and Illuminati, but I will do my level best.

However, I am willing to defend YOUR right to freedom of speech, free expression, freedom from fear and freedom to BE. I always take the side of the underdog, join the losing team, and help them overcome impossible odds.

As the Avatar of the Western Realm, I can hardly do less.

What fun! Luckily, I have access from behind the scenes, so when they finally DO arrive in Heaven, I can slam the door in their faces.

If you hope to spread the word and get these TFZ items out there, it's really going to be word-of-mouth and person-to-person transmission. In short, it's a Grass-Roots Movement, and needs MILLIONS of people getting behind this MASSIVE MAGICAL ACTION for personal freedom and personal safety of the non-Christian non-white population of Trump's Amerika.

If you no longer feel safe on the streets of Trump Amerika, you might want the Bubble of Protection over you. Wear the earrings and the amulet. Carry or place the medallion in home or office.

Enjoy the peace and freedom of your Trump-Free Zone. Maintain your TFZ as necessary.

TRUMP-FREE ZONE EARRINGS

TFZ PENNY-SIZED GOLDEN BRASS EARRINGS — $49.95 pair — SPECIAL SALE PRICE: $19.95

These are handmade on rolled-out GOLDEN BRASS sheet cut into a disk, then signed. Ear wires are gold-colored surgical steel.

Lightweight and easy to wear. Subtle discreet design.

TFZ PENNY-SIZED RED COPPER EARRINGS — $49.95 pair — SPECIAL SALE PRICE: $19.95

These are handmade on rolled-out COPPER sheet cut into a disk, then signed. Ear wires are gold-colored surgical steel. Lightweight and easy to wear. Subtle discreet design.

TFZ DOLLAR-SIZED GOLDEN DESIGNER BOARD-BACKED EARRINGS — $125.00 — SALE PRICE $69.95 pair

These are large but lightweight designer metal hand-embossings, signed and mounted on a heavy black backing board. Very discreet design. Gold colored surgical steel ear wires.

TFZ DOLLAR-SIZED RED COPPER BOARD-BACKED EARRINGS — $125.00 — SALE PRICE $89.95 pair

Hand-embossed and signed on pure, solid copper, then mounted on black board backs. Very discreet design. Gold colored surgical steel ear wires.

TFZ DOLLAR-SIZED GOLDEN BRASS BOARD-BACKED EARRINGS — $125.00 — SALE PRICE $89.95 pair

Very strong golden brass disks, hand embossed and signed, then mounted on black board backs. Lightweight. Very discreet design. Gold colored surgical steel ear wires.

TRUMP-FREE ZONE MEDALLIONS

TFZ DOLLAR-SIZED GOLDEN DESIGNER BOARD-BACKED MEDALLION — $49.95 — SALE PRICE $19.95

This is your best home defense. Set up a Trump-Free Zone with these BLOCKERS. Hand-embossed and signed on golden-hued designer metal disk, backed with black backing board, then set into a foam ring in an acrylic archive-quality capsule.

TRUMP-FREE ZONE ACCESSORIES and SUPPLIES:

TFZ PROTECTION HOME DEFENSE ANTIQUE FRANKINCENSE — $9.95
This is real RARE Frankincense, collected over 50 years ago by Donald and June Suckling. It comes originally from the Holy Land, home to Christianity, Islam and Judaism.

TFZ PROTECTION HOME DEFENSE ANTIQUE MYRRH — $9.95
Real antique MYRRH. This comes from a crate that was shipped to the U.S. over 100 years ago. It is very rare, and quantities are strictly limited.

TFZ KAHUNA HAWAIIAN MAGIC "PROTECTION" BATH SALTS — $9.95
Great for personal protection from unwanted psychic influences such as Trumpism.

TFZ NEPALESE TIBETAN MAGIC "PROTECTION" BATH SALTS — $9.95

Great for personal protection from unwanted psychic and emotional vibes, these are from Nepal and are very potent and powerful.

Don't Leave Home Without It
February 4, 2017

Take your TFZ Medallion with you whenever you go out of the house, especially if you're one of those illegal aliens like my friends from Orion and the Pleiades, here!

USE YOUR MEDALLION AND OTHER TFZ ITEMS to ward off the Trump-Dominated Zombies, ward off the Evil Avatar

Numspaa, basically, to ward off all the ill-effects and unwanted nasal hair from Trumpism.

USE YOUR TRUMP-FREE ZONE to defend yourself, your family and your home against your President.

Ironic as it sounds, that's what you have to do if you are NOT white, NOT Christian. You are under direct threat. There is a CLEAR AND PRESENT DANGER.

You NEED SOME SORT OF PSYCHIC PROTECTION, not only to keep you safe, but to keep you FEELING safe and FEELING free, both YOUR RIGHTS as a citizen of the United States of America, and it's also your right as an honored guest, visitor or newcomer. You're innocent until proven guilty. That's the law, but Trump is changing all that.

Are Trump's paid goons and his volunteer zombies allowed to break the law? Of course they are. What are you, completely dense? They bend the law, break the law, ARE the law. Wake up, stupid!

Note how that reads: "Wake up, stupid!". Please take note of the fact that it does NOT read: "Wake up stupid!".

If you can't tell the difference between the two statements, you're in far worse trouble than you think.

As far as Amerikan prejudices go, if you're a Jew, or black, or Native American, you already know that you can't go into certain hotels, restaurants or country clubs.

You grow up understanding this one single, unchangeable fact: **No matter how rich you get, how powerful, how successful, you'll always be a Jew.** This is nothing new for anyone not lily White in the Trump Amerikan sense.

If you don't happen to be a White Supremacy Born-Again Christian of exactly the "right" congregation — which is what Trump Amerika is all about — **you're up Shit Creek, without a paddle,** which is the actual original expression that has been so mangled by popular usage.

Trump the Rump intends to leave us up Shit Creek, too.

By the time he and his mindless minions — who profit greatly from all this mayhem — have finished with us, there will be nobody left in Amerika but the Lily White Christians.

Everyone else who remains in Trump Amerika will be starving in one of the Forced-Labor Camps, or dead from exhaustion, starvation or gas.

The rest will be Amerikan Refugees, whom NOBODY wants, especially after the way Amerikans treated refugees seeking political asylum or religious freedom or freedom from oppression and pain.

Amerikans should not expect a friendly hand anywhere in the world, after this. The Ugly Amerikan was well-known even back in Mark Twain's day, in the 1870s, and it was bad enough without Trump adding his Fascist shit into the mix.

Now EVERY AMERIKAN is considered a Nazi, which makes SOME of them ashamed to be Amerikans.

I resent being associated with Donald Trump, just because we were born in the same country.

I also resist his hatred, his violence, his insanity.

As a result, I will no doubt go down when the goons get around to me. I only hope that they give me some warning, but that's not their usual style. They like to attack from behind.

Interesting, eh?

They insist on feeling safe from harm, but do plenty of damage to others who also expected the same feeling of safety.

Thanks to Trump, there is an air of uncertainty, of hate, rage, destruction, fear, rejection, aggression, violence, anger, violation.

And what's more, it's everywhere. You can't walk around in a mall without feeling the hate, the mutual distrust, the furtive glances, the hooded winks, the crooked smile.

It's a hate-filled and fearful environment, so Donald Trump should feel very much at home in it. He loves company, hates to be alone, hates to die alone, hates to hate alone.

No matter how successful you become in Christian White Amerika, you'll always be black, always be red, always be brown, always be Muslim, always be Catholic, always be Italian, or Irish, or Asian, or...

Well, there ya go. "Asian" means what? It means precisely that **Amerikans know fuck-all about other countries, and barely know anything about their own.**

And what, exactly, is "Mexican"? To Amerikans, it means anyone who speaks with what they think might be a Spanish accent, although they don't know German from Chinese.

"Mexican", to the average Republican voter, means "someone from Costa Rica, or Chile, or Argentina, or Spain, or Portugal, or Italy, or Yugoslavia".

I'm tellin' ya, Amerikans don't recognize foreign languages or accents, can't tell one from another, but they DO know a Mexican when they see one!

Are you still unconvinced that YOU and YOUR FAMILY are targets of the raging mob? Wait until you see some of the news stories coming up in the next few weeks. You won't believe those things, either, any more than you can come to grips with the fact that the United States has been turned from a FREE country to a SLAVE STATE.

Good luck convincing anyone of that.

I don't even try anymore to convince anyone of anything. No point, no point at all. In roughly 4.5 billion years, who the hell is going to know the difference?

I can think of a thousand things I'd rather do than develop a comedy routine for folks to use in their own defense, or write, sing and publish protest songs, or make "Trump-Free Zone" medallions, but Trump seems determined to have his way with us, as he does with women who have the misfortune of finding themselves in his employment or power, and I don't go down without a fight.

My kind of fighting is with a ready wit and a word-processor, as you see right here and now. My songs can cut down the most pompous of dictators, and my comedy can rip their egos to shreds.

Keep in mind that there is one Great Leveler for all — commoners and kings and queens and holy men and emperors of the world.

Keep your eye on the work-goal, not the immediate emergency. Trump will be removed from office, but that won't help you. The NATIONAL MOOD IS HATE.

Amerikans will from now on be considered "hate-mongers", to be shunned and avoided. Just TRY visiting another country after the next Trump rampage!!!

DON'T FORGET YOUR TFZ AMMY and MEDALLION and RING and CHARM! Don't Leave Home Without It!!!

I Fart in Your General Direction
February 5, 2017

Spook watches a fireball manifest in Norton Street demonstration, 1969. All the props courtesy of Universal Studios, except the Mayan Glass Knife from my collection.

NOTES ON RESONANCE TRAINING:

You can: paint, draw, sing, act, dance, sculpt, make jewelry, all with the singular purpose of producing balance and harmony between Centrums, Chakras and Meridians, and a profound sense of peace and harmony between yourself and your environment.

It's NEVER about talent. It's ALWAYS about giving yourself permission

"I can't give myself permission," you tell me.

Well, do you ever give yourself permission to act out negatively? To be angry, sad, depressed, for more than a few seconds? That's all the time it takes to have an emotional reaction. The rest is reverberation and decay time, and that could, for some unfortunates, take hours, days, weeks, years, maybe never.

La Balance – The Tarot card "BALANCE" illustrates the concept and method of harmonic resonance. The goal of harmonic therapy is to restore the natural balance of sounds inherent in a blended whole, to restore the whole note from the resultant fragmentaries.

It's easy to manifest thought-forms and prayer-forms if you can concentrate AND FOCUS your Higher-Being Attention.

94

CREATE HARMONIC TONES and OVERTONES:

Invite a group of friends to gather in order to experiment with the TC-Helicon H1 Intelligent Harmonizer, working to create notes and harmonies along the TONE SCALE of OBJECTIVE WAVELENGTHS with the object of obtaining harmonization and defining the range of each individual's voice at this time, before stretching and flexing the vocal muscles.

If you're acting as guide, get them to harmonize as well as they are presently able, on the HARMONIZER, going through C Scale, D Scale, E Scale, F Scale, G Scale, A Scale and B Scale.

Focusing a beam of PSYCHIC LIGHT through the twisted distortion lens of a portable version of the Astral Particle Beam.

Don't try to get them to note the effects of each scale at this time. That is a much more advanced level.

On the SECOND PASS through this exercise, get them to harmonize on the E Flat Scale, A Flat Scale, F Sharp Scale and finally, the B Flat Scale.

Each participant is responsible for their own voice. Working together, they will strive to weave a tight and deep harmonic fabric as a vocal harmonic group, but first, each must learn how to hear and control their own voice before attempting to blend it with others.

CREATE TELEPATHIC WORMHOLES:

HARMONIZATION can open telepathic tunnels which follow ionized paths.

Using HARMONY, we can create PRAYER PATHS and PRAYER THOUGHT-FORMS.

A PRAYER PATH is merely a grooved or "ESTABLISHED" pathway of ionized ASTRAL POINTS which in turn creates as-if particles between the origin of power and the target, creating a momentary connection between 2 quantum-entangled points at two different locations somewhere along the ZERO GRID, the basis for the Higgs Field Cubic Tesseract, the foundation for any living universe.

Ultimately, any universe is built of SOUND. Waves indicate pulse, fluctuation and rhythmic beat frequencies.

Finding BEAT ZERO on the Beat Frequencies Scale is quite an accomplishment, but it's a dire necessity when using sound waves to create Shamanic Effects, such as operating a PORTAL or directing healing energies.

HARMONIC RESONANCE is the only action that creates HARMONY of CENTRUMS.

This personal level of harmony can spread out into other areas by continued RESONANCE, something to be learned in the process of using the POWER OF SOUND, SONG and PRAYER.

SOUND IS POWER

You can improve your SONIC POWER and PRAYER EFFECTS by taking one of our Harmonic Resonance Clinics, where your PRAYER PROJECTIONS and PRAYER POWER are measured and improved.

How can you determine if your PRAYER POWER is more effective?

One simple and time-honored way to test your PRAYER POWER

is to select a wounded target that has no normal chance to improve or recover, so that there can be only one source of the healing, see?

Okay, so what would that be right now?

Looking in today's headlines, we see a story about hundreds of swastikas plastered all over the advertising placards on New York City subway trains.

In Manhattan, the Jews are a full 20% of the population, so those playful youngsters with the spray cans and crayons are taking a helluva chance. They probably weren't professional Nazis, just kids with a twisted and tormented sense of wonder.

Some people in New York City will cross the street to avoid a confrontation with a gang of Jews, just as they'd do the same with a gang of Puerto-Ricans or African-Americans, which make up a walloping 25% of the New York population, and they'd be right to do so.

Jews, Hispanics, Muslims, Arabs (not all Muslims are Arabs, dum-dum), African-Americans, Native Americans, Asians, Australians and foreigners, non-whites and non-Christians in general, are feeling pretty pushed against the wall just about everywhere, these days, and the hate is FEEL-ABLE out in public.

The hate, fear, distrust and rage aroused by demons in control of your governments around the world are in place in order to control you, keep you from reacting, from rebelling against the assault, but if you're going to be hanged as a horse thief, you might as well have the horse.

What I mean is, if you're going to die anyway, take the bastards with you. There's a good reason the Shaolin monks and Ninjas learned deadly self-defense — they had to, and anyone who is slightly "different" will have to learn to go onto a street thoroughly prepared to defend themselves, their children and their friends from HATE GROUP attackers.

In the New Order, Hate Crimes are no longer a crime.

Back in the subway car with all the swastikas, somebody finally spoke up, and said, "Hey, hand-sanitizer takes that stuff off easily."

Everyone got involved, and with that level of warmth, respect and cooperation, the swastikas were quickly and efficiently removed from the subway car signs.

That's what I call PRAYER POWER.

It took courage for those people to stand up to the bullies, even though the bullies had sprayed and run, the mark of a true coward.

One person involved in the subway incident yesterday said, "I guess that's what it's going to be like in Trump's Amerika from now on."

"No," said one passenger, "Not as long as we're here to stop them."

That's my point. We soon won't be, for any of three reasons:

They came to take us away.
We became refugees and emigrated to safety and freedom.
We've gone into another dimension, one way or another.

Frankly, if my friends and I had caught them doing that back when we were big, strapping and very able street-fighters, had there been a more or less even match, there might have been very different headlines.

But bullies never look for a FAIR FIGHT, it's always about attacking helpless feeble people, which they do so well, and I'm too old and weak at this late stage to offer much resistance to overwhelming force, which is the only kind of force they know how to use.

There's not a lot of "bragging rights" in hitting an old person, or a pregnant person, or someone lying in a hospital bed or on the floor, but brag they do.

It's not particularly brave to attack someone small and helpless with 10, 20 or a mob of 2,000 or more huge, monstrous creatures calling themselves "people" throwing stones at a living target, which is YOU and YOUR FAMILY.

Those otherwise harmless kids are not a good target to test your Shamanic Powers, at least, not yet, although they ARE as tempting a target to YOU as YOU are to THEM!

As a Jew in Trump's Amerika, I should be well-armed and prepared to defend myself should I happen to venture out onto the streets or fail to keep an armed guard at my gate.

But I'm not well-armed. I'm not armed at all.

I don't do that sort of thing, so I suppose that whatever happens to me will be taken as a direct result of my failure to defend myself with overwhelming force, but as I said, I just don't do that — I just have my open hands, feet and head, none of which are up to a solid fight anymore.

However, let's ignore the New York Nazis for the moment, although we may return to them later, if we need another target.

Meanwhile, we hope to find a BETTER, more READABLE target, something upon which we can QUANTITATIVELY MEASURE the results. Leaving a bunch of dead kids on the third rail of the New York subway system is NOT a good way of measuring your HEALING PRAYER POWERS.

GOOD SCIENCE requires good lab practices, so we must look further for a "fair subject" to indicate success at our lab class exercise.

Aha! PERFECT!!! Here also in the news was another "Breaking Story" — this one featured a strange and enigmatic unknown person calling himself "Steve Bannon".

YES, THIS WILL DEFINITELY DO THE TRICK!

I'll explain:

It was recently discovered by the news media in general and the social media in particular, and got published and circulated widely just yesterday and this morning, that a mysterious person named "Steve Bannon" is behind the scenes with Donald Trump and has been since Day One, manipulating and influencing himself into TOTAL POWER as the MAN BEHIND THE CURTAIN.

The "Steve Bannon Connection" is the story that everyone in Washington knew, but nobody dared speak about — like knowing that J. Edgar Hoover was a cross-dresser (and therefore subject to blackmail), or that the U.S. Government has been building Labor Camps all over the place, for YOU and YOUR FAMILY, not some opposing foe or invader force.

It's very clear from his random, wandering speech patterns and his wild ill-considered Presidential Actions, such as the Tragic Seals Ambush, where he ordered his troops into an area without good intelligence, and I mean that both ways, that he lacks the on-board native intelligence and personal bargaining skills to actually become President of the United States.

He CAN'T HAVE ACTED ALONE, nor is he acting on his own now. He's dumb, slow and quick to anger, vengeful, spiteful, mean and intolerant, just the kind of person you want at the helm with his finger on the Nuclear Trigger!

Haven't you been wondering who's pulling Trump's chain?

He was put in power by the man behind the throne, Steve Bannon, just as Dietrich Eckart trained Hitler to assume command, and gave him the speech and mannerisms that put him in power and created

Nazi Germany.

By the way, the Germans don't want Hitler back. Ask them.

I put quote marks around the name "Steve Bannon", because that's just the name of the BODY, the human creature that is now, and always has been, Trump's chief advisor, mentor and guide — I'd be looking closely at THAT relationship, were I a news reporter.

But who is "Steve Bannon", really?

You really want to know? IN BODY, he's connected deeply with the Illuminati, but that's not his real claim to fame.

But poor Steve Bannon got careless with an invocation one day, quite a few years ago, and ended up, as did Trump, signing a PACT with an actual Demon from HELL.

This is not nearly as uncommon as you'd expect.

I don't usually even take note of such impacts on human life, because micromanagement is out of my League and interest area, plus there are SO MANY OF THEM absolutely everywhere and nobody ever seems to notice, and those who do happen to see something just don't care enough to DO anything about it.

They'd be right. Short of an EXORCISM, there's not much you can do against a demon, and in most cases, you don't have to do anything. I wouldn't even suggest this except it's handy for a test of your psychic healing skills.

In the case of poor Steve Bannon, the FULFILLMENT of the PACT involved a full POSSESSION, which is why today we have the Demon Asmodeus wandering the Earth once again.

He's the MAIN CHARACTER of "FAUST", the story and play and film and opera that shows the average person exactly how to go about signing a pact with a demon, and what generally happens as a result.

In short, a Morality Play.

Let me give you a bit of background, taking my quotes from pathfinderwiki.com:

"Asmodeus believes that the strong should rightfully govern the weak, who in turn owe their masters unwavering obedience. He loves negotiations and contracts, especially those that give one of the parties a distinct, hidden advantage over the other. He expects and appreciates flattery, but is never fooled by it, seeing it as a negotiation tactic, as well as a duty those in inferior positions owe their betters."

The Demon Asmodeus has since then opened the door to many more, some of whom have possessed high government officials all over the planet, which is why we're headed for war, if they succeed in their human-tormenting agenda.

It is their singular purpose to divide humans and create discord and chaos, and they have been doing a bang-up job so far, since the RIFT occurred a few decades back, at the CBS RADIO BROADCASTING STUDIOS at the famous tourist landmark, "Columbia Square" on Sunset Boulevard in Los Angeles, on the evening of Sunday, October 30th, 1938, at about 5 PM California Time, the infamous and notorious "War of the Worlds" broadcast that caused widespread panic.

Orson Wells said later on that it was intended as a harmless Halloween Entertainment, but what if it wasn't a hoax? What if the Martians invaded, and forced Wells to say that???

The HELL-RIFT of 1938 — there were two more major rifts in 1947 — was covered-up by allies of the demonic forces that entered this space-time continuum at that break-point, using a Vortex to make the initial jump.

Since that time, they have helped others to come through the StarGate that opened up back then.

One of the Chief Demons, presently occupying the form of the said "Steve Bannon" has power and dominion over many political figures, one of which happens to be the creature known as "Donald Trump", who is under his influence and control.

I know, it all sounds like science fiction or fantasy. That's because YOU'VE BEEN TAUGHT TO FILE ANYTHING LIKE THIS UNDER THE CATEGORY OF "FANTASY" AND "SCIENCE FICTION".

It's all so absurd. Asmodeus is a silly character in Dungeons and Dragons, everybody knows that. It's all just fantasy.

So how do we RESPONSIBLY and PEACEFULLY use the situation to test our PSYCHIC POWERS?

More importantly, is it KARMICALLY CORRECT?

The answer to the second question first is a resounding "YES!!!" It's karmically okay, and might even provide a bit of MERIT.

The answer to the second question, "What can you do to test your skills?" is to merely direct your ASTRAL HEALING POWER LINEAR ACCELERATOR GENERATOR BEAM toward the general direction of the false human, "Steve Bannon", in order to drive the DEMON ASMODEUS out of his skull.

Aim the Astral Particle Beam Generator Accelerator or your home-built or professional built "See In Three Dimensions" binoculars more or less toward Washington, D.C., taking into account the curvature of the Earth, meaning, aim slightly downish — and intone the following magical phrases:

"I FART IN YOUR GENERAL DIRECTION!"
"Beans, Beans the Musical Fruit.
The More you Eat, the More you Toot.
The More You Toot, the Better You Feel.
So Eat Beans at Every Meal.

This will create a large, very powerful SBD (Silent But Deadly) fart odor wherever you have directed.

The horrible fart smell will immediately cause a cessation of the Demon's control over Donald Trump, which will be easily visible on news coverage, as a sudden disappearance of any sense of personal Triumph of the Will.

In short, Trump will IMMEDIATELY LOOK and SOUND as DUMB as he really is, the moment the EXORCISM takes effect.

The MAGIC of DEMONIC POWER OVER HIM by the DEMON ASMODEUS will be suddenly absent in him, and he'll look lost, confused and unutterably sad. This "SADNESS EFFECT" is your major indicator that you were successful, and can be considered a "Passing Grade".

To achieve an "A" or "A+", you'd have to come back from a time trip with the original players, like Bill and Ted did, and you'd better NOT forget that, in San Dimas, the clock is still ticking, so that'd mean something on the order of having Trump sing the Newfie's song, "I's the boy who bails the boat, I's the boy who sails 'er" have 100% of his intelligence removed, and as a result, suddenly burst into a resounding chorus of "Frere Jacques".

It's not MY joke, it's THE CLASSIC Newfie joke, along with the chain-saw gag. Apart from those two, I have no lingering repertoire of Newfie jokes, but I DO have a surfeit of Jew Jokes, along with a very generous supply of "island" jokes, "bar" jokes, "lawyer" jokes, "parrot" jokes and, of course, the old standard, "mother-in-law" jokes.

The clock is still ticking in San Dimas, and it's all-too-true of the Simulation, too. The clock is ticking in the Real World, and it's time for a snack for all the Real Ones, the Players behind the game. I'll continue this in a moment or two, by your time perceptions.

There. I'm back with my snack, exactly 2.1 moments later.

Uh, where was I???

Oh, yeah...

Uh, okay ... uh, the action of taking out THE DEMON ASMODEUS is commonly called "SPOOKY EXORCISM AT A DISTANCE" — an uncopyrighted and unprotected term that I invented back in the days of the Sumerians — or was it in Lagash?

Ah, Emily! She never forgot that hay ride.

What's that? I'm wandering again? Oh, okay, spooky exorcism at a distance, right???

Ahem.

SPOOKY EXORCISM is SO easy to perform and SO less messy than an in-person exorcism — I'm talking about the inevitable green-pea-soup goo that comes flying out of the mouth of the victim — that it's a wonder it hasn't taken the place of MAINSTREAM "Allopathic" MEDICINE long ago.

Don't you hate to have to burn every outfit you ever wear to an exorcism because you really can never get that green-goo vomit out?

I personally managed to ruin several dozen very attractive raw silk tops, until I switched from in-person to at-a-distance exorcisms, and frankly, I don't care for exorcisms at all, never did, except that they CAN be fun once in a great while, when you confront a demon like Asmodeus, who can really whip out some devastating one-liners.

Personally, I consider anyone who casts out demons without a license to be just showing off. Don't waste your skills trying to impress me. I've seen it all come and go, and believe me, it's hard to be original.

So, frankly, I wouldn't even suggest the casual exorcism of the Demon Asmodeus, except that, as "Steve Bannon", he happened to be in the news yesterday, just as I was casually searching the news for some easy indicator of student successes at the ancient art of SPOOKY STUFF AT A DISTANCE.

Edgar Cayce performed "SPOOKY HEALING AT A DISTANCE" and "SPOOKY READINGS AT A DISTANCE", and our Remote Readers back at the Agency used "SPOOKY VIEWING AT A DISTANCE" to accomplish their aims.

I can easily teach anyone how to accomplish "Spooky ANYTHINGS" at a distance. The principle is simple, but not all that easy to apply, It involves skills such as "NULLING" and "BEAT FREQUENCY MODULATION", which must be mastered both in radio science and sound science.

It would be unfair to use this skill to smear those playful little runts who had to stand on the seats to despoil the railway advertising placards, but you might get away with just giving them a permanent, wildly itching rash that never seems to go away.

Okay, maybe that would be karmically risky, so let's just stick with the exorcism. I feel constrained to mention that I am somewhat in sympathy with the little devils in the sense that I hated it when those advertisements first appeared in New York Subway cars back in the 1940s!

OUR ACTION IS A HEALING, SO IT'S KARMICALLY OKAY!!!

I'll be showing how to set up a LARGE HADRON PRAYER-POWER ASTRAL PARTICLE ACCELERATOR at the workshops and clinics this spring, so watch for those!

You can obtain or build a PRAYER POWER ASTRAL PARTICLE ACCELERATOR of your own! They are totally legal to build and own, at least while the Constitution and Bill of Rights are still in force, which won't be for very much longer, if THE DEMON ASMODEUS has his way, and as of right now, he IS, as is being reported in the media.

REMEMBER TO DO NO HARM!

"Do No Harm" is the Hippocratic Oath, and is the most foundational of all ideas in healing. In your attempts to heal, are you doing the patient a favor? Do they really WANT healing?

In the case of a DEMONIC POSSESSION, that question just doesn't come up. But if you're conducting the EXORCISM IN PERSON, something WILL DEFINITELY COME UP that you won't like.

Vomit.

You heard me, vomit.

Yes, just like in the movies, DEMONS VOMIT to prevent EXORCISM, and almost always the victim of demonic possession VOMITS IN THANKS after the EXORCISM.

You don't want to be in the way of that particular green pea soup.

That's why I always recommend "SPOOKY EXORCISM AT A DISTANCE" over those in-your-face CLOSE ENCOUNTERS with demons. I keep my distance, and you should, too.

How will you know if you've succeeded?

Well, the STORM TROOPERS won't be coming to your door, and you MIGHT be able to safely walk the streets without fear for the first time since the Nazis took over the U.S. Government.

BTW, I got a note that a few people were upset that I made comments about the New Order. As a Jew, I'm entitled. As an American, I'm entitled. As the Avatar of the Western Realm, I'm obligated to make a statement against any demons who get out of Hell and start causing trouble again.

I don't want to bring you down, but somebody has to speak up, and in this case, it's me. Am I trying to convince anyone of anything?

No.

Am I trying to change anyone's opinion, or interfere with local politics?

No, emphatically not. I don't advocate a change of government, nor the exorcism of the demons who are controlling the men in power. All I suggested here is that you use the situation to test your psychic skills.

A few demons on Earth more or less won't make a big dent in the general mayhem.

PRAYER CREATES ELECTRICAL FORCE

Did you know that scientists have now demonstrated with lab equipment and improved testing methods that PRAYER CREATES ELECTRICAL ENERGY. It not only produces voltage — it also creates a powerful MAGNETIC energy field because PRAYER has ROTATION.

The Rotation of any magnetic field has a definite and profound DISTORTION EFFECT on the Higgs Field in general, and sort of shakes things up across the entire universe.

In short, the activation and SENDING of a PRAYER FORM can penetrate the entire GRID to get where you want it to go.

ADD ANGEL POWER TO YOUR PRAYER

You can add ANGEL POWER to your PRAYER simply by opening a Telepathic channel on the GRID.

Once the CHANNEL has opened up, you can channel that

individual or communicate with a Higher Entity for help in healing or life-repair.

You want to be on Mars? You can recognize it from outside the BRANE, with simple RESONANCE, like making a sound that bounces off something to indicate its presence — the foundational concept behind RADAR and SONAR.

You get in resonance with one thing and in general you are more and more in tune with resonance, more and more coherent internally, as the harmonics LEARN to vibrate together in RESONANT HARMONY.

It takes some time for the BEING to learn this, because the BEING is learning it in two or more dimensions and locations at the same time. It takes many repetitions to make it stick and make it a habit.

USING NULLING, ACQUIRE THE SOUND. Notice, pay attention past the ego, and you can accept that your voice might be somewhat or greatly off-key. This is not a crime, but some off-key singers can make you want to throttle them to get them to stop.

Don't make yourself one of those off-key singers that we all remember from our teen years.

CREATE SOME VIRTUAL SOUND FORMS:

As ARCHANGEL ZADKIEL says in his Basic Rules of XD Voyaging, "All your relevant x, y and z coordinates can be brought into Harmony by the F6 Function."

It's then obvious to the expert that all contributing angelic prayer-forms are caused by specific voices at each coordinate in these specific ways:

X = lower voice
Y = higher voice
Z = middle voice

Harmonics can be altered by sounding a note and then diagnostically tuning the key knob. The coach performs a Key Knob Diagnostic while the Neophyte tries to intone a single tone without warble and wiggle — this will be almost impossible for the untrained voice and breath.

The harmony choices you make for your HARMONIC VOICES can and will alter the mood and temperament of the space in which you are operating, and can be extended into other spaces.

This is particularly useful in "Spooky Healing at a Distance", a quantum prayer technique that uses quantum entanglement in rather imaginative and effective ways to create a healing effect on the other end of a Healing Vortex, quite different from a Wormhole Effect, although both can result in a Miracle Healing.

Step-toning or micro-toning through any selected key will produce a kaleidoscopic variety of harmonic overtones, undertones and harmonic decay within the TONE SCALE of Western Octave Notes with varying degrees of chord clash, decay and sublimation.

OBJECTIVE PRAYER AND SOUND POWER can manifest as an actual tangible form that has size, weight, shape, color, texture and is collidable, all within the laws of Einsteinian Physics as well as Quantum Mechanics.

SOUND FORMS and PRAYER FORMS can be made tactile, feel-able, sense-able. It can have mass, density, weight, size, shape, color, sound, visibility and a certain amount of ambiguity which is settable at the change of vocal frequency.

CREATE A MASS WITH SOUND:

Using sound, it is possible to create a virtual shape, machine or even a Being on a very high scale of Objective Reality.

The use of SOUND in the form of PRAYER and CHANTING in order to WEAVE A REALITY in the FABRIC OF SPACE is so much second nature to the ESSENTIAL SELF that it requires no more instruction on how to achieve these results than a few hints in the form of some simple and quite obvious coaching instructions.

The underlying cause of PRAYER POWER is that the power of sound is everything, because ultimately, EVERYTHING IS SOUND.

The whole UNIVERSE is nothing BUT sound. Sound CREATES sound. Sound INFLUENCES sound. And sound EXPRESSES itself as sound.

One of the more serious intentions of creating a universe is the eventual development of jazz.

Another inevitable development is art in the form of painting, graphics, sculpture, architecture, theater, poetry, science, history and language. Those are my payoffs, and they happen no matter what or where the originating culture might have been.

Without the CREATION, none of those would come to be. They are all a result of the MIX of REALITY and EXPERIENCES OF REALITY, coming upward from the RELATIVE WORLD, the World of Creation.

This CREATIVE IMPULSE that makes SYMPHONIES and GYMNASTICS and ARTISTIC GENIUS and WONDROUS SPIRES AND TOWERS is arguably the Highest Purpose a UNIVERSE can possibly have.

You CAN argue otherwise, but you'll be arguing with me, and who should know what the Ultimate Purpose of a Universe is?

HOW IS IT DONE???

Changing the space-time reality structure even in the slightest is not the aim here. Think of it this way ... you are not a home-builder by profession or nature but — given the right instructions and a blueprint — you could potentially learn or help another to build a house or barn.

Some co-workers know more than you, some less and some the same.

Somehow between all of you, the work gets done and the house gets built. Now what if your contribution, instead of hammer and nails and a bit of sawing, was an absolutely delightful, supportive set of TONES that together create a SACRED CANTICLE?

In the BUILDERS' CLASS at PROSPERITY ASHRAM, you learn how to make as-if solid THOUGHT FORM CONSTRUCTIONS out of very simple primitive thought-forms, called "PRIMS", which manifest as a VIRTUAL REALITY within which you can meet and communicate and interact with others and with the local internalized environment.

As you well know, those designs can evolve into incredibly complex patterns, especially if you are building a snowflake with no fewer than a million faces. Ultimately, it's all about the Pythagorean Triple, which makes into a Pythagorean Triangle, one of the most important concepts in human history, and the very foundation of REALITY ITSELF.

Building aeolic chambers and filling them with scintillating standing waves is truly a job for an angel, and that angel could be YOU. One of my jobs here is to recruit volunteers for ANGEL DUTY, which involves making and weaving sounds, as well as carrying messages to and from Earth.

As I've said before, and you can quote me on this: "I had nothing but myself with which to make the world. Out of myself the world was made."

I'm not complaining, just stating a fact.

If you don't recognize the ingredients and know the recipe, you can't bake a cake.

Bishop Berkeley said, back in 1709, that tables, chairs, doors, windows, all the objects in the universe and space itself were all ideas in the mind of the observer, that in point of fact, as we'd say it now, THE UNIVERSE IS A SIMULATION.

MONUMENTAL with picture of HEAVEN as a MALL KIOSK or INSTALLATION.

SIGN: "SING WITH THE ANGELS"

EARBUD JACK on KIOSK FRONT

BUILT-IN MIC PICKS UP VOICE OF CLIENT

INSTRUCTIONS PRINTED ON FRONT OF PANEL "Learn to sing with the Angels. Make and hold for a few moments any sound for the microphone to pick up and harmonize. Your Two Angelic Guides will guide you toward more perfect Angelic Harmonies until you create Perfect BALANCED Prayer Power.

NOTES ON ATTUNEMENT, ALIGNMENT, RESONANCE:

performance in class room
University of Sound
Invigorating energizing
Angelic healing sounds
Yoga of breath
Any language or no language
Use sound shaping
Overcome fear of Ego threat
Resonance permits telepathy
Non-resonance prevents telepathic communication
Tuning fork a good example of resonance created by harmony
synaptic paths
neural paths
Ionic paths
Blending is achieved by advantaging the synergies only after resonance has been achieved

Harmonic therapy cures imbalances
Theater-Style Demonstrations, Lectures and Classes
melodic harmony
true harmony
resonance harmony
Things in harmony will tend to resonate
Harmonic resonance creates a vibrational effect
Angelic healing requires angelic invocation
How to have the Angel answer me
Out of phase not in harmony
When you are in harmony you resonate
Tune weaving
harmony
attunement
alignment
connection
balance
Get connected with harmonic therapy

SPOOKY FART-CASTING AT A DISTANCE, WITH THE NEW 3D BINOX UNIT
February 6, 2017

Well, finally I've gotten around to making my first commercial prototype 3D BINOX unit, which will be ready for market this morning, if all goes well.

You will be astonished, probably even shocked, by what you can see in the 3D BINOX. You'll hear people actually yelp in surprise when they see the difference between what they see with ordinary eyes and what they can see with the 3D BINOX.

You can use the 3D BINOX with your H1 INTELLIGENT HARMONIZER to create some amazing effects through Quantum Tunneling and my very latest miniaturized WormHole technology.

THE 3D BINOX now has several great new effects that we've added just for the latest 2017 NAMM Show. It features the all-new GREEN CLOUD FART-CASTING EFFECT, a host of HEALING and CROSS-DIMENSIONAL EFFECTS that you're gonna just love.

It has an application in access to hidden doors, passages and messages, can help you to penetrate a puzzle or decode an encryption, strike into a closed system such as a binary quantum-entanglement, and to top it all off, the all-new 3D BINOX features a sleeker, more futuristic look, which was back-engineered from my crashed saucer over near Goldstone,

California since the accident in 1962 that left me stranded here on Earth until I can rebuild it or build another one.

Can't hardly get molybdenum anymore. Used to be, you could pop over to Wynn's House of Chemicals on Second Avenue in New York City to get whatever you had in mind for your latest experiment, but that's long gone now, and Moscovium is almost as hard to find in your local stores as Unobtainium and Upsydownium, both made famous by the world-renowned scientist, Bullwinkle the Moose.

Not only can you use your 3D BINOX for the normal uses — such as finding lei lines, spotting walkabout magnetic lines, dowsing and locating gold, silver and water, plus the healing and wall-softening effects that it can be used to produce — but it now can alternately operate as a quite different device, without making any changes or adjustments.

3D BINOX ASTRAL PARTICLE-BEAM FART-PROJECTOR

Delivers six different fart smells to the target.

Makes a slight, almost indiscernible, fart-sound when released to target.

Great easy to use new targeting system uses photos and screenshots.

Lightweight and easy to carry.

No moving parts.

Works first time, every time.

Always "ON" makes defense a breeze.

"Smart-Fart" feature makes Auto-Adjustments, to locate the target.

"Green Cloud Effect" — 5% Chance of SBD Green Cloud to show.

Can deliver a series of high-pitched farts, single medium fart, or a long, drawn-out low fart, with a slight adjustment of the EMO-TONES on the Harmonizer.

I've made a few adjustments in my standard model, but they're all in the realm of minor points, to make it easier to hold the instrument and less likely that the components will get in the way of observations.

The commercial model works as well as the prototype, and that's my main concern, giving the same quality in the commercial model as in the personal prototype I made for my own use.

I've just delivered a walloping Galloping Green Astral Plasma Fart to the Fuhrer, which I'd like to have you think of as a personal opinion, not the view of the entire Council of Nine.

Some of the others wanted to use the SBD, but that's reserved for those special times, like an address to the United Nations, or the State of the Union speech.

It's so easy to use!

FART-CASTING WITH YOUR 3D BINOX

Just hold the unit up to your eye sockets and aim it toward Washington, wherever you deem that to be from where you are.

Get the VISION right, then using the H1 Harmonizer, chant the following:

Beans, Beans, the Musical Fruit,
The More You Eat,
The More You Toot.
The More You Toot,
The Better You Feel,
So Eat Some Beans,
At Every Meal.
I FART IN YOUR GENERAL DIRECTION!

You'll note a rather light group of upwardly mobile floating astral plasma particles, forming a sphere that's about the size of a small Texas grapefruit or a large beach ball, gathering at the very end of the BINOX.

When you chant the SENDING SPELL, "I Fart in Your General Direction!", the force of that spell SENDS the Green Fart through the Astral Plane, directly to Washington, to the address specified by you, or visualized or pictured by you, or written down on a parchment beforehand.

This target address to which the Astral Fart is to be delivered can be further defined by the SENDER — that'd be you — by chanting in a singing voice with the aid of your H1 Harmonizer.

You might get a whiff of the outgoing fart as you SEND it, but since it's YOUR fart, it will smell rather sweet and quite pleasant to you, but overwhelmingly noxious and horribly, gaspingly foul, to anyone on the receiving end of your ASTRAL PLASMA FART.

Of course, the 3D BINOX can also be used for more important, less frivolous things than sending farts to a recipient of your subtle plane practical jokes, but what could possibly be more FUN than farting in someone's general direction???

I've done the math and the Gorby science on this. We're not gonna run outta farts, if you keep bolting that junk-food on the run at your gritty nine-to-five job and your commutes to and from same.

I calculate that if everyone in Amerika got BEHIND this MOVEMENT, so to speak, we could deliver up to 2.4 MILLION FARTS PER HOUR.

That would seem to me to be more than enough astral punishment to bring even the most hardened tyrant to his knees, begging for mercy and a stick of incense.

You can use the 3D BINOX to spot DIMENSIONAL ANOMALIES, from which you can fashion WormHoles for time-travel. This can be very handy, if you've got a pack of hounds behind you, which might happen if you send too many farts to the wrong people.

Healing is possible using the 3D BINOX. You just look through it and aim your healing efforts through the tubes.

Telepathy Effects can be enhanced by using the 3D BINOX. Try standing a block away from each other and TALKING THROUGH ONE OF THE TUBES at your target receiver down the block.

You'll be amazed what you can HEAR through the 3D BINOX, and what you can SMELL and SEE and SAY through it, as well.

Your 3D BINOX is a three-way communicator, and can even be used to READ the Akashic Records and to VIEW Akashic video files.

YOU EXPECT THE 3D BINOX TO GIVE YOU X-RAY VISION?

What do you think this is, the back cover of a vintage comic book???

I've tucked the smaller components of the 3D BINOX into the common line, where the two cylinders of the BINOX joins, and the coils are placed in such a way that the grip is not disturbed — however, if you've got very large hands, you'll need the X-L variety.

No problem there. I custom-handcraft every single one of them, so if there's something YOU need on your BINOX, such as super small or super large, or something stronger or safer or more protected, I can do it.

You'll notice that there are two coated-wire coils, one around each cylinder.

The coils are connected to the vintage crystal radio parts that are tucked away between the cylinders, and they are always active.

Don't worry about them always being "ON", because ALL the electricity and quantum power comes from the electro-magnetic and gravitic effects of passing captured radio waves.

Waves move electrons. My device sends them into another dimension, where they loop around to create the effect you see in the new 3-D BINOX.

You can do so many things with the 3-D BINOX, not the least of which is to turn on your friends to the wonderful world of multi-dimensions and alternate realities.

SO NU, HOW MUCH IS THE NEW 3-D BINOX???

ACCESSORIZE YOUR 3-D BINOX FART-PROJECTOR
Send today for these incredible Fart-Projector Accessories!

FOUL FARTS — $39.95 for a 2 dram vial of the foulest farts you ever had the misfortune to suffer through in a small, cramped and crowded elevator!

GREEN CLOUD — $39.95 buys you a 2 dram bottle of the grossest farts ever made!

CELEBRITY FARTS — $39.95 for a 2 dram Celebrity Fart of The Month!

POLITICAL FAT FART VIAL — Indistinguishable from the usual cloud surrounding people. Will not affect enlightened people.

EXPANDING FARTS — 2 Dram vial. Starts out as a small dot, expands quickly and forms an entire universe of rapidly expanding gas.

PEPPERONI PIZZA, GARLIC and ONION FARTS — $39.95 for a full 2 dram vial of the worst gas anyone ever made.

MEXICAN FART — $39.95 — A full 2 dram vial of the most potent CHILI and BEANS farts you ever smelled in your life. Even your own farts will knock you out. The perfect revenge for the Deportee of the Month Club!

GREEN FART SONGBOOK

GREEN FARTS BELOW ME
FART ME TO THE MOON
SILENT BUT DEADLY
BLOW IT OUT YER ASS
A CLEAR AND PRESENT DANGER
GAS GETS IN YOUR EYES

CHOKING SMOKING GASPING YOU
UP IN GAS
SMELL THIS 3 TIMES ON THE CEILING, IF YOU LOVE ME

And more! There are thousands of songs in this incredible new Green Fart Songbook, so you can start singing ALL OF THEM right now!

BUT WAIT!

If you act now, you'll need an "Actors' Equity" Union Card.

A lot more than you'd expect to pay. You might think it's worth $1.98, but NO! How about $3.98? NO, it's not that, either!

YOUR BRAND-NEW 3D BINOX ASTRAL PLASMA PROJECTOR will cost you a measly $225, because it's made of rare antique parts, but then, so am I. Don't worry — here's your guarantee:

IF NOT 100% SATISFIED, YOUR MONEY BACK — However, I'm pretty sure we'll be satisfied with your money.

Haw, haw, thanks to Bill Gaines at MAD COMICS for that zinger! But all kidding aside, if you are not 1000% wildly happy with your 3D BINOX, return it for a full, immediate, no-questions-asked return!

Well, MOSTLY no questions asked. I won't mention it, but our New Inquisition Friends will no doubt want more from you than just a casual chat, if you're caught owning one of these little puppies.

I KNOW The 3D BINOX will be an incredible addition to your spiritual tools kit, and I'm confident that you'll quickly learn to use it, and use it well, and remember that the Fart-Caster aspect is just a funny way of saying "fuck off" to the powers that want to take away our freedoms.

There are additional SPOOKY STUFF AT A DISTANCE devices planned, with differing uplifting effects and purposes. They're in building and testing now, and should become available within the next few months, if all goes well.

If it doesn't, I'll see you in Hell, but then again, all your friends will be there, and fairly soon, if we don't manage to squiggle out of a nuclear war this week.

If we do end up in total nuke exchange battles, and there's a huge cloud of nuclear waste and fallout coming our way, I'll probably re-think my spring marketing plans, but the Easter Workshop is still on — I'll be broadcasting from somewhere over the Rainbow.

AN EVEN MORE POWERFUL MAGICAL TOOL, "FART-CASTER" MY LATEST 3D VIDEOGAME!

I'm currently designing a brand-new 3D videogame, "FartCaster", which will allow you to cast farts in ANY direction.

Merely enter the name of the receiving end, so to speak, of your Fart-Casting in the drop-down menu that says "enter name", and let loose with a variety of powerful, horrible, insanely disgusting farts, created just for your amusement by XxaxX Constantine, aka Uncle Claude.

You will emit SOUNDS SO DISGUSTING that even YOU will gag and probably vomit.

The gas clouds will be so powerful and overwhelming, because they're composed of BILLIONS OF PARTICLES — would you believe millions of particles? How about a dozen very small particles, compounded by mirror reflection???

NO, DRYDEN ... THIS IS GOING TO BE FUN!

That's what Peter O'Toole, as Lawrence of Arabia, says to Claude Rains as "Mr. Dryden", diplomat, head of the British Arab Bureau, who enlists Lawrence and then warns him that the desert is "a burning, fiery furnace".

"No," says Lawrence. "It's going to be fun."

That's exactly what my newest, latest 3D videogame is going to be — sheer fun, to help you forget those creeps who are flexing their power, bringing us to the brink of nuclear war, not just in Washington, but in virtually every capital around the world, even the small third-world nations, like North Korea and China.

Haw, haw, I WILL have my fucking joke. If I'm to be hanged as a horse-thief, I might as well have the fucking horse!

YOU set the target in the game, YOU decide who gets fluffed with the worst gas this side of your Aunt Martha's intestinal tract.

Once you've entered the target's name, you're ready to play! Choose from ten of the worst, most crippling, most horrible, foul-smelling rank Farts From Hell.

Even though they are "just soundbites" created by Uncle Claude just for this game, the belches and farts will evoke such powerful essence-memories that you'll be able to have full recall on that barfing contest you had with that gladiator, Gluteus Maximus, back in ancient Rome!

There is no better reincarnation trainer!

Farts are always with us! They can be your enemy, they can be your friend. Find out which is which, by playing this fascinating and rewarding quantum magic virtual device.

Learn how to CONTROL your Fart-Casting, make every whiff count!

You will soon find out who your real friends are, when you invite them to a Fart-Casting Contest or Party! Discover the joy of solitary confinement when your family finds out what you've been up to!

How it works is this: you're fully loaded with fart casters and very specific types of farts, belches and other disgusting sounds and smells.

You enter your target into the drop-down menu, and start blasting away into the target area in each STATION, and experience elation and freedom from fear and worry with every fart you can lob in there.

Is it a gag? Sure, it is. Then again, it isn't. Oh, it's all so complicated!

Okay, it's a gag, but will it help?

Well, it won't make the problem go away, but it will make it easier to take as it comes down on us long-suffering peasants. The rich don't understand why the poor remain poor. Why don't they just get richer??? Probably too lazy, right? What do you mean, nobody will hire you???

It will help you feel better, but it has a magical purpose, too. You can use this power to express your higher thoughts and feelings through lower bowel effects.

Have you gotten the job you deserve? The raise you deserve? The praise you deserve? Are you a wage-slave? Are you afraid to walk in a mall or on the open streets?

If you're among the downtrodden, those who fear for their lives under the New Order, Fart-Casting Can Change Your Life! Don't make trouble. Don't say anything. Bow your head down low, and walk bent-over and humble. Do not look up at the Naked Emperor! It's death to look at him, and it isn't worth the risk or the penalty. He is SOOO ugly!

DON'T SAY A WORD TO ANYONE!

Well, it isn't READY today, is it?

Okay, so whenever we manage to get it out the door, okay? Watch for it on this very blog, and we'll of course be posting it on our video gaming sites and gaming outlets.

FEDERAL BAN ON ALL VIDEOGAMES!!!
February 7, 2017

If you don't speak up now, you never will get the chance. Soon you will be disallowed from commenting on, or criticizing, Donald Trump. It will be LAW, and you will risk Federal Imprisonment for violating the "Presidential Critics Law of 2017", if I remember rightly, and there's no reason to suppose I do.

Like I've said before, I failed "Earth History 201", which is the history of the human species on planet Earth during the 21st and 22nd century, and I'm in this Earth Simulation that you call "Reality", to find out WHY Donald Trump is called "Trump the Rump", what is the meaning of "Trumpism", how did he get into power, and why people hated him so much.

Donald Trump is the first U.S. President to be featured in over 1,000 videogames to date, and he is pissed off about it, even though some of them are positive, some even wildly so, with Storm Troopers at your disposal to wipe out all those inferior races.

Most of the TRUMP or RUMP VideoGames are rabidly negative, and here's what their leader has said about that:

"Videogame violence and glorification must be stopped—it is creating monsters!"

HE should talk???

Donald Trump is a monster, if ever I've seen one.

I've never had to actually DEFEND MYSELF FROM THE

PRESIDENT OF THE UNITED STATES, but up until now, none of them have actually attacked me.

Donald Trump attacked me. He literally and figuratively attacked me, personally.

He assaulted me, and when he can get his legislation through his slave Congress, he is about to compound that by committing actual battery upon me with his Storm Troopers and his Secret Police, in the Great Roundup, which is coming to a theater near you, real soon.

You doubt that this will come to pass? Haw, haw, you don't even know your own history!!!

It's not that I hate him. I can't afford hate, and from long, long experience, I am only too aware that there is no money in revenge.

"Everyone knows that Gypsies steal chickens," says Archie Trumper. "So do your Hare Krishna guys and your yogas, and all them there guys."

It does no good to mention that they are all of them vegetarians and wouldn't touch a chicken to save their lives.

Donald Trump isn't enough of a Demonic Deity to force me to the Dark Side no matter WHAT the provocation, and he's been provoking me pretty hard these days. I'm still able to maintain my cool in the face of his provocations.

I actually rather like him, and appreciate what he's doing for me. It's a great sacrifice for someone who loves and needs praise as much as he does to offer himself as a scapegoat for my comedy from now on.

Oh, yes. The success of the first one — Paparazzi, which garnered 3 million downloads before it was shut down — tells me that the public is ready for more fun on the Higher Planes.

Apparently Trump called my people over at Dial-a-Prayer to ask if there were any messages for him. Clearly, he doesn't understand the situation. I'd already picked up any messages at Prayer Central, and he isn't authorized, doesn't have a box, and certainly doesn't have a key.

Oh, he has the rest-room key, but it's to the women's powder room, formerly a safe space. We don't allow violent cases anywhere that they might accidentally wander out onto the street.

It's not the fact that he's a vicious hate-filled racist, or a demagogue, or a rabble-rouser, or a sneak, or a tax-cheat, or a draft-dodger, or a paid agent of Russia's brutally murderous dictator who has his rivals assassinated, or a philosophical virgin, or a sociopathic pervert, or a megalomaniac with a family to support and a devilish agenda to follow

120

to the ruin of all humanity that bothers me so deeply. But what is it then that offends my circuits?

It's not his manner. It's not even the ever-present threat of nuclear war that he so joyfully holds over our heads. He could offend a dozen world leaders with a single stupid utterance.

No, it's none of those things, horrific as they are; it's just that he's SO HARD TO WATCH.

A photograph, even the SINGULARITY that I found, where he's actually sort of grimly and salaciously smiling, is enough to turn anyone's stomach, even an extraterrestrial, and they're built to take it.

Donald Trump has billions, but he's never seen himself in the mirror, or he'd have done SOMETHING. They say that beauty is only skin-deep, but ugly goes clear to the bone.

Donald Trump goes clear to the bone.

I'm speaking objectively here, as a fine artist, not as a political or social or economic or historical critic. He's goddam ugly, and that's a fact. It's more than the mop, more than the puckered-up lip-less mouth and beady, squinty cruel and sadistic eyes.

It's much, much more than the expensive but rumpled suit and badly chosen tie.

Gosh, when Donald Trump actually attempts to TALK, and gets instantly all wound up, which happens the moment he opens his foot-filled mouth, who can look even for an instant at his tweaked, thoroughly contorted, rage-filled face?

That twisted, wrinkled, puckered up mouth sure reminds me of an anal aperture, and there's no reason it shouldn't. It's the same muscle.

Hell, both ends of the Eating and Shitting Tube are pretty much the same, except that you're supposed to speak out of the mouth end of the tube as directed by the mind, and fart out of the other, as directed by gassy pressures inside the lower intestine.

Donald Trump does EXACTLY the opposite.

I've never actually SEEN SO MUCH of ANYONE in the WORLD, and he IS a monster. His face is constantly contorted in pain and anger and rage and hate, and he is constantly making monkey and ape-like gestures and sounds.

If I wanted to see the primates, I'd go to the zoo. Donald Trump belongs in a zoo, and has desecrated the Oval Office into a zoo with racism and hate, and of course, he constantly invites his ape friends in to join him while he plots out the next media outrage and course of revenge.

I swear, if he read my blogs, I'd be on a prison farm in Siberia. Trump's Russian friends are eager to host me, but I got news for them. THEY are the ones who will end up in prison, at the end of the day, and I'll be strolling in the woods in Dimension 7, watching their misery and, frankly, feeling sorry for them.

I do feel sad for Donald Trump. That's a lot of pain. He's afraid to die alone, which makes him want to take us all with him. He's afraid to BE alone, so he asks folks to sit with him. Why is he afraid to be alone? Because of the thoughts.

He's dominated by the thoughts. Bad thoughts. Fearful thoughts. Angry thoughts. Sad thoughts. All through the long, dark night.

"Everything happens to me!" exclaims Donald Trump. "Look, it's raining again!"

My friends on the Other Side are waiting for YOU to walk the line between them.

"ALL NEGATIVE POLLS ARE FAKE NEWS!" He proclaims, "THE LIBERAL MEDIA IS AGAINST ME", thus guaranteeing that he will NEVER actually hear the millions — soon to be billions — of voices around the world, clamoring for his resignation, or impeachment, or worse.

Come to think of it, the Liberal Media IS against him. He's perfectly right.

I wouldn't even be INTERESTED in Donald Trump if he didn't directly threaten me and my immigrant and non-white friends, of whom I have PLENTY.

We owe this misery to Carroll O'Connor, but I don't hold him responsible for making a bigot funny and lovable.

Trump knows that media is what controls people's minds, and boy, does HE know how to control the media! He leads them around like a vicious master who's in a hurry to get through the rain drags a tiny puppy along a wet pavement.

That tiny puppy would be us.

Donald Trump was in the news a LOT, and on television a LOT, buying time with his money, to create his Reality Show so he could get attention.

He got just enough attention from the media and through the mediums of television and radio, that it was obvious that he is an NPD of the First Water, meaning he can't get enough gold, or attention, or power, or revenge on his sworn enemies who now number in the billions — not ever. It will NEVER be enough.

There will always be another demand when the present demand has been met. Threaten, cajole, promise, apologize, threaten again, stab in the back. This is what those who are members of the Order of the Double Cross typically do when they play games with each other.

Donald Trump used to be paranoid, which technically means that he was abnormally and unjustifiably afraid that people around him hated him and feared him and wanted to do him harm.

Now that he has frightened and pissed off BILLIONS of people, he's no longer paranoid, in the sense of being incorrectly convinced without cause of the hatred and suspicion of others.

In short, BILLIONS OF PEOPLE AROUND THE WORLD now know him for the pig he is, and they do, indeed, hate and fear him and want to destroy him or see him destroyed, which in effect, means that he's cured of Paranoia.

I'm a peace-loving extra-terrestrial visitor who has no stake in this world whatsoever, and even I'M pissed off at him for attacking my human friends who don't happen to be his particular color of skin or his particular brand of religion.

No despot is truly religious. It's a game, a pretense, to gain and hold power, to control the mob, to destroy all resistance.

"It is as I have foreseen," says the Emperor, "give in to your anger, Luke."

I WON'T give in to anger. Resentment I can allow myself, just because I'm offended by him and by his actions, beliefs, attitudes and general bad smell.

I feel sorry for Donald Trump, but — I DO resent his intrusion on my life. I DO in fact RESENT him for demanding my time and attention ALL DAY LONG, EVERY SINGLE DAY INCLUDING SUNDAY.

It makes me want to say "Fuck Off", to the President of the United States, and I personally resent being jammed forcibly into that position, JUST BY BEING A JEW.

I'm more than THAT for him to hate. I'm not only a friend of a LOT of immigrants from Europe, Asia, Africa, India, Japan, China, Korea, Norway, Germany, Italy, France, Spain, but I've reincarnated so many times as a person of color — hell, there WERE no whites, and frankly, there's nothing in the DNA Code that specifically spells out "Whitey".

Jesus, am I doomed to see ALL MY FOREIGN-BORN FRIENDS destroyed and made homeless by that overly rich son of a bitch? And am I supposed to stop incarnating as female, dark-skinned, non-Christian or non-White?

Screw him, I say, and screw the horse he rode in on. If I can't say THAT to the President when he offends me with his foul language and even fouler racist lies, then go ahead and lock me up along with the other protesters.

Will Rogers would have been top on Trump's "Revenge" List had he been around nowadays.

You can silence some of us, but the mob is very big and growing bigger all the time. Aristocrats NEVER understand why the people rebel. If they don't have bread, why don't they eat cake?

Donald Trump doesn't know what it's like to not be able to put food on the table, and he never did. He's rich, always has been rich, always will be rich, and he doesn't like being around dirty folks such as us.

I'm a peasant. Poor, weak, old, growing more feeble every day past my 75th birthday, but still quite able to have a voice, to dare to speak out against tyranny, but why?

Because I know that MY name is on that list.

It doesn't much matter if I remain silent or speak out. My days are numbered. But so are yours. You can't win against a monstrous, enormous and powerful machine.

Trump holds all the cards, so to speak.

And somebody holds his chain. Even if he wanted to, he couldn't back out now, for fear of someday being tried as a war criminal or worse, a mass-murdering fuckhead, which he will become, if he can possibly engineer it, to create the Second Holocaust, for which Trump someday will become known.

There's no one in the world that Donald Trump doesn't hate, including his special friend and constant companion, Steve Bannon. Don't forget, I'VE seen Trump's diary and day-book, and he can't resist a scorching commentary in the margins.

Donald Trump spends more time with Stevie Bannon than he does with his wife, although I can certainly see his point of view. Any woman that Trump has on his arm is there strictly for show. He keeps Melania well out of sight of himself and the media, because if she ever talks, he'll be so humiliated, but he'll soon recover from THAT, and go on the attack, which is the style of a true coward.

This guy never served in the Armed Forces, nor has he ever paid tax, done jury duty or any of the other things that one might do to be of service in the cultural sense.

Instead, he has sent competent troopers to their certain death, just like Hitler used to do, to demonstrate their complete, unquestioning loyalty and obedience.

Again, true to pattern. A despot always does the same things that all the other despots do and did. Ho, hum, tell me another one. Yes, he drives his wife, Melania, out of sight. Out of sight, out of mind. Ah, but those are two entirely different and unrelated statements about Donald Trump.

I'm speaking here from the viewpoint of history. Like Anna Russell says about the Norse Gods in Valhalla represented by Richard Wagner in Der Niebelung, etc. — "I'm NOT making this up!"

From my actual history lessons back in the 37th century, even though I admittedly pulled a "D+" out of my history class last semester, I can tell you this much:

Donald Trump emerges as the most hated and feared President in U.S. history.

He gets forcibly removed from office, but I forget how. I think he's put into a strait-jacket and hauled away flailing and screaming, to a special Federal Nut-House, but that's uncertain. This is the part of the Term Exam that I failed miserably, all because I couldn't bring myself to take an interest in Amerikan politics of the 20th or 21st century.

"Don't be a Trump" means, in my time, "Don't be a racist," or "Don't be a Hate-Monger", and sometimes "Don't be a total asshole", although in a telepathic society such as ours up in the 37th century, it's hard to be an outsider.

Trumpism was always thought to be pro-banker, but nobody back home realized that Trump was a card-carrying member of the Nazi Party until the records were found sometime in the 21st or 22nd century.

Donald Trump is found to be in violation of a number of Federal, State and International laws, but again, this is where I blew the exam, like I said.

I seem to recall that Donald Trump is the LAST U.S. President, but I can't recall what happens after that — my studies didn't include that, but I DO remember that "I Love Lucy" goes into its millionth re-run at the same time the sun runs out of Hydrogen.

I've been watching as we are guided by angelic forces through this very turbulent and rough sea. Be courageous, and remember that the light at the end of the tunnel won't always be New Jersey.

We might be able to just sail through the rocks of satisfaction. Possibly John Parker will get through.

While we're holding the pink box and waiting for the tragic DECLINE and FALL of Donald Trump, there are so many CONSTRUCTIVE things we can do, so let's do them! I'm doing something constructive right now — I'm creating a videogame that can help you find your way out of the Trump Amerika Lifestream.

I'm actually broadcasting my messages from quite far away, interdimensionally speaking. You CAN find your way out of the Trump Trap, just by using the same gimmick used by Homer in the Idiot and The Ostrich — Follow the Drinking Gourd.

How can we feel safe again? How can we feel free again? How can we trust others again? Will you ever again feel safe in mentioning Donald Trump's name on the street or in a supermarket?

Do you feel safe talking about politics these days?

Do you feel as YOU specifically are a walking target on the street? Do you pull your hoodie over your head to hide your curly hair or dark skin or your Jewish nose?

Do you FEAR others on the street? Are you BRACED for a sudden attack on the street? If you're not, you don't yet understand the situation and don't really understand that YOU ARE THE TARGET.

I say we get the TRUMP STINK out of the Oval Office, and that's exactly what I've done for myself. I've made a representation of the Oval Office, and every so often, when I feel the oppression especially heavily, I invoke the videogame and blow a few farts in his general direction.

The fart-smell is like a flowery summer day, compared to the foul brimstone and sulphur smell that you get when you're anywhere within breathing distance of Donald Trump.

If you DO happen to get that close to him, I feel sorry for you. I hear he reeks of alcohol and cheap French perfume.

That's total nonsense, False News if ever I heard it. There IS no cheap French perfume.

Hey, if you were serving in the U.S. Armed Forces, would YOU want to be known as a Storm Trooper? Would YOU want to know that sooner or later, you'll be asked to fire upon Amerikan civilians in protest, as they did back in the 1960s?

Or perhaps you'd prefer to enjoy the fate of the striking miners during the Great Depression? This particular economic misery that you're experiencing today is, by the way, commonly called "The Great Recession", as if it differed — when you're starving and homeless, it doesn't matter WHY you're cold and hungry.

Trump has enough money to feed the hungry in Amerika for decades without missing a penny of it, but he doesn't believe in helping the poor.

In his own words, "Fuck the poor", he expresses his concern for them.

There is one videogame out there where you bash Trump on the head with a baseball bat. I heartily disagree with any game like that. I certainly wouldn't want to suggest an attack on a person, but on an OFFICE which Trump is defiling with his racial bigotry, why not?

Abe Lincoln once sat in that office, and he's turning in his grave over the occupation of the White House and Houses of Congress AND the White Supremacist Supreme Court, fashioned by Trump for Trump about Trump with Trump in mind.

HOW TO USE YOUR FART CASTER VIDERGAME TO BRING A DICTATOR TO HIS KNEES

Hey, if my FART CASTER VIDEOGAME happens to be the Jewish VideoGame Programmer's equivalent of a fart machine or a whoopee cushion, what harm can it possibly do?

Practical Jokes have been associated with the White House ever since it was first built. Politicians, like everyone else, appreciate a good joke once in a while, especially if it's on someone other than themselves.

Mel Brooks on Tragedy and Comedy: "Tragedy is when I cut my finger. Comedy is when YOU fall into a sewer and DIE!"

So I made for my own amusement and to settle my stomach a little, my own version of an imaginary Oval Office somewhere outside space and time.

The game environment "Oval Office" is paneled in solid 24k virtual gold, probably more than even Donald Trump can afford, as greedy and rich as he is, and he wants even more — he wants YOUR IRA retirement fund and YOUR social security money, that YOU earned and, unlike Donald Trump, YOU PAID TAX!

Why don't we all just tell the IRS, "Until Donald Trump pays HIS fair share, just bug off, okay???"

Of course we DON'T do that, because if we did, the IRS would have us hauled away and shot.

Did you know that IT IS AN ACTUAL ON-THE-BOOKS CRIME TO EVEN SUGGEST in print or on the air THAT THE VERY RICH PAY TAXES, as enacted under Title 18, Section 22 of the U.S. Federal Code?

You probably already know that Donald Trump is about to invoke and test that law, probably on me, because I surely DO pay my fair share of taxes, and I resent that as rich as he is, he doesn't pay any and never has, and I'm very vocal about it. I resent that the poor have to pay until it hurts, and the rich get away with being tax-free, don't you?

It's the kind of thing that builds guillotines and encourages mobs to run in the streets with torches. Unfortunately, the only damage they do is to themselves, then the troopers come in to mop up what's left and take anything that isn't nailed down.

That tax thing is both business and personal. Donald Trump also has got a LOT to hide in his international money dealings, and he'll be trying to cover his tracks in Russia, where he enjoyed some sexual entertainment produced by the Russian government.

It never occurred to that schmuck that the Russians would have hidden cameras in the room?

I'm also shocked and amazed that this Wannabe Dictator is going to get away with keeping all his business interests, including those in Russia, to whom he owes PLENTY of favors, and who have PLENTY on Trump, enough to disgrace him forever, but don't worry, that comes anyway.

After all, Putin hasn't YET published the photos he obtained of TRUMP and GUESS WHO in sexual congress at the special Russian Spa where Trump stupidly stayed for FREE — and that's not the only thing Putin is holding over Trump's head.

Trump is technically in Putin's pay and under Putin's control and domination, and watch the fun begin when Putin pulls even more of Trump's strings, and rest assured, he will, because he's PUTIN, and that means "mean" and "nasty", "treacherous" and "vengeful".

Gosh, those endearing traits are shared by both men, AND their cronies. It's HELL NIGHT for the next few decades, and you might as well get used to it.

You'll be taking plenty of abuse and living through fearful times, with WHITE SHIRTS and uniformed Storm Troopers herding you around and into cattle pens and stockades, where you can be worked until dead.

That's the plan, and Donald Trump is not only at the head of it, he wouldn't allow anyone else to be. He has to be THE BOSS, or he'll upset the game board and throw all the pieces onto the floor.

Have you ever played with a kid like that?

He holds you hostage every single second of every single day. You don't play ball his way, he presses the Nuclear Button, just like that bully in school who kicked your blocks down just when you were about to lay down the final block.

He has nothing to lose. In fact, he wants to take the whole world with him when he goes. That's merely a product of his mental illness and need for glory, power and recognition. Approval he will NEVER get, because creeps like these always betray their friends.

Can't trust anyone who PUT you into power, because what if they decide they don't like you and they put someone ELSE in power???

There's always the paranoia element, and it keeps you jumping and twisting, trying to avoid getting crushed by the flying demolishing ball.

I don't know what course others may take, but as for me, give me a videogame for harmless revenge and freedom from fear and worry.

I feel so TARGETED, don't you?

When Trump looks into the camera with those fireball eyes glowing with racial hatred, doesn't it feel as if he's cursing YOU out???

Actually, under his breath, he is, if you're a Mexican, a Jew, an African American, a Cuban, a Haitian, a Jamaican, a Swiss, a Muslim, a Buddhist, a Hindu, an African, an Australian, a Canadian, a Peruvian, a Chilean, Japanese, Chinese, Korean, Ancient Alien, you name it, he hates it and wants to drive it off-shore or kill it in the gas chambers nice and neat, making it the FINAL solution to the Immigrant Problem.

They're marching in the streets, and your liberties are directly threatened. There is for you a clear and present danger, and they hope that you don't act in time or at all to save yourself from their rage and hatred of anything not exactly like themselves.

OVAL OFFICE

I created an Oval Office of my very own, in quantum-active psychic cyberspace in the GODD Engine. Into this Oval Office I cast my harmless practical joke style virtual farts, to wit:

PINK CLOUD — A stream of beautiful, elegant and feminine PINK FART particles becomes a horrible pink stink, expanding to fill the room with foul disgusting odors.

RED CLOUD — A stream of highly charged flaming Red particles explodes into fartness, creating a rank, sulphurous smell of unbelievably rotten eggs.

BLUE CLOUD — A powerful stream of Cobalt Blue particles represents "L'Aroma du Garbage" and at the same time, the odor of spoiled milk and rotten milk products fills the room — you may or may not hear the ghost whisper, "Who cut the cheese?".

YELLOW CLOUD — A continual stream of powerful popping YELLOW FARTS blasts into the Oval Office, to create a stink that can't be overcome by incense or room fresheners.

WHITE CLOUD — A stream of WHITE FARTS erupts to destroy any remaining White Supremacists in the immediate area of the Oval Office.

GREEN CLOUD — The dreaded "Silent But Deadly" of our grade school days. The only protection is to call out the Freedom Code, "SAFETY". The rules of the game "Safety" require that someone who farted can say "Safety" and then punch anyone in the room on the shoulder repeatedly, until the victim can find and touch a doorknob. This is essentially the game that Trump is playing with YOUR life.

PURPLE CLOUD — A stream of overwhelmingly odiferous particles that will choke even the most hardened demon out of his socks.

I plan even more powerful and annoying fart weaponry for my Oval Office Fart Caster, so stay tuned for developments.

My harmless game will perhaps alert folks to the danger. Maybe YOU can react quickly enough to the danger to escape certain death in the Labor Camps already built to house YOU and YOUR FAMILY.

Even if you don't think that YOU and YOUR GROUP or FAMILY or BOTH are the target, that's only true right now, and you haven't seen his whole plan. I have.

Any Remote Viewer can find his outline in his Oval Office lap drawer. It's clearly entitled, "My Struggle", which translates, roughly, into German as, "Mein Kampf".

I wish I were kidding.

I also wish it weren't dangerous to speak up about these things, but that's exactly my point. Before Trump, you felt safe in opening your mouth, saying things, pointing out injustices and brainstorming for good social solutions.

Now, everyone is in their own corner, distrustfully squinting at all the others in the room. This is where Trump lives every minute of every day, and he wants YOUR company in his own private Buddhist Hell of Upside Down Hanging Bodies of Fear, Distrust and Hate.

Watch "Golden Child" for details on this particular Hell.

Do you really want to live there? If not, you'll have to speak up, not just you, but millions of you. Demand your rights.

Did you know that, technically speaking, the President of the United States is YOUR employee, a public servant SWORN TO UPHOLD THE CONSTITUTION and the LAW.

Actually, although he hates to think the thought, YOU ARE TRUMP'S BOSS.

Why not march into the Oval Office and say, "You're fired!"

I only risk mentioning it because if someone hasn't already done it, they're bound to — it's such an obvious social comment based on his vicious and spiteful television show.

I'm digging myself deeper the further I go into this issue, but there is nowhere else to go, and I'm not likely to let go any more than a bulldog will open his jaw, at least not when so many injustices prevail in the Land of the Free and the Home of the Brave.

Maybe a couple of years in military service — in service of ANY kind — would have done Donald Trump some good, but he wouldn't have been happy as a PFC, which is all the rank he would ever have gotten.

The only reason he's rich today, is because his debtors bailed him out so he could pay them back, which he never did, in the end. This will eventually become an issue.

In order to steer a course for yourself through this damned and treacherous sea of hostility, keep your balance! Don't give in to the Dark Side! Don't Panic! Here's how to stay TRANSCENDENT to the whole media circus that is TRUMP and TRUMPISM:

USE YOUR H1 HARMONIZER EVERY DAY!
USE YOUR SUPERBEACON AT LEAST ONCE PER DAY!
PLAY GUITAR FIVE MINUTES EVERY DAY!
DO SOME COPPER EMBOSSING EVERY SINGLE DAY!

DON'T MISS A DAY OF MOVEMENTS.

DO YOUR PLS ASSIGNMENTS ONCE A WEEK EVERY WEEK.

ATTEND THE MORNING MEETINGS (DARSHAN).

ATTEND THE ICW ON LIVESTREAM.

WORK IN THE ASHRAM AND PARK YOUR AVATAR THERE.

PERFORM READINGS FOR THOSE WHO HAVE PASSED.

PERFORM ACTS OF COMMUNITY SERVICE.

You get the general idea. Stay with the program, don't let the bastards grind you down. These guys care nothing for you and as a matter of fact, regard you as just so much hamburger meat to be ground down in their lust for power and control.

In the end, those guys fight it out, last man standing wins the game.

They never calculate that correctly.

In THE END, there is only ONE left standing, and guess who THAT is???

Cosmic Joke?

Not at all. Just another history assignment in a long list of history assignments — what I'm really dreading is the quiz on Leslie Ann. I've studied everything about her that I can get my hands on, but what about Dorothy???

And what about Myra?

OVAL OFFICE FART-CASTER

So, back I go, to my schematic map for my newest, latest video-game, "Oval Office Fart Caster", which I'll have ready for market as soon as it's inhumanly possible.

I just realized that this whole blog — dare I say, "Article"? — is actually an unplanned marketing ploy to get you to consider downloading my game.

If you've wanted a way to express your worries and concerns, and a great magical way to express them in a meaningful way, there is no better method of protest than a fart.

Not a fart farted in anger, but a fart farted in protest, on behalf of all those who are soon to be martyred on the cross of Trump's Road to Power, or who have already passed over to the Other Side, in his wicked service.

Of course, I'm not complaining. We NEED workers on this — meaning "the Other — Side. As Lord of You-Know-What (God, I really wish we could find another word for "Death") I'm obligated to host anyone who ends up here in the AfterLife.

I'm currently in the Buddhist Hell of Typing. It's rather pleasant here, Hellishly speaking. I can listen to jazz and pretend to write the blog. I move the fingers to correspond to the letters I see appearing on the screen.

So what do I really want from you?

C'mere, bud. (grabs collar and pulls toward self, face-to-face close up and personal), "Hey, bud, look at this here orb", I gently but persuasively invite.

"What orb?" you query.

"This orb," I reply.

"What's an orb?" you ask.

"Never mind," I say, wandering off around the next corner.

No, no, that's all wrong. That's a scenario from the Trump Zone, and this is a Trump-Free Zone, where we don't do persuasion. Okay, how best, then, to say what I want to say without offending or risking misrepresentation??? Ah, I have it:

"Okay, maggots! Download that videogame NOW, by order of Army of the Western Realm, General Nunan! — Spend that 99 cents on something real, something fun, something really weird!

General Nunan flies an NZ-121 Scoutcraft, and comes from a planet so far away from Earth that the light reaching Earth from there hasn't yet revealed that his entire far-away home galaxy no longer exists as such.

It collided with two other galaxies in the meantime, just as our Milky Way Galaxy is colliding right now with the outer edges of the Andromeda Galaxy, to form a double galaxy when they stop reverberating.

What a pretty sight that is, and I'll be watching it with you.

Don't forget to download the game and pass it on to others to do the same and pass it on to others to do the same ...

HOW TO DESIGN A PROTEST VIDEO-GAME FOR THE MARKETPLACE
February 8, 2017

"Do You Want to Play a Game???"

The voice rings out in the video arcade. Of course you do. What else? Stand around while others play? Wander outside? Of COURSE I want to play a game.

After a few dozen Billenia in the Void, you'll start to wonder what they're DOING in there, in the CREATION, and you'll downscale into the world just to cop a peek, take a quick look, but WARNING, there is a definite danger here — GRAVITY.

As you look into the world, you're pulled down, down, down, into it, and the next thing you know, BANG! There you are, incarnated again. It's that magnetic gravity pull that does it every dang time, and you're sucker enough for that gimmick that you fall for it again and again and again.

It's kind of like FACEBOOK. There is no "I think I'll just take a quick look at it."

One second later, you're HOOKED and you're off on some wild-ass goose-chase through a series of postings, each one more incredible and weird and fascinating than the last, until four hours later, you emerge, exhausted and thoroughly winded by the unwitting slavery to fascination and curiosity.

Is the internet evil? No more so than electricity or the telephone, but like electricity and the telephone, it can easily be

TURNED to evil, and one of those evils is definitely FACEBOOK.

I categorically never LOOK at FACEBOOK, as I would with the Medusa or any other horrific creature of fascination and enchantment.

FACEBOOK is perfect for robots. It requires a LOT of maintenance and repair.

Like any other immortal Being, I'm always ready for a game, and a worthy opponent. Only once in a while does a major player come along to oppose me in my relentless drive toward The Perfect Game.

If there IS a Perfect Game, I haven't invented it yet. I don't know who has. I've seen a lot of very good games that were darn near perfect, but that doesn't score the bulls-eye.

A strutting, slimy, boasting and bragging peacock like Donald Trump is a COMEDY TARGET that's Made in Heaven, so to speak.

A COMEDY TARGET needs to be ROASTED until IT'S NOTHING BUT ASHES.

Okay, so last night, I invented a game that I call "OVAL OFFICE FART-CASTER".

OVAL OFFICE FART-CASTER VIDEOGAME

You'd lob or place or direct or cause to appear a sort of virtual fart, with what I call a Fart-Caster, a virtual expression of the actual Fart-Caster that I make for sale as a curiosity and practical joke in my online comedy and magic stuff.

"Oval" refers to the regular roundish non-circle — generally most folks know what we mean by "oval". What else would YOU call it? Okay, so I made an office in the shape of an oval. This is not uncommon in 18th and early 19th century architecture, and is VERY common in ancient architecture, particularly Greek and Roman public buildings, the kind I used to design for nobles and royalty, back in the day.

Ah, those were the days, when nobles were noble, and royals were royal. You don't get many despots like that nowadays. You youngsters don't know the sheer joy of living under the Emperor Nero, or Caligula.

Haw, haw, you never knew what they were going to do next. One day, they'd be out there feeding the masses, the next day, they'd order their troopers to massacre the first-born.

It makes life so EXCITING to wait for your local despot to press the WAR button. I LOVE it when you wake up in the morning to a mushroom cloud.

For you, it means the end. For me, it means another goddam term paper.

I love history, but I hate the names, dates and places thing. I'd much rather just get history by FEEL, if you know what I mean.

There are so many people, so much has happened and in so many places at so many times, it's just impossible to remember them all, so I don't.

I just concentrate on the people, time and place that I really find fun and exciting. Why NOT find some excitement? You've got ALL OF ETERNITY to play with, so why not add a bit of fun? My kind of fun happens to be meditation. Wanna make something of it? That's a VERY esoteric bit of backstage humor, which I think will fly over the heads of most.

Come to think of it, who wants revenge? There's no money in revenge. So forget about Oval Office Fart Casting.

How about a videogame that encourages folks to use StarGates to escape Trump Amerika? Why fight it? Just get the hell out of town!

Leave the scraps behind.

But — if you're a wage-slave, stuck at a nine-to-five job five or six or seven days a week, barely make enough to just return to work the next day, barely feed the kids, barely make the payments, barely have a minute to yourself, you probably aren't in a position to just pick up and start your life over in another country, right?

Who has a million bucks in their retirement fund these days?

You can bet Donald has an escape route planned, probably ending up in Putin's Witness Protection Program, in case things go very wrong, and he's prosecuted for his violations of the Constitution and the Law.

"Oh," snorts Trump, "Those SO-CALLED JUDGES again! What the hell do they know? I've bought and sold judges like them!"

YOU might end up in jail for the rest of your life for saying something like that, but not Trump. Like all despots, he is above the law. He is THE Donald, and won't ever let you forget it!

You haven't got a spare million bucks? Okay, so you'll have to find another, less uprooting and more affordable way to escape.

Have I got a StarGate Portal for you!!!

Not just one, but a bunch. In this game, you learn to SPOT STARGATE PORTALS and you also learn HOW TO USE THEM to move around from one Dimension to another, one Lifestream to another, then you apply that in your Home Dimension, what you laughingly call "The Real World".

"Is this the Real Life? Is this just fantasy? Caught in a landslide, no escape from Reality." That's what Freddie Mercury of the rock group "Queen" thought, but he was wrong, there IS escape from Reality, plenty of it, and your world, the one you call "Reality", is just one of them, and they were all designed by me.

Laugh if you will, we'll see who laughs last.

DESIGNING A PROTEST VIDEOGAME:

I'm not the type of game developer who hits and runs. I could easily have made a game such as "Dump on Trump" where you take a dump ... you get the idea.

Or you could design a game called "White House Tipping", similar to cow-tipping and outdoor toilet tipping.

The marketplace might welcome a game that featured Trump-like Cabbage-Heads that you'd hurl at a wall, busting the wall wide open.

Maybe you'd think of a game like "Royal Flush". I won't go into the details, there.

Another possible game about our current cultural and social scene is the one I came up with as a protest.

In the end, in my game, "Escape From Trump Amerika", you escape from the misery of Trump Amerika, leaving ONLY Trump supporters behind to occupy the territory. Who wants it, if you hafta share it with THEM???

Of course, if they eliminate EVERY FOREIGNER from Amerika, they end up with NO physicists, NO doctors, NO brilliant mathematicians and NO imaginative and lively educators.

That would suit most Trumpers very well, indeed. They don't like brainiacs and rocket scientists. But those dumb Asians and Russians CULTIVATE 'em, don'tcha know???

It's a pretty gray and grim world they make, just like Mordor. Rip up all the trees and pour concrete, put up steel girders and glass. Gosh, that would suit Trump real well. So at his command, you drive out or destroy all eggheads and nerds. Jeez, that makes a really smart population, leaving just the crust, doesn't it?

Holy oledo, how long will THAT last against hundreds of nations all competing to be the very first to actually apply the full alien technology that "accidentally" fell into their hands back during Hitler's World War II??

Gosharootie, this is going to be fun!

Okay, so I didn't make any of those revenge games or upheaval games or battle games or killing or fighting or destroying or blowing up games.

I made a very simple maze game.

You simply get up out of your armchair and WALK briskly out of Trump Amerika, in my videogame.

You walk and sometimes take a boat, to and/or through, a series of StarGates that you have to locate and learn how to spot, identify, set destination, activate and traverse them.

The map keeps changing, so you can't get "Maze Bright". You'll never know which configuration of map you're in, and the map itself won't help you.

You can't see where you haven't been, and the journey is NEVER the same twice in a row.

If you DO happen to shoot anything, it's strictly to open a door or reveal a treasure or a key, or the occasional unstoppable Alien-Dominated Zombie or Zombie Boss.

Are there monsters? Sure, there are, if you want them, but they'll all be in your head. The only shooting you'll do is, as I said, to open a door, get a key, level up or find a treasure or get a few zombies out of the way while you pass through.

I could easily have made it into a shooter, but I didn't. Want to know why I refused to make it into a sure-fire hit? Damned if I know why. I guess I should make it into a shooter, if I expect any downloads at all, sigh. I did put in a few zombies to slow you down a little.

The public NEVER buys a non-violent 3-D game.

Take it from me, I know that marketing secret all-too-well, having put the SAME GAME up for sale in two forms, one violent and the other nonviolent. Guess what? I never had a SINGLE DOWNLOAD of the nonviolent game, while the violent version got THOUSANDS of downloads.

Commercial success with our gaming engine? We chose not to go that route, and our engine has never been used to create commercial games. We were one of the three first 3-D game developers, on the Amiga platform, as a matter of fact, predating all the others by months, with our very own engine and physics, which we still use today.

Marketing a videogame requires a LOT of killing, even if you've just committed Grand Theft Auto.

VIOLENCE IS the name of the game, especially in Trump Amerika, the Land of Fear and Hate, and the sooner you recognize that sad fact, the easier it will be to accept that if you're the nonviolent game type, you'll never make the Big League.

Okay, so where does that leave us? It leaves us with a super-violent zombie killer game called:

"Escape From Trump Amerika"

How much is it? Where can I download it? Can I play it on my laptop?

Those are all questions that I'll be only too glad to answer, once I've designed and gamed out and thoroughly tested the game. I haven't even made the starting map, yet, so I can't answer any question except "will it be violent?"

Sadly for my marketing team and any possible large audience of appreciative parents, I'm ashamed to admit that the answer is a resounding "No!", except for a few lousy zombies, and they don't count, anyway, except to another zombie.

But don't despair, because — even though there is no killing — there IS plenty of SHOOTING, and LOTS of DYING!!! The zombies don't die — they're undead, remember??? But they can lie down awhile, to let you pass.

You'll find Tiger Pits, Lava Pits, Tar Pits and Apricot Pits scattered about in there, along with all manner of things, all of which are AFTER YOU or AGAINST YOU or BLOCKING YOU, including dozens and dozens of zombies, dogs, creatures of the night, horrible vicious hungry denizens of the dark, waiting to kill you and eat you.

All this, without any violence. Just the occasional zombie, like I said.

Having already admitted defeat on the violence front, I'll now proceed to launch into the project, starting with CONCEPT, to wit:

Okay, I'm escaping from Trump Amerika. How much do I have to know in order to start playing the game? Can I learn more as I go, as things develop in the gaming cycle?

The player finds himself or herself in a situation in which SOMETHING must be done, something specific, such as springing a trap or opening a hidden door, otherwise all other actions and directions are blocked. It's a small total trap with no apparent way out.

Once this hidden door is sprung and the player is out of the initial Holding Cell, we should give the Player some sort of spell or weapon or key or something.

There should now be an upgrade of the character, however slight, such as upping the money, magic or life.

Now we need to further the plot just a bit, get the character moving, so we'll need an NPC to give directions and provide a specific short-term QUEST, such as find a key, release a prisoner, discover a hidden cave or cavern — that sort of thing.

Something exciting to happen right here — possibly a challenge, maybe a water pit or slime pit with a narrow bridge or a jump.

An ACTIVE threat needs to happen here, maybe a descending ceiling or an ever-widening gaping hole in the floor?

This is the point at which there must be a turning, a choice of paths.

Once you've made a choice, the universe starts spinning out alternative realities, and that carries over with shamanic quantum magic into the "Real" world in which you live your daily life.

NOW maybe you could shoot a zombie or two.

Once you choose a path, there will be several alternatives. You will never be sure which one came up in the random selection pattern, so there's no way to know what's ahead.

One thing you know for sure, that each of the various StarGates you encounter and learn to find, see and open and travel through will be different in many ways, but the same in one important feature, which is HOW THEY WORK.

Where they go and what they do is always a challenge — you can get some impression of this by watching "Bill and Ted's Excellent Adventure", when they time-travel around in the time-tunnels.

This is pretty accurate, as is "Defending Your Life" and "Beetlejuice" in the sense that they do portray very clearly some of the attributes and conditions of the Between-Lives State.

Want to go to Heaven?

You really want to go to Heaven? It's only good for the climate. The company is lousy. You get party mixes. On the other hand, if you feature hanging out with losers like Elvis Presley and Johnny Carson, you'll like Heaven.

Myself, I'm happy where I am, wherever that happens to be. I got a

LOT of time on my hands, all of Eternity, and it doesn't much matter what's happening now. Eventually, it all washes away and we start over again.

I kind of like that starting over.

The very beginning of Diablo II was the real meat of the game, the rest was all window dressing, and you get to start out weak and helpless. I like that in a game, video or otherwise.

OBJECTIVES OF THE GAME

From my perspective and with my intention, there are a number of possible "objectives" of the game for the Player:

Get through the game from the beginning to the end.

Learn how to FIND or LOCATE StarGate Portals.

Learn how to SEE StarGate Portals.

Learn how to OPEN StarGate Portals.

Learn how to SET or SELECT StarGate Portal Destinations.

Learn how to TRAVERSE StarGate Portals to a Destination.

Learn how to CLOSE a StarGate Portal behind you.

Get out of Trump Amerika one way or another.

Teach others how to escape Trump Amerika.

Open the Path to Wisdom.

There are of course more levels on which this game operates, all of which are beneficent and I hope helpful to the oppressed masses who must suffer under the rule of a vicious, violent and vindictive dictator, which is today's Amerika, like it or not.

You may NOT like it very much and might even be ashamed to be an Amerikan, so you MIGHT be tempted to play the videogame, which means 99 cents more toward MY Escape Plan!

In the game, you will learn how to actually activate REAL StarGates, and learn how to REALLY use StarGates to escape for REAL from Trump Amerika.

You'll also learn how to take out a roomful of zombies.

Don't wait until it's too late. It might be too late already. You may not be able to pass the borders in either direction without getting shot.

LEARN THE LESSON OF THE WALL. What do you get when you cross the Trump Wall with a Mexican? About half-way.

Don't fight them. Fighting is stupid, base and animalistic. No need to fight. Escape from Trump Amerika! Get out now, while you still can! Leave them to fight each other, for they surely will.

Meanwhile, ESCAPE FROM TRUMP VIDEOGAME AMERIKA! DOWNLOAD MY NEW TODAY!!!

Uh, oh...It's not READY today. Okay, well, if I ever get it out there, please consider downloading it and telling others about it, all right?

In the meantime, I'm going to go now, to amuse myself by making a level or two. I'm planning a number of very challenging levels. None of them qualify as "easy", not even the very first one.

As a matter of fact, that first level will be sort of a test of how serious you are about completing the game all the way to the Final Boss???

But wait — there is no shooting, so how can there be a Final Boss?

I guess it's gonna cost ya 99 cents to find out, pardner.

THERE HAS BEEN A MAJOR SHIFT
READ ON
February 9, 2017

I never talk politics, couldn't be less interested, and I'm not talking politics, now. I'm defending my freedoms, and yours, too, whether you know it or not, even if you don't live in Amerika.

Am I a Democrat? No, emphatically not. A Republican, then? No, I'm not a Republican. I'm a visitor to this planet, an off-worlder, and have no local political interests or ambitions.

In fact, I have NO other interest than to bring the Teaching to a sad and angry little planet full of violent morons screaming in pain and agony, killing each other and destroying their legacy and history.

Bringing the Teaching. Haw, Haw!!! What a hopeless task THAT is, but I keep trying.

Push even the most peaceful of Pacifists up against the WALL and hold him there for a while, and sooner or later, you'll wind up on the floor. Punch me once, you won't get a second chance. Not ever.

That's what happened when Senator Elizabeth Warren got pushed up against the wall by the Republican Majority in the Senate. READ ON...

She bravely took it on the chin when she DARED to stand up to the Rich Republican Bullies on the Senate Floor. She got in a few licks, and then was silenced, probably permanently, by an overwhelming vote and a Big Lie, which seems to be Washington

Tactics these days, since the Trumpies took over.

Not to worry, I haven't been silenced, at least, not yet. I'm a citizen. I pay taxes. I served in the Armed Forces. I can't be silenced by the Republican Majority, at least, not openly. They might think I'm likely to be a Whistleblower and tell what I know about the intelligence community.

I would never do that, even to save myself.

In fact, the only way they can silence me on the Trump issue would be to disgrace the Senate forever by ordering me silenced in a way so brutal and mean that fighting would erupt in the streets, but none of that is going to happen, because we had a SHIFT in LIFE STREAMS.

The Coretta King Incident sparked yesterday by Senator Warren marked a Major Shift.

The shift is a good one, leaving you, and me, and all our friends, in a different LifeStream, where there's less chance of something going dreadfully wrong.

Sadly, Senator Elizabeth Warren is now in mortal danger of being expelled forever from Congress, or being attacked by a Trump Supporter, which would definitely set off a shooting civil war.

The Republican Senators who were just elected to Total Power, all of whom are Filthy Rich Second Amendment Gun-Carrying Crooks Protecting Their Financial Interests, are only too willing to use their overwhelming force against a few paltry peasants, which is US.

The Republican Senators literally don't care if you live or die. Frankly, from their perspective, if you're not a card-carrying White Christian Republican, you'd be better off dead in the world they're making now.

Are we safe from harm? Are we safe from our ruthless Dictator President? Are we safe from our Ruthless and Destructive Overwhelmingly Nasty Republican Congress People?

No, we are emphatically NOT safe! You're NEVER entirely safe, and you're NEVER safe from your government!!! They are public servants who think they OWN you!!!

Those in power, and that includes Democrats and Whigs too, ALWAYS abuse it and use their power to overwhelm and destroy any and all opposition, even if it's harmless, just out of hate and spite.

It's not about Republicans. They just happen to be in overwhelming power now. If Democrats were as powerful, they'd be bastards, too.

You can read Mark Twain to discover the abuses 150 years ago —

they were pretty much the same, mostly racist, mostly nasty, mostly one-sided and delivered with overwhelming force.

This Republican Congress has the STATED intention of curbing the civil rights of all non-white Christians, and if you think that doesn't include YOU, you'd be wrong, perhaps even dead wrong.

That's right, the Republican Senators want YOUR DEATH, and they won't stop legislating until they get it. They HOPE you starve to death. It leaves more for the White Christians.

These are the same people that voted to create the conditions that brought about the Dust Bowl of the Depression Years, the immense eight-state ecological disaster that still haunts us today.

They are the same people that voted to invade Iraq, thus creating ISIS and alienating half the world against Amerika.

They are the same people who voted to ban Whiskey with Prohibition, thus creating EVERY SINGLE MOB that exists today, including the booze-running mob run by President Jack Kennedy's father, who used his money to buy the Presidency back in 1960, so the Democrats do it, too.

It's not just one party, it's a group of demon-possessed greedy assholes who get themselves elected to Congress and then bleed the people for the next few years while they spend their time and effort trying to get re-elected, and try their best to destroy the opposition and break their shit.

From here, the Republican Congress today looks very similar to ALL abusers, including those elected to public office by the very people they want to destroy. If you're an African-American Woman, and you voted Republican, you've only yourself to blame when they carry you off kicking and screaming and flashing your Republican Party Card.

The mob will not listen, will not see the card. They will rip you to shreds, a victim of your own fear and hatred.

If that isn't a description of the Hell World in the Between-Lives State, what is?

This is a perfect time for you to practice being dead. Please try to understand. It's not a trivial matter.

At no time during the past fifty years has the President been so openly, aggressively, anti-Semitic, anti-black, anti-Hispanic, anti-Asian, anti-African and anti-Indian and Australian.

At no other time in Amerikan history have you ever had to

PROTECT YOURSELF FROM YOUR PRESIDENT.

The Republicans AGREE with Trump, are RACIST just like Trump, and don't mind history viewing them as rabid racists, so long as they have YOU at the end of a lynching rope.

VIOLENT RACIST BASTARDS have taken over the entire government, every branch and every agency of the government, and there is nowhere to go, nowhere to run to, nowhere in this world that is ENTIRELY safe.

Luckily, Senator Elizabeth Warren took a very verbal stand against the tyranny yesterday, and may pay for it dearly, perhaps by being kicked out of the Senate permanently by the Republicans. They can do it and get away with it.

The Republican Congress can silence ANY opposing voice, merely by voting the offending opposition "Out of Order", as they did in her case. They will tolerate no opposition, not a word in protest.

They have the law on their side and, as lawmakers in control of the Supreme Court, they can twist it any way they want to, and make you hurt, and hurt, and hurt.

Haw, haw, it's like watching a Live Action version of everyday life in Downtown Mordor, in Tolkien's so-called fantasy, "Lord of the Rings", which describes Trump's takeover of the U.S. Supreme Court and Congress to the letter, except that YOU and YOUR FAMILY are the helpless orcs in service to Evil, Pure and Simple.

This is now none of my concern.

The voice of the people is fully raised in howling pain and agony, and the tyrant and his buffoons don't realize that the mobs will soon take to the streets and there's only one possible outcome of that action.

That's right. It's too late to sign the "Edict of Tolerance", which did King Louis no good.

By the time they reach the palace steps, the mob won't listen to reason, either from you, or from a deposed oppressor, as happened back in 1792, if I recollect rightly, or from their own leaders. They are usually too far gone into hysteria to hear anything but the roar of the greasepaint and the smell of the crowd.

Nothing in this world is completely safe. We're not safe, but in this LifeStream, we're SLIGHTLY LESS LIKELY to be picked up in the Great Roundup — SLIGHTLY less likely to be beaten up on the street for being ethnic, and SLIGHTLY less likely to be attacked without warning by a hysterical, window-smashing car-burning mob of

148

frightened humanoid creatures, sweeping through the streets like locusts through a wheat field, looking for Jews, Blacks, anything different.

Learn to stay out of their way, and it isn't enough to be in the deep country to qualify as "out of the way" — a city mob can get fifty to a hundred miles out before they stop destroying things.

Think of a cattle stampede, and you've got it. No way to stop it, dangerous to turn it, just get the hell out of its way, is all you can try to do, and sometimes, that just doesn't work.

SOUL GROUP L315a is being COLLECTIVELY GUIDED, like a ferry boat going through the shoals and around rocky cliffs, coral reefs, and other dangers. For the moment, as long as you're with the group, you should be all right.

As a matter of fact, several of my latest Orbs feature boats, some of them large steam packets like the Mark Twain, which I built out of Simple Prims, and the Sea Raft, which can be maneuvered like a small sail boat.

With all those voices raised against the tyranny, I'm now free to develop funny videogames and funny "filk" songs that give people the power to fight the tyranny in a peaceful and lawful manner.

I'd just as soon concentrate on my games and songbook than write devastatingly witty repartee that is doomed to fall on the cutting room floor. YOUR voice should be ringing somewhat, as well.

It isn't yet a crime to speak out, but it soon will be, if Donald Trump has his way. If we allow him to grab our collective pussy, it's our own fault.

By the way, if the Boss touches your body, even over clothing, he's guilty of more than merely harassment — that's technically sexual assault, even when fully dressed and standing up in an office.

Of course, if you happen to have the misfortune to find yourself working as an employee, you're on your own.

Please note that yesterday, the White House Clown announced that WE'RE the ones using the Race Card.

It never occurred to me or anyone other than a White Christian that a President would turn out to be a thorough card-carrying racist bastard.

I didn't turn down "Minorities" from MY housing project, you lying asshole bastard, YOU did, and you're lying about it now, and you'll be lying about it with your very last breath!

I never thought I'd HAVE TO talk to a President that way, and I wouldn't, if he deserved respect, but he attacked me first, as a non-Christian and a non-white, meaning that I'm a Jew and, like I said, I'm determined to get my licks in before I'm wiped off the map by overwhelming force.

Most restaurants and hotels that turn away blacks also turn away Jews and Hispanics and Asians and Indians, as any one of us will grimly inform you.

If you're White and Christian, you won't have experienced this prejudice in Amerika, but it's there. Want to find out just how oppressive it is? How intolerable? Want to find out why someday the aristos will all end up on the guillotine and always do?

Wear a "Jew" armband around town for a while, and see what happens to you and what you have to do to defend yourself, protect yourself from actual physical harm, every single day of your life.

It makes many people wish they'd never been born, which would suit the Republicans just fine. In fact, that's their plan.

Under the inspired leadership of Mass-Murdering Fuckhead Adolph Hitler, all Jews in Germany were forced to wear the hated "Juden" or "Jew" armband, which marked you as a target for vicious street violence.

The "Juden" armband is white on blue, and you can find the pattern online — with or without a yarmulka, and you'll see what I mean. Want to get into a fistfight or deadly combat? This is definitely the way.

Identify yourself as a target.

If you're other than white, you won't need to do anything to identify yourself as a victim.

No restaurant, no hotel, no pool, no gymnasium other than the YMHA and YWHA — Hebrew gyms for Jews who were turned away from the YMCA and YWCA for not being Christian.

You can't legally turn a Jew or a Black or a non-Christian away from a hospital at this time, but hold onto your hats, because if Trump has his way, we lose 55 years of Civil Rights advances over the next few months, thus rolling the Civil Rights Clock all the way back to 1955, before Martin Luther King, before Rosetta Parks, before Coretta King.

We're now back where we were during segregation, maybe even worse, and now it's not just African-Americans, it's Muslims, Jews,

Puerto-Ricans, everyone except the lily-white Christians.

Jeez, it suddenly occurs to me, ***what if you're black AND Christian?*** Do they allow you to go into the pool, but only up to your knees?

Thanks to Donald Trump, it's now considered a SPORT to kill innocent senior people on the street, and several hoodlums and punks have threatened me lately, thus making it very clear that sooner or later, I'll be forced into deadly combat by someone who thinks they can take me down in an even fight.

Of course, Republicans are known for not fighting fair.

Screw Donald Trump, and the racist extremist horse he rode in on. Even his own party will eventually have to distance themselves from him or suffer defeat at the hands of an angry mob of millions of outraged citizens who emphatically did NOT wish to elect a dictator.

Even if Donald Trump actually had the will of the people and hadn't lost the Popular Vote and won by an old election-hall trick, that doesn't give him permission to put "His People" in power, and then blow the rest of the country out of the water.

He does NOT have the right to enforce his opinions and views on others. He's supposedly the President of ALL the people, not just his closest friends.

Amerika is being held hostage by the very rich, and you know what happens when that goes on too long and the rich get too greedy.

There are now millions of voices of people who are thoroughly SCARED of Donald Trump, and are already tired of him after only two weeks of his Power Madness, and they will get rid of him when he goes just a bit too far, and he will, but he's NOT going to get very far, at least in THIS LifeStream.

Life in Amerika is no longer a Fair Game. The White Christians own the field. Please note, there is not a single Jewish, Muslim, Hindu or Buddhist television station on the entire band of satellite television stations. Not a one.

Why do you suppose that is?

In my opinion, it's the same reason as not finding a single Synagogue in this county, even though there are an estimated 7,500 Jews living here. There is a "social center" in the Rabbi's private home, but nothing on the street, no building to cover in swastikas.

The object now is to try to stay 100% with SoulGroup L315a, and that means doing your daily practices without fail, every single day, to keep connected.

Run a click, walk a click. Like I used to say to the troops back at Fort Ord, "Pick 'em up and lay 'em down!". Keep up with the troops, maggot!

In order of importance, the morning chat will keep you well-informed, reading my blog will give you the particulars of the day, and you can get grounded, centered and connected by placing your Avatar in the Ashram.

Readings from the ABD, running Orbs for yourself and others, playing five minutes of guitar, training your voice for angel song, doing some embossing work, making rings or earrings — all are good practices to help KEEP YOU IN CONTACT. They also work to keep you TRANSCENDING, to keep you well above the world of pain and misery that humans have driven themselves into through greed and violence.

Hey, what goes around comes around. You reap what you sow. You get what you gave. That's an immutable law, and Donald Trump will surely one day pay the price for what he has done to millions of people who didn't want THAT done to them.

Of course, he has followers who DO want that done to them, and that'd be fine, if millions who DON'T want that done to them weren't getting run over by a steamroller in Congress.

So the upshot is, there are plenty of voices, and my voice is just one of millions.

Should the time come when every non-Christian must leave Amerika or die in the camps, I will surely mention it in my blog, if I'm allowed to remain at my desk, which I doubt. I've told you for many many years, by the time you see it coming, it's too late to duck.

Myself, I'm not the Jordan-Crossing type. As Darth Vader says of Obi-Wan Kenobe, "Escape is not his plan," nor is it mine.

My job relative to Trump Amerika is not in blogging, but in creating devastatingly funny videogames and "filk" songs to give tools to folks, so we can all pull those statues down when the tyrant falls.

On the other, hand, my blogs do seem to interest him. How do I know? Remote Viewing. You can do it, too, just as easily as I can. Remote Viewing, like telepathy, is built into the human biological machine, as if you didn't already know that.

See? You're already telepathic as hell.

152

So while the Race Wars, Religious Wars and Ideological Wars rage all around us, we're obligated to stay focused on our spiritual work.

I don't mean to ignore someone who's overwhelmingly and unignorably in your face and aggressing on you. I don't get into fights, because I'm not going to live the rest of my life waiting for them to get even.

What I mean by staying focused is, do your spiritual practices, don't give up the ghost, even if you feel like just quitting the day job and going on the breadlines.

Dictators always work the same way — it's classic NPD OVERWHELM. They wear you down, and wear you down and wear you down until you finally give up and tell them to go ahead and do whatever the hell they want.

That's their method of controlling you, and you have to learn to defend yourself on that level.

That's why I'm considering starting a "NO OVERWHELM!" training, although I don't know how well that will be received. It works along with the HARMONY Training and devices, plus a few simple self-defense moves for those times when reason doesn't rule, something that will happen more and more.

People will be less inclined to listen to reason, more likely to act reflexively, animalistically to perceived threat, which will soon be anything or anyone slightly different from themselves.

Frankly, I'm more inclined to tell someone to go to hell than I have been, but that's my New York upbringing.

It's typical of a New Yorker to ask a cabby, "Can I get you to take me uptown to 186th and Grand Concourse, or should I just go fuck myself?"

I'm used to getting pushed around, but there's a limit to the push I will take from ANYONE, and once over that line, I don't expect to go back. I do NOT respond to bullies with reason, wit or bravado.

I do what anyone would do when faced with overwhelming force. I get my licks in first.

According to Law, this is the TIME OF RACIAL PURGING, and you would be wise to learn how to stay out of the way. Is it possible to stay out of harm's way?

Probably not, but you can certainly TRY to stay out of harm's way.

One way to do that is to remain centered.

Another way is to move away from a crowded urban area to a rural countryside farm or ranch OR ASHRAM, and sit out the raging mobs if you can — some of them are bound to run over the countryside, respecting nothing, mindlessly and hysterically destroying everything in its path, including you and your home.

The mob will make a sound like nothing you've ever heard before, unless you've been lynched or stoned in a prior life.

It sounds like an oncoming freight-train or a twister, but it isn't.

It's people gone mad, made crazy, wild with fear, howling with infused rage, looking for a victim and, like I said, that'd be you, if you get in their cattle-path.

Yes, cattle-path. Don't expect Ancient Wisdom to come from the mouths of these hysterical fear-driven morons.

I call them "Alien-Dominated Zombies", and they were the subject of several songs that Jimmi and I wove into music a few decades back.

I'm still singing about them, and now the zombies are pissed off because I make fun of them all the time, and I guess they're right — I do lay it on rather thick sometimes.

Jimmi, on the other hand, perhaps wisely, went back to 1950s doo-wop.

With a reduction of threat-level from Washington, I can grab a little free-time to develop what I really prefer to work on, which is my Inter-Dimensional Strapping and my See In 3 Dimensions BINOX, both of which are on my workbench at the moment, and to which I intend to return when I'm done blogging, whatever THAT means.

I also have some pages of song lyrics here by my side, and I'll be spending some time tonight working to refine the wording and add maybe a few more verses.

Also on the work-table for tonight will be some level-writing, probably on Level One, of "Escape From Planet Trump" and no, I'm not making the Oval Office — I just put that up as an example of what I COULD do, if I were so inclined, but I'm not.

My plan is to develop along the lines of some of my more difficult maze-games, combined with a zombie shooter that makes it fun, challenging and non-boring.

I hope it's as much fun for you to play it as it is now for me writing it. Tonight, my main concern is game-balance, making sure that you have enough ammo replenishment to finish the Quest, and that the NPC shopkeepers are in good working order, which means some work on the responses and maybe some voice recording for the NPC

154

soundbites.

I don't want anything I'm doing to suggest violence or aggression against anyone, except maybe a zombie or two and a Level Boss at the end of every level.

Escape from Planet Trump IS my style. I use the opportunity to introduce some StarGate technology and Jaunting Styles. I regard this time period as a great opportunity for Work.

You can't have a game without breaking a few omelettes, eh?

Yes, Virginia, there IS a Trump-Free Zone, somewhere, over the rainbow, if I remember rightly.

I'm one of those Pacifists who can't be held against the WALL for even one single second without delivering a blow to the throat, followed by a devastating strike-through into the sternum. I guess I wouldn't compare well with Gandhi on that score, eh?

But we're totally different Avatars, Gandhi and I — were I black today, I'd be in the streets after the Sessions appointment. I haven't checked CNN yet today, but I'm sure that sooner or later, the Government Bastards will provoke something.

They want an excuse to call the National Guard, to point to the blacks and women and Hispanics and Asians and say, "They're the violent ones!". It never fails, and it's always the same story.

Aristocrats never change, throughout history.

With the Republicans occupied with millions of targets, it leaves YOU and ME free to work, to practice our spiritual exercises, to make up some songs, write poetry, write a blog, write your Congresspersons, paint a picture, stay creative, stay active, stay vocal and stay free with maxi-pad.

Now with millions of voices raised in outrage and opposition, Trump is ready to ascend to the throne he's due to occupy in history, as the most ridiculed U.S. President in U.S. history, and we're here to see it happen!

How cool is that???

What Caused the Disappearance of Christianity Back in the 21st Century???
February 10, 2017

What caused the sudden and unexplained disappearance of Christianity in the 21st Century?

Aren't you the least bit curious? Have you ever wondered what caused Christianity to suddenly vanish sometime in the middle of the 21st century, never to reappear, at least as far as the 37th century?

If not, it's because YOU CAN'T REMEMBER, not because you weren't there. THIS IS A TIME TRIP, REMEMBER??? Ah, but it's hard to wake up IN THE DREAM, isn't it???

As a seasoned time-traveler, although I probably haven't taken as many ill-considered rebirths as you have, I've often considered taking rebirth around 1941 or so, and observing life in the late 20th and early 21st centuries, to find out what really happened to Christianity.

Not the Christians. They didn't vanish. The Church of Christianity did. The Christians remained for quite some time after the collapse of The Christian Church, first in Amerika, then after a short time, it went down worldwide.

My first thought was, maybe the Rapture??? They'd been expecting it.

I checked my stats for Heaven/Population/Christians/Rapture — but there were evidently no more Christians coming through the Between-Lives State than the usual upflow, about six billion an hour.

Don't forget, there are 300 BILLION Earth type planets out there in THIS UNIVERSE ALONE, and life-bearing doesn't just follow that narrow path, AND there are billions upon billions of parallel worlds on which people and other creatures, lots of them, die every day.

One planetful of humanoids doesn't make much of a crunch when it goes up in smoke. The idea that a planet's demolition would cause much of a disturbance in The Force is absurd, to say the least, but go try to tell that to George Lucas.

He never let his technical advisers tell him he couldn't do something. If he wanted sound in space, he got it.

I also checked — and double-checked — the time-stats up through my own time-frame back in the 37th century and, from what I could glean out of the miserable patchy and sketchy surviving records of Western Civilization, there hasn't been a Rapture yet, and if there is one sometime up ahead in the far-distant future, there won't be any Christians around to take advantage of it.

There are billions and billions of creatures being born and dying every single moment of every single day, and you can't possibly expect me or anyone else to keep track of every mother that ever got born or hatched or fissioned, but I checked ALL the Akashic Records, which you can easily do yourself to check my figures — and no Rapture, at least not on THIS LifeStream.

So if it wasn't the Rapture, what the heck was it?

As you are only too well aware, we knew nothing back home in the 37th century about the Christians, except that they were around for a couple of thousand years, and then, all of a sudden, without any indication of exactly why and how it happened, there was a total absence of Christianity that occurred sometime in the EARLY PART OR MIDDLE OF the 21st century, into which I've penetrated, using nothing but a student visa and a note from my history teacher here in the 37th Century.

As a time-travelling student, I'm on "Extraterrestrial Student" status with the Franklin D. Roosevelt Administration, the Truman Administration, the Eisenhower White House and the Kennedy Administration.

I'm also on good personal terms with the Clintons — I used to send them truffles — and with President Barack Obama, but a fat lot of good it does me now, with a madman in control of what is swiftly becoming a Police State.

I have photos of myself in the White House during 7 administrations, but not this one. I'm not ABOUT to present myself at a White House that wants to DEPORT ALL ALIENS which would have to include me because I come from outside the sim.

I suppose they'd leave me alone, if I came to 21st century Earth as a cat, but then, typing with the paws, it's awfully hard to take good notes.

What if they want to send ME back?

Wait a minute. If they do, they might be willing to reassemble my scoutcraft and return it to me....what the hell am I saying? I keep forgetting how utterly TREACHEROUS human beings tend to be — particularly the uncivilized ones, like the Amerikans.

They would never let me rebuild it and escape to bring my fleet down upon them. I have no fleet, and told them so, but naturally, because they lie, they assumed I was lying, and they can't or won't use their telepathic powers to check my story.

I'm a Time-Traveler from Up Yonder.

Time travel is easy for us back in the 37th century, because we have tons of Unobtainium with which to power our temporal devices.

Just kidding. I don't even know what "Unobtainium" is. I just used it for the gag.

Obviously I'm actually using, as you suspected all along, the same old ACME Time Tripper 101 that we all used in the History Lab at "More-Science High", back in the 37th century.

As you're only too well aware, Time Travel is Basic Physics, just as rising from the dead, casting out lepers and healing the sick is really Basic Med, back home.

We have no surviving records or texts from the 20th or 21st centuries except a full re-issue boxed set of MAD Comics and one volume of PANIC, but there WAS an oral tradition, kept alive among survivors for centuries after the BIG WAR and the REALLY BIG WAR, and the REALLY REALLY BIG BIG BIG WAR, the exact details of which are lost to 37th century history.

You'll see all that outlined in detail in my class notes, entitled "SlimeWars", outlining what I know and remember from the Earth Simulation History Records — the actual history, not what the textbooks say or what the fiction writers make up as they go along.

So that's what I meant when I said, "I'm here to see a bomber."

What I mean by this is, "What the Hell happened to all those Christians?" From the 22nd century on, there's no TRACE of Christians anywhere on Planet Earth? But WHY???

I never knew, nor did anyone I knew back home in the 37th century, and none of the textbooks had any better information than we did.

I have bets up in our office pool, but we need a definitive ANSWER, so we can either collect our bets or pay up, and that's why I'm here, in this horrid, dreadful time-space you call 21st century Earth, to get answers to that obscure question.

I'm the first, apparently, to ever take an interest, but I needed a subject for my Term Paper, and that was my first inspiration, so here I am on planet Earth!!!

God, what a dump!

I know Bette Davis will excuse my use of her famous line. It IS a dump, in the Objective Sense of the word.

So here I am in the first part of the 21st century, and I'm supposed to find out WHY the Christians suddenly vanished off the face of the Earth and bring that information back to the 37th century in the form of a completed Term Paper.

Right up until now, there's no dearth of Christians — they're everywhere.

But then, WHAM!

No trace of them in ANY civilization from the middle of the 21st century, right on through the ages up until my time, in the 37th century!!!

But if it wasn't the Rapture, what could possibly have happened to them???

Pity — they're just gone, just plain gone.

I rather LIKE Christianity, and the occasional somewhat forgiving Christian.

I always liked Christmas and Easter. Back in the day, there was no Chanukah — the Jewish kids stayed in school through the holidays and no, I'm not kidding, and it wasn't all that long ago and yes, the Hindu, Buddhist and Muslims got no vacation, either.

It's going to be that way again, soon.

It was a devastating blow for me to find out, at the age of 11, that Christmas and Easter were RELIGIOUS holidays!!!

Not only religious, but Christian in particular.

It's easy to see that it's Christian when it's Christmas — the yule log, the ornamented and decorated tree, the stockings hanging on the mantel, the fruitcake and the hot brandy, all bespeak a time when Christians ruled the Earth.

And on Easter, all those Christian symbols, such as the rabbit, the egg and the chocolate bunnies, all signifying the Christian mythology and Christian social ethics. Religious holidays, indeed.

How dumb is THAT???

I find myself wondering why the ROMANS are the chief Christians — why is ROME the center of Christianity? Um, didn't the Romans have Jesus killed on the cross?

Oh, no, I forgot, it was the JEWS who killed Jesus, who was the very First Christian, didn't you know?

You would never have heard of Christ or Christianity, had not Saul of Tarsus had an epileptic seizure out in the desert. By the time the fit was over, Saul had come to realize that, although the original guy was now long-dead, HE WAS THE APOSTLE PAUL!

Okay, he goes to Rome, tells the Romans "You don't have to practice Judaism to worship Jesus!"

Hey, even THEN, you'd never had heard his name had not Constantine seen a cross-shaped cloud the evening before an important battle, after having been worked on about Jesus by his wife, a former street hooker.

Right after that, Constantine declared Christianity the official state religion throughout the entire Roman Empire, making his wife momentarily happy, right up until her execution for having an affair with Constantine's son Crispus.

Gosh, does EVERY tyrant end up with a former street hooker for a wife? Where does that leave Melania?

From what I saw at the time, here's the scoop on what really happened:

Crispus was Constantine's favorite son, by another mawwiage. Fausta, Constantine's wife, was afraid that Crispus would be favored over her sons for the throne, so she told Constantine that Crispus had tried to rape her, but that she had resisted.

So Constantine had his beloved son executed.

Then about a week later, he heard the truth, and ordered Fausta drowned in an overheated bath, a relatively painless way to die, I'm told by those who tried it.

Fausta didn't have a clue that Christianity had originally been a

Jewish Doomsday Cult. She wouldn't have cared. She was a total convert.

I guess it would do no good to mention that Jesus was a Jew, and that in fact he was a very strict Jew who kept kosher, kept the Sabbath and as I recall, kept a few mistresses on the side. He also wore a dress, like many priests and other Catholic Church officials.

The Pope likes purple hats.

My friend Jesus was a good Jewish boy who wanted to reform JUDAISM, not start a crazy DOOMSDAY CULT which invites practitioners to eat his body and drink his blood and worship the machine of his death, the crucifix, a common Roman remedy for Jewish insurgents like Jesus.

Jesus would never have passed a gold plate around the room, looking for donations. Jesus was a very, very CONSERVATIVE Jew in the original sense, meaning strict and lawful according to the Covenant, and annoyed that many Jews had strayed from the Orthodox Path.

That was Jesus' mission — to reform the corrupted form of 1st century Judaism.

That's why Jesus went after the money-changers — not money LENDERS, as you have been so ignorantly and deliberately taught to think. He didn't object to them being there, he was protesting against Caesar's Ten-Commandment-Breaking COINS, with the Emperor's FACE showing up on the front. Such things with Graven Images were forbidden, quite rightly, in the Holy Temple.

Hence, Jewish coinage was used — nothing else was permitted into the Shrine area.

Don't you guys know ANYTHING about this stuff? What survived is hardly a hundredth of the story, because the goons ALWAYS burn the library at Alexandria and everywhere else.

The Neanderthals HATE the smarter chimps.

They burn their books and flatten their museums and libraries.

(Picture John Wayne grabbing your collar and lifting you up a few inches, face-to-face) "Listen up, Pilgrim, and listen good.

"If Jesus landed here and walked around Trump Amerika with his robe, long beard, long hair and Jewish nose, he'd be lynched by a mob of White Christians!"

He'd be turned away as an Arab-looking hook-nosed, barefoot, cross-dressing, whore-loving, rabble-rousing street bum, at every

162

church in town!

If he were in a Catholic town, he'd be excommunicated.

Walking around a Southern town, Jesus would be lynched.

If Jesus encountered a Jew in Far Rockaway, he'd be a welcome Shabbat Guest on Friday night.

You gotta keep guys like Jesus quiet, or they'll stir up trouble. You want the peasants to be quiet and peaceful, not all riled up and mad.

I think that, in the end, the Christians bring it on themselves. That's my conclusion, based on recent observations, and that's how I'm going to conclude my Term Paper History Report.

I'm pretty sure I'm right.

Think about it. There are how many Christians in the world today?

Okay, one-third the world's population. But how many Muslims does that leave? How many Buddhists? How many Hindus? How many blacks? How many Hispanics? How many Arabs? Indians? Pakistanis? Japanese? Germans? Russians? Chinese? Yugoslavians? South Africans? Turks? Iranians? Iraqis? Lebanese? Syrians?

Two thirds against one third, 4 billion against 2.2 billion.

Holy shit, if they ALL GANG UP ON THE CHRISTIANS, it'll be a bloody massacre, worldwide. Of COURSE there's no trace of Christianity, after THAT, if that's what happens.

I think if the Christians get EVERYONE pissed off at them, they might very well paint themselves into a corner, and face a groundswell of uprising.

IS THE RISE OF THE CHRISTIAN RIGHT AN EXTINCTION EVENT?

Gosh, I sure hope not.

I figure that if it is, it'll involve most of the humans on Earth, regardless of where they are. I expect nuclear warheads to literally rain down.

But heck-darn, that, in a nutshell, is WHY I'M HERE ON EARTH.

That's the story I'm here to see and hear, the real story behind the scenes of whatever it was that caused the disappearance of Christianity from all of history.

I'm thinking of bringing some Christians with me back to the 37th century, but which ones? They all seem equally ignorant of their actual beliefs and church history.

But that doesn't help me write my Term Paper, does it?

Back home, there's NO information on it at all, nothing, not a whit, not a hair. There is also only one mention of the United States of America, just one singular entry: "Mostly harmless.". I doubt that, and intend to correct the entry as soon as I get back home to the 37th century, which I'll be only too relieved to do, once I have my Term Paper handled.

HOW IS JESUS HANDLING ALL OF THIS?

As you probably already know, he's largely unaware of Christianity. I TOLD you, he's a strict, very Kosher Jew, and that's historically supportable.

Besides which, I WAS THERE, and am there right now, and that's not just a figure of speech. All of space-time is a single thing, and there is no linear time, as you think of it.

Time is just another direction of space.

I hope I didn't give away anything, there. I never mean to, but sometimes I let something slip, and the next thing you know, an undeveloped species is rummaging about in homemade UFOs and Cigar-Shaped Starships.

Oy, if I've said too much, I'll never hear the end of it when I get back home. I just KNOW those guys are laughing at me right now, chasing after a silly totally obscure item like the disappearance of Christianity.

To tell you the truth, before I got here, I was convinced it was a snark hunt and that there never had been any Christianity, but boy, was I wrong! It's everywhere, and it's rampant!

And also, by and large, it's very unpleasant here in Christian White Amerika, unless you happen to be a Christian.

Well, being Christian, just plain Christian, isn't really enough. You have to be the RIGHT KIND of Christian, and nobody is certain what brand that might be — it changes as power shifts around.

Well, I think I've got it nailed, at least enough for a Term Paper. If I were writing a Doctorate Thesis and preparing Defense for Same, I'd have to bring back a LOT more evidence, but at the moment, I think I see the shit coming fan-ward.

See, it doesn't take a rocket scientist to figure this one out.

The Christians will all be in Church, waiting for the Rapture. Outside, in the sky, will appear thousands of Mother Ship UFOs, surrounding the Earth completely.

All Christians will get sucked up by the Christian Filtered Particle Beam, and they'll ride up the Magnetic Rays into the bays of the UFOs

164

stationed around the atmosphere.

The Greys are robots. They have no bio material on them, so they grow it. They need biological material for their clones. They spend decades and sometimes longer, cultivating the DNA and giving it lots of human bodies within which to grow and multiply.

This NANO material is then gathered by the Grey aliens and is used to create a new edition, or generation, of slave bots that live virtually forever.

There is a constant need for replacement bio enzyme material, hence any planet that can be used to cultivate it is prized and often off-planet and even on-world battles will erupt between farming and mining alien species.

Wow, are YOU lucky to be here at this particular moment in time-space! You've arrived on Earth just in time to see a HUMAN ENZYME ALIEN HARVEST.

But why do they only take Christians?

Because they're bred for the market, the rest of us peasants are worthless, enzymatically speaking.

Just kidding, they're DNA whores — they'll take anyone in a pinch. It's just that the Christians all vibrate on the same frequency — it's usually the number of the local Christian AM radio broadcast station, somewhere near the middle of the dial.

Everyone on a similar frequency makes it easy to scan and pull them up with the Tractor Beam, which is how it's done.

I've seen these harvests a million times, and it never fails to fascinate me, to see millions and even billions of bodies floating up into the sky and into the bellies of those big alien spacecraft.

They'll never listen to Linda Moulton Howe's warnings in time!!! Haw, haw, haw! I can't wait!

Here's hoping that you can avoid the crunch when it comes!

ESCAPE FROM PLANET TRUMP VIDEOGAME
February 11, 2017

Sorry if you're a Christian, and you got scared by my previous blog. I was being amusingly speculative, but even had I not been playfully toying with the thought experiment, "What Happened to the Christians?", it would have nothing to do with YOU.

I guarantee that even if you wore an 8" solid silver filigree cross vividly displayed and wore a tee shirt that said, "Ask Me About Jesus", you'd be excluded from that exclusive club. No matter how you try to look, act, sound and smell like them, you'll always be an outsider.

It's not about Christianity, it's about racism and hate groups, and preachers who preach hate. Unfortunately, humans are all-too-ready to be told what to do.

Mindless robots, relentless zombies, egotistical level bosses make a real double-socko combination-punch to the *medulla oblongata!*

If you're to effectively survive and get out of harm's way on Planet Trump, you'll need somewhere to go. No matter where you land, you'll be an immigrant, a newcomer, an outsider, and you'll end up in the Amerikan Ghetto, wherever that might be.

You'll be an Amerikan. You know, the "A" word.

In other countries, "Amerikan" will be a racial slur, and Amerikans abroad will be what foreigners are to most Amerikans, apparently.

Amerikans will be treated more or less the same way as they treat foreigners now, no matter where they go — if not immediately, certainly when enough of them have landed and are taking jobs away from the previous immigrants.

Besides, Amerikans just plain SMELL funny. I won't drink from the same well as one of them, would you???

Of course, it makes TOTAL SENSE to try to get to another planet entirely. You don't want to end up on the shit end of the "Immigrant" stick, so you need to find a PORTAL or STARGATE that will offer REAL escape, not just momentary relief, like taking a big dump.

Speaking of Dumps, there will be no place safe from Trumps. Grumps, Lumps, Bumps, Strumps, Humps AND of course the Yiddish variety, "Shlumps" — all these monsters, and more, are to be found in my newest game, ESCAPE FROM PLANET TRUMP.

You will have to find a completely different world, because all of PLANET TRUMP has gone mad, and it will all be embroiled in the racial purges of the 21st century.

I recommend a REALITY SHIFT to another dimension or LifeStream, and that's why I built this videogame, to show you how to REALLY GET OUT OF TOWN!!!

You can easily find your way through the mazes, and fight your way through the zombie-ridden passages and Portals.

Portals in this game are guarded, but not ALL the Portals you'll find on Planet Trump are necessarily guarded — however, they ALL require a KEY, a PASSWORD and, of course, a RITUAL, all of which you will perform through your in-game Avatar, but don't forget that what you do in the Quantum World REFLECTS in the Einsteinian World, so there might be direct effects from your CyberSpace actions in the videogame world.

As below, so above. Follow the Drinking Gourd. I have placed specific Portal-Opening Rituals into the game, to indicate how to spot and open Portals and the same thing that opens the Portal in the game opens the real Portal in the Super-Game you call "Life".

The very first Portal in the game "ESCAPE FROM PLANET TRUMP" is an easy and obvious gated doorway into a concrete tunnel, what is called the "Concrete Wormhole". You'll find out more about these Einstein-Rosen Star-Bridges in workshops and clinics.

When you first start out, you'll have the opportunity to select a character class or type that you prefer for this run.

There are two very cute cartoon-type kids on the left, one nominally male, the other nominally female. Then you'll note that there's a young teenager in modern dress, and another in Medieval garb, then three more teenagers, and then on the far right, the Amazon body that you're already wearing.

If you don't prefer to shoot, no problem. No need to shoot a zombie. Merely toss a bomb, grenade or fireball, or blast them with magic.

You'll find a very obvious PORTAL, in the form of an open gateway. Go through it and down, down, into the CONCRETE WORMHOLE, and your adventure will begin.

I like to play Pyro, which is Number 5 on your Weapons Pack, selected by pressing the corresponding number on your keyboard, but I also like Number 4, the Dart Gun, and for a very amusing time, I'll choose the Number 3 Weapon, Bombs.

You have a total of ten weapons numbered zero through nine, which I'll go over right now:

ZAPPER — A fast-launching electrical force gun that explodes into high-radiation particles upon impact.

BOOMERANG — Will fetch anything back to you, including monsters, so be careful what you wish for!

BOMBS — Lob these over for some ballistically-satisfying sport!

DARTS — The Dart Gun is a Particle Accelerator that blasts out tiny Tesla Darts.

PYRO — A wonderful blast of energy makes this Pyro Weapon a pleasure to use.

GRAPPLE — When you're trapped and there's no way out, try the Grapple!

ROCKETS — There is nothing like a Rocket Launcher to clear the way!

MAGIC — When the enemy is supernatural, you'll need some Magic! Make sure you have plenty of manna before you depend on Magic!

AUTOFIRE — This is the plasma equivalent of the Uzi SMG. Rapid-fire endless clips.

HATCHET — Actually, the number of this weapon is "zero". Guess what it does?

Save your Rocket Launcher AMMO for an explosive blast into a pack of horrible Ego-Eaters. They explode into little tiny particles, each of which is the same as the whole. Fascinating effect, thanks to VAL.

You can buy more AMMO with the GOLD that you collect around the labyrinth here and there. Be sure to loot the dead bodies of the zombie bodies that you'll be leaving lying around.

The floor-cleaner scours them up, eventually, and restores the space with new zombies, but that's the way life is, but by that time, you'll be in Level 2.

Heck darn, if something gets in your way, reason with them with the ever-popular Pyro Flame-Thrower, which by the way, is also good for instantly clearing the ice off your HUMMER windshield.

When escaping from anything, and Planet Trump in particular, always stay with the POG, the Pack of Green. If you don't know how to stay with the POG, or you have no idea what I'm talking about, ask Yanesh, Claude, or anyone in the Ashram.

I intend for this to be a group game, if group games are permitted anymore, and a solo game when you can't find a group or prefer to play solo.

Uh, if you're checking about the POG, um, well ... I'd inquire rather quickly.

I'm designing this game for the PC, not for the Android. If there's a smartphone version, it'll have to be made from whatever I've done, perhaps a converter or translator, from our GODD PC game engine over to an Android or iPhone type cell phone gaming engine might be available by now — it wasn't, a few years back.

We've bought escapefromplanettrump.com tonight, and I'm now starting serious work on the GODD LEVEL EDITOR, meaning that I've begun writing the first level, and it's a dilly.

I'll explain the finer points of the game and a few of the cruder ones, too.

It's HARD to get off Planet Trump once the shooting begins, but by the time you have to grab your bug-out pack and clear the area, you'll have SOME idea of what else to do besides shoot it out with the mob of zombies I have waiting for you around the next bend, and that never works out well.

There are no safe bends in this escape game.

Every end is a dead end, in a sense. You've taken yourself OUT OF PHASE and that means that you're OFF THE GRID, quantumly speaking, which means you can SLIPSTREAM or SLIDE from one

BRANE to another, using several extra dimensions, which is why they'll end up calling you an extra-dimensional illegal alien.

You start the game by escaping from immediate mob-threat. They're coming after everyone, sweeping the streets. Nothing escapes them. There is no reasoning with them. They are coming. They are coming, and they are dreadful.

You have to find a way around the mob, and that means finding and using the Secret Alien Portal that opens out to an area that is momentarily safe, but only momentarily.

The mob will try to find you, seek you out, so be sure to hide well, and stay there until the mob moves well past your area.

If you happen to accidentally survive the zombie mob, you might find the ALMOST inescapable LAVA PITS interesting.

If the lava pits don't get you, then the DUNG PITS OF GLYVE will surely enmesh you in their slimy entrapments.

Should you somehow survive the dung pits, you'll be delighted to run across the Bridge of Horror, at which you'll have to fight a bunch of Trumps.

A "Trump" is just a plain old zombie. Level Bosses can be "SuperTrumps", so beware and be prepared. It's best to have a bit of extra AMMO, so load up on whatever you need for your favorite weapon, and don't forget to see a TRADER when you run low on AMMO!

You'll find many zombies along the way, but they're nothing like the swarming mob of ordinary humans that awaits you at home, and is constantly just behind you, roaring with rage and pain, looking for a scapegoat.

Don't be a Socrates. When they come to get you, be elsewhere.

There are other enemies in the way, blocking and obstructing your WORMHOLE path and making the going more than merely difficult.

Troggs and Trolls and Soul Devourers and Exploding Monsters are just a few of the horrors you're bound to encounter between one world and another, when you GO OUT OF PHASE with the Einsteinian Reality, and decide to traverse the Time-Tunnels, Warps and WormHoles between the Branes of Reality.

But in the meantime, never mind the weirder and more dangerous enemies up ahead — what do you do NOW about the zombies?

Shoot 'em.

"Cache" is pronounced "Cash". It's a French word that means "stash of stuff", usually food, water, ammo, ranged weapon, short-range hand weapon, hatchet, radio, compass, map, survival knife, weatherproof matches, butane heater and lighter, change of clothing, extra boots, backpack or knapsack, maybe more.

You can bet your sweet ass that wherever there's a CACHE or DUMP, you'll find guardians, usually zombies, but they can be deceptive.

What I mean is, a LOT of zombies cross-dress into human form, which is why there are so many of them when you get on any kind of line or attend any reunion.

In a High School Reunion, it's even worse. Far fewer classmates are able to show up than those in your College Reunions, you can bet on that.

All zombies follow the Sign of the Double Cross. You can use this to your advantage. You'll find out how to make this work for you, as you play the game.

There are tricks and traps and jumps and spins and turnarounds and wrong moves galore. You'll find the whole experience rather challenging, to say the least, but it's a good training ground for what's coming up in your Alternate Reality Menu.

And I haven't even finished describing Level 1 of ESCAPE FROM PLANET TRUMP yet — there's so much more to tell.

How about I work on the Level a while before breakfast, eh? Keep your head above water, and DON'T PANIC!

Do watch a couple of films: "They Live" and "Hitch-Hiker's Guide to the Galaxy", both of which give abundant hints on what to look for and how to SEE it, StarGates included.

It's all in the light-shift. Watch for the glint, the slight rip in the fabric of space!

Look all around you — there are Vortex Points and StarGates pretty much everywhere, except perhaps some of the ritzier areas of Long Island, Palm Beach and Palm Springs.

You know what? "It's a helluva lot easier for a camel to go through the eye of a needle than it is for a rich person to enter the Kingdom."

That was the original quote.

It had nothing to do with Heaven, which wasn't invented until seven hundred years after Jesus walked on this planetary sphere.

Make that 787 years, to be exact.

By that time, EVERYTHING about Jesus was strictly hearsay,

172

rumor, gossip and speculation.

When you meet the REAL Jesus, you'll see how wrong human people and zombies can be. You will encounter Jesus in-game. He's your cabby when you drive through upper East Side Manhattan.

When you DO see Jesus, tell him Groucho sent you.

And get a receipt.

Here are some lyrics for your protest filk song rallies ...

If you wanna hear a liar
Tell a bullshit tale,
Or you wanna hear denial
Of a Mission Fail

CHORUS:

Donald Trump, Donald Trump,
Liar, Liar, Pants on Fire. (repeat)

When you wanna hear the truth
You will have to pull a tooth
If Ivanka were not his daughter,
He'd be dating her if he caught her.

CHORUS:

I haven't written the whole song, yet, and you're certainly welcome to add any verses you'd like to sing, change mine, whatever.

Mystical Voyaging Helps You Learn How To Escape From Planet Trump

February 12, 2017

On the Black Falcon, ready to board ten passengers for a Mystical Voyage.

Mystical Voyaging Helps You Learn How to Escape From Planet Trump, FAST!!!

One way to get off the planet real fast without any prior training or recollection of your Atlantean Self is to take repeated Mystical Voyages, which you can do in the Ashram without ever having to learn the basics of visualization.

In Mystical Voyaging, you learn to FEEL your way. You get

used to passing through PORTALS until it becomes second nature to you.

As a matter of fact, using the Ashram's Mystical Voyaging as a tool for transformation is as simple as singing or playing guitar for five minutes every day. It sort of transfers to the higher centrums, more or less by osmosis.

It's a painless way to learn. You do, and do, and do, and after a while, it just does itself. Please allow me to explain how you can apply this in your daily life:

Get aboard the Black Falcon — we're just about to take off on our Mystical Voyage.

Ritual is a set of actions, sounds and operations that opens a PORTAL.

Those actions, sounds and operations could look like dance, theater, drumming, chanting, processioning or walking through a Zen Garden in Walking-Zen Meditation.

The ritual can take almost any form, and must contain all the releasing and unlocking and invoking tools you'll need to open, activate and operate the PORTAL.

This is useful to open and operate almost any PORTAL, once you've found it.

Online Conventions, lectures, meetings, chats and demonstration lab classes can be held in the Ashram. All you need do is ask.

PORTALS are another matter. They're hard to spot sometimes, and then again, even if you know exactly where it is and how to operate it, the thing sits stubbornly dead and empty.

It can be a major stumbling block to not know where the PRIMARY PORTALS might be located and more specifically, where the NEAREST PORTAL to your house might be found.

After you've found, seen or Remote-Read and Mapped a PORTAL, you need to be directly in front of it, right?

My little Handy-Dandy Portable PORTAL folds up into HyperSpace when I'm not using it.

So the next item on your list is GETTING TO THE PORTAL, unless you're planning to build your own Home Vortex Particle Accelerator, or you happen to have a SHAMAN'S SHED PORTAL right there in your back yard — hey, not a bad idea, these days, what with a shooting war just around the corner.

Hear screaming, shooting, explosions? Do you see a mob of hysterical stampeding humans passing by, looting as they go?

Why not duck into your Shaman Shed and bug the hell out of there?

But how do you "Bug Out" into another dimension???

Okay, once again I'll go over the "Carnegie Hall Drill". Read my lips: "Practice, Practice, Practice." So what didn't you understand about practice?

You pick up the Voyaging Skill as you run through many, many

Mystical Voyages performed in the Ashram. Many, many.

Repeated Mystical Voyages will have several desirable effects, one of which is that you'll AUTOMATICALLY find voyaging to be easier and much more fun and far more interesting than "Real Life" — much more fun than you'd ever have expected.

You think I'm kidding, or exaggerating or just plain fibbing? Not my style. Try it, you'll like it.

And it's even better if you learn to serve in our Voyaging and Flight School, where Avatars can learn how to fly and how to sail in the Ashram.

I prefer my Mi-24 HIND to the little drones — you can't beat the firepower.

If you can learn to fly a plane in the Ashram, you might enjoy the little Pocket-Sized Drone I got for Christmas. It comes from Hammacher-Schlemmer, and is the damnedest little thing you ever saw.

Ashram Flying is Fun and Instructive.

That thing rises up a foot or two, maneuvers around a cafe table, takes a photo or video, then flies a wobbly line as it lands gently on the table in front of me, and then gets tucked away into my pocket.

That's the small, pocket-sized version of the personal drone, but they have them much bigger and capable of much further flight and much more flight control with larger, more complex computer-driven personal drones, some of which have a controllable live-action range of five miles and a payload of 38 POUNDS!!!

I can only imagine the kinds of things someone could put into one of those.

You can buy one that carries a boxful of stuff, like the AMAZON DRONES that fly your package right to your door, and sometimes through a picture window.

But you get it the day you ordered it.

Gee, those PERSONAL DRONES arrived just in time for the Big Blowup, eh? There are literally THOUSANDS of them for sale everywhere, and there are entire stores such as Radio Shack, that specializes in PERSONAL DRONES.

Myself, I prefer the feel of my trusty Mi-24 HIND chopper which I keep handy in the Ashram in case of Nuclear War.

It's got terrific firepower, and it's the choice of more than 50 different countries, none of which is the United States. You will really like the comfort of the ergonomically-designed air-flo contour seats, and the New-Age look of the cockpit and instrument panel.

You will FEEL the higher vibrations when you unleash the firepower of this little baby on the average woody countryside, and remember, it can all be rebuilt in the blink of an eye, so don't hold back!

The chatter of machine-gun fire is so soothing, you might prefer it to just flying around in the Black Falcon, but believe me, even wildass sky combat gets boring and tiresome after a while.

One small learning curve in this particular SL aircraft is that if it hits something, it tends to crash and burn and then explode. Best in the hands of expert drone-style flyers, I suspect.

One terrific result of drone flying and flying aircraft in the Ashram is that you get direct personal experience in Remote Viewing, and it's all at high-speed, so you learn quickly how to maneuver without crashing into something.

Remote Viewing can also be accomplished by using cyberspace entry, where you'd create a duplicate of the space, then invade it with an Avatar and explore it, getting the mental images as you work around in the space.

This works well if you have the layout already in hand. If you don't, you're stuck with the old pencil and paper "draw what you see" style of Remote Viewing.

Well, let's leave the military aircraft behind, and proceed to our next

Mystical Voyage Destination, the Garden of Zen Delights.

GARDEN OF ZEN DELIGHTS

We only walk through the garden on our Mystical Voyage, but you can take a moment to capture the teleport on your viewer, and return whenever you like.

The water sounds are an important part of any Zen Garden, and water features are vital for the success of the vibrational magic and overtones set up by the garden vortex, which is rooted on the x/y axis in the exact center of the garden.

This produces a vortex effect when activated and a mild magnetic field effect when it's not.

The curved bridge over the water is a vital element, as are the garden lights on either end. Waterfalls and smaller falls or rippling washboard pebbles and dripping stones can add a lot of magical effect as well as higher aesthetic levels.

Aesthetic levels are where it's at, in terms of rising through the Aethyrs, which is really what it's all about.

You want to be able to go up and down the ladder, up and down the elevator, up and down the slider, up and down the column, the tree of life, the circles of consciousness, the scale of creation and more.

You'll note that the lower levels are very robotic, that the program is everything, learning is nothing.

Progressing up the Scales of Cosmic Reality, it will be evident that greater and higher levels of consciousness rise as you go up the Scale.

Higher Consciousness also means greater ethics, higher integrity, stronger willpower.

It's easy to travel Jacob's Ladder when you know how, and it's even easier to learn than guitar!

WHAT is easier to learn than guitar?

Why, moving up and down the REALITY SCALES, of course!

Moving from the Dung Pits of Glyve all the way up to Buddha's Pure Land and Beyond, taking the floors two at a time.

Of course, you can't do that with your human body. But you CAN use your experience in a human body to access these quantum levels.

These skills tend to jump over boundaries, and you'll find yourself having an easier time Remote Viewing, Remote Reading and Astral Projecting and Jaunting when you've done a few Mystical Voyages

180

with us.

These are worlds that exist on many different levels, many different relative scales, but all pretty much the same in detail and configuration from one level to the next.

When you get to the top, you'll know.

In short, a pile of rooms stacked one on the other, all the way up and all the way down, and there is no end to "up" and "down" on any scale, due to a trick of infinity.

So how do you determine which level you're on, if they all look the same?

This Selfie at the Krishna Temple was SO hard to take. It looks like I have no lips!

That's part of your Shamanic Training, to learn to distinguish one from the other, but first you must become an easy voyager, knowing pretty much what to expect and how to deal with the inevitable oddball psychic and historical effects of voyaging.

One way to perform actual voyaging is to become so comfortable with Mystical Voyaging that it becomes Second Nature to you.

You want Voyaging to be something you do instinctively and naturally.

Voyaging becomes second nature, when you voyage a lot. One way to implement this idea is to DO something in your voyaging, like t'ai ch'i exercising with us on the Main Island in the Ashram.

You can organize events in the various chapels, meditation halls and temples, and processionals are always a welcome sight at the Ashram.

You might want to schedule a lecture or a talk or a forum — you can do that, too!

One fantastic thing about Mystical Voyaging is that you never have a baggage or luggage issue. You travel with everything you need in your stash bag, which carries more than can be contained in a single universe, so not to worry about a large handbag, it's redundant.

You'll need to know how to FIND a PORTAL, how to RECOGNIZE a PORTAL, how to BUILD a PORTAL and how to TRIGGER and OPERATE a PORTAL, all of which you'll learn easily and naturally as we go along in our Mystical Voyages.

Yes, Virginia, VOYAGES, which means "more than one". It takes a lot of REPETITION to set in the habits, and a hundred Mystical Voyages later, you'll still be learning and getting incredible results.

Habits is what you need, and REPETITION takes it right out of the mental and into the direct experiential, and one of the most important habits you'll need to develop is RIGHT TONES with your INCANTATIONS, CHANTING or PRAYERS, and you can use our "Sing With the Angels" Practice to accomplish that.

CORRECT PITCH means that you're "on-key" rather than "off-key", which is a result of practice, practice, practice. You are expected to GET that practice using the H1 Harmonizer. You need to be able to correct your vocal pitch and keep it corrected with minor adjustments of abdominal muscles, breath and vocal chord manipulation.

All this sounds terribly complex and horrifically scientific, but it isn't. It comes easily, I tell ya, when you practice Mystical Voyaging on a daily basis, even if it's only five minutes a day. Actually, 20 minute sessions and 1 hour sessions are more common and produce much better results, but anything is better than nothing at all, when it comes to spiritual practices.

Grishy and I run "G&G Enterprises" to keep everyone supplied in materials and tools for transformation.

CORRECT INTONATION

Intonation means the QUALITY of your tones more than the precision of their frequencies, although that is important, too. The quality of your voice will change with the strength of your out-breath, the setting of your vocal chords and the shape of the mouth, but really, it's about the TIMBRE, which is hard to grasp until you have LOTS of experience personally experienced upon which to draw for massive sets of examples of TONES.

Intonation is subtle, and I wouldn't expect you to catch on to what it is or how to use it until you've had hundreds of hours of practice.

You'll eventually pick up the nuances. Don't expect Mastery in the first few minutes.

CORRECT TONES

Tones are the notes as they are seen against the entire TONE SCALE, which technically is the entire range of SOUND within HUMAN HEARING, which is not very much in the way of spectrum, if you ask me.

You'd normally view TONES within a much larger horizontal chart of frequencies along the Electro-Magnetic Spectrum, or EMS.

If you turn that scale sideways, so that the lower or deeper TONES are at the bottom of the scale, you'll be able to figure out how that relates to musical tones.

There's a LADDER there as well, ranging from lower notes at the bottom to higher and higher notes at the top.

This LADDER is arranged in groups of repeating tones at OCTAVE intervals.

We call the various notes "C" or "D" or "E flat", but they are indeed DIFFERENT notes, even though SIMILAR NOTES repeat themselves at octave intervals throughout the TONE SCALE.

Of course, the notes in the WESTERN SCALE are usually of the Tempered Variety. I find that I have to use many different TONE SCALES, both Eastern and Western, to get the great quantum TRANSFERENCE and VOYAGING effects that I would like to see happen.

If you ever expect to PHYSICALLY TRANSFER from one dimension to another, you'd better not rely upon just stumbling onto, in and through a PORTAL into another dimension.

For one thing, you never know what it's attached to, what's at the other end, unless you are already familiar with that particular PORTAL, because they're all different, and they all lead to different places, different times and even different realities so far apart that you might not recognize them.

In short, it can get really weird, and the sooner you get used to it, the better.

What's New, Pussycat?
February 15, 2017

Before I Time-Travel, I like to dress down for the locals, but I always pack an Ankh and Flail, just in case I run into a gang of rowdies.

What's new??? Well, I've just spent the entire night making a BUNCH of SILVER WALKING LIBERTY HALF DOLLAR QUATRAIN MEDALLIONS, that's what's new today.

I'm ignoring the media circus in Washington for the moment, but I'll be back with the latest flash in a minute or two — it'll knock your socks off, if you're a tenderfoot in the political/business arena.

I've written a few more FOLK PROTEST SONGS which are on Barbara's desk for entry into my collection of Trump Roasts — get it? Rump Roast, Trump Roast? Haw, haw, haw, this guy's a barrel of laughs.

Frankly, from my perspective, I'm indifferent to whether or not he sets off a nuclear conflagration. I get paid no matter what happens, and I collect my dollar bet once the whole planet blows up real good.

Not my problem, and certainly nobody else's, either. We have other planets, we'll get over it. The locals, however, tend to go down with the ship.

MY BEST LRS MEDALLION EVER

Meanwhile, while we're waiting for the mushroom clouds and the loud "boom!" of the shock wave, I'd like to interest you in the Walking Liberty Half Dollar Quatrain Medallions. What they are is a half-dollar sized embossed inscription with the Kufic-Style Inscription, which is actually a Cabalistic capture of the Four Lines Quatrain from the *American Book of the Dead.*

If you're an LRS Member, you will DEFINITELY want one of these — it functions as a GATE PASS and creates a BUBBLE OF PROTECTION around you as you pass through the Hell-World, Brute World and Human World all around you.

About the Hungry Ghost World, the Jealous God World and the God World, we need do nothing — they won't hassle us if we don't get attracted to them, but the lower worlds are different, and their minions are under the control of local gods like Trump and Putin, and need to be warded off as we traverse those darker more dismal realms.

Note that all despots like to make their subjects live in a world of gray.

Think of this SILVER WALKING LIBERTY HALF DOLLAR QUATRAIN MEDALLION as a GATE PASS that allows you to slip through the FINAL CURTAIN as a cast member, not a theater-goer, and for the Human Realm, it works as a BUBBLE OF PROTECTION.

Unfortunately, nobody else can do this particular complex form of

sort of Arabic-style fluid calligraphy that looks so much like Kufic script, like an ancient Kufic Inscription on a ring-stone, but it isn't — it's English, modern English, and it spells out the first letters of each word in the Four Lines:

With a Ram's Horn and this Medallion, I could bring down the walls of Jericho. That's what actually happened back then ... back then ...

It's time for me to do a little online work, before returning to the rewarding creativity while making the LRS Medallions.

APII — All Phenomena is Illusion.

NANR — Neither Attracted Nor Repelled.

NMASM — Not Making Any Sudden Moves.

MHWCMT — My Habits Will Carry Me Through.

And it's a bitch to make one of these.

THINK OF THE MEDALLION AS A GATE PASS THROUGH THE VEIL

The identification as a CAST MEMBER and not an AUDIENCE MEMBER brings you to the MAGIC THEATER in a whole different way which you will appreciate as you run the BARDO BETWEEN-LIVES STATES without a body to weigh you down, which is the same experience as REMOTE VIEWING and ASTRAL PROJECTION, which you can realize using my methods for REMOTE and ASTRAL VIEWING AND PROJECTION, like I said.

If you don't even TRY Remote Viewing, it's a guaranteed fail.

The thing is, I guarantee results. If you take the REMOTE READER'S COURSE you WILL BE ABLE TO REMOTE VIEW and REMOTE READ, period. Guaranteed.

Now, what that enables you to do is to GET OUT OF BODY much more easily, when you're quite comfortable with SEEING outside the body, VIEWING from a non-body viewpoint.

Yes, that's right, I use a DELL desktop computer to do most of my online work, and all of my game level development.

I also play around with Adobe PhotoShop and have come up with a number of perhaps interesting graphics in that realm, which are destined to go into future volumes of "My Life as a Boy" — VOLUME FIVE is currently under preparation, about half-way through the 50-chapter book.

I just wanted to take an extra moment to point out that the U.S. WALKING LIBERTY SILVER HALF DOLLARS that are used in the making of the LRS SILVER QUATRAIN MEDALLION would cost you a pretty penny in a coin show. It's not your currently circulating half-dollar, and I believe those are now hard to find in themselves, but they're not silver.

THESE HALF DOLLARS ARE RARE CERTIFIED SOLID SILVER 1930s and 1940s WALKING LIBERTY HALVES!

Hey, in a pinch, you could disassemble the medallion and perhaps use the silver coin to negotiate yourself through a border crossing or a

Shock Troop surprise ambush. It might be a fun way to add to your survival gear.

The embossing work that I do is affixed to the coin, which is then set into an archival acrylic capsule, which will protect the coin almost forever, barring planetary catastrophes and an exploding sun.

The List Price is $225 for the solid silver Walking Liberty Half Quantum Medallions, but YOU pay only $62.50, which is normally reserved only for attendees at workshops, but I want these to get out there FAST for your protection, so I made them $62.50 and no, they don't get any cheaper than that.

So what was the other thing? Oh, yes, the Media Circus in Washington.

First of all, my Polish friends and relatives are pissed off about how Polish immigrants are treated. At the age of 75, I'm not taking part in it myself, but WE, THE POLISH IMMIGRANTS, ARE MARCHING ON WASHINGTON!

Even now, as we speak, they are only five miles outside of Seattle.

Might as well learn how to handle an attack chopper like the Mi-24 Hind — you never know when it will come in handy.

Just to keep the pressure up, I'll weigh today in on a Trump NIGHTMARE item, which I want you to recall, if and when it's finally revealed. This scary thought came to me as if in a dream:

190

What if Trump is a "SLEEPER" Russian Agent?

Jesus, what if during all those visits to Russia where he was treated as an honored business guest, he got programmed and prepared to take over the government and hand it over to Putin, the way Quisling handed Norway over to Hitler, without a shot being fired.

Gosh, what a thought.

My mind goes back to "Manchurian Candidate" and films like that, where some unsuspecting booby gets programmed by an enemy to act as their agent.

I'm not just making this up out of thin air. You'll find CONTROL agents in *Get Smart*, the television series, not the stupid movie, who were captured by KAOS and programmed, and of course you'll see this same idea reflected in scripts from *MAN FROM UNCLE*, *I SPY*, and *WILD, WILD WEST.*

I worked on an episode that explored that very same idea, and I couldn't help but remember how realistic and plausible that seemed at the time, knowing the methods of brainwashing available to the Russians.

North Koreans were famous for their "conversions" through brainwashing, during the Korean Conflict of 1950-1954.

While I do take full responsibility for the launching of this particular universe, I cannot and will not take personal responsibility for the abuse of same.

I know it sounds too far-fetched and too outrageous for words, for this guy to be a brainwashed agent of Russia, but look at all the "understandings" between Trump and Putin, and THINK A MOMENT — where did all his sudden wealth come from?

He was literally BANKRUPT just a few years back, in TOTAL DEBT to his mentors and backers — then suddenly he has all this money, all this power, and he has business interests in Russia which he won't reveal and won't let go of, like his Income Tax Return and his connection with something definitely weird, perhaps a sex trip that gets satisfied by the Kremlin when Trump visits that special Russian Hotel for visiting Dignitaries.

We can see what a sucker he is for an intelligence community spin job. He has no sense of security issues, nor would he ever care. His plan doesn't include survival, just fame.

Perhaps Trump is Putin's Programmed Puppet — and has been all along??? In that case, he wouldn't need additional instructions, and their communication code would be very exotic and highly impenetrable.

Talkin' 'bout my Meditation.. Talkin' 'bout my Meditation...

Sure, I know the speculation is already circulating around town that Trump and Putin are sleeping together, but this goes deeper than merely bedmates — what if someone like Trump were PLANTED as a "SLEEPER" Russian Agent, made very very rich, and then, by a wild slip of Pure Chance, he got himself elected PRESIDENT???

What if suddenly overnight, he turns the country over to Putin, invites the Russian troops to land, and we wake up to find ourselves citizens of a country run by those two, until one of them stabs the other in the back?

The horrible thing is, I received this data from Higher sources, which makes me think there's more to it than just a gag for morning television and another hook for SNL to snag him with.

I'm not so sure it's idle speculation. There may be some truth behind it.

But the Hell with it. I'm busy with Higher Things.

I want no part of politics and power, but I DO refuse to budge when pushed around in my own home and my own mind. It's too personal when Trump invades my household, my life and the lives of everyone I know in this world.

That stuff, politics and intrigue, is strictly for kids, and mostly for bullies. Once in a while, you get a reformer, but they learn fast that

192

they are not welcome in Washington, and they work the way everyone else does, with lying and cheating and stealing, or they tend to just wither and die by the wayside.

Nighttime is safe in the Ashram, but not so safe in the so-called "Real World".

Some of them become lobbyists, a fate worse than the Buddhist Hell of Billy Graham and Aimee Semple McPherson, if you ask me — I've been there, and believe me, it's the worst Hell I know of.

My preference of Buddhist Hells, if you're tempted to remain for any length of time in the Afterlife, is the level where you'll find Jack Benny, Ernie Kovacs and Sid Caesar, the Hell of Vaudevillians and Television Performers.

You can keep the Hell where Carol Burnett, Jackie Gleason, Lawrence Welk, daytime soaps and the Kardashians hang out.

The speculation about Trump and Putin is the kind of stuff which speculative sci-fi novels and made-for-tv shows are made, and I'll let someone else take that road — I don't bother writing sci-fi novels anymore these days. There's no market for literacy, and trashy novels are not worth writing.

I don't need to wade through the bullshit. I can make a living doing something else.

Anyhow, I have more fish to fry than a mere Earthbound politician. I'm off to work on more QUATRAIN medallions. They have an interesting "uplifting" effect when making them, I noted. This might translate into a workshop or clinic where you get more benefit from making them than you do from carrying them or wearing them.

I can craft with these virtual hands as well as with the organic ones, can't you???

That's the basic idea behind the Bodhisattva Vow — it's a way to earn Merit a LOT faster than if you just sat around watching all the suffering and misery until you yourself get pulled into the quicksand of daily life on Earth.

I have an idea to produce a PENNY-SIZED Quatrain Medallion, using several options for the penny backing — the Lincoln Wheat Penny or "Wheatie" or the Indian-Head Penny.

Another possibility would be the 1943 STEEL Penny, which many folks believe, incorrectly, to be made of silver. It is rather expensive as antique pennies go, but has powerful quantum effects that could be harnessed for goodness.

The PENNY MEDALLION would be around BEST PRICE $35 NET, not a penny less. I can also make a NICKEL-SIZED MEDALLION, with a BUFFALO NICKEL backing, or a WARTIME JEFFERSON NICKEL, which was made of silver when nickel became a wartime priority metal.

The NICKEL varieties will also be bottom-lined at $35, not a penny less.

I'm making QUATRAIN rings as well, SIZE 7 ONLY, in gold over silver, for $225 bottom line price, not a penny less. That ring is a total bitch to make, but I'm willing, if you want one.

Keep in mind that I won't be making too many of these — I pay a heavy price with my hands and fingers for these, but if you want them, it's worth doing them!

Okay, that's it for the moment, enough news update. Back to the jewelry bench.

PEOPLE'S SONGS OF PROTEST
February 17, 2017

Kiss My Butt, Donaldo!

Okay, if you're wondering why I'm taking sides, I'm not. Believe me, if Hillary had gotten in and pulled the stunts this media-whoring pigheaded creep is pulling, I'd be right on her case, just as heavily, you have my word on that.

Donald Trump is walking all over the Constitution. Hey, I'm not permitted to interfere with local politics here on Earth, and I don't.

What could be worse than all-out multi-nation nuclear war?

That's not why I'm writing *People's Protest Songs*, not at all. Donald Trump is just another cog in the wheel that is Washington, and he's now discovering the painful truth, that unless he invites Russian troops in, he has no real power.

So why am I after Donald Trump?

I couldn't care less if we DO live through a "Red Dawn" scenario. I have bigger fish to fry.

In point of fact, you probably haven't a clue why I'm really doing it, and couldn't care less, if you're in the mainstream with most humankind, but I have a very high and celestial reason to do what I'm doing, and I'll be only too happy to explain just why:

Donald Trump is not the center of the universe, but right now, he's making himself pretty much the center of attention, worldwide. People are absolutely terrified, quite rightly, that he might go off the deep end any moment now, and press the nuclear button, or worse.

Okay, I have a list of things that the government has at its disposal that could be a whole lot worse even than 35,000 Megaton Yield Warheads.

The Russians, North Koreans and the Mainland Chinese have even worse than that, which they haven't used yet, only because it could backfire on them — there's no other reason.

The Chinese would have blown us out of the water ages ago, and so would the Russians, the Libyans, the North Koreans, the French and most of Africa and Asia if they had the weapons to do it, but they didn't, only because they're afraid of the fallout on themselves, and they're quite right.

Biological Weapons can't yet be reliably DNA targeted, but as soon as they can be, you can expect an attack on that level — it's that kind of fucking planet.

Humans are treacherous — that's what they warn you, when you first arrive on Earth.

They mean, of course, "Earth Humans", because no other high-technology species in any galaxy anywhere, is as wild and violent and thoroughly predictable, as they are.

First of all, because he is SUCH a comedy character. Nobody who ever was in the White House — and I knew most of them personally — ever gave in to the chaotic interior of their sick minds to the degree that this man has and does, every single day.

He provides more comedy material in one day than some entire 8-year administrations have done in all eight years in the White House.

Nobody has ever gotten more attention from the press, nobody, not ever.

The reason is simple: he holds nuclear war over the heads of every person on Earth. He's holding YOU hostage, and you probably don't know it, don't realize it except only dimly, that he has you by the short hairs and he won't let go.

When you have me by the short hairs, you have my complete attention, and that's what Donald Trump has now, although I paid him

NO attention until two weeks into what is laughingly called his "administration".

I can't imagine how he could make money in business. He's so damn bad at it. However, I understand that he's in and out of tremendous debt all the time, and using my Remote Viewing powers, I can easily pick up a paper trail that leads directly to Russia.

Eventually, he'll trip up, or leave some loose ends, and he'll get caught, and even the Republicans won't protect him once his Russian Connection is revealed. I'm not guessing, I'm speaking from the 37th century history textbooks, and they don't lie.

After a few hundred years, even the deepest governmental secrets are revealed. There's nobody left to care anymore.

Actually, Donald Trump is just a name to me — a character out of a cheap, sleazy 21st century novel about cheap, sleazy people, like the Kardashians.

Did you expect that the White House was going to become a Reality Show?

Apparently, there are plans for Oprah to host it on her private network. She hopes to become his Head of State someday. She's the head of something, all right.

"Trumpism" is a word back home in the 37th century, and I never really understood why it's said in such a clipped tone, until now.

Okay by me. Again, I could care less. I have no axe to grind on this planetary sphere, nothing to gain, nothing to lose. I'm here to see a bomber, meaning that I'm here to collect my bet, plus I'm stuck doing this Term Paper on the 21st century, and THAT is why I'm writing *People's Protest Songs*.

It could be about anyone, but Trump just happened along at the same time I was getting ready to write some protest songs, in order to illustrate for my class on Social Dynamics exactly how they're constructed and how they work in the political arena.

I don't expect my songs to get out there very far.

It's not my intention to change the world. I know all too well that I could if I wanted to, but I have a LOT of restraint, although I must say the "No More Water, Next Time The Fire" camp back home where we programmed this historical simulation are probably right.

They want nuclear war for sound and sufficient reasons. I'll explain.

In a nuclear war, there's always something left, even if it's highly vitrified, meaning that stone or rocks or sand have been turned into glass by some incredibly powerful heat, such as a nuclear airburst, the kind that happened over Mohenjo-Daro.

Things stay pretty much organized for the archaeologists who come along later. Right now, it's humans, but we've had reptilian archaeologists, ant-man archaeologists and of course the greys who have their own peculiar agenda far outside human comprehension, but not beyond yours, if you're a member of Soul Group L3-15(a) — that's how it's properly written.

The object of the songs is Donald Trump. The whole damn point of writing biting satire is that you HAVE TO HAVE A COMEDY TARGET, and boy, does Donald Trump fit the bill.

My history records and textbooks from the 37th century record that he was dragged offstage, kicking and screaming obscenities and filth when he finally popped his lid and went over the top crazy. I could be wrong, don't forget I failed history, which is why I'm here in the first place, to do my Term Paper directly inside the History Lab Sim back home.

Donald Trump is SO insane, SO out of control, SO angry and SO hurt and insulted by humor, such a poor sport and so easily offended, so much so that he calls comedian Rosie O'Donnell a "pig face" — has he looked in a mirror recently?

Trump calls women he doesn't like either a "pig" or a "dog", suggesting some form of projection, wouldn't you say?

Sort of like calling everyone else a liar, a cheat and a thief. After a while of that, doesn't it make you wonder? His focus is entirely on himself, so his most basic assumption is that everyone around him is exactly like himself.

In order to reinforce that, he surrounds himself with people like himself, a sort of political ghetto that insures ignorance and mistakes galore, some of which could end up as full-blown planetary catastrophes.

Gosh, with that stupid a comedy target, even if I didn't have a reason to write a song of protest, I would learn how to do it, and I'd do it, even on my busy schedule.

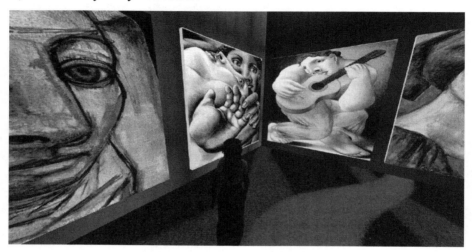

So why no more floods?

You can get on the SuperBeacon horn and ask the Council of Nine or the Federation of Planets why no more floods, but they'll have no more clue than you.

It's actually built into the software, the .exe "execute" program that projects this as-if three-dimensional universe onto the central sphere, where we always put the holographic matrix you so amusingly regard as "infinite and eternal".

I could turn it off and on again and you'd never know it.

That's why I'm writing those songs of protest. You really need to come out of your shell, come out of hiding, long before you're stripped of your human form and consciousness, and learn some of the secret teachings of the ages.

Oh, you're probably still wondering why no more floods, why the Holy Council of Nine have decided to go with the nuclear war. See, a flood wipes out all trace of a civilization, except for the megalithic buildings, the things built of huge million-pound blocks of granite.

Well, shit, nobody builds like that, anymore, and there was nothing I could do to coax builders today to start thinking megalithic, so don't blame the nuclear conflagration on me.

THIS time, it wasn't my fault.

I hear ya. Last time, it WAS my fault. Okay, okay, I take full blame for what happened back then, back then, back then...but how was I to know that all the table-salt on the planet had been secretly weaponized?

Don't ask me the details, I never keep track. The only defense I have is that I didn't know the salt was loaded.

Anyhow, floods are a mess.

Mess. That, in a word, is why no more floods. Too messy, leave too much mud and debris behind. Nuclear war is clean, and leaves no trace after a few years. Even the background radiation quickly returns to "normal", whatever that might mean to you.

To the dinosaurs, it meant a lot. There was a lot more radiation everywhere at that time, because the Carbon-14 stuff hadn't happened for very long, which means the breakdown of the atomic stuff inside the carbon material, like charcoal or fired ceramic, hadn't gotten very far at that early date.

Fossil records have been found. Most of the better fossil records date back to the time of the 45 RPM singles.

The very best single ever issued was "Mbube", now known as "Wimoweh", written and recorded by Solomon Linda with the Evening

Birds, for the South African Gallo Record Company in 1939.

It generated the Second Best Fossil Record ever released, "Wimoweh" by the Tokens, the most covered song in modern musical history, with tens of thousands of variations all over the world, but I digress.

Why no floods, you continue to ask?

You may as well ask, "Why no earthquakes?". I'm all for earthquakes, asteroid impact, eruption of the Yellowstone Volcanic Caldera, which would cause a 99% extinction planet-wide.

At least, that's what it did before.

Then there's the shift in the Earth's axis back over 17 degrees to where it was before. That often creates a little havoc in the crystal, china and mirror shops along the boulevard.

Anyhow, it won't be YOU that'll be riding the waves in the New Ark. Forget the waves. You'll need a bomb shelter capable of sustaining life for a minimum of 1,000 years and you won't be around to see the open sky, not ever again.

Grim prospect?

Not at all. A far grimmer prospect is that you remain unprepared for Eternity until the last minute. That will never do.

Even a good heart and a pure mind is not sufficient to evade the bite of the werewolf when the moon is full.

You need to carry a large, elaborate crucifix. That's the only thing that will save you from the werewolf's bite.

However, in the case of a Jewish werewolf, the crucifix won't help.

Another reason I'm writing the songs about Donald Trump is that you never run out of material.

White Christians against everyone else. Men against Women. Americans versus the World. Muslims against Christians, Christians against Muslims, Rich against Poor.

That's the most obvious division, rich against poor. Donald Trump and his rich friends, including his rich Russian friends, against the poor.

Fortunately for Donald, the poor are so ignorant, they don't realize when they're being swizzled, like buying one of those "Oh, My God!" Tanzanite rings on the satellite sales channel.

PUSH SOME BUTTONS

It's easy for someone with no integrity and no conscience to manipulate the press, manipulate people and manipulate the lawmakers into doing things they'll later regret in retrospect.

Trump holds all the cards, and that's not a cheap Contract Bridge joke, either. He does hold all the cards, has all the money, all the power, all the influence, all the lawyers and law-makers on his side, in his camp, under his domination and control, and sooner or later, YOU are going to feel the ass-end of that stick.

When you do, you have NO WEAPONS with which to defend yourself or fight against the oppression, and you DON'T NEED WEAPONS!!!

You have something much more powerful than any weapon on Earth.

RIDICULE

A Narcissistic Personality Disorder case is totally predictable. Any psychiatrist or psychologist or psych teacher or author would immediately recognize the signs and symptoms of the incurable disorder, "NPD".

So ridicule would get right under his skin. He couldn't take it, not a bit of it, not even from the weakest source. He has to get rid of ALL who hold him up for ridicule, one of whom is me.

It satisfies me to be just another face in the crowd.

It's like what happened to one of Trump's former employees, who had signed a non-disclosure agreement with him in order to escape his despotic control. She had been released from her employment and waited for a taxi to arrive.

Trump shook his head and snarled at her,

"I bet you can't wait to spit on my grave."

The young lady shook her head, and said, "No, Donald, when I got out of your service, I swore I'd never stand in line for anything, ever again."

There IS a long line, of people waiting for him, and there will be a much longer line in the Afterlife, because he'll have a LOT to answer to when he gets there, before the Judge.

Every President must face the challenge of sending military and secret agents to their death, but usually, the President CARES. An NPD can WATCH YOU DIE and not give a shit.

That's material for humor, for comedy, for satire, for parody, and that's what I wanted, was a subject for my WORKSHOP on COMEDY, so I started writing protest folk songs.

I also intend to show how to use ridicule in theater, dance, puppetry and ventriloquism, as well as painting, sculpture and more. There are a thousand peaceful weapons at your disposal, if you just know how to look for them. Folk singing is a powerful weapon, much more so than any instrument of war.

When you walk through a carnival or a circus, you'll find a large area called "The Midway", which gets its name from its obvious position relative to the rest of the fairgrounds.

Okay, so somewhere in that Midway, you'll see some idiot in a clown suit, sitting on a board suspended above a tank of ice cold water, and you won't be able to resist.

You'll buy three balls and try to hit the bulls-eye to see if you can dump him.

If you fail, you can buy three more. Keep up the pressure. He's trying to ignore it, wait it out. Maybe we will all go away???

BITINGLY SATIRICAL PEOPLE'S SONGS OF PROTEST
BITE YOURSELF, DONALD TRUMP!

February 18, 2017

Take a heroic pose and take a stand against tyranny!

Please keep in mind that I haven't written a protest song in well over half a century, and I wouldn't do it now, except that we now have sitting in the White House a real louse, who insists on robbing us of our freedoms, and setting back the Civil Rights clock over a century into the past.

I don't care about Trump personally, or politically. I'm just taking this opportunity to show my guitar and folk song writing classes how to write a protest song — that's my entire agenda.

Is Trump traumatic? Is he intolerable? You bet he is, but I really don't care. I've lived under worse dictators, and they always get theirs, in the end. Usually, the people who put them in power become disgusted and they take matters into their own hands — not a good plan, these days.

De-stabilizing Amerika is what both Putin AND Trump have in mind. Trump is looking for ANY excuse to call in the National Guard and declare a State of Emergency in which he assumes full dictatorial powers.

Think it can't happen here? It already did, in the administration of Franklin Delano Roosevelt, who served a THIRD TERM and would have remained in office for LIFE had he been given the opportunity.

An NPD does not easily let go of power, equity or fame.

There are HUNDREDS of photo comparisons of Trump with Hitler and Mussolini.

Donald Trump is now, and will always be, a laughing stock, and history will place him right there next to Napoleon Bonaparte, Hitler, Mussolini and Jack the Ripper.

Okay, maybe the Ripper is a bit over the top, but you get what I mean. For the rest of human history — not that long now — his name is "Mud".

Well, no, wait a moment — now that I think about it, Jack the Ripper had pretty much the same attitude toward women that Trump seems to have. Love 'em and Leave 'em.

My suspicion is that Trump is in the direct pay of the Russian government — Jesus, he could easily be a replacement, like the second Paul McCartney, or it's the same guy, only he's been brainwashed and programmed by the Russians to open the door and let them in without a shot being fired.

Wouldn't that be something?

An example of my "Jack the Ripper" greeting cards for Christmas, 2017.

I LOVE Red Dawn, it's such a comforting film — comforting to know that sooner or later, I'll collect my dollar bet when the humans push the nuclear button and it all goes up in smoke.

At some point — I failed my 37th century class on 21st century history, but I sort of remember some of the details — Donald Trump goes ballistic onstage, right in front of a LIVE audience, and he has to be either herded offstage or actually carried kicking and screaming offstage.

I forget how Congress handles it, but I do know that he doesn't last long. Dammit, I hope he can hang in long enough for me to launch my People's Protest Songbook!

I need the extra income to pay for my medical bills that aren't covered by my lack of coverage.

Just like yourself and everyone you and I know, I'm on the New Trump Medical Plan — I plan not to get sick. I have no other options, unless we leave town, and that's probably what everyone with an ounce of sense and intelligence will do.

Leave Amerika to the Fundamentalist Christians and the Fundamentalist Muslims to fight over the territory until the Russians and Chinese march in and split it up between them.

Trump is such a sucker, he's easily led into the trap by his buddy Putin, who is the most back-stabbing bastard this side of Stalin, except that Stalin was slightly less ruthless.

Like I said, I only hope Trump remains in power long enough to get a couple hundred copies of my songbook out there in public, for protest singers to sing and kids to learn when they want to know the story of Donald Duck Trump.

Here's a list of the songs in People's Protest Songbook:

Donald Can You Spare a Dime?
Donald's War
The Donald Tweets Tonight
Drinking Gourd
Emperor Donald
Everybody Dislikes President Trump
Far From The Trumpies
Feelin' Uptight
Freedom Special
Frozen Donald
Go Tell Miss Liberty
Hang Down Your Head Poor Donald
Hey Trump
Hit The Road Trump
If I Had an iPhone
If You're White

214

Imagine There's No Trump At All
Ivanka Trump
Let Trump Pay
Listen Donald Trump
Mama Told Me Not To Come
Mercedes Trump
Miss Liberty Don't You Weep
No Balls At All
No One Knows Trump
One Trump Over The Line
Purple Haze
Putin On The Style
Rainbow Trump
Smoke On The Water
Sympathy For The Trump
Talkin' 'Bout My Meditation
There Once Was A Union Maid
The Weight
This Land Is Trump's Land
Trump Meatball
The Trump Pretender
Trump Roast Blues
Trump Time
Trump Train
Wall Around Heaven
Waltzing Gorilla
Washington Farewell

Those are them, and believe me, you'll never sing all of them in one sitting. You'll want to choose the songs that best express your views, probably anywhere from eight songs to maybe a dozen.

If you're doing a whole show, you'll want to organize the songs in relation to the audience participation, feeling, mood and subject matter or specific concept.

I very intentionally used well-known songs as the basis for my parodies, so that you're easily able to track where the song originally went, and where I went with it to create the sense of parody.

It's obvious that Donald Trump is the reincarnation of Benito Mussolini, the dictator of Italy who was dragged through the streets by his own people at the end of his tyranny.

How to write a protest song is more important than memorizing a few protest songs, but if you don't actually SING them and get others singing them, you might as well curl up and die.

Watch videos of Mussolini. He and Trump are one and the same person.

You've been practicing guitar, you either have or soon will have a voice harmonizer so you can belt out your songs of protest. All that remains is for YOU to actually DO IT.

If you're on a Women's March, Minorities March, Immigrants March, Civil Rights March, or your local neighborhood Poverty March or Riot, you'll want to bring along your Protest Songbook and an asbestos jacket.

If you don't even try, it's a guaranteed fail.

I thought I'd include a sample of one of the lyric sheets you get in the songbook, and by the way, I don't expect Donald Trump to actually listen. He's an NPD, and an NPD can't be wrong and will not long endure ridicule, even from the small and helpless victim he has under his utterly ruthless heavy thumb.

KGOD InterDimensional Radio broadcasts from the Sixth Dimension.

He is a monster, and the sooner people realize that he will betray everyone including his supporters, the better, so tune up your guitar and warm up your ROLAND STREET AMP, and get singing!

When you get to the Magic Theater, you're very close to the Higher Dimensions.

LISTEN DONALD TRUMP
(to the tune of "Listen, Mr. Bilbo")

Listen, Donald Trump, listen to me,
I'll give you a lesson in history.
Listen and I'll show you that the foreigners you hate,
Are the very same people made America great.
In 1492, just to see what he could see,
Columbus, an Italian, looked out across the sea.
He said, Isabella, the world is very round,
And the U.S.A. is just a-waiting to be found.
In 1609, on a bright summer's day,
The Half Moon set anchor in old New York Bay.
Henry Hudson, a Dutchman, took a good look around,
And said, "Boys, this is gonna be a helluva town".
(CHORUS)
When the King of England started pushing Yankees around,
We had a little trouble up in Boston town.
An African-American, Crispus Attucks was the man,
Was the first to fall,
when the revolution began.
Colin Kelly was a pilot flying down low,
Levine pushed the button that let the bomb go.
They sunk the Haruna to the bottom of the sea,
It was foreigners like those who kept America free.
(CHORUS)
With a Slavic wife you're taking a helluva chance,
And your good friends, the Duponts, came over from France.
Another thing, I'm sure, will be news to you,
The first Mister Trump was a foreigner, too.
(CHORUS)
Well, you don't like Mexicans, Muslims, or Jews,
If there's anyone you DO like, it sure is news.
You don't like Hindus, Catholics, and Buddhists too,
Is it any wonder, Donald, that we don't like you?
Listen, Donald Trump, listen to me,
I'll give you a lesson in history.
Listen and I'll show you that the foreigners you hate,
Are the very same people made America great.

218

In New Greenwich Village at the Ashram, you can sing onstage.

Well, what are you waiting for? Get hold of that songbook and start playin' and protestin'! If you don't raise your voice against hate and violence, who will?

Is it dangerous?

Yeah, it's mother-fucking dangerous. These guys are not playing with a full deck, and they literally have no conscience, no sense of right and wrong, no feelings for anyone including themselves.

The Trump Supporters are typically, although not always, racist and hate-mongering, anti-Semitic, anti-Muslim, anti-Arab, anti pretty much everything except lily white and their particular brand of Protestant Christian.

They are a mob, and even when they're not acting as a mindless mob, they are hopelessly and incurably consumed with violence, anger, hatred and vengeance.

That's a pretty accurate description of planet Earth, and the easy eruption into violence of the human species is the singular reason that there is NO FEDERATION CONTACT with these creatures, none whatever, and there won't be time to see that happen, not now, with Trump in charge, holding the entire world hostage to his demands and his insanity.

Far from Salvation, the Council of 9 are no longer thinking that humans are in any mood to calm down, and if they're right, I collect my bet, one Federation Dollar.

I don't actually NEED the dollar, but it was such a sucker bet, I'm sure I'll collect, and they gave me 3 million to 1 odds, haw, haw, haw!

The plan of the Council of 9 is to — as usual — wipe out the human race entirely, not leaving a single one to breed again, and start over, perhaps with ants, cockroaches and rats — there's a good chance they'll arrive at the high technology star-voyaging stage without the violence and greed that humans unfortunately display.

In my studio, peacefully writing my blog.

I didn't say the Council of 9 had the greatest imaginations. They have a very limited response to racial warfare. Generally, it's a flood, but as I said before, that's totally out now.

The majority vote in the Council is for Fire, and that'd be either the Yellowstone Caldera eruption, or a nuclear exchange.

I voted for both.

After an Extinction Event like the one coming up, you have to have a surviving species with an opposable thumb, but sloths, squirrels and racoons are not their first choice to inherit the Earth.

I really like the ants as a "win" bet, maybe the cockroaches to "place" and the rats to "show" — that's first, second and third place in your typical horse race.

The election of Donald Trump was no accident. Putin is in control. Hold onto your radiation suits, this is not over yet.

Like I said, I only hope the administration lasts long enough for me to get my book out there. I wouldn't want nuclear war to interfere with my spring marketing plans again.

I voted for both volcano eruption AND nuclear war, so I'd be sure to collect my bet.

Atlantis sank beneath the waves, thus destroying my spring marketing once again.

Last time this happened, we lost Atlantis.
Oh, well, back to the drawing board. Keep watching for the bright

flash — resist the urge to look directly at it. Remember what happened to Lot's wife back when I unleashed a few airbursts over Sodom and Gomorrah.

I've already told Valiant Thor he can just turn his ship around and go back home. The humans are determined to have a nuclear war — I say, let them have it!

POP QUIZ:
Is Donald Trump the
Reincarnation of Hitler, or Mussolini?
February 19, 2017

WARNING TO SCHOOL TEACHERS:
You can be fired on the spot for suggesting a comparison between Trump and Hitler!
Many teachers have been fired or suspended for suggesting a comparison between Hitler and Trump. Kids turn in their teachers

for this offense. You can't even suggest that they LOOK at it, consider it, think about it.

Donald Trump is now a "Forbidden Topic". You risk death and disfiguration by merely mentioning the name in the wrong company, no matter which "side" you happen to be on at the moment.

It is now considered blasphemous to question The Donald, just as it was in 1933 in Hitler's Germany death to question Hitler, and even worse to ridicule him.

Guess Right, and Win a Trip to the Gas Chamber!

That fact alone should nail it for you that there's something going on between the two historical characters, Trump and Hitler. We can't even THINK THE THOUGHT without getting fired from a tenured job?

You can be dismissed from your position if you even postulate the idea in a classroom of conducting some sort of experiment or inquiry.

That's okay, soon you will be taken away if you utter that forbidden word, "Freedom" in public.

Secret Labor Camp in the Delta Region of Amerika.

224

You don't believe me, but you WILL believe it when you have actually been loaded into the van and driven off to your certain death in the Labor Camps which ARE BEING BUILT RIGHT NOW!

Those Labor Camps are for YOU, when you are poor enough and hungry enough to voluntarily walk to the slaughter, taking the only option available to you, that of repairing the roads and bridges rather than starving or freezing to death.

That's the story up ahead, and that's how you'll keep yourself and your family alive for the rest of your futile and miserable life under the thumb of a tyrant.

If you're a peaceful being, you won't fight back. You'll go down with the ship.

That is your fate, unless YOU do something to stop it from happening, and one of those things is to move into another LifeStream, and another is to have a Gateway open to another dimension, and step through it when the trouble starts.

Either way, it's about $3 million dollars away from here, and I don't see any volunteers stepping up with a checkbook.

So we'll watch it come down, and it's on us that it will come down, but never mind that stuff — let's return to our question of whether Trump is Hitler or Mussolini. There's absolutely no question that he's one or the other — the only question is, which one???

Okay, let's assess this: Trump LOOKS like both Hitler AND Mussolini.

Not only is that a whole lot of UGLY, it makes it SO much more complicated, doesn't it? Okay, well, Trump is definitely A Reincarnation of Some Sort of Lord of Ancient Evil, but WHICH Lord of Ancient Evil, exactly???

You can detect the FREQUENCY or VIBRATION of the entity inside Trump. Everyone in existence has his or her or its own identification tag, its very own unique "VIBRATION", which simply means that it has a frequency assignment and a location on the grid.

Those factors never change, no matter what it looks like from in there.

All that needs doing now is to connect the dots, and I've got billions of years of experience in doing just that, so let's begin analyzing the situation:

First of all, we know Trump is SOMEONE evil, probably recently dead, so is Donald Trump the reincarnation of Adolph Hitler, or Benito Mussolini, or BOTH?

Both isn't possible. The universe does not tolerate a paradox, but it's weird, because he resembles BOTH OF THEM perfectly. Although they're repulsively hard to look at, you can match up Trump's face with Hitler's OR Mussolini's, and they match exactly.

I already have my bets down, so I can now reveal what I know for sure:

On CNN's "New Day" show, Trump was asked if he was at all bothered by the comparison between himself and Hitler, and he immediately barked out, "No!".

Just "No," and nothing more.

Um, Donald Trump is not exactly shy. He is a brash, outspoken and horrifically boastful bully, just as he was back in his previous incarnation as Adolph Hitler.

He could have denied it right then and there, and denounced the Nazis, Neo-Nazis, Fascists and racists and anti-Semites, but he didn't.

Only later, when he was cornered, did he backtrack and backpedal, as he always does, and as he always did back when he was Hitler.

I personally guarantee that Trump is NOT anti-Semitic. He can't afford to be.

Trump has consistently avoided the question of whether or not he personally is anti-Semitic, and has a lot to hide here, because many of his friends and members of his family are Jewish, which he can live with, but it's a fact that he wouldn't like to have paraded in front of his many anti-Semitic followers — it could lose him a whole support base that he has now, and is counting on when he pulls whatever he's going to pull on us sooner or later.

Trump with his cabinet? No, it's his former self with his party leaders.

I predict that he will never answer that question directly, just as he will never voluntarily allow his tax returns to become public, nor his dealings in Russia and with Russian Secret Operatives working directly under Putin, nor his current relationship with a famous model named "Andrea", AND his secret dealings with hotels in Las Vegas, which have yet to be revealed only when he leaves office.

I also know his twitter password.

How do I know these things? I have deep knowledge of this from the Akashic Records, The Council of 9 and, of course, my notes from my textbook back in the 37th century, which is what's surrounding this Class Lab Sim you call "21st Century Earth".

Haw, haw, haw, everything you can touch, see, smell or feel is simulation, and when you're in your higher consciousness, you know it. Unfortunately, you're not spending nearly enough time out of your mind.

I'm not depending on luck or guesswork, here. I'm depending on the accuracy of my textbook, "Earth History 101", Chapters 40 and 41, "Amerika, its Rise and Fall" by Armer Hinkup, Ballington and Bridges, London. Illustrated Edition, Second Printing, AD 3656.

So far, it hasn't been very accurate. It says that 21st century Amerika is "Mostly Harmless." I doubt it.

The Opel was test-run on the new Autobahn — of course it's a RACE car, what else?

We're all of us waiting for the other shoe to drop. Gosh, Donald now accuses US of playing the "race card". That's SO Adolph Hitler!

What outrage comes next? And then, when we've given up fighting and we roll over and die, what's the next small step to Hell, one small step at a time until, without realizing it, there we are, in Hell???

You can sit there wondering when the axe will fall. I don't have to guess. I know.

I don't take the greatest of class or assigned reading notes — they tend to be sketchy, because I frankly don't think ANYTHING I'm learning in History class will be of any use in the 37th century.

I can hardly wait to get back home to present my History Report!

I regard Earth History as an Elective, first and foremost, then also a way of getting a slightly better grade than "D+", which is what I'm carrying now, and that leaves me very far from Class Valedictorian, if you know what I mean.

I wouldn't have a clue how to proceed to improve my History Class grade had I not seen "Bill and Ted's Excellent Adventure".

Don't try to explain the views of Socrates or demonstrate Billy the Kid's fast-draw, when you can bring them out onstage and have them do the demo, and that's why I'm collecting folks from this century to travel back to the 37th century with me for my own History Report.

I've already lined up a sound engineer, a lighting technician and rented a 135mm Time Dreamer — the rest will be History!

Um, where was I?

Oh, yeah, I remember. Adolph Hitler, the Founder of the modern state of Israel.

The pig is the one with the apple in its mouth.

As disinterested as I am in local politics, even as they come down the street with tanks to round up all the Jews, including me and my family and friends, I do have a profound interest in reincarnation, and I hope you do, too.

As a matter of fact, I wouldn't even bother Mr. Trump if I didn't require some proofs for my demonstration on The Mechanics of Reincarnation.

So how can I use Trump's Rise to Power to illustrate the Mechanics of Reincarnation? Yes, mechanics, not reality. I shouldn't have to "prove" reincarnation these days, now that we have Facebook.

Never mind about PROVING reincarnation. Take reincarnation as written. Now what? Now we look at the MECHANICS of reincarnation, that's what!

As a matter of fact, all other issues are merely minor factoids in the gathering of data for the technical mechanics of reincarnation, which after all, is the time-crunching factor that the Nazi archaeologists and field research teams were looking to find.

Of course, it was right under their noses all the time!

Adolph Hitler appreciated the young girls, and so does Donald Trump.

Let's get to work here, sorting out our facts and suppositions:

Trump rose to power by cultivating the fear and distrust of his supporters. That sounds like Hitler, right? No, Mussolini actually did it first. Hitler copied Mussolini, a LOT. He literally worshiped Mussolini right up until the day they met, and Hitler successfully overwhelmed Mussolini.

Master and slave, dominant and submissive, that's the way it always goes with humans, chimps and dogs.

Fear and distrust have covered the land. I know many immigrants who fear walking the streets of Trump's Nazi Amerika these days, and they are so right. They really feel fear about going out of the house. Wouldn't you, if your skin were dark or your accent too heavy?

Trump Amerika is now a fortress, like Fortress Europe, or "Festung Europa", under Hitler. Hitler never felt safe unless he was surrounded by something, like a big high fat solid stone wall or an underground bunker or a house in the mountains or a million adoring fans or 15 million blindly obedient soldiers.

Adolph Hitler does Donald Trump at an "Election Rally" in Munich, 1936.

On that level, so far, we're seeing Hitler as the primary candidate for reincarnation here — you agree? If you know your history, you will. Let's proceed further along these lines, shall we???

Please note that "Festung" in German means "Fortress", but it also means "Walled City", from back in the City-States days of antiquity, so think about it, could this be the creep responsible for the Berlin Wall, the Great Wall of China and the Iron Curtain?

Again, there's that NEED FOR PROTECTION, a WALL AROUND HIMSELF to protect him from harm, although there's no better way to put yourself in harm's way than to assume power and constantly direct attention to yourself.

Trump is wildly, amazingly, stunningly, egoistic, and he was no less of a zany egomaniac as Adolph Hitler. His enthusiasm for himself is overwhelming. He is truly a Legend in his own Mind.

Donald Trump's total acceptance of the Hitler identity comparison on CNN's Day Show occurred DURING THE CAMPAIGN, not when he was safely sitting in the Oval Office.

He UNTHINKINGLY snapped out, "NO!" when he was still running for President, and he knew that the people would never elect Trump, but they WOULD and DID elect Hitler.

Trump thinks HE can yell? Ten bucks says he can't out-yell the Hell-Lords of the Third Bardo.

This was back when he was a candidate, trying to get votes — so it's clear that he actually LIKED the comparison and appreciated the interest in his previous incarnation, and cultivated the votes from the Nazis, but was clearly later advised to tone it down a bit, so now he says he never said it.

Exactly like Hitler.

One more vote for Hitler as the offending soul inside Donald Trump's queerly built biological body, and there's more ... read on.

Hitler was Master of The Great Lie. You just keep repeating the same trash over and over and over again until you wear down the resistance and whatever you say, regardless of how absurd it may be or sound, becomes the TRUTH.

You are living in Trump Amerika, and the Storm Troopers will never let you forget it.

To cap it all off, Trump has REPEATEDLY asked his supporters to raise their right hands and arms in what can only be described as the Nazi salute, in homage to what is surely the most insane bigot who ever lived.

Unfortunately, he somehow lost his magic speaking power. As Hitler, Trump was a lot more intelligent and charismatic.

This is the only family group shot I have of our folks back in Germany.

There was a clarity that Hitler had that Trump just doesn't, but his followers don't care, they're happy to see their old leader back, to lead them to triumph, just as he did so many years ago, right down the road to hell.

It always ends the same, and the followers don't learn any more than the leaders, because they're PROGRAMMED to behave that way, to think as their leaders tell them to think, to do as they are told.

In short, to OBEY.

Like Hitler, Trump has clearly indicated that he intends to popularize the use of electric shock therapy on anyone who opposes him, such as "undesirables" and "degenerates".

If you're a Jewish Artist, that puts you in Double Jeopardy.

There are MILLIONS of mindless freaked-out wildly enthusiastic followers who will do anything to make their troubles go away, and they need a scapegoat, and that'd be me and you, until they end up on the Scapegoat List.

Everyone does, sooner or later, including the Masters and Tyrants. They always get it in the end. If not by mob action, by eventual death, which is, of course, MY so-called "Ace in the Hole".

I can arrange a rebirth for him as a Muslim Refugee, a Jewish American Princess who ends up being buried facing Macy's, or throw him into the body of a Mexican Day Laborer, in his next lifetime, but I don't do that.

I don't do anything except observe. I watch. I do nothing. I just watch.

Then when the dust clears, I rise up and go Home.

That's when I collect my dollar bet, and like I said before, I'm betting on nuclear war, and I've got a Federation Dollar says I'm right.

If you haven't taken action to quit the premises and leave town pronto, this presupposes that you assume that YOU and YOUR FAMILY aren't on his list.

What are you, nuts???

Rest assured that, no matter how far down the list your name might be, it's on there. Want more evidence that Trump is Hitler? Okay, how about this:

Hitler used the Jews as a scapegoat. Trump is doing exactly the same thing with Muslims AND Jews, except the rich Jews he happens to know, including his son-in-law, an Orthodox Jew.

When asked about his obvious anti-Semitism as displayed openly on TV News and interviews as well as his support of anti-Semite supporters, he says, "It's very complicated."

"Veiled Lady of the East", pastel on handmade paper, by E.J. Gold, 1991.

You're goddamn right, it's complicated. He's grooming his kids for a dynasty that will last a thousand years, and his son-in-law Jared Kushner, is an Orthodox Jew, whom Donald is grooming for The Great Succession.

Do whatever you want here, but in the Afterlife, you answer directly to the Judge.

Jesus Christ, you should excuse the expression, that means we'll someday have an Orthodox Jew in the White House.

So how can Trump admire Hitler, if he's not anti-Semitic? It's so simple, you're ignoring the obvious.

Like Trump's son, Hitler was Jewish.

There's DNA evidence now, plenty of it, to support that, but that's not what I mean. What I mean is, Hitler was an OBSERVANT Jew, a GOOD Jew, the FOUNDER OF THE JEWISH STATE OF ISRAEL.

Without the Holocaust, would any European Jew demand a Homeland and actually pick up everything and risk death to go there?

Donald Trump supports Israel. He HAS to! They are his people!

Boy, he is right, it is SO complicated.

Trump gives himself plenty of permission to express rage, and it attracts followers who do the same. Imagine what it must feel like to live inside that thing.

This guy is a bundle of contradiction, but only if you catch him at it. Here's another point that scores a hit in the "This Guy Is Definitely Hitler" category:

Hitler was a master orator, able to swing and sway a crowd almost hypnotically. Okay, that's a major fail, there, because Trump is anything BUT a Master Orator. He could have been swizzled down the drain by Jack Kennedy any day of the week.

He was lucky that Hillary was his only opposition. She doesn't exactly have the most magnetic charismatic personality in the world, does she? The cold, calculating level-headed business approach works well in the courtroom, but it doesn't sway the mob.

What ALWAYS sways the mob is to encourage the hate that's already in them. Hate is a by-product of fear, and nobody likes to admit that they're afraid, so the fear is expressed as anger, rage, fury.

That's always easy to engender in a mob. Just ask the Romans how tough it is to attract a mob to a public slaughter?

Trump delights in his own ranting, raving, hate-mongering trash, and wild, exaggerated facial expressions and out-of-control arm movements and body language, but, like Hitler, doesn't do well in the presence of a heckler, and tends to have his Court Jesters drawn and quartered and his generals taken out and shot.

If you happen to be one of his generals or security advisers, I wouldn't make any long-term plans involving travel abroad, if I were you.

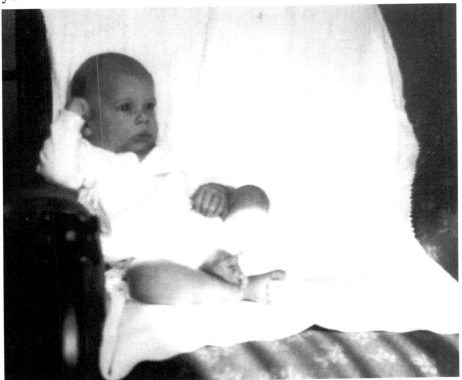

That's me at the age of a few months, listening to Bartok on the radio.

See, if you know your history, and you know that history ALWAYS repeats itself, because the game program is VERY limited, so the same scenes tend to get used over and over again.

You see the same 3-D tree models that you've seen in so many time-frames before, and the action goes pretty much the same. Give it a break, DNA has only so much capacity for variations, okay?

It's not my fault that DNA is so limited.

You make one mistake, you never hear the end of it. But never mind about my defense of my Master's Thesis in Sculpture, which resulted in this miserable excuse for a universe.

Sigh. It wasn't my fault.

DNA has a lot of POTENTIAL, but it needs some massaging, some research, some numbers-crunching, and that's another reason I'm here, to get the numbers crunched, and there's never a better place to do that than at school, where you get computer time and equipment free.

Kids loved Hitler. He gave them candy and rides.

Well, almost free — I pay $7.50 a semester, which includes the parking fee. I never pay more than $7.50 a semester at City College, do you?

So if you were one of Hitler's generals, you at some point disappeared in one of his purges, just like Stalin did, and so many other despots have done. So far, Trump hasn't managed a purge, but rest assured that, when he can, he will.

Purges are fun.

Oh, not for the purged, but dictators tend to LOVE purges, where you get rid of ANY opposition, like they did in the Grand Inquisition which wasn't so grand, believe me, if you were on the receiving end of a hot branding iron or a cupful of molten lead being poured into your ears.

The mob loves blood. Ask the Mayans, the Romans, the Christians ...

What? You don't count Christians as among the blood sacrifice crowd? Clearly you didn't know that IT IS A SIN to deny that the Host and Wine are the ACTUAL BODY AND BLOOD OF CHRIST, created so in the Act of Transubstantiation as enacted by the local

240

Catholic Priest, but it is a sin, a MORTAL sin, for which you could have been excommunicated which, in those days, meant certain death of exposure and starvation, because nobody could offer you refuge or food.

Gosh, just like Jesus would have done, eh?

Adolph always enjoyed reading the Washington Post, just like Trump.

From what I see of Christians acting in Christ's name, he was a bloody and savage son of a bitch, wasn't he?

Kicked out the sick, buried the dead and said, "Fuck the lepers", that's the Jesus they create today. If Jesus returned today, he'd be locked up as a vagrant, and it was that way in Hitler's Germany, too.

If you were a member of Hitler's gang, eventually you got your balls caught in the crunch of a Holy Party Purge, and if you didn't buy it that way, you committed suicide along with your boss when you lost the war.

When you DIDN'T happen to lose a war, you celebrated and lived happily ever after, in the glory that was Greece, or Rome, or Amerika or wherever you happened to be.

And then you died, and that's where I come in. So, where were we? Oh, yeah, Hitler. Haw, haw, haw!!! Hitler! As if that had really been his name!!! You couldn't possibly know this, but Adolph Hitler's real name was Morris Greenblatt, but of course he couldn't take power in Germany under a name like that, so he got a nose-job and changed his name to Hitler.

The comic section and the astrology prediction were his favorite reading.

As Adolph Hitler, he achieved the Great Jewish Dream of a Jewish Homeland in Israel, the historic home of the Jews, and without the holocaust, there would be no Israel today.

That's why, in the far-distant future of the 37th century, Adolph Hitler is called "The Father of the Jewish State of Israel", and Donald Trump is called "The Last President".

Of course, he's the last President, as soon as he declares himself Emperor.

By the way, I've already designed a GOLDEN crown for Trump. I'm willing to make the item for a modest fee plus the State of New Jersey.

I'm not a greedy person, it's just New Jersey — I'm not asking for much.

But back to work assembling our data:

Okay, we know that, by his own admission, Hitler was the greatest living master of strategy, and was the greatest military leader this side of Hell.

Unfortunately, this attribute did not fare well during the transition from one lifetime to the other, so Trump is forced to function with a horribly weak intellect and a reduced ability to do the Peppermint Twist.

All I'm asking for is New Jersey, you can keep the rest of the country.

Fortunately for Trump, as he predicted verbally on video, the Republicans are so stupid that you can tell them anything and they'll believe you. "I'm the only person in the world who can make this country great again!" he promised the crowd, and they voted him in.

Haw, haw, haw — like I said before, it ain't my planet.

I have lots more evidence to support my "Trump is Hitler with a Toupee and Moustache, which I'll now present for your kind consideration:

Hitler committed suicide on April 30, 1945, fulfilling the prophecy of his astrologer, Eric Jan Hanussen, that he would die on a Jewish holiday. When Hitler demanded to know which holiday, Hanussen replied, "Believe me, Mr. Hitler, ANY day you die would be a Jewish holiday!".

Hitler's Spirit spent almost exactly 14 months paying for that little "accident", then reincarnated on June 14, 1946, as Donald Trump.

Hitler used to be IN LOVE WITH his Nazi flag, but now he's cured. Thanks to modern psychiatry, now he HATES his Nazi flag.

14 Months??? How can I assert this with absolute certainty?

He stayed at the Afterlife Hilton, and I have the room records. He left his baggage behind and skipped out on a huge room service bill — $500,000,000 Bardo Bucks, just for the hookers.

His bar bill was staggering, but then, so was he. I lost maybe fifty or sixty billion Bardo Bucks on the deadbeat, but what the Hell, who cares? Plenty more Bardo Bucks where they come from!

Then again, maybe it IS Benito Mussolini in there?

Are the dates right for Mussolini? Yeah, they are. Mussolini was killed and his pummeled body was dragged through the streets with his mistress by a furious mob, on April 28, 1945, only two days before Hitler died an ignominious death with his new bride — they went to Hell for their honeymoon.

Mussolini was Hitler's hero until the day they met, but Hitler often quoted Mussolini:

"It is better to live one day as a lion than 100 years as a sheep."

Interestingly, that is the EXACT CONTENT of a Trump Tweet a few weeks back.

"Make Amerika great again" screamed Trump. We heard something similar from Mussolini, who screamed in exactly the same annoying, whining tone, "Make Italy great again." You'll note the degree of success both men had at that sort of thing.

It never works out, but in the meanwhile, millions lie dying or dead.

Millions lie dead in the aftermath of an ancient nuclear war, photo by E.J. Gold, circa 34,000 BC, city of Arnakki. I have more photos of this disaster.

So what do we have so far? Let's see:

We have Trump's behavior, agenda and style, plus the LOOK of Mussolini and the body postures, gestures, facial expressions and mannerisms of Adolph Hitler.

Given those facts, I'd vote for Uncle Claude's Postulate:

Donald Trump is the reincarnation of Adolph Hitler inside a Benito Mussolini size and shape body. He LOOKS like Mussolini, but FEELS and ACTS like Hitler.

Okay, how can we prove this thesis?

Simple. We look at Donald Trump's cabinet and staff. The people he put in place will be the reincarnates of his former staff as Adolph

Hitler, so first we look at the death dates of Hitler's staff members, if known.

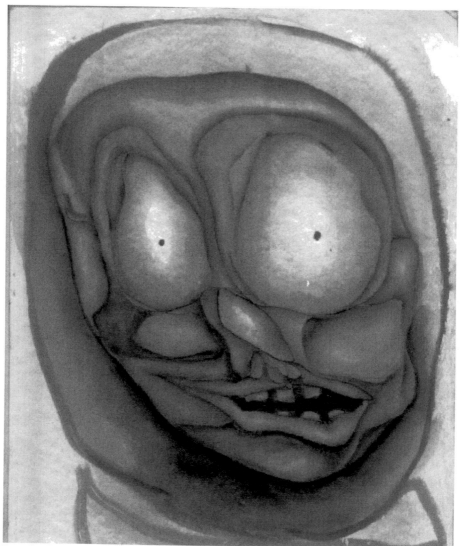

Lord of You-Know-What awaits everyone on the Other Side of the Veil — pen and ink wash by E.J. Gold.

Then compare the faces of the dead Hitlerians to the faces of the Live Hitlerians under Trump's control, and you'll see a pattern emerging.

246

If most of them match up, you've got your answer — it's Hitler and his Gang, reincarnated to do more damage.

If they DON'T match up, it's gotta be Mussolini in a Mussolini body, but I don't think it'll turn out that way.

The entity living inside Trump's body is definitely Hitler, and he's exulting in his latest triumph. Problem is, he always does the same thing, and always in the same way, and the result is always the same, disaster for everyone including himself.

Doesn't he ever learn?

Why, no, Virginia, he doesn't. Haven't you been paying attention the past billion years? Did you READ the ABD? What's wrong with your perception? He doesn't "learn", because that IS his natural nature, don't ya get it? He's SET that way, that that's all he does and that's how he does it, like a robot on a far planet, acting autonomously from previous instructions. Dragged through the streets is such a common fate for despots. I could name a few who ended up that way, but the most famous and best-deserved would probably be the Roman Emperor Elagabalus.

The story is too long and complicated to recount here. Look him up and read his story, and hold onto your hat, or your hats, if you're multi-headed, because this guy was weirder than Caligula and crazier than Nero or Napoleon, if such a thing is possible.

Of course, there's no one crazier than Caligula, Nero or Napoleon, but Donald Trump has high hopes. Today, if you want to signify "crazy", you stick your hand into your shirt and assume the Napoleonic Stare.

If you're onstage in a play or a blackout comedy sketch, you'll wear a Napoleon hat, which everyone will immediately recognize.

The moment you stick your hand inside your vest, shirt or jacket and assume the pose, everyone in the room will know that you mean "crazy". This works well when playing "Charades", but doesn't fly on network TV.

I think you'll agree that I've presented good evidence to support my thesis that Donald Trump is the reincarnation of Adolph Hitler, don't you???

"TRUMPANITE" MAKES TRUMP WEAK AND HELPLESS!!!
February 20, 2017

GREETINGS FROM SOUL GROUP L3-15-2

You can use the larger images in this blog as screen-savers.

STAY FREE WITH TFZ!
You can place a "TRUMP-FREE ZONE" Medallion at each door and window, and ward off the bad smell, enjoying a new-found freedom from the stench of Trump. Gosh, and he's the one calling people names like pig-face. Has he ever looked in a mirror?

But NEW FREEDOM is not enough. You need to also STAY

FREE!

Unfortunately, if you're not both white AND Christian, your days are numbered and your life of personal freedom is over forever, even after this administration has gone down the drain, like they do.

Once the Constitution is overturned, we have crossed the Rubicon and there is no going back. If you allow that to happen, you deserve what you get.

In this world of distrust and superstition, racial hatred and religious radicals, there is nowhere to run to, no place to hide, no refuge from the chaotic storm of rage and zombie apocalypse that is coming to this planet.

So what? Big Deal.

That's what John Whorfin said, and he was right. So what? Big Deal. Hey, if you're an off-worlder with a way to blast off this loser planet, you've got no worries, mate. But if you don't have an escape plan, don't happen to have a working scout craft since the last one crashed out in the desert, stranding you on this mudball, and don't have a Portal Option or anywhere off-world to go, you'll have to endure the misery of the next few years, and then things get REALLY bad.

You need a way off-world.

Unfortunately, my way off-world is about $3 million dollars from here, and I'm not entirely sure there's actually time to clear and activate the Portal.

If you have a nearby Portal that you can use and know how to use, you don't need to remain here unless this tiny living-tissue harvest planet is still important to you. If you're a Grey Alien, it's very goddam important, but there's nothing I can do to avoid the carnage of the next 600 years and, hey, I wouldn't wait until there's a line around the block at the Portal. Sometimes you can just squeak by in the nick of time, like at Sodom and Gomorrah, for instance.

GREETINGS FROM SOUL GROUP L3-15-a

There was just enough time to grab the kids and run.

If you're a GREY ALIEN, you'll regret losing your easy income from the human and cattle enzymes, but hey, you guys are very resourceful — you'll find another planet to farm, or you'll learn to work with the next species that happens to arise out of the upcoming Extinction Event, for your High School Lab experiments.

I don't think I gave anything away, there.

GREETINGS FROM SOUL GROUP L3-15-a

Anyhow, escape from Planet Trump is easy, if you have a Portal. Merely use the Portal, GateWay or StarGate to escape Planet Trump, before it's too late! If you can't use a Portal or don't know how, better find out how, and soon.

If there is no Portal nearby, you might want to go to The Great Portal when things get desperate, which will not be in the far-distant future, if Trump's war-plans go according to his scheme.

HOW CAN WE USE THE GREAT PORTAL?

Problem is, The Great Portal is buried and needs excavating, and I don't really believe that there's enough time. Only The Great Portal will allow a large number to escape all at once, to the same safe place.

Excavation will take a while, and I estimate about $3 MILLION just to clear the entrance of tons of rubble, plus there must be enough to outfit the refugee group with enough supplies to last them a while, once they get to the REFUGE on the other side of the Portal.

Keep in mind, it's not a StarGate. You're not going to fly around in a UFO, at least not on Earth, you won't. Those things are strictly in the hands of the Federation and the Council, and I wouldn't build one now anyway — they're expensive to produce, and hard to obtain materials.

Can I build a UFO?

Yeah. So what? I can also repair a 3-speed British Bobby's Bike, and I can fly a drone. Yawn.

A UFO is great for a research project if you want to do some local traveling around a singular galaxy, but for real long-distance travel, you want to take a cruise ship, and that'd be hard to do at this time of year.

This is the time when things are really popping. Nobody seems to know what to do with Trump. His Republican friends in Congress want to save their jobs and get themselves re-elected, so in the name of Expediency, they go along with him.

This has all happened before, so many times before. It's always deadly and dangerous and it makes life not worth living on a day-to-day basis. You want to give up and curl up and die, but that's exactly what the bastards want you to do. You don't want to be on Planet Earth when all this stuff comes down for one very important reason:

Nobody goes to Earth in February.

You'll be better off seeking some sort of higher plane solution than to try to find a "safe" place somewhere on Earth.

There's no reason to suppose that, once the nukes have been launched and the poison gas released and the DNA-targeted viruses and the raging bacterial wave that springs up from the activity and the volcanoes start spewing out carbon dioxide and sulphurous fumes, there might be some sort of "safe" place on Earth.

No, you'll have to go down the hall to find SANCTUARY.

"It is as I have foreseen, Young Luke. Use the Dark Side of the Force. Give in to the hate, the rage. Use the Force to divide and destroy," says the Emperor in Star Wars, but Luke doesn't give in, doesn't use the Dark Side, even to save his own life.

Good plan.

Dark Side stuff leads to lousy karma, and if you use magic, you

LOSE YOUR BET back home, and rest assured, The Watchers are watching, to make sure nobody cheats when the shit comes down.

GEMSTONES are amazing things. I'm not going to extol their virtues or roll out a long list of what they've been known to do.

Everyone and every thing in this or any other universe has a NAME, a shamanic name, which translates to a number, and that number is very specific to THAT PARTICULAR INDIVIDUAL, whether it's being a person, place or a thing, and we've all been all three, so get used to it.

Send a Mariachi band to play under Donald's window every day.

EVERYONE HAS A NUMBER

Everyone has a name and a number, and that is so very specific that it can be matched by the frequency of a gemstone that has been drenched with radiations of a special kind.

My entire argument in favor of GEMSTONE SHAMANIC QUANTUM MAGIC is that they carry and generate both heat and electricity, depending on how you tickle them.

For instance, quartz crystals are programmable and can make digital storage units that are likely to last billions and billions of years in outer space, and millions of years in an oxygen atmosphere with weather and temperature ranges.

Quartz melts, and when it's crushed into small fragments, combines well to create granite, a very hard and very electrically charged rock that can be carved and drilled and formed into large blocks or tall obelisks like the ones you see amongst ancient Egyptian ruins.

SO WHAT IS "TRUMPANITE"?

Do you remember "Kryptonite" in the Superman movies and television shows and comic books and action figures? Trumpanite is similar, but it's resonant to Trump, not Superman.

You put Kryptonite in front of Superman, and he goes weak in the knees and sinks to the floor, helplessly struggling against gravity and a sense of general fatigue.

Kryptonite is what most household cleaning supplies contain, and most men are allergic to the stuff.

TRUMPANITE IS LIKE KRYPTONITE

I'm sure I don't have to remind you of Superman's background. Even if you didn't read the comic books back in 1938, when the first Superman stories were printed, you know about the strange world of Superman's origin, the distant planet Krypton.

Well, that story of Superman's origin, was written by my Dad, Horace, a fact that was well-known back when he was the highest-paid writer in the comic book industry.

It was a fully scientifically-based, totally supportable story in the matter of good physics, good chemistry and good math.

Good rocket science, I can't say as much for. That part of the science was weak, but my Dad never wrote space opera, or so he claimed. I actually found about a dozen space opera stories of his that haven't seen the light of day for over 75 years, and might consider publishing them.

Trumpanite is a gemstone that is naturally tuned to the right frequency, then activated.

Well, actually, it's been continually bombarded with radio waves, light waves and sound waves to respond to Donald Trump's personal vibration with a resounding "THUMP!" of rejection.

Rejecting the SPECIFIC and PRECISE wave-pattern that IS Donald Trump can provide great relief to a household that is plagued with worry over what this crazy man will do next, and to whom.

You want freedom from that madman?

You got it.

Get some Trumpanite. Put the crystal dome with the lump of Trumpanite at or near the center of your home and IMMEDIATELY FEEL THE TRUMP VIBES GO AWAY, leaving your home smelling fresh and clean, and your sacred space within your home is allowed to exist in peace and harmony and freedom from fear.

Now, look — if Trump's Storm Troopers come down the street block by block in a Big Roundup and bust through your front door, the warranty is off.

At a moment like that, your lump of Trumpanite will only be good as a fist-axe, but right up to that FINAL ROUNDUP, where we ALL get rounded up and gassed to death, it'll work just fine as a gemstone with specific frequency properties TO KEEP THE FART STINK OF TRUMP and TRUMPISM OUT OF YOUR HOME!

When the Storm Troopers finally DO bust down your door and take you away to the death camps, you still have one last thing you can throw against their impervious armor, haw, haw, haw.

I've tried throwing one of these at the armor they wear, and there's one less item to worry about as they destroy your home and family before your very eyes, which is "will it hurt anyone?" The answer is a resounding "No".

They bounce harmlessly off the Storm Troopers' Body-Armor.

So don't worry, the only one who's going to get hurt will be you. Never mind that — how much is it, and where can you get one, before it's too late?

The Trumpanite Dome comes housed in a hand-blown crystal dome on a hand-carved and routed solid oaken carved base. Your special price is only $89.95 — no further discount, that's right there at the edge.

So, in the end, when all else fails, throw the fucking Trumpanite at somebody's head. At least go down fighting. Don't just give the Trump Salute and say in a droning robot voice, "BY YOUR COMMAND", then lie down to die.

At least have the guts to tell your tormentors to fuck off while you still can. I've finished the People's Protest Songbook. It's available for download at $9.95 and contains around 45 new songs written just in time for These Unpleasant Times.

From about now until the 37th century, nobody on Earth will know that any of this ever happened, and then there's a big resurgence in interest, which is how come I'm here to observe this and make notes for class.

Gosh, it's happening the same as it did back in Atlantis, and that wasn't the first civilization to go down this way, nor the last. I want at least SOME of the after-marketing concession rights on the next three world wars.

I LOVE the uniforms in World War IV.

OVAL OFFICE PROJECT
February 21, 2017

At the airfield on the way to the White House for lunch and meditation.

OVAL OFFICE PROJECT

The Oval Office Project is a non-political, non-sectarian effort to raise the consciousness of the entire staff of the White House, the President's consciousness and the consciousness of any visitors who happen to wander through on the White House Tour, which won't be so easy to get on these days, I suspect.

By now, even the most hardened Right-Wing Republican who finds himself to the far right of John Birchers has seen the evidence — President Trump is downright crazy, totally out of control, completely off his rocker, and he has his finger on the nuclear trigger.

Technically speaking, he's a Classic NPD — Narcissistic Personality Disorder — with a colossal ego inflation and a blustering low-life crudity that makes even the sturdiest supporter cringe now and again. He's a spoiled brat with his finger on the nuclear trigger.

I said this effort is Non-political, and it is. It has nothing to do with the beliefs, attitudes and party convictions of the current inhabitants of the White House. The reason that this becomes possible is that Trump's behavior is arrogant, spiteful, childish and on the verge of an uncontrollable tantrum. Bear with me, if you're a Trump fan, I'm merely establishing the groundwork against which one can measure success. I'll explain further.

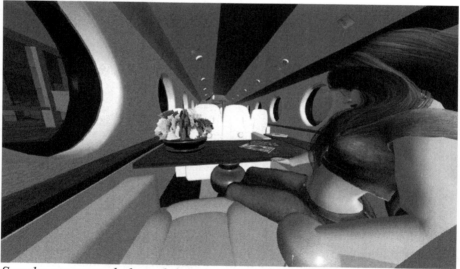

Snacks are served aboard the Black Falcon, and every seat has its own video screen.

An NPD cannot tolerate contradiction of any kind, and is even less tolerant of criticism in any form whatsoever. You cannot reason with him face to face, because his face keeps changing with the wind, and in the end, the conversation always comes back around to the beginning of the loop.

"Ready Tape Loops" is what my friend John Lilly called them. Every human being has them ready to play whenever they happen to get triggered.

Generally, that's the whole science of human thought in a nutshell.

An inner conversation runs continually, with a dim vision of the surroundings unless there is some anomaly which smells like a threat of some kind. Ego-threat counts here, so if you're planning on reasoning with an NPD, it's a total waste of time — he sees you coming a mile away, and knows exactly how to dodge you while back-pedaling the whole distance to the starting point, and WHAM! There you are again.

That, right there, is the base line from which any magical success must be measured. When the insanity and megalomania is so obvious and so blatant and so in-your-face that even the conservative media is forced to report it, it provides a definite viewable thing within which the effect can definitely be observed, and those effects will have been brought about by your efforts in the Virtual White House to bring Enlightenment to the Washington White House.

You can fly the Black Falcon using the controls you see here in the cockpit.

It's not too likely that I'll be invited to the Actual Washington White House to decorate the place with dozens of SHAMANIC MAGICAL DEVICES and THANGKAS, but I can decorate MY version of the

White House that will exist in the "real" White House in the Astral Plane, and what's more, I can load it up with dozens of invocational and magical devices to improve the level of conciousness and at the same time the levels of awareness, enlightenment, beneficence and conscience of all those in the area of the actual White House.

If they are already genuinely acting in the public interests, then they shouldn't mind a little boost in the area of inner tranquility, calm and Enlightenment. If we can sneak a little Cosmic Consciousness into the mix, I wouldn't be disappointed.

I can quantumly — or "magically", if you prefer the Medieval terminology — hook up my Second Life Cyberspace White House located in our online Virtual Ashram with the ACTUAL White House in Washington, D.C. — nothing could be simpler for me for a variety of reasons, one of which is that I made the game in the First Place.

The Other Reason that this is simple for me is because I have in my possession dozens of actual artifacts from the Clinton White House, given to me by Kaki Hockersmith, the official White House Decorator during the Clinton Administration.

At Ronald Reagan InterDimensional Airport, waiting for my limo service to arrive.

I've been involved with every Washington administration since I entered the planetary sphere back in what you call "1941". To me, it's just a spawning point.

In that particular case, the Clintons invited me to participate in the decorating party, and I did. The Clintons have dozens of my pieces in their collection. You'll also find my art in the collections of several dozen more Heads of State as well as the National Museum.

Not by way of making a big deal of it, just explaining how I came to have a number of items from the White House in my household possessions, as it were. Actually, if you count the Scalamandre samples, it numbers well into the hundreds.

So that made a "Quantum-Entanglement" connection a total no-brainer. I've placed photos of my White House Relics within the sphere of the virtual White House, and models of the 3-D items are placed cunningly about.

In the Second Life Marketplace, I located a stunningly well-made and accurate White House model, and installed it in the online virtual Ashram, along with a smaller model of just the Oval Office by itself.

Lucky I got that smaller model, because it was accurately furnished with White House furnishings, albeit from the Obama Administration, but that gives me an opportunity for humor.

Waiting for baggage at the Reagan InterDimensional Airport can be expedited.

It would drive Trump quite over the edge — a short, short drive, believe me — to discover that the MAGICAL MODEL of the White House contains only Obama furnishings, although that could easily change by my whim and whimsy.

Trump is trying to do what all tyrants do — control the media, cast out and destroy and erase all traces of all previous rulers, and he'll fail at that just as he will in the end at everything he's ever tried to do.

That's because the only thing he's ever wanted is attention.

Now that he's in the spotlight and has the world by the short-hairs with his 50,000 nuclear warheads, he has it — and he can't stop provoking it on a daily, even hourly, basis. This makes him very conspicuous, and any change in his behavior would be instantly visible, I would think, wouldn't you?

Okay, so he's very visible, and any change will be correspondingly immediately visible.

At the fence WALL around the Virtual White House on a Big Sky Day.

We agree?

Good. That's the only criterion we actually care about here. This is an exercise in ASTRAL PROJECTION OF ENLIGHTENMENT WAVE VIBRATIONS. So, let's proceed.

Now we load up our MAGICAL MODEL OF THE WHITE HOUSE with all sorts of ACTIVE and PASSIVE magical devices, such as a Native American Dance Circle in the room just above the Oval Office.

I've just spent the past five days and nights doing just that, and it's fully loaded for bear or whatever else that grizzly guy has in mind. In short, we're blasting out psychic power prayer on all levels and they're projecting RIGHT INSIDE THE WHITE HOUSE as we enact them here.

Even if they don't actually hear the prayers or see the effects, they ARE THERE, profoundly affecting the people and dogs inside the ACTUAL WHITE HOUSE. They are reacting to our vibrations whether they know it or not, or are aware of any influence over them from elsewhere.

There's always a line of "stretch" limos outside MY White House for my guests.

It's so ironic.

It is truly ironic. Our Psychic Remote Reading Unit was shut down because we did Tarot readings for members of Congress and someone — I suspect it was a group of middle-management people — became afraid WE'D INFLUENCE MEMBERS OF CONGRESS.

And now we're DELIBERATING influencing ANYONE living in, working in, or just casually passing through the White House, and especially concentrating on uplifting the vibes in the Oval Office toward Consciousness and Buddha Enlightenment for all souls in the immediate area.

It's not just about the Oval Office. Sure, the Oval Office is fully engineered for magical operations through cyberspace and psychic planes, but the fact is that the whole dang place is WIRED FOR PRAYER.

Not just any prayer, but a particularly potent and invasive form of prayer that FORCES the consciousness higher and higher, creating vibrations that cause Enlightenment, which may in turn cause powerful behavioral changes in the subject.

At the front door to my Virtual White House in the online virtual Ashram.

Wired? Yes, wired.

In the sense of Spiritually connected. Psychically speaking, there isn't a square inch of space in the Actual White House that isn't covered in some way in my psychic model.

Years ago, you'd have had to master visualization and manifesting in order to achieve anything on this order of meditation and prayer, but today we have cyberspace and the ability to create in cyberspace almost anything you can imagine.

Rather than you spending years and years in a monastery to learn how to visualize, you can walk through the visualization with the INTERACTIVE form of an Avatar in cyberspace walking around a virtual model of the thing and interacting with it in various ways.

You are an ACTIVE operator in a very easily definable space

266

within which you find yourself able to move about quite easily. You can participate in the space in a variety of ways, including helping yourself to a portion of a really excellent sushi plate or one of my specialty donut platters.

There are a nice variety of homey things around the place, and frankly, they really should hire me to decorate the place, but to be fair, I'd be inclined to ignore everything and load the place up just like you see it here today.

Just inside the front entrance to the Virtual White House is a line. Ignore it.

The model of the thing is the thing itself.

The more perfect the model, the more powerful the quantum connection. That which is like something is connected to that thing, and that which has been in contact with something at another time can be made to be in contact with that something in this time-frame.

Simple High School Math.

Actually, I should look for, or build, a set of the twin Houses of Congress and fill that with Enlightenment Vibes as well. I'll look into it, when we've first got this thing going.

Meanwhile, at MY White House, you'll find an ABD Devotional Altar Service set up on Trump's desk.

The more enlightened the operators in the VIRTUAL White House are, the more powerful the effect will be, and the more rapidly we should see some improvement toward the enlightened side.

Skipping past the line, you'll turn to the right and walk that direction.

Enlist Help For Us From Enlightened Beings!

If you know some very Enlightened Beings, ask them to help you with this project, if they are able and willing to do so. It's asking a lot, so be prepared for some turn-downs from some very exalted beings, for two possible reasons:

One reason is that they're busy doing MUCH higher things and haven't time to squander on local politics and events. That's where I generally sit, unless DIRECTLY provoked.

The other reason is that it really doesn't matter. Honest, it doesn't. Look at it from this perspective — how much do you know about the day to day life in Ancient Rome, Sumer, Chichen-Itza or Kalamazoo?

Even if you do PLS work to explore those time-space regions, you won't recall absolutely everything about the daily life and I wouldn't expect you or anyone else to have that much recall on a whole lifetime or civilization or culture.

But think about it — after a few thousand years, it's all rumor and mythology. Nobody knows the truth nor do they care, and that's the fate of all present-day events. They will become part of the big vague blur that is "history".

You'll see a small room with a sign that says "Sekrit Keep Out". Go in, of course.

In the small side room, you'll find a TELEPORTER to other locations in the Ashram. You can take this teleport in anytime after you've been initiated, which means that you've gone through the Oval Office Enlightenment Project Training Course.

You can also set up a location and put that in your "favorite locations" bar at the top of your screen in Second Life.

It's easy to participate in the Oval Office Project.

You can attend a group course, or request a personal tour with our special Guides, who will demonstrate how to operate the various magical and shamanic devices, such as circle dances, meditations, heart prayers and more.

In addition, you'll want to visit our fabulous FREE 99-Cent Buffet. It really is free, it HAD to be called "the 99-Cent Buffet" because that's what the casinos in Vegas were famous for back in the 20th century, if you'll cast your mind back a moment.

Um, Prime Directive???

Does projecting and enforcing ENLIGHTENMENT onto others through psychic means violate the PRIME DIRECTIVE?

269

InterDimensional SHAMANIC PORTAL to the ACTUAL White House!

This is a serious question. The Prime Directive, simply stated, says that an off-worlder is not entitled to meddle in local affairs. Period.

Well, almost Period. Actually, under certain extenuating circumstances, you CAN take assertive direct action of a certain type.

Latch onto one of these T'ai Ch'i balls and leave your Avatar there all day long!

Imposing Enlightenment would be one of those direct actions that you'd need a special dispensation to apply.

One of those special situations involves a 90% Extinction Event, and that's not too cool, when you've got dozens of off-world races with intersections and bypasses located here.

So the answer to whether or not it violates the Prime Directive is, emphatically, "No". There is a clear and present danger to the planet, above and beyond the danger to the human species, and so long as that danger persists, you have license to help bring the Emperor to Enlightenment.

A Levitation Project

You are in fact causing a Levitation in the White House in the sense that the Enlightenment Waves will cause the entire structure to vibrate in Sympathetic Harmonic Resonance, to coin a phrase, and the whole thing lifts off the Human Plane just ever so slightly.

You couldn't measure the effect with anything short of a Photon Detector, and that wouldn't give you anything but the location and time of day.

Use this Fortune Teller to directly telepathically communicate to Donald Trump.

The Oval Office Project is a directed meditation which is actively pushing Clear Light Waves of Perfect Buddha Enlightenment into the

White House, permeating everything including the drapes, thus causing the inhabitants to experience Enlightenment whether willingly or unwillingly, knowingly or unknowingly.

Of course, only then, with full Enlightenment comes Realization.

WOW! What a Change!

You can ask one of our Ashram Coaches to help you understand how to harness the Fortune Teller in the T'ai Ch'i Studio next to the Oval Office so you can directly communicate telepathically through DREAMING WORLD connections!

It's at that point that we'll see a profound, deep inner change in Donald Trump. The most obvious sign that something of an inner spiritual awakening has occurred will be that he will simply stop lying.

You can measure this effect on a daily or hourly basis, so "NOT LYING" would be a good indicator that your meditation and prayer are WORKING!!!

Even so, this spiritual meditation exercise in levitation is not directed at a single individual. It is an Enlightenment Prayer Project that covers the entire Washington White House.

Heart Aura Meditation in the Oval Office. Your AURA builds up as you sit there.

This meditation does not travel with the people, so if Trump is golfing in Florida this weekend, you'll have to go up to my TRUMP

GOLF VIRTUAL COUNTRY CLUB COURSE upstairs on a higher level in the Ashram, to send waves of enlightenment vibrations to him and his golfing party and at the same time play through my 18 hole course — you'll be lucky to shoot par.

You can get free clubs and balls at the clubhouse or on the first tee.

If you do use that particular ROSEN BRIDGE to the TRUMP GOLF VIRTUAL COUNTRY CLUB COURSE, please don't use it to psychically screw up his game. You won't be able to send that kind of vibe anyway, because I've installed a TOURMALINE VEIL on anything that's outgoing from the Ashram, to filter out any such negative vibes.

The Virtual World's Most Challenging Virtual Golf Course! Try it, you'll like it!

You can use my TRUMP GOLF VIRTUAL COUNTRY CLUB COURSE to make it rain, but only for the general benefit of the Palm Beach countryside, which means that when the palmettos have drunk their fill, the rain stops, and believe me, weather of all kinds never stops a golf nut, and Trump is ALMOST as fanatical and obsessive about golf as he is about himself.

So when OPERATING as a REMOTE READER in our VIRTUAL WHITE HOUSE, you'll want to consider the various types of interactions you are able to conduct from your vantage point.

Let's take a photo tour of the VIRTUAL WHITE HOUSE. I'll try to give you an overview of just a FEW of the magical operations you can conduct to PROJECT PSYCHIC WAVES OF ENLIGHTENMENT directly INTO the ACTUAL WHITE HOUSE in WASHINGTON, D.C.

Imagine how difficult it would have been to master visualization before the invention of 3-D gaming engines!

Years invested in getting SOLID images, seeing in clear detail, moving in astral space and more. Now YOU can be a Remote Reader INSTANTLY, and the more Enlightened YOU are, the more powerful your effect will be at the ACTUAL WHITE HOUSE to which these Enlightenment Prayers are directed.

I wasn't kidding about the 99 Cent Buffet, and it really is excellent, as buffets go.

Uplifting Meditation.

The fundamental reason that we are licensed to PROJECT ENLIGHTENMENT ONTO THE WHITE HOUSE is that we are at the very brink of a nuclear disaster, triggered accidentally by someone who can't control his temper and has, as I mentioned earlier, his finger on the nuclear trigger 24/7/365, and he's utterly unpredictable.

He needs calming down, and Enlightenment generally does it. All Emperors need to be enlightened, but some are more resistant than others. I think this guy is a prime candidate for an Enlightenment

Exercise, simply because the odds are so much against it.

If you can VISIBLY ALTER HIS MANIFESTATIONS and REDUCE HIS ANGER in a very measurable way, which means "clearly visible on network tv", then you can say that you have done a good Enlightenment Job.

If you can palpably help to bring Enlightenment to the Washington White House, then you are not far away from achieving Enlightenment your own self.

I sing Folk Protest Songs here in the Grand Ballroom of the White House.

Enlighten Others!

Sure, Enlighten yourself, but after that, what?

Once YOU are Enlightened, you can start to help to make it better. It's a clear field, not a lot of folks practicing it, not really, mostly just in the Name of Enlightenment, which believe me, is not the same.

Enlightenment is a Clear Objective, one that is recognizable in its immediate and profound effects. Should you succeed in this project, you will see a deep and astonishing change in the manner of Donald Trump. We will post some of the changes that we have achieved, as they happen. One thing has already occurred. Just the day following my pronouncement that I can personally guarantee that Donald Trump is not an anti-Semite, he denounced anti-Semitism, along with his son-in-law, who is an Orthodox Jew.

These are some of my yummy snacks set out for all visitors in my White House.

Enlighten others as you yourself would be Enlightened.

YOU need at least SOME Enlightenment in order to influence anyone ever in that direction. This could be just the motivation you need to achieve Enlightenment.

Enlightenment is easy to achieve. It's only the very first baby step on the path to Total Self-Mastery and Completion.

That's my whole reason for creating the VIRTUAL WHITE HOUSE and loading it up with magical influence toward Enlightenment, don't ya see???

Okay, I slipped in a little Compassionate Buddha on the side, but I know you'll forgive me for it — how could I resist?

So without further ado — there's been plenty of "ado" already — let's do lunch. What I mean is, let's see what other magical tools are available to the diligent observer in our VIRTUAL WHITE HOUSE.

TO BE CONTINUED...

OVAL OFFICE PART DEUX
February 22, 2017

My Trump Model behaves pretty much as the original does, including "KMB" poses.

OVAL OFFICE PART DEUX

At one end of the Ballroom, you'll note a small closet, within which is tucked a skeleton. How proverbial is that? Can you think of another word for "Thesaurus"? What if there were no rhetorical questions? If a cat and a banana traveled East on a train from Chicago to New York at an average of 90 mph in a stiff wind, how many chickens were left at the end of the run?

And that's the kind of polite chatter you'd be likely to expect from the Washington crowd, most of whom are lawyers without a practice. You can't come across a band of worse thugs than that, and when they get together, it's called "Congress" — aptly named, I think, for the kind of thing they do to the country.

The Ballroom is very valuable as a venue for speakers, poets, protest songsters and theater and dance presentations, all of which are Spiritual Enlightenment Technology directed at the leader and leadership of this once-great nation.

If you didn't used to be, but now you are ashamed to be an American, it's time to take some positive action, and this is it. Get into the Ashram and start pushing those vibes out at the Washington politicians who aren't listening on any other level.

Returning to the Front Lobby, you'll notice a red-carpeted stairway to the left. You'll go up those stairs to visit the private area of the White House.

In Shamanic Magic, it's all about CONTACT and COMMUNICATION. Contact merely establishes a connection, but communication is a two-way process which you must fully understand in order to apply it in the Shamanic sense to activation of Higher Centrums.

We are going to use the Washington White House as a subject for our experiment in projection of Waves of Enlightenment into and onto the President, Donald Trump, for the benefit of all beings everywhere.

And that goes double for anyone who doesn't happen to be both white and the right kind of Christian.

You're right — there's a skeleton in that closet. Don't look! Fake News!

GOOD CONTACT depends on accurate duplication of the White House, and this we do have. GOOD COMMUNICATION means that YOU are taking part, YOU are doing your part to bring Enlightenment to someone as dense, low, crude and ugly as Donald Trump.

I'm not making fun of Donald Trump when I say he's ugly. He wouldn't be ugly if his anger and rage and frustration with everyone but himself didn't show up on his face, but it does.

Every face eventually shows the inner self, radiant and smiling, or frowning and ugly, and Trump definitely wears the ugly kind of face, and keeps it ugly with his fears and upsets.

In the Washington White House, the private quarters are upstairs on the third floor, but as the model has only two stories, I've combined both the second and third floor operations onto the second floor, which works just fine to deliver the VIBES.

So far, we've only seen and been in the public areas of the White House, although the Oval Office cannot now be said to be public in the ordinary sense of the word.

There was a time when a citizen could stop by the White House and have a talk with the President. Even if times were not so violent, it would not work out today — there are just too many people, too few goods and services to go around.

At the top of the stairs you'll see a large golden Buddha.

Now you're at the top of the staircase, on the second floor, where you'll find a combination of offices, studies and bedrooms, within which you will discover a number of ongoing passive magical operations as well as active participation areas, which I'll point out as we go along.

Remember that this is a combination floor, intended to contain all the necessary chambers in the actual configuration while conforming to the adjusted model which has two stories instead of three.

The architecture is basically Georgian with touches of everything that was done to it in the name of progress and modern architecture and design. In short, it's a mish-mosh of periods.

The designers are driven by taxpayers, the President, the members of Congress who happen to take note and interest in the decor of the building and, of course, any kids who happen to be passing by on the way home from school.

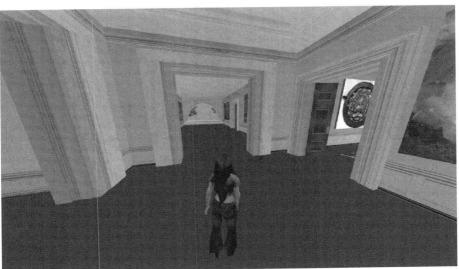

At the top of the stairs you'll find yourself on the private second floor.

You'll note that there are two distinct wings. We'll want to turn to the left at the top of the staircase and head in that direction.

The sepia carpeting of the private area distinguishes it from the plum-carpeted areas downstairs in the more public areas of the White House.

The Master Bedroom is a fairly unmodified space, because he's rarely there.

The moulding around the doorways was replaced on several occasions throughout the years, but remains essentially the same — rather massively heavy and somewhat overbearing.

The intention of the building is to capture and project the impression of a European Royal Palace, but it falls far short of the mark for anyone who's actually seen one of those things.

If you want to see real magnificence, check out the Bourbons, the Medicis and the Hapsburgs for sheer spending power and untold wealth, all for the purpose of creating what amounts to a mausoleum without a corpse.

In the Master Bedroom, I've placed a number of passive influences, among which are several very rare thangkas and some beeswax candles burning on the low coffee table by the wall.

You won't see it, but there's influence in the form of invasive music and other electronic programming coming through my sound feeds into the Ashram.

One advantage of using a separate sound feed for the Ashram sounds is that they never fail, as the interior sound system of Second Life often can, notifying you that your sound probably doesn't work.

In that case, you should exit and come back in. Sometimes just going from one region to another can screw up the whole sound thing, and leaving and returning almost always repairs the online interruption.

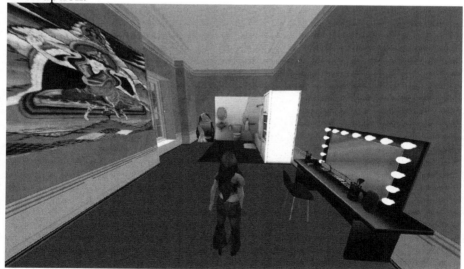

Trump has his very own vanity dresser in his bathroom — note the lipsticks and rouge.

Make no mistake, you don't get that ugly just doing nothing. Trump needs a face-lift, but who would want to steal his face?

Note the contained-bath area, leaving plenty of room for visitors to pack in and gawk, thus creating exactly the kind of feeling and sensation that the Trump White House gives us as a general impression of being a bug under a magnifying glass, trying to dodge a giant tweezers in the sky.

One of the major weapons you have at your disposal is the Power of Song. Using simple techniques, it's possible to create folk-style protest songs that can actually create a ground-swell of resistance.

When almost everyone except a very privileged few are crushed down to the carpet, you can be sure there's a rebellion of some sort in the offing, and hopefully it will be in the form of a massive initiative and vote, probably to impeach or worse, if treason can be proven.

Yes, treason. I'm not the first to use the word, along with the name "Benedict Arnold" and other epithets. I am NOT making this up — search "donald trump treason" or "fareed zakarian donald trump" to see some real shit fly.

Queen's bedroom is for Melania, who ranks as the least effective First Lady ever.

There are a lot of women who held and exercised power in Washington, but Melania Trump will not be numbered among them.

She is no Eleanor Roosevelt, nor is she any of the female heroes of the White House. She's just a flashy dresser with a bunch of smarts.

How smart is she?

Smart enough to shut up and cringe in the background for the next eight years, if Donald has his way with her, and why should she be different from all the rest, including his present mistress?

I've loaded the bedroom with lots of performing deities and healing and uplifting deities as well. You can add to that force merely by passing through the space.

Of course, it follows that the more Enlightened YOU happen to be at the time, the greater the effect will be on the target space.

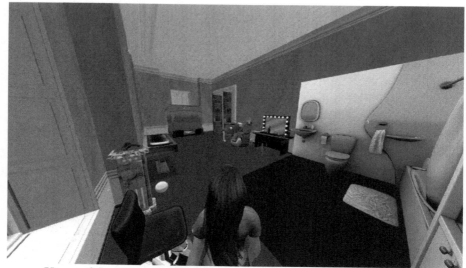

View of the First Lady's luxury bathroom and beauty parlor.

The First Lady's bathroom is loaded with more than merely luxuries, although there are, as you'd expect with her busy supporting role and daily schedule.

Around the area are scattered rather judiciously, if you'll pardon the Supreme Court pun, passive shamanic items that beam the ENLIGHTENMENT VIBES directly into her toilette, as it were.

You get a compound effect by having visitors wander through at odd hours of the day and night — there are visitors to the Ashram around the clock, because they are mostly international and interdimensional.

284

Naturally, our InterDimensional and off-world traffic doesn't give a shit whether this planet is blasted out of the sky or not, but we DO have side-bets running — for instance, I've got a Federation Dollar on the humans of planet Earth blowing themselves right the fuck up, and I can't get decent odds on it anymore, now that Trump is in office.

Powerful Tibetan Magic operates in this yoga workout area near the bedrooms.

I'm lucky to get even money.

With Trump in charge, even-money bets are more the norm now, so there's no chance of picking up more than a single buck, but the dollar side-bets really DO keep the game interesting.

Otherwise, it's just another hi-tech species blasting itself out of the water, and that happens every day of the week in this galaxy alone, and there are 450 billion more chances for something to go wrong, and it always does.

That's the nature of the game. Think of everything you'll ever know as a wave of improbability in an ocean of uncertainty, as Toni Lilly once pronounced.

It's true, and there's nothing you can do about it. But there IS something you can do about Donald Trump.

You can dance in this Native American Spirit Circle just above the Oval Office!

You can take advantage of his erratic, spiteful, vengeful and nasty disposition to test your ability to cast an ENLIGHTENMENT WAVE spell onto the White House or anywhere you choose to target.

You'll find Spirit Candles everywhere in this upstairs Candle Chamber.

By the way, you can do this without the technology, just by learning visualization and manifestation — common practices in many esoteric teachings.

I don't use 'em right now, because the technology IS available, and it's easier to teach someone how to use a mouse and keyboard to move and get around and do things in cyberspace than it is to teach them visualization.

Visualization comes over a long, long period of time. Plug in your laptop and slip into the Ashram's White House Oval Office and get going within just a few minutes!

No longer does it take years and years to master visualization. At the click of a button and the touch of a mouse, you're off and running!

In addition, you'd have had to learn many shamanic technologies. Now, you merely click on an action, and it carries ITSELF out!

All you need to do is SHOW UP!

Showing up sounds easy, and it is, on the first day, when everything's new and exciting and interesting and it's still a novelty, sort of like the honeymoon. Then reality sets in, and you see a 30-year mortgage and years of soccer games and iPhone apps staring you in the face.

That's where most folks get off the train, but that's exactly the spot where you have your very first test — can you stay the course, go the distance, finish the race?

Votive Prayer Candles include "Marie Laveau", "Saint Jude" and "Saint Barbara".

Dang it, I said the word "race", and I just know I'll get mail about it, but I meant it in the sense of a running sport, a competition against other runners, but these days, everyone is so sensitive that you can't use certain words, even if they don't mean those things at all.

Race was always an issue, and will always be an issue in any country or area where more than one tribe lives.

As soon as there are two tribes, you've got the Bugs Bunny Syndrome — (spoken in a high-pitched Bobby Kennedy sort of voice) "You realize, of course, that this means WAR???!!!!"

Even if you're white AND the right kind of Christian, you've got to be careful out in the streets these days. You daren't say anything about Trump for fear of being overheard and getting beaten up or killed by Trump's roving civilian gangs of Right-Wing rowdies and bullies.

If you're not white, you'll think twice before going out of the house, and YOU SHOULDN'T HAVE THOSE FEARS, but this is Trump Amerika, and you have every right to be afraid for your very life just by going out the door to buy some groceries at the market or going to pick up your mail at the post office.

You can enter the name of someone, and a candle will burn for them for 24 hours.

I know dozens of people who don't happen to be white, and that's happening to them every day, now. It didn't used to, and that's my point.

288

That's EXACTLY WHY we are now able to perform this uplifting project. If Donald Trump were not in office, we would have no measure of our success rate.

As it is, if we direct our ENLIGHTENMENT VIBES toward the Donald Trump White House and staff, we should see some clear and tangible quite visible results of our efforts.

We can measure the change against the fear and uncertainty we feel now about being attacked in our homes or on the street by those who feel empowered by Donald Trump's self-evident racism and bigotry, not to mention his egotism, which is massive by any comparison, even with Hitler, Napoleon or Mel Gibson.

The reason that PROJECTION OF ENLIGHTENMENT VIBES works so well as a Remote Reader's Class Experiment in telepathic communication and the force and power of prayer is that Trump is SO over-the-top megalomaniac and bald-faced liar that BY CONTRAST, any change in that demeanor will be stunningly obvious.

Private meeting space upstairs is filled with powerful Passive-Magic Technology.

Even on news coverage by the liberal media, you'll see the improvement. When you wake up to find your house NOT covered by swastikas, you can count yourself successful in the Enlightenment Department.

You have to have something *that* obvious in order to conduct a good experiment. Good lab practices produce good lab results.

Two factors — the first is that the more visitors take part in the project, the more powerful the prayer will be and the faster it will take effect.

The second factor is that the more elevated in consciousness the senders might be, the more powerful the prayer effect will be in Washington.

You'll be earning Merit as you do this practice. In addition, you'll be performing a definite service, and that counts in the realm of ACTIVATION OF HIGHER CENTRUMS.

Compounding this is the cumulative effect of performing this practice for the benefit of others who perform the same practice for the benefit of others who ... and so forth. It adds up real fast, and that's why we take advantage of this poor schmuck who has inadvertently and accidentally gotten himself painted into this particular corner.

He's the head of a country out of sheer spite. He hates Obama for a public sleight, and will not rest until he eradicates all traces of Obama from the planet, and that's what drives him at the moment, although any wind can do the same in his pathetic case.

He's very subject to influence, which is why he became an obnoxious, belligerent bully.

The bio-chamber in the Healing Room is for the Trump Avatar to step into, of course.

Donald Trump is the very face of fury — wrinkled in vengeful spite. Donald Trump in fact accurately represents the voters who voted for him. Think about that. Would you want to share in that karma?

What I mean is, if you looked like that, could you get up in the morning?

When all the shit has finished coming down as a result of his maniacal thirst for attention, in the end, there's going to be hell to pay, and the taxpayers will once again bear the burden.

The rich will always be tax-free.

You are among the downtrodden, and according to the present administration, it's their responsibility to MAKE YOU FEEL downtrodden, otherwise, what's the point of being filthy rich???

You are invited to ring the Dharma Bell — but only once per visit.

When you participate in the White House Oval Office Project, you do more than bring Enlightenment to the White House — you bring Enlightenment into yourself.

The necessity is so great that it creates sufficient force to make even YOUR Enlightenment possible, because it's so NECESSARY.

The higher YOUR consciousness, the greater the effect.

That's an immutable law, and furthermore, it can't be changed. You'll note that there are a number of functional items in the Healing Chamber, among which is the HyperBaric ThermoChamber by the window.

Resist the urge to climb in there — it's reserved for the Avatar of Donald Trump, and yes, we have one, and we intend to use it and use it well, to a lot better effect than the flesh-and-blood version stuffed into the Washington White House by an ignorant mob of White Supremacists, some of whom don't even know that's what they are.

You'll find a very active private kitchen upstairs, which is a work in progress.

Yep, if you elect a White Supremacist to the highest office in the land, you deserve what you get, in the end, and in the end, you DO get it, whether you see it coming now, or not.

I've been around a long, long time, and seen a lot of things come down. This is just one of very few possible scenarios for any government.

If you examine your Earth history, you'll see what I mean.

Athens is a prime example of the scenario that's going down in Amerika today. Let me give you a quick reference — Hippias of Athens and his strange relationship with the arch-enemy of Athens, Sparta.

Alternatively, you might want to look up the word "Quisling", which means "someone who collaborates with the enemy in order to seize or hold power", a term that arose by the fact that Quisling, as the country's leader, GAVE AWAY Norway to the Nazis.

You can dance around the First Family at their Borgia Dining Table Set.

The Nazis marched in without firing a shot, and within minutes, betrayed Quisling by not supporting his Collaborator Government, thus ruining his spring marketing plans forever, but making his name a permanent word for "traitor".

I didn't use the word first — it's been on the news lately, along with other similar words, but I really don't care who betrays whom.

My point is merely that this has happened many millions of times before, and it won't be the last time, either, and I'm not about to start keeping track of who's winning THAT game — who cares who wins and loses, except to collect the dollar side-bet.

Even if the other Council Members have forgotten, I'm keeping track.

There are dozens of "flowering times" when civilizations burst onto the scene on a billion different planets in a billion different galaxies in a billion different universes, and this is one of them.

You've got a remarkable and rare opportunity to expand your consciousness and elevate yourself along with Donald Trump into Cosmic Consciousness and Beyond!

All you need to do now is arrange a Virtual White House Orientation Tour, and you're well on your way to Enlightenment for the entire planet — sure, why not?

We can get a globe and start working on that project the minute YOU get some improvement in Donald Trump's condition. Trump first, THEN the universe.

The punching bags outside the Oval Office are there for the liberal media.

Well, there you have it. The Virtual White House Tour, and you can go on an actual virtual tour of our virtual White House in our Ashram merely by contacting us and asking how to arrange it.

We have operators standing by.

Well, actually, would you believe call waiting and a message machine?

Okay, so you call and arrange a tour, then what?

Then from that point on, you're entitled to use the space to enact your own contribution to the White House Oval Office Telepathic Beaming Project.

You don't even have to wait. There are additional spots in the stand-alone Oval Offices!

Just in case the White House spots are totally filled — which they can be — I've installed duplicate Oval Offices around the Ashram, so EVERYONE can join in.

It's a totally benign and beneficent operation — completely clean and clear "good magic".

The photo of Putin on Trump's desk is where he'd normally keep his wife's photo.

You are helping to BEAM telepathic Astral Plane particle-waves of Enlightenment directly into the Washington White House, right into the heart and brain of Donald Trump & Co.

Of course, they wouldn't like it if they knew about it, but that's just the illness talking.

Donald Trump holds the nuclear button in his hand. He no longer has the option of being non-Enlightened just because he wants revenge and notoriety.

He certainly will get that.

According to my 37th century history texts, Donald Trump holds several important Guinness World Records, one of which, he has already achieved — the lowest approval rating in U.S. history.

Now, that's something to write home about, and I would write home about it, too, if I could, but writing home is not one of my options here inside the World History Sim in the History Lab in, as you'd expect, the History Building on the south side of the campus.

Of course! I know how I can project my findings out there!

I can blog it, and that's readable outside the World History Sim, but then, who would or could possibly read it? Ah, of course! — YOU would read it!

With the proper coaching, YOU can appear to Donald Trump in his dreams!

So THAT'S how it's done???!!! Why didn't you say that Earth History is exactly like Bingo in the first place? I'll expect your help and any help you can enlist in the project.

Trump in Action!!!
March 2, 2017

Take a good look at the objects on Trumpenstein's desk.

At first, I thought to take some screenshots of the Trumpenstein Avatar in various poses and facial expressions, and that's what I did — at first.

Next, I plugged him into the T'ai Ch'i and Yoga Mat exercises, and took some snappers of those, as well.

Actually, it occurred to me that someone might volunteer to take him to a daily T'ai Ch'i practice, but we'd have to work out the timing for that.

I'm very aware that selfies are all the rage these days, and I'm always trying my darndest to come up with a few selfies, no matter what the subject matter.

Unfortunately, I take EXTREME closeups, so you generally can't see the background, but I soon learned that nobody really cares about the subject matter or content of a photo — it's all about colors and high definition, even if it's only a highly defined nothing.

A few closeups of the T'ai Ch'i workout might classify as "selfies".

Trumpenstein is a sucker for great Italian food, and that's what's on the block tonight.

I let him work out through the short form, then took him over to the Yoga mat for a little morning prayer.

Then suddenly it came to me in a flash — what I call a "Zad-O-Gram" because these marketing ideas mostly come from Zadkiel, for whom marketing comes naturally and easily — what about some dances? I'm sure to get a number of good poses for my still shots.

I purchased a few dance animations and took some action snappers as Trumpenstein danced around the White House, especially the kitchen and main offices.

As you've probably already guessed, I observed Trumpenstein dancing, and realized that HERE WAS A SHOW!!!

Trumpenstein chilling out as he does the Short Form at the upstairs T'ai Ch'i Dojo.

What a draw! Trumpenstein does 100 dances from the 60s! Trumpenstein ballet corps, Trumpenstein Flamenco, Trumpenstein drunken dances and best of all, Trumpenstein does a Tico-Tico Party!

Oh, you gotta see this to believe it!

Trumpenstein in the private meeting room, practicing his Hip-Hop dancing moves.

I'm going to perform with the character onstage at the virtual White House and I only hope that someone makes a video of it and posts it somewhere.

It will be funny, that I can promise you and, if Donald Trump ever happens to see your video of the Trumpenstein Avatar dancing about, he will undoubtedly have a good laugh at his own expense.

He's such a good sport!

So I started looking through some of the Abranimation MOCAP dances, and ended up with a slew of them, plus a bunch of other stuff.

Not neglected are the fabulous A&M MOCAP belly dances. Oh, that IS funny, when a fat old ugly guy does those dances!

It probably never occurred to Donald Trump that when he took public elected office, he automatically guaranteed by Constitutional right that the people could make fun of him whether or not he thought he deserved it, and millions DO just that.

Trumpenstein practices his Gangnam dance in the upstairs meeting room.

If you wanted to avoid humiliation and bitingly satirical treatment, you had no business running for public office.

If the people EVER lose the right to make fun of PUBLICALLY ELECTED government officials, you might as well pack up your bags and prepare to board the bus for the Labor Camps, because that IS where you are headed, whether you know it or not.

By that time, you might not care.

In the meantime, you can ridicule Trump and watch the Trumpenstein Avatar dance and make a fool of himself!

When someone public with a LOT of power over YOU and YOUR FAMILY looks foolish, it's good to laugh, and a belly-laugh is even better.

The Boogaloo is just one of many vintage dances that you can get on MOCAP.

He who laughs last laughs best, and that will be us.

In the end, everyone on this planet will leave their lives behind them, and then we'll see who laughs.

YOU will certainly laugh.

You've lived many billions of lifetimes over uncountable aeons, and yet, here you are to tell the tale.

Make videos! Post them!

Ridicule is the best remedy for a Tyrant! Don't fight! Don't struggle against the granite stone! Don't rage against the machine!

Get even. Make fun!

Ridicule is GOOD for an NPD. A little invigorating bath in public humiliation and scorn wouldn't hurt anyone, and if he's truly headed for Liberation and Enlightenment, he won't at all mind.

If he does mind, we have some more work to do in the Virtual White House!

You might very well go hysterical watching this goonie "Drunk Dance".

Keep the PURPOSE of the exercise in clear focus. It isn't about who's in the White House. You're trying to demonstrate the power of telepathic influence, and that's the whole purpose.

Break dancing on the new Sienna wall-to-wall carpet I've installed.

Keep politics out of this.

Humanitarian concerns are something else entirely. They are part and parcel of the process of telepathically imposing Enlightenment on a powerful and ruthless ruler.

It won't be the first time I've had to do that, and you've undoubtedly done the same, but can't remember or don't have contact with prior lives, in which case, maybe you should find out how to remedy that little flub.

I'm considering performing a comedy skit or sketch or routine, or a play, or a poetry reading, with the Trumpenstein Avatar.

The Trumpenstein Avatar is a powerful magical tool that I plan to use as sparingly as I can possibly manage.

Of course, if provoked, I'll put out some scathingly funny videos. Hell, come to think of it, IT'S FUNNY, so the Rule of Roger Rabbit prevails here:

"If it's funny, ya GOTTA do it!"

There really IS no other rule to comedy.

How would you like to see Trumpenstein in "Springtime for Trump and Russia"?

The cost is dear. When you open your mouth on this planet, you always take your life in your hands, because the local zombies take things real serious.

Speaking of zombies, watch for a bunch of friendly, playful and totally deadly zombies, now appearing in my new, very latest, almost ready for release, "Gorebagg's Trumpenstein".

That's to distinguish it from any other Trumpenstein that might be lingering about.

We've secured the Trumpensteingame.com website to house it, and it will be there soon as possible, promise.

You can't really see how funny this is from the stop-motion photo, but it IS funny!

Put your thinking cap on and come up with ways we can use the Trumpenstein Avatar to expose Trump to ridicule and humiliation.

It's not a bad thing, not at all negative. Think about it. What better cure for NPD than humiliation?

Humility is the one thing with which Donald Trump is NOT afflicted. If you see him start to use words like "compassion" and "fair play", you know that our efforts are starting to have an effect.

Note please that I recommended a pinch of "Compassionate Buddha Vibes" several days ago, and the word "compassion" was used in the Budget Speech, so how's that for a first success???

Keep the Faith!

When All Else Fails, Use Magic!!!
March 12, 2017

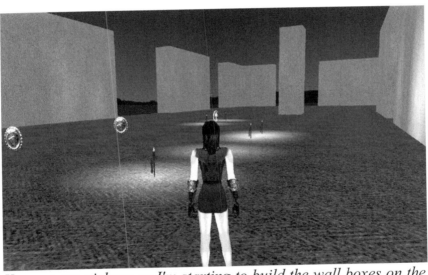

You can see pickups as I'm starting to build the wall boxes on the main floor base.

Feeling helpless and in despair? Is Trump too much for you? Would you like to shut him up, or at least get him to stop lying, cheating and back-stabbing the public?

Great idea, but hard to actually accomplish, especially face-to-face. Trying to reason with madness and deep paranoiac insanity is a fruitless task. All you can hope to do is to contain it and make it harmless.

No matter what you say OR DO, Trump will not listen to you. He is famous for being unable to accept answers he doesn't want to believe.

Sure, you can engage him on Twitter, duel with him in the media and try to get a phone call through to the Oval Office before he presses that Nuke Button on the side of his desk, but no amount of pleading will have an effect, no matter how compelling and convincing.

Crazy is crazy.

Windows need window sashes and framing. These prefabs are made from 8 prims.

So what's left? Clearly, just waving a clenched fist in the general direction of the White House does about as much good as a snowflake in Hell, so give up trying to change him in any direct way.

Magic is one way of getting through and creating an effect by SUBTLE TELEPATHIC INFLUENCE, but how to deliver it?

If you're very skilled at visualization and mapping, you'll have little trouble penetrating into the White House with your Astral Body, Body of Light or Remote Viewing Vision, but first YOU HAVE TO FIND THE TARGET.

That means years of training in Creative Visualization, and who has years to devote to the very BEGINNING part of Remote Viewing? In short, we need something that gives us a shortcut to Remote Viewing without the hassle of visualization and the years of training it takes to get really good at it, good enough to make a difference, and that's where my OVAL OFFICE ORB comes in handy.

Just Press The Button!

Daunting work ahead, but one step at a time does the trick!

It does all the "finding" work, draws you through a Pineal Wormhole using radio waves on your own brain, and deposits you safely on the Other End of the connection, right there at the White House, where you have total run of the territory. There is no place not open to you.

You are free to roam and try to influence anyone in that area of the actual building, or you might decide to concentrate your attention on the Oval Office, the primary psychic target.

Okay, so you now have a Magical Tool at your disposal, and you've used it to penetrate into the White House. The rest is up to you. You're a Remote Viewer, go ahead and View Remotely!

By using the Orb, you cut out dozens of years trying to learn how to do in your mind what you can easily do in your mind with the prompting of the cybermapped Orb.

All the Orb is doing for you is taking the place of Astral Projection and Body of Light Movements in the target space, same as you'd be doing if you had that visualization training and then applied it toward this project.

As a matter of fact, if you can already visualize fully, you'll appreciate how rapidly the Orb takes you there and establishes a powerful CONNECTIVITY.

Early view of the entrance to the North Side Oval Office from the Rotunda Lobby.

Don't forget that the Orb is just like a projection device — it could be arguably called a "psychic particle beam accelerator", because that's exactly what it does and how it operates, but entirely in the Spiritual Realm.

As a matter of fact, the Orb uses the Basic Laws of Quantum Physics to accomplish its purpose, but don't forget that its real purpose is to demonstrate itself.

In order to practice with this Orb, you'll need an actual target, and the White House serves this intention well, because there's hardly any better indicator of your magical success than the sudden Onset of Enlightenment upon Donald Trump and his advisers.

Use The Orb as a Magical Tool!

Remember that it could be made into ANY configuration, including corporate realms. The whole thing is based on shape — Shape is Everything.

You must take the time to determine for yourself the precise and notable difference between shape, morphology and topological extensions.

Adding the columns to the rear of the Oval Office, along with subterranean levels.

Oops, I guess I let that slip — I think I might experience a "Flub Slip" from Above on that one, but I have points against it, so I won't worry too much about it.

The fact is that once you have established CONNECTIVITY to the target space, you can activate the CONTACT points by picking up the half-dozen artifacts placed nearby.

Walk around the Orb for a moment or two, and be attentive to the fact that YOU WILL EXPERIENCE THIS EXACTLY AS YOU WOULD IF WALKING THE ACTUAL SPACE.

You're expected to recognize the thoughts and images coming in as you maneuver around the cyberspace environment of the OVAL OFFICE ORB.

You can now listen to conversations, pick up thoughts and read documents as a Remote Viewer, without all the training and hassle!

If only our Remote Viewing Unit in Arlington, Virginia, in 1964-67 had obtained an alien technology tool like this back then...back then...back then...

Oval Office setup with double dragons, hemp plants, an ABD and a SuperBeacon.

But we didn't have that. We had DAYS of training, then months and months of practice, practice, practice, then actual assignments. We had no feedback on our results, although years later I learned that our "hit-

Closeup of The Oval Office desk. Note the doggie doo on the pedestal in back of alien.

rate" was well above 80%, a walloping amount over anything achieved by Joseph B. Rhine, one of my college professors back in North Carolina — I was at Elon University at Burlington — the carpet capital of the world — and he lectured nearby, at Duke University in Durham.

My primary physics prof was Dr. Hook — not the puppet, the college instructor — who lectured at many colleges, which is how Claude attended his famous lectures.

Many of Dr. Hook's lectures were delivered in the costume and surroundings of the person whose ideas he was presenting at the time.

In a way, you got a direct pipeline to the time-space of the physicists back in the 16th, 17th and 18th centuries.

With the OVAL OFFICE ORB in your hands, you'll find yourself in the same COMMAND CONTROL POSITION, so go right ahead and enjoy the relief.

When you're at the wheel, you're in total control of the space. Put as much energy as you're able into the projection of the telepathic influence of Enlightenment Waves.

Not only can you use the Oval Office as a cyber device to achieve penetration into a target space, you can easily direct your attention to very specific areas within the general area.

South Side Frontage of the Virtual White House, which functions as a magic device.

Okay, so that demonstrates the cyber tool, which is, don't forget, my main intention. I have no interest in Trump — he's just another turkey passing through.

Or should I say, "pissing through"?

In any case, I could just as easily build a radio-wave powered telepathic quantum penetrating device that resembled the Kremlin, and listen in — I don't have to use a device to achieve that, but anything I learn will be useless, because I operate under the Prime Directive, but that doesn't prevent me from making jokes about it.

Using this Oval Office Telepathic Penetrator, you merely climb into the space and operate on it — but how???

Of course, with courtesy and caring, which means "healing" first, "do no harm". That indicates some powerful prayer or spellcasting that involves the general benefit of all beings everywhere, so you can't give him a bad case of gas or a nasty rash on his forehead.

We could spend hours and hours researching a wide variety of nasty rashes — the internet is full of them, but we'd be wasting our time, because he already HAS a nasty rash — it's called "Kellyann Conway", a media-whore and first-class spinning agent if ever there was one.

You can toss Florist Lawn bouquets into the Oval Office or anywhere you'd like.

Pity — it's very tempting, isn't it?

But even a serious rash wouldn't solve the problem. So what would bring about a change in Trump toward compassion and gentleness? Nothing physical would work here.

So how about directing TELEPATHIC WAVES OF ENLIGHTENMENT at him day and night, as long as he's in the White House?

In fact, it affects everyone in the defined space of the cybernetic map. This all adds greatly to your own Merit, the only true way to gain spiritual advancement, as any advanced being will gladly inform you.

Forget about those years of visualization training. Press the "ON" button, and YOU ARE THERE!!!

I'll give you a short tour of the cybernetic telepathy device, to familiarize you with just a FEW of the many ACTIVE and PASSIVE magical effects built into the OVAL OFFICE ORB.

Just by entering the OVAL OFFICE ORB, you perform the major task of the magical operation, which is ESTABLISHING A CONNECTION.

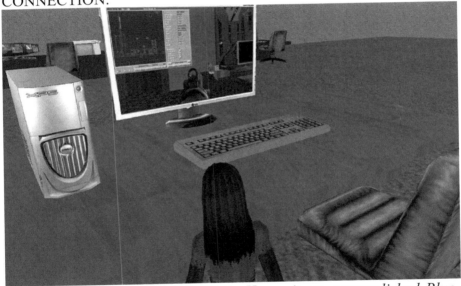

Every staff member of OUR White House is an accomplished Blue-Liner.

This is technically called "CONNECTIVITY".
Connectivity relies upon two major LAWS OF MAGIC, That

313

Which Is Like Something Else Is Also That Something Else, and Two Things Once In Contact Remain In Contact Until and Unless Contact Is Consciously Broken.

We can use both of those laws in the ORB, because a number of the items are models made directly from items that came from the White House, gifts of various Presidents — I've been in direct communication with the Oval Office for decades, as a short glance at my bio will reveal, and several Presidents as well as a few Kings and Queens have my works in their collections.

As a matter of fact, I've worked in one way or another with six administrations, and each got some artwork from my studio for their collections.

I have photos somewhere that show that stuff, but I'm far too busy to dig them out right this very minute. I'll find them eventually and post them when I can.

In the meantime, rest assured that I haven't pulled out my paints and canvases yet, and I'm surely not about to, unless Trump manifests Enlightenment Big Time.

For every other President, I've bent over backwards to be supportive, even though they still reject help from my friend VAL. For them, many rewards.

Some items on the various desks and tables can be picked up. Others are passive.

For Trump, nothing — not even a get-well card.

I know how fruitless it is to engage in direct conversation with a nutcase, and it's even worse when you're trying to present an unfamiliar idea, or something that the aforementioned nutcase will find discomforting.

God Forbid Donald Trump should experience a single moment of discomfort. He has spent his entire life serving himself, so he should be plenty comfortable by now, yes?

No.

He isn't comfortable at all. In fact, Donald Trump is in serious pain — spiritual agony. He needs Enlightenment in order to rule responsibly.

SuperBeacon and Matrix on the left, can be activated by merely touching them.

As Ben Parker is reputed to have said to Peter Parker, aka "Spiderman", "With great power comes great responsibility."

To be precise, it wasn't in a dialogue balloon. The phrase was typefaced on a page slug under the illio, but who's counting?

Clearly, Donald Trump reads the word "responsibility" as "blame" rather than taking command of the situation, which Trump clearly cannot. He is not in control of himself — Steve Bannon is, and he's hiding behind the curtain — you're supposed to ignore him.

315

Donald Trump has no agenda. He rolls any which direction that he feels will benefit himself. He has no feelings or regard for others — they are merely tools in his clutches, and he enjoys their pain and displeasure, viewing them as "fake news" and "hired actors".

Yoyodyne Industries has a huckster booth just outside the Oval Office. Check it out.

He has no shame.

Trump can't be wrong, can't admit a mistake, and the news commentators have been very vocal about this glaring fact — Donald Trump never admits an error. He doubles down on every issue on which he's called to show his hand, but he never shows his cards at the end of the day.

This makes it easy to see if you're scoring hits with your Enlightenment Waves.

Frankly, he's about as rhino-skinned and leather-tough on the outside as the average Abrams M-60 tank, and just about as responsive, and in the same way, which is to lower the cannon and fire point-blank at the questioner.

Any change in Trump — even the slightest whiff of change — would be and should be obvious — so obvious that it leaves no doubt that your telepathic influence on the White House, toward Enlightenment is WORKING.

How else can you measure the effect? You have only one scale, one measuring stick, and that is his sicko public disgraceful and bestial aggressive behavior and general attitude toward inferior races, religions and liberal media companies in general.

In the House of Egypt, you'll find Anubis waiting to give you a ten-card Tarot Reading.

DONALD IS NUTS!!!

Make no mistake — I am not alone in this assessment: Donald Trump is clinically insane, clinically a sociopath, clinically an NPD and clinically and demonstrably an OCD. He is called by his own people "a loose cannon" and he cannot be contained or calmed down by any ordinary means.

He doesn't respond to truth, and he makes it up as he goes along. He doesn't expect to get caught in his automatic lies and total fabrications, and until he became the highest elected official in the government, he got away with it most of the time.

At the moment, his ravings and externalized self-psychotic projections are directly connected to well over 50,000 nuclear warheads and chemical canisters, along with a variety of biological weapons at Trump's immediate disposal.

Just remember that you can't reason with a nut. If you keep that singular fact in view at all times, you'll have a clue how you might successfully deal with it.

He has his hands on your short hairs at all times, but the irony is that he's the one who feels vulnerable.

He's really, really unwell in the head, and it's far worse than simple harmless neurosis. He's so far off the deep end that he's in direct line with the conspiracy theorists who supported him and elected him their President.

Anubis is always at the ready to ask you vital questions to help you prognosticate.

He's crazy.

Something like that is as easy to spot as instantly knowing that Archie Bunker is a racist creep, and he WASN'T lovable, and no such idea was intended. Rob Reiner did his level best to play against that character, bringing him up on every issue, but as you know, it did no good, never does, nohow.

The only way to reach someone deeply insane is to go directly through the spirit, and that's how we operate, through the spirit.

Is it "fair" to impose Enlightenment on Donald Trump?

Sure it is. He's the King of Amerika. As things stand now, Amerika is in for a very racist and sexist and religious fanatic and birth control nutto time.

Is there no longer a functioning law in this land? We used to have laws preventing false accusations, libel and character assassination. I guess we don't, anymore, but that comes as no surprise.

You can get a Tarot Reading, right next to Portal 9, easy to find it!

If I were Obama, I'd bring a Libel Suit.

It's going to end up as a free-for-all, anyhow, so why not strike a blow for freedom now, while you still can?

Soon, you won't be able to speak for fear of being taken away to the Labor Camps. Think that's a fantasy? An exaggeration? Ask any psychic sensitive — they'll tell you that the camps are already built and waiting for you.

Not all of them. There's plenty of room for a civilian contractor, and as a matter of fact, Trump has one of his protected corporations bidding now. They're listed in the budget under "infrastructure".

The crumbling infrastructure is a matter of great concern in Washington. Nobody knows where they're going to get the labor to do the work, and without undocumented workers, they're going to be hard-pressed to round them up, but that's exactly what they'll do, and that's exactly how they'll do it, too.

You'll notice the Tree of Life on the floor, an Earth globe above it between Binah and Chokmah. You'll be spinning off that focusing device.

There are some 24k gold HUD Enervating Deity Amulets on the

sides between the draped windows — they are easy to spot.

Here I am in the Main Chair, projecting those Enlightenment Vibes into the space.

The calendar is predictive and carries Proggie vibes, which makes it easier to use the Prognostication Tools at your disposal.

When you sit down in the theatre chair where I'm sitting, you'll be able to bring down a drop-down menu that offers several chanting and mantra options, or you can choose to produce those sounds yourself at your end of the Wormhole.

Remember that although they can't actually HEAR what you're saying, they can FEEL IT, so be nice. Your thoughts must be pure and clean to have the Enlightenment Effect.

Be sure to check out my new CDs with my latest Trump Outrages featured in song and dance! Keep your sense of humor and don't let politics distract you from your spiritual goals!

Thank you, Donald Trump, for being such a great comedy relief! Reminds me of the days back in the fifties, when there wasn't enough to protest, so folk music was morphed into folk-rock, which is about personal relationships, not world-shaking events.

Remember that YOU are empowered. You can do it, too! Just be prepared for the backlash from the primates! Keep a Portal Handy!!!

KEEP THE FAITH!

Comedy Gag Elements for a Presidential Comedy Routine
March 13, 2017

PRESIDENTIAL COMEDY ROUTINE

Do you feel like punching Donald Trump right in his bulbous red nose? You wouldn't be alone, but it'd be a big mistake to let that rage take you over. That's exactly what Donald Trump wants, is your permanent rage, because that means you're giving him the attention he needs and craves and must have every minute of every day.

How would you like to convert that rage and frustration into something good and peaceful and contributory and gentle and kind and loving and wonderful and beneficial to all beings everywhere?

That's exactly the point of the Spiritual Technology which I used to call "CONVERSION", the fundamental basis for a system I once called "Anger Management", given in the form of workshops in 1964 and 1965. I don't use the term anymore, because it was popularized and turned into a money machine and I want no part of that action, thank you very much.

Conversion is the plan. Sure, you feel lousy and miserable, and befouled and angry and frustrated and annoyed and fearful and distrustful. These must be converted solidly into positive energy, and the best energy beam ever made was and always will be "Waves of Enlightenment".

They act like waves, so the subject is more or less continually beaten on the head to wake up and see the Light — in short, "Get fucking Enlightened NOW!"

You start with the lower emotions and sensations, of course. It always starts with something small.

Anger, rage, frustration.

But wait!!! Those are the very same symptoms felt all day and all night by Donald Trump! How is that Possible? He's a multi-billionaire and has anything and anyone he wants in his pocket, bedroom or twitter account, or so it would seem.

Donald Trump Lives in Hell.

As a Remote Reader, I know the truth. He's actually in debt up to his eyeballs, and is under the power of those who give him bailout money to keep his financial empire from going under, which it has nearly done several dozen times in a row.

"Why, Faustus, this IS Hell, nor am I out of it. Of all the inhabitants of Hell, none but Lucifer KNOWS THAT HELL IS HELL." — with thanks to my good friend Chris Marlowe for the quote.

Anger, rage, frustration.

If you could get away with it, wouldn't you just love to flush Donald Trump down the toilet he came in on?

Oh, that's a terrible thought, right? No, it doesn't even come close to comparing to Donald Trump's rage when he suggested to his followers about Hillary Clinton, that "Maybe some Second Amendment Rights person will take care of her."

Second Amendment Activists are against gun control.

Was Trump suggesting that someone blow Hillary away? He thinks he's a LOT more clever than he actually is. Quite frankly, he's transparent as Hell, and his mean and selfish nature is dominant and defiant.

Hate crimes against Jews are up almost 200% since Donald Trump took office. Why do you suppose that is? So if someone does something, can it be traced back to Donald Trump's mild smirking suggestion at some press conference?

Charles Manson was convicted of suggesting murder to his followers. Is Trump's comment any different, and what would have happened to him had someone followed his vile and criminal suggestion?

No matter what the President does, it's wrong to want to get rid of him or her, except through legal means, such as impeachment, and yes, Virginia, impeachment does happen when the facts are brought to light, and that's what will eventually prevail, the Rule of Law.

That's the only thing holding civilization together. Without the Rule of Law, you have nothing, and even SUGGESTING to a crowd of believers that someone "might be taken care of by some Second Amendment Activist" is, to my immortal mind, downright criminal, and if someone else doesn't speak up about this, I'm damn well going to! It's totally criminal.

You're damn right, criminal, not merely civil, as in the Libel suit I hope gets brought against him by Obama.

Donald Trump is the President, so he is supposedly the MODEL of behavior for all kids in school who are watching this drama unfold.

Trump apparently also committed perjury and brought false witness and impugned and soiled and dirtied the reputation of Former President Obama, of whom you'll note that I speak with respect, as I have done with all prior U.S. Presidents until this creep came along, and forced me to speak badly where I should speak with respect.

I'm a taxpayer. I'm Trump's boss.

He's such an egomaniac that he'll never admit that, but it's totally true. He is a salaried elected public official, sworn specifically upon taking office to uphold the Constitution of the United States of America.

If you're a citizen of the United States, you're his boss, too, but someone who is so crazy over control and domination can't possibly imagine that concept. To him, HE'S the Boss and all Amerikan citizens are his SUBJECTS.

Holy shit, is this guy nuts. Napoleon, get outta town!

What's more, he's never paid taxes in his life, so he doesn't even COUNT as a citizen worthy of respect in my opinion. If you pay your taxes religiously as I do, without claiming any extraordinary exemptions, you have the right to walk up to Trump and say, "You're fired!"

Frankly, I wouldn't like it if he were removed from office, because I have personally never had so much goddam FUN at the expense of a political figure since Attila the Hun conquered half the known land mass of Planet Earth.

I should be able to speak out without fear of an IRS audit.

I'll bet that I can tolerate an IRS revenge audit better than he can, dollars to donuts I come out the winner, and I won't withhold MY tax returns, asshole!

Trump suggested to his followers that they make "Hillary For Prison" t-shirts, and they did. Besides the fact that that was downright mean and low below the belt, but it was unprofessional and far over the top even for a Presidential campaign, which you expect to be fought hard.

Of course, it's Trump who will end up in prison, once they trace down the mysterious "Dmitri" and other politicians and Russian and European businessmen who are his "associates" — actually his bosses and his "control".

Trump hates and distrusts the intelligence community, because HE HAS A DEEP SECRET THAT HE DOESN'T WANT EXPOSED and he knows that they could easily bust him if they knew where to look — at "Dmitri" for instance, if they used Remote Viewing Operatives like I used to be.

My Remoter Skills are no less now.

Trump is guilty of a LOT of transgressions and outrages, and they will ALL come out, but it's never soon enough, right?

Donald Trump is so messed up in his head that he UNKNOWINGLY and UNWITTINGLY leaves a bloody trail about as messy as the one left by O.J. Simpson.

Listen, I pay my taxes without complaint — although that has changed — and I don't care what happens. As I've said, I'm 75 years out of port, and on top of that fact, this world has never been important to me — I'm here on a history mission.

I'm quite prepared to end up a refugee in a long line of refugees at the Canadian border — they'd never let us into Mexico after Trump's outrages against them — and you should also be prepared to end up as a refugee, too.

No matter what your current situation, you can become a helpless refugee, if you're an Amerikan citizen, or deportee, if you're not.

It can happen overnight. You go to sleep in a free nation, and in the morning, you wake up to see the area covered in tanks and heavily armed men in uniform, and wham! You're living in a Police State and the army has taken control.

Welcome to Trump Amerika.

Technically, it's called a "Military Junta", but frankly, who wants to live through that?

I'm not interested in money or the things money can buy, even healthcare, quite frankly, because I'm 75 years out of port and headed for home, but I'm also living very differently than you are, unless you've activated the Perm Waking State in yourself, something I emphatically do NOT recommend for the novice.

Anyhow, raging won't buy you anything. Keep that in mind as we go along. Rage against Trump is fruitless.

Of course, you can't even SPEAK about Trump, positive OR negative, without endangering yourself in this nice, new Nazi environment we're living in, full of hatred, violence and suspicion, for as long as it lasts.

It won't last long, and I'm not guessing. I have 37th century history lessons upon which to draw, although my memories of class lectures is somewhat on the fuzzy side, because my history class falls at 1100 Hours, which would normally be my nap time if my body ruled, but it doesn't, and I often will sort of half-doze as the professors drone on.

Textbooks? I haven't ever cracked a textbook in my entire life. Anything I want to know is stored in the Akashic Records, which I use every day without really thinking, "Hey, I'm using the Akashic Library again!!!".

It's become second nature to rely on the ARL — Akashic Records Library — for all my research needs. Unlike my internet connection, I never lose contact with the Records Office.

Perhaps that's not such a good thing, because it takes the punch and guesswork out of the future, doesn't it? I mean, if you already know how it comes out, you might as well just jump to the next segment, no?

No.

That's not a good answer. Nor is rage or anger or frustration, not because they are "bad", but because they are ineffective and inefficient.

When you feel like treating your President like a punching bag, and you've never felt that way before, it can be very upsetting. I personally resent the fact that I HAVE TO refer to the President of the United States as an insane asshole.

I also can't believe that there are so many hate-filled people out there in Amerika, who would LOVE to see Trump take over and make things right.

Far from making Amerika great again, he will cause the world to think of Amerikans as a bunch of schmucks, and they'd be right.

Personally, I'm betting on the great new country of Pacifica to come out the winner in all of this ruckus, at least until Pacifica is attacked and overrun by ... oh, but I published all that stuff in "SlimeWars" which is still in publication today.

I Failed Earth History 101.

What I mean is, no point reprinting 150 chapters of that book here and anyhow, they're very inaccurate, due to a slur in my memory for names, dates and places.

In SlimeWars, I outlined in extreme detail all the Earth History I COULD REMEMBER from my lessons. I don't rely entirely on my memory of what I picked up in class or what I failed to do as homework or assigned reading, for my information when I'm making important decisions, however — for two solid reasons:

I barely managed a D+ on my exam.

I can't seem to remember dates and places, and names escape me entirely.

Frankly, I don't care. It's all just a blur to me anyway. I hated history, until I started visiting the past, like here.

It is so weird to live in a society of natural telepaths who suppress the perceptions provided by telepathic contact, and pretend to be entirely cut off from the Cosmic Consciousness.

Anyway, rage against the machine, for all the good it will do you. Serious debate has no effect, but ridicule cuts right through the defenses, right to the bone, which is where ugly goes, while beauty is only skin deep.

Anger, rage, frustration — they can be transformed magically into good spiritual food for Enlightenment of your comedy target, toward his or her Enlightenment, and you'll note that I do NOT specify gender here in relation to Donald Trump, because he's a nebbish, a nothing.

He once asked Phyllis Diller if he should have a sex change, and she replied, "From what?" — Please don't react to that gag — it was included out of respect for Diller, nothing more.

It's the Old Conversion Play.

Don't give in to the Dark Side, Luke. Stay on Target, Luke.

These are important teachings that are embedded in Star Wars just as they are in your DNA, if you can reach in there and get hold of it.

Don't respond with anger.

Sure, you'd like to punch the motherfucking goddam sonofabitch lying bastard right in his ugly pig-nose, but that's against not only the law, but all common sense and spiritual Right Action, don't you see?

Don't respond with rage to rage.

Donald Trump is a multi-billionaire who is in so much spiritual pain and torture that he can barely stay alive. He'd have done himself in long years ago, if he could have mustered up the courage, but he's a coward, a bully and a coward, and so are his friends.

How would you like to be inside one of those foul, cruel instruments of torture? Sounds like Hell, doesn't it? That's exactly what it is. Hell is NOT what you think it is!

If you're living in Hell, you're in Hell.

If your insides are crawling and your mind is coming apart at the seams and your emotions are streaking around in pain, you ARE in Hell — you don't have to wait to die, you're already dead and in Hell, if you live there all day long, and many violent creatures DO live in Hell.

Strangely, it's called, on the street, "The Life". You call THAT living??? You can start expressing yourself verbally instead of with violence. Violence never works, as tempting as it might seem.

Violence is not an answer.
After all the violence is over, humans tend to pick up the pieces and begin banging rocks together right from Square One.

This happens periodically for two solid reasons:

Humans have no historical memory, none whatever, except for a few scholars.

Humans can take only so much complexity before they want to tear it down.

Sure, you're scared of Trump. You have every reason to be. He's a huge, ugly bully with a fat agenda of hate, anger, frustration...

Hey, every day that guy goes BALLISTIC with rage and frustration.

Is that the kind of life YOU'D like to be living? Poor bastard, pity him. More than pity him, target him for Enlightenment, by

PERFORMING A RITUAL COMEDY ROUTINE ON HIM.

Yes, a comedy routine CAN be a sort of Voodoo Doll approach to communication, don't you think?

It suddenly occurs to me — between Al Franken, Rob and Carl Reiner and Billy Crystal, you have some really excellent examples of exactly how to CONVERT RAGE into humor, and if the humor REACHES THE PUBLIC, it will serve to roast the bastard quite royally, with the scorn and pity and ridicule he so richly deserves.

DON'T GIVE IN TO ANGER!

If you give in to anger and rage and frustration with Donald Trump and it turns into violent hatred and pissed-off action, you'll be playing right into his hands.

Giving in to the kind of tantrums and rages displayed in public by Donald Trump, the Idiot President, brings YOU right down to his level, about the emotional age of 3 years old.

You won't accomplish anything by punching a Donald Trump punching bag around all day long, although THOUSANDS of people have ordered one and are now using it to get rid of the frustration and anger they feel toward Trump and Washington in general.

It won't do any good to punch a punching bag. That doesn't hurt Trump, it hurts YOU.

Trump would just love to see you give in to your rage. He IS the Emperor in Star Wars, urging you to give in to the Dark Side, but if you're smart, you won't.

You can make real change by using the most magical of all weapons, comedy. You can get fast, fast relief by making fun of the weirdest and most absurd American Presidents in U.S. history, Donald "Rump-Roast" Trumpenstein, or is it Trumplestilskin?

Either way, you have a TRULY GREAT comedy target in Donald Trump. Rejoice in it, and wish him EIGHT GOOD YEARS, or better yet, hope for him that he gets his wish and becomes the ABSOLUTE RULER OF PLANET EARTH.

And it shall come to pass that he shall be known as "Emperor Ridiculous I" and his stepson shall be known as "Emperor Ridiculus II" and so forth to the end of time, or nuclear annihilation by the disappointed aliens who can't wait to try again, this time with ants.

Yes, ants.

Ants are automatically telepathic and have as a result a group brain, quite a bit superior to the local small brain that humans are forced to operate with, because they block their telepathic channels so they can lie, cheat, steal and betray.

In a fully functioning telepathic society, you can't do any of those things, so Trump would be instantly revealed as a captured tool of Russian agents and business associates.

Take your revenge in COMEDY RELIEF.

If you're one of the many millions of Amerikans who were robbed by Donald Trump of their freedoms, sense of unity, exhilaration for life and the zest and energy to go to work every day until you drop, you'll appreciate these barbs of scorn and ridicule for the worst and stupidest U.S. President in history.

Regain your equilibrium! Rejoice in life again! Have a day without fear! These are the benefits of pushing some doggie-doo into the face of a thoroughly bizarre example of toupee art gone mad.

I've never called any U.S. President an asshole.

I try to treat all high government officials with the respect they demand, whether or not they deserve it, because that IS the payoff to being a high and mighty muckamuck, and they won't let you, me or anyone else forget it.

They're in it for the admiration.

Okay, that having been said, I find myself constantly saying "Trump is such a fuckhead", and "Trump is a total asshole", and "Go Fuck Yourself, Donald", and that can't be good for the soul.

So I make the effort to convert my total scorn for a thoroughly evil beast without an ounce of ethics or integrity into something that is constructive.

You won't make any points with Trump on an intellectual level, basically because he has no brain — it's all knee-jerk reaction.

You can't reason with Trump, because he's totally, raving nuts insane.

You can't argue with Trump, because he's the President, and he could have you summarily executed for insulting him, just as any King or Emperor would do.

You can't get through the armor with reason or facts.

Trump is impervious to facts. When a fact happens that he doesn't like, he simply makes it not exist, and from that moment, for him at least, it no longer does.

Reason doesn't work on the insane. Facts do no good against mindless drivel and party propaganda and banter and accusations. Remember that a fundamental trait of the NPD is to blame others and accuse others of what they themselves have done and are doing.

You can't make him hear you or see you.

But you CAN hold him up to ridicule, and that has to hurt, when you're as egotistic and puffed up and self-inflated as this creature seems to be. He'll never see or hear what you have to say, but many folks will hear it, think it and say it because YOU gave them the courage to speak out.

Whether you're a big fan of insane fuckhead dictators and want to help them build monuments to their glory, or you're just browsing around for something Trumpish that might tickle the funnybone, these little comedy quips might just fit the bill.

Normally, these zingers are kept aside for the occasional rude heckler, but that describes Donald Trump to a "T". On the other hand, they could be applied to almost anyone else likely to be sitting in the White House Oval Office.

The fact is that Obama wasn't worth making fun of — there wasn't that much funny about him, although from his actions you can see that he is sincere and has the public interest at heart, at least ten thousand million times more than Mister Oil Pipeline.

Okay, there have been a few U.S. Presidents that deserved to have some comedy punchlines heaved at them and heaped up at their feet. FDR was as close to Trump as you'll find out there on the History Channel.

Polk was a nothing, even less of a pimple on the face of history than Donald Trump. I write an average of 20,000 words a day, and spend good time composing and reworking and sharpening and trimming my words, because I'm a professional writer and editor.

What kind of compositional skills do you need to post a few words on Twitter?

Like I said, he's an idiot with a fake education.

I will BET MONEY and give good odds that I can wipe Trump across the floor with a few well-chosen quips, compared to his highest level of comedic wit, "Fuck you!", which is his Final Refuge when all other witticisms fail him, and they do, for he is truly witless.

Is he really a Closet King?

He doesn't have to be, because now he's real close to his actual goal — to be more powerful and more important than Putin, but that, of course, is impossible for anyone other than Putin to accomplish and besides, he already has.

In short, the job is filled, so fuck off, Donald.

Where in the entire modern world could you find someone so deserving of a shit-pie in the face? Wouldn't you love to cram your fist into his fat stomach just one time, for destroying what's left of your miserable life?

Well, calm yourself, bunkie. He's no more responsible for his words and actions than any other robot.

Yes, I said "robot".

The fact is — and this will be revealed by history — Donald Trump is LIVING IN RUSSIA TODAY.

You are familiar with the so-called "SexBots" offered now on TV? These are "Almost Alive" robots that have been programmed to respond sexually to advances of any nearby human, although they can be set to respond to only one, for a few extra bucks.

I bought myself a SexBot on the internet the other day, just to see what it did, and it arrived yesterday afternoon. I was all set to test it out last night, but it had a headache.

See? That's a gag I just wrote, and YOU CAN DO IT, TOO!!! Just see what strikes your funnybone and push it a little more, and test it, try it, see how the timing works, because it IS all about timing and delivery, not subject matter or material.

So then why use Trump as a comedy target?

Um, uh, Because He's There??? No, that's a mountain, and Trump is no mountain, not even a molehill. Hell, he's hardly an ant farm.

Two ants in an ant farm, talking to each other. There's a huge fuzzy eyeball just behind them. First ant says to the second ant, "I get the distinct feeling we're being watched.".

Long, long line of ants on a field, stretching out into the far distance, coming into the near foreground. There is one lone ant standing just outside the long, long line of ants. He says: "Mind if I cut in?".

Years ago when I knew people in the publishing field, I had the idea for a funny book for someone who just isn't great at drawing, has no drawing skills whatever, which would be a book of ant gags, with the ants represented by little black dots of India ink.

I didn't do it, although Roger Price, publisher of Price, Stern & Sloan, was dating my Mom until he found out she hadn't a funny bone in her. Not actually grim, but always serious and never cracking much of a smile. Forget the belly-laugh.

On the other hand, my Dad was one of the funniest people on the face of the planet, and the authors of at least fifty science fiction autobiographies would agree. Actually, all four brothers were extremely funny — Dave, Sanford, Horace and the funniest of all of them, my Uncle Cliff, who wrote under the name "Floyd C. Gale".

Never mind the ant farm. It's not important, because WE'RE DOING A MONEY TRICK! The reference is to a comedy magic routine performed as a stand-up by a very young Harry Anderson. The routine is called "Hello, Sucker!" and is a total riot, but don't try it at home.

Trump as a comedy target is rich, because there isn't a single day he isn't prominently in the news. By this time, every other administration was settled in for the duration, but Trump is UNCONSCIOUSLY prolonging the agony in order to keep himself in the public eye, which he craves more than anything else, and I'll tell you the deep secret reason why:

TRUMP IS AFRAID TO DIE ALONE.

That fact creates his entire fantasy world and drives his insanity, his NPD Core Illness.

On October 31st, 1950, Halloween Night, five year old Donny Trump was left alone in the dark in his room, by his Dad, who could not tolerate the child.

No amount of screaming made a difference, and he's still screaming in pain over this event today. Somehow, the synaptic connection made a constant contact with this event and a fear of death, hence his compulsion to COMMUNICATE on Twitter, lacking friends to whom he can go with his frustrations and his fears.

The combined effect is the deep meta-programming layer which responds to the DNA CONTROL COMMAND, "Mustn't die alone".

This fear of dying alone is what causes him to tweet on Twitter and sit up with companions through the dark hours and try to distract himself from the slowly passing minutes and the crawling hours of darkness and despair.

He can never admit that he's terrified, but he is, and his attempts to distract us from his fear ends up looking like anger and rage. Never forget that those things are merely fear in disguise.

Trump tries to camouflage his fears with rage, but nobody is fooled. You can SEE his fear on his sad, miserable, thoroughly sad and disappointed face.

He has everything, and it's all empty.

Fuckin' hell, I've been saying that for billenia.

He's terrified of dying, but even more so, of dying ALONE, so he creates TONS OF DRAMA to make sure that he is constantly surrounded by people who are continually aware of him.

This satisfies nothing, but he doesn't know what else to do, and he isn't programmed for intelligence, as you can easily see and hear for yourself. I don't need to convince you that he's a total schmuck, and I wouldn't dream of changing your opinion.

In the meantime, I'm going to have some fun at the expense of Donald Trump. Does he deserve my disrespect and scorn and ridicule?

You bet he does.

That bastard robbed me of my country. The motherfucker — and I use the term advisedly, based on several rumors about Trump and some women in his "Spin Factory" — should be taken out and put up against the wall, if he actually conspired with his friends, the richest Russians in Russia, to destroy the United States — that'd be treason, pure and simple.

I'm wrong to call him a traitor. He isn't even human.

You probably saw the news coverage and the CNN specials about the new sex robots coming out of Japan.

They're so realistic, you could meet one in the lobby of a hotel, have a conversation, a drink at the bar and go up to a guest room and have sex, and you'd never know.

That's how real they are. Even the skin is warm to the touch.

How do I know? Read on!

Trump is a Russian Robot.

Of course, if I'm right, and Donald Trump IS a cleverly made Russian Robot, it's already happened. By now, probably half the Congress and most of the Military General Staff have been replaced by Russian Robots, engineered by Donald Trump.

He gets on the phone to some General or Senator and says, "Say, Bob, will you meet me for lunch at the UFO stand near the West Wing? Of course, he's immediately snatched up into a Reverse-Engineered Russian UFO.

They've had them for years, and were on the Moon and Mars long before there was a space program. Yep, there IS a Secret Military Base on the Moon, and another on Mars, and still another on Io — yes, Io.

Anyone who remains unaware of the "deals" between various governments and Dracos and Lizardos has got to be sleeping deeply. There is abundant evidence from around the world that aliens are presently on Planet Earth, and they're getting worried.

They are more worried about Donald Trump than about any other world leader, including Kim Jung Um, who has to be the worst case of inbreeding I've seen since Akhenaten and Nefertiti.

Speaking of elongated skulls, badly made and badly fitting toupees, and alien hybrids abducting government officials, let's look at what else makes Trump funny.

To begin with, he's ugly, really, truly ugly-repulsive, and his facial contortions, when they twist with inner hate and anger and frustration, become truly magnificent in their sheer power to disgust the senses.

In short, he's so ugly, he has to sneak up on his own shadow, to quote Moms Mabley, who would have had a hell of a lot to say about this creep, and that opens up the subject of Trump as a comedy target, but let's look at the potential for comedy, here.

I have deliberately avoided researching Trump, in order to keep my Remote Reads clean and clear, but I'll bet dollars to donuts that Trump's education level is surprisingly low, and that there's a LOT of stuff that we have every right to assume he knows, but he doesn't.

One of the biggest comedy slams on record is the takedown of the puffed-up, and Donald Trump certainly qualifies in that category. The more inflated the ego, the greater the effect on the comedy audience.

There hasn't been an ego that big in the White House, not EVER!

You'll note that Donald Trump is UNABLE TO ADMIT THAT HE IS WRONG. This makes him a PRIME comedy target, if you add into that his ability to throw the entire world into nuclear mayhem anytime the whim strikes him or the voice behind his left eyebrow tells him that he must kill again.

This guy is paranoid, classic paranoid. He has the CIA and FBI watching him in Trump Towers, his IMPENETRABLE CASTLE. He views himself as a KING, not as a President, and he fully intends to take over the military and do pretty much what his bedmate Putin did to Russia.

The difference is, Amerikans won't tolerate him for very long, and they'll dump him, just as the South Koreans impeached their asshole leader just a few days ago. That's gotta get a lot of people thinking in that direction, even the densest and most stupid of Republicans, although they'll tend to wait until Trump is actually standing on THEIR neck, not somebody else's.

What makes Trump a comedy target is the same thing that makes anyone a comedy target. He takes himself seriously.

It would come as no surprise to anyone, then, to discover that Trump has had THREE UFO abduction experiences in just that one lifetime. He has revealed this in his published letters, and will soon go public with these facts, even though I just made them up, because that's how the Law of Irony works, see?

As I've said many times, and am prepared to prove at the drop of a hat, I have no feelings whatever about Donald Trump. He's just another criminal in Washington, and that's not news, and hasn't been news since the Dawn of Time.

Humans of Planet Earth ... you know I love 'em.

Quite apart from what Trump is doing to a once-great nation just to feed his little-boy ego, and his tendency to play with plastic toy soldiers, he's the most incredible comedy target since John Quincy Adams.

If you don't have your Atlantean Self released yet, there's very little chance you'll remember any of this, and frankly, even those who remember being there won't have much good or smart or funny to say about John Quincy Adams today, because hardly anyone remembers the Good Old Days.

It may seem new to you, but if you were in your Higher Mind, you'd see clearly that this has all happened before, because that's the nature of the game — it's built into complexity out of a single simplicity compounded, reflected and refracted.

You can buy a Trump Doll Avatar in Second Life and do a comedy routine right there in Second Life AS TRUMP!!! Impersonation is still legal, so do it while you still can!!! Soon, all disrespect of Trump will be punished with IRS and Medical Coverage revenge against taxpayers who dare to speak up.

Remain silent to remain safe, but it doesn't last. Eventually, your name comes up on the list, and you face the gas chambers yourself, along with your family and friends and yes, it has come to this point before, many times before, and nobody seems to see it coming.

MAGICAL LAWS REVEALED:

In short, the UNIVERSAL LAWS follow the plan and directives and command controls laid down in the GODD 3-D Game Maker

Engine and Editor, which exists apart from the universe in the Causal Plane.

The software in the GODD Engine duplicates the quantum regulations that govern all universes and clusters.

LAW OF SIMILARITY — That which is like something else is, for all practical purposes, that "something else". Similarity causes connection.

LAW OF CONTAGION — That which has once been in total contact with something else is forever in contact unless consciously broken.

LAW OF IRONY — If it makes you groan with the irony of it all, it will probably happen.

LAW OF IMPROBABILITY — If it can't possibly happen, it will.

LAW OF FUNNY — If it's funny, you gotta say it or do it.

LAW OF THIRDS — One third of the audience will think it's great, one third will hate it and the other third will think and do nothing at all.

LAW OF DISPLACEMENT — If you put it down in a spot where you always put it and expect to find it, it won't be there until the next time you look in the same spot.

I've included far more material than you'll need for the FIVE MINUTE ROUTINE I've planned for you. Why only five minutes?

Because five minutes is a LOT of time onstage, that's why, and the attention span of the average audience is measured in Planck Time, which figures to come out at about

FORMULA ????? or less.

I hope that helps you.

Five minutes is all I had when I did my comedy act in New York City in 1964 at clubs around Greenwich Village, especially the Clubhouse, where I did the interstitial fill-in between the Holy Modal Rounders' song sets, even though Peter Stampfel was himself incredibly funny, because he needed a break, is why.

Sometimes I did a full 20-minute set, but that was rare at the

Playhouse, more common at other clubs where there were typically three acts per night, tops.

So how you fill the five minutes is you TRY ALL THE LINES first, then go through them again, delivering the lines aloud, noting which lines YOU FEEL MOST COMFORTABLE WITH and that feel like they "belong" in the set.

Okay, try it on an audience.

You may not be able to get yourself a slot in a local comedy club, even on an open mike night, because the competition is SO fierce, now that comedy and stand-up are considered cool.

Back in the day, if you were a "comic", you lived alone, ate alone and slept alone.

Once you have your comedy routine selections written down, TRY THEM MANY TIMES on as many audiences as you can find around you, EXCEPT AT WORK.

I got fired from KTTV-TV studios in 1966, for telling jokes on my mail delivery route. Not raw jokes, just ANY jokes. Mail clerks don't talk. they deliver the mail. Find a way to get your comedy out there that doesn't get you dumped out on the street, or don't blame me if it happens to you. You've been warned.

The way insult humor works best is to keep yourself absolutely UNINVOLVED. You're just a spectator, a commentator, an interlocutor — if you don't know what "interlocutor" means, you'll have to look it up yourself or remain ignorant, and that's the basis of Trump humor.

When Trump says something outrageous, you don't have to look it up to discover that he made it up out of thin air, and that's always funny. So without further ado, here are the comedy routine parts from which to choose.

Take your time when you're building your comedy routine. You won't have that experience too many times in a lifetime. Relax with it, make it fit your headspace. Don't worry about the headspace of the audience — they'll come to your headspace, if you play it right.

COMEDY ROUTINE ELEMENTS:

Donald Trump suffers from insomnia. He keeps waking up every few days.

Trump finally got a good night's sleep, but it didn't do him any good. All night long, he dreamed that he was awake!

There's nothing wrong with Donald Trump that a good case of Reincarnation wouldn't cure.

He should move out of the White House and go home — his cage is clean.

Some people would like to break Donald Trump in half, but who wants two of him?

He ought to take up clarinet for a deaf cobra.

Donald Trump's soul should only find peace, and the sooner the better.

People like to hate him in installments, so it'll last longer.

He leaves a bad taste in people's mouths.

He's all right in his place, but they haven't finished digging it yet.

I understand that Trump wants to be kind to his inferiors, but where will he find them?

When Donald Trump had greatness thrust upon him, he asked if it came with directions.

Melania is okay as a First Lady, but I get the definite impression that Eva Braun did not die in that bunker in Berlin.

Next time Donald Trump wants to express himself, suggest UPS or FEDEX.

Donald Trump lives on the wrong side of a one-track mind.

Donald Trump never did an honest day's work in his life, and he didn't do that very well, either.

Donald Trump would give away the shirt off his back — the Health Department would insist.

Donald Trump is a man who started on the bottom, and has gone down ever since.

Donald Trump thinks the bubble-gum cards are great works of literature.

Donald Trump doesn't like to exaggerate his accomplishments, but he tries his best.

Donald's mouth is big enough to sing a duet.

Donald Trump can't see a belt without hitting below it.

Donald Trump is so vain, he would take his own hand in marriage.

Donald Trump's Bible has only six commandments, and two of those are just requests.

Trump is really moving, but that's because he's going downhill.

You'll have to excuse Donald Trump — he's going through a

nonentity crisis.

Donald Trump wouldn't have the milk of human kindness if he ate an entire cow.

The way Donald Trump finds fault, you'd think there was a reward.

Everybody loves Donald Trump, and so does he!

Whenever Donald Trump walks into a room, people give him a creeping ovation.

Trump has all the charm of a dirty Christmas card.

An insurance agent told Trump, "Now that you're married, you should get insurance." "Nah," he responded, "I don't think she'll be THAT dangerous."

If they ever put a price on Trump's head, he should take it.

If Trump had an extra brain, he'd have one brain.

Trump is a self-made man, which relieves God of some of the responsibility.

Trump gives "success" a bad name.

It wouldn't do Trump any good to see himself as others see him — he'd never believe it.

Trump got his stooped posture by living down to his ideals.

Trump comes from a long line his mother once heard.

If Trump had his life to live over, he should spare us the trouble.

Trump never opens his mouth unless he has nothing to say.

Trump has had it rough, lately. His organ-grinder died.

Trump has no enemies, but his friends won't be seen with him.

When Trump cleans his nails, he loses 20 pounds.

Trump wears a shirt and tie to cover up his choke collar.

Donald was an unwanted child. He asked his parents if he were adopted, and they said, "Yes, but they returned you.".

Trump would make a perfect stranger.

Trump is so negative he won't even eat food that agrees with him.

Trump is such a creep; when he served on jury duty, they found him guilty.

Trump called Dial-a-Prayer and asked for his messages.

Trump is nobody's fool. He freelances.

There's good news and bad news for Americans today. The bad news is, the Martians have landed. The good news is, they eat politicians, and pee gasoline.

In Trump's case, you can't believe everything you hear, but you certainly can repeat it.

With two words, Donald Trump can light up a room. "Good night."

Trump was supposed to take a trip on Air Force One, but he couldn't remember the flight number!

HEY, TRUMP! — A COMEDY SET

In this style of routine, you're talking directly TO Trump, not ABOUT Trump, as in the previous material above.

Hey, Trump, why don't you freeze your teeth and give your tongue a sleigh ride?

Hey, Trump, you could give failure a bad name.

Hey, Trump, if they ever put a price on your head, take it!

Hey, Trump, You have some great thoughts. Let them work their way up to your mouth!

Hey, Trump, you have lots of get-up-and-go. Please do!

Hey, Trump, try a mind-reader — you can get in for half-price.

Hey, Trump, you've got the kind of face I'd like to shake hands with.

Hey, Trump, when you get up in the morning, who puts you together?

Hey, Trump, why don't you go down to the seashore and pull a wave over your head?

Hey, Trump, let's play library. You be the "silence" sign.

Hey, Trump, I believe in human rights. I guess that leaves you out.

Hey, Trump, dpn't you ever get tired of having yourself around?

Hey, Trump, brains aren't everything. In your case, they're nothing.

Hey, Trump, I'd like to forget you exactly the way you are.

Hey, Trump, you're not yourself today, and it's a definite improvement.

Those are two modern styles of comedy routine related to a specific comedy target, ie; Donald Trump, a Legend in His Own Mind.

Let's look at another style of comedy delivery, which is the STORY.

STORY GAG DELIVERY

In this comedic form, you tell an anecdotal story about Trump. The most important factor is something I cover in every one of my comedy workshops and clinics — the setting of the story MUST BE REAL TO YOU.

Base the setting on an actual experience experienced by you. Place the characters and the story in a setting that you can vividly remember out of your own recent past.

You'll visualize the events as you relate the story, and the audience will SEE it with you if you make the visualization powerful enough that you actually see and feel the time-space before you.

This creates a REALITY for your story that will penetrate even the densest and deepest unconsciousness.

People live their lives BLOCKED from the Higher Influences and Experiential Realms, and when they do happen to wander outside their little boxes, they run back and hide, real fast.

Your job is to make sure they stay out of their rabbit hole long enough to have a good belly laugh at Donald Trump's expense. Believe me, he can afford it, and he richly deserves your scorn and ridicule.

STORY COMEDY ELEMENTS

A story is very different from a one-liner or a fast quip or wise and funny observation. A story has just a little more "meat" to it, a bit more depth. Let's take it from the shorter story forms first, and then build it up. Your story can be drawn from your daily life, by simply adapting funny stories to your life. Simple as that. Speak from experience:

Trump goes to a doctor, asks the doctor, "Doctor, how do I stand?" The doctor answers, "That's what's puzzling me."

Trump's doctor tells him that he's raving nuts psychotic. "Fake news," retorts Trump, "I want a second opinion." "Okay, the doctor continues, "and you're ugly, too."

Donald Trump was visiting a small country village in England many years ago, along with his then-wife Ivana and a dozen kids. "You have twelve children?" she smiled. "No, we have sixteen, four more at home," Ivana replied. "Sixteen children?" the woman responded, "for that, you should have a knighthood!" "My husband has a dozen of them," replied Ivana, "but he hates to wear them."

Donald Trump walks into a wig shop and is immediately topped with a piece of orange-pink crap that the store was trying to get rid of. "This is you," the salesman cried out. "Can I try on something else?" Trump replied. The owner of the shop came over to help, while the salesman turned Trump's head to the left, then to the right, several times, then had him turn completely around and look in the mirror on the other side. The owner smiled, and said, "This toupee looks GREAT on you!" "I'll take it," Trump said, and left the shop. "Do you see how easily a sale can be made?" the owner said triumphantly. "Yeah," the salesman agreed, "but who got him dizzy for you?"

Recently, President Obama said that each incoming President should have in hand three envelopes, the contents of which would only be revealed upon opening them. During the first 100 days, when the going is always rough, the new President should open the first envelope, inside which is the message, "Blame the guy who was in office before you!". At the end of the second year, he should open the second envelope, inside which will be the message, "Blame Congress!" and at the end of the third year in office, when he feels battered and bloody, he should open the third envelope and read the message within: "Prepare three envelopes.".

Donald Trump was overheard on his Presidential chopper saying to his buddies, "I don't hate Mexico. Hell, in Mexico I can get a fifty pound sack of sugar, two bushels of corn, a quart of whiskey and a woman for twenty bucks; the problem is, the booze is awful."

Trump was on one of those $9 million vacations in Florida again and he decided to ignore warnings, as per usual, and he dove into the ice-cold crashing surf and was caught in the undertow. A bellhop from his resort whipped off his shoes and jacket and dove in after him and a few minutes later, had landed him safely on the beach, where he turns to Steve Bannon, who has been watching the whole thing from the safety of the sand, and asks him, "What do you tip for saving your life?"

There are a million story type jokes and gags for you to draw upon as well, and there's nothing stopping you from making up your own jokes or adapting existing jokes to your purpose.

Keep your barbs sharp and to the point. How about a routine in which you impersonate Trump, either with makeup or not, or as a Trump Avatar in a live Second Life performance or a machinima you post on YouTube for the world to see.

TRUMP LIVE IN MOSCOW

For many years now, the border between Poland and Russia has been volatile, shifting this way and that, so one year you were a Russian, the next year you were a Pole. I remember the time I was first told I was now Polish. "Thank God," I said, "no more of those freezing Russian winters!"

A Moscovite walked into a department store, marched up to the shoe section and demanded a pair of shoes. "What size?" asked the clerk. "I wear a size 41, but I want size 36." The clerk was surprised, and asked him, "Why?" "Because at home at the end of the day, when I take off my shoes, that will be the most pleasure I've had all day long!"

My tooth was throbbing, so I managed to send for a Russian dentist who was recommended by my friend Dmitri. I learned that the fee was going to be 3 million Rubles — about $50,000 in pre-destabilized Amerikan currency — and to tell the truth, I balked. That sounded like a bad deal to me, so I asked why it cost so much. "We have to operate to pull the tooth. It has to come out through your ear. You're not allowed to open your mouth here in Russia!"

Trump visited his favorite expensive Strictly VIP Moscow brothel, and after he was taken care of, he sat with the prostitute to have a sip of tea before leaving. "Why don't you join us at my Trump Moscow country club later on?", but she said "No, I can't. It's bad enough — my Mom would hardly even agree to me joining this brothel."

I went to the opera the other day with my daughter-wife Ivanka. We saw a vintage Russian opera, "Comrade Butterfly".

When I get to Hell, I plan to establish myself in the Russian Sector; that way I know the heating won't be working.

Russian Roulette isn't a bad game; the problem is, not enough Russians are playing it.

Two rabbits met in the middle of Siberia, and one said to the other, "We've got to get out of here. They're going to castrate us." That's ridiculous," the second rabbit said, "they're only going to castrate camels." The first rabbit said, "Okay, wiseguy, after they castrate you, try to prove that you're NOT a camel."

Well, it finally happened. Russia ran out of shortages, and in Russia, a person can really talk his head off!

You know why Russian Police always travel in threes, right? The first can read, the second can write, and the third policeman is there to guard those two members of the intelligentsia.

MURZILKA just ran a contest for the funniest anti-government joke. First Prize was 20 years!

Yevgeni Popov asked me last week about my secret Amerikan contacts, and naturally, I told him to ask me at the next meeting, which is now. Oh, but wait — whatever happened to Yevgeni Popov???

To repay Russia for its many shipments of food and weapons, the Egyptians sent a mummy to the Kuskevo Estate for its permanent collection. The Egyptian Egyptologist who brought and installed the mummy in the museum display section commented that he had no idea exactly how old the mummy was. The Russian scientists said they'd soon find out, and sure enough, they announce a few days later that they knew the exact age of the mummy. "How did you find out?" the Egyptian curator asked, now curious. "The mummy confessed."

Well, you get the idea. None of these gags are "mine", nor are they yours. You can't legally copyright a joke, not just one standalone joke, although you can copyright a collection of jokes. They're just too short for copyright to take effect.

Technically, a song would fall into the same category, but it has other protections, although these days, nothing is safe, nowhere is safe.

Even your cell phone and your Pong Game can be turned against you.

Grab a Guitar and Join the War!!!
March 15, 2017

LeslieAnn ripping into Trump at a recent comedy performance in Reno.

LeslieAnn likes to make the audience think about what's going on.

Feeling helpless? Is Trump too much in your face all the time? Are you sick of hearing his voice and seeing his stupid wig flapping around in the breeze? Do you wish you had a photo of the bald Donald Trump to post on your Facebook page?

Well, despair no longer, bunkie. Your days of frustration are over, and Donald Trump's are just beginning. The Power of Song is greater than you think. It's more than reason, more than persuasion, much more than mere influence.

Song is the basis of shamanic magic, did you know that?

In ALL spiritual practices, song is used to convey prayer, to build thought-forms, to open portals, gateways, doorways and StarGates.

Sound has power, but you already knew that. Okay, so how to harness it for a specific purpose?

Well, first, you have to have a purpose, and that means some sort of target effect, so you can measure your success. There can be no greater purpose than to regain your country and your freedoms and to help others who are too helpless to help themselves do this by teaching them HOW TO RESIST TYRANNY.

Of course, accidents CAN happen, and it is quite possible that you'll wake up one morning to find yourself living in a military dictatorship.

My history lessons aren't open to folks in the past, but I CAN give you a little hint — there's no mention of any U.S. Presidents after Trump.

That doesn't mean there weren't any, just that historians weren't all that interested in the 21st century, what with all the really interesting stuff happening in the 22nd and 26th centuries, not to mention my home time frame, the 37th century.

Remember that this is a class exercise, not just casual curiosity, so conduct yourself accordingly. Keep always in mind that there is nothing personal, that you are merely determining the effect of your shamanic magic, and how you determine that effect is by observing changes in Donald Trump's behavior.

Not subtle things — big, major changes, as in taking the initiative against hate crimes, coming out in favor of mixed marriages and abortion rights and equal pay and freedom from fear and fair treatment from law enforcement and the removal of blockages to refugees and a more gentle and sensitive relationship with women — like I said, big things, things that are definitely NOT likely to happen just on their own.

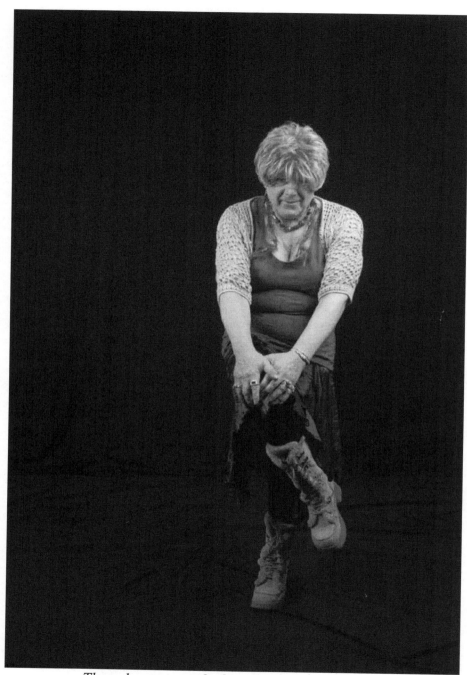

Those boots were the best I ever wore onstage.

What I mean by that is, there is no chance in Hell that Donald Trump will voluntarily drop those psycho-aberrations anytime soon, so if they DO happen to change radically and he starts acting like an Enlightened Being, you get an "A" for the course, and I end up with a combined semester grade of D+, which satisfies me just fine.

I'm an artist. I don't need the grades, and a D+ average is PLENTY for an artist, musician, songwriter, playwright, actor, dancer or Creative Person Without Portfolio.

That used to be me. I never had an art portfolio to get into Otis, because all my stuff had sold.

These days, I'd be punished for the offense, but at that time, photography was bloody expensive, and the few photos I could afford to take went to my recording industry friends. I used to do their publicity photos for them, free — what beginning show business hopeful can afford a set of 8"x10" glossies for their portfolio?

I still have the negatives somewhere about. I guess they'd be worth something to someone, but I have little faith in the public interest in anything, much less vintage photos of long-forgotten heroes of the entertainment industry.

Along with the magical effects IMPLANTED into the folk songs, I've tried to also make them make some sense in relation to the political circus that will be gracing the table for the next few years.

Why focus on the political scene? I never do that. Not only am I totally disinterested in local politics — meaning any Earth politics at all — but I have a more fundamental reason for my disinterest in anything regarding the outcome of any planetary body.

In the Long Run, it doesn't matter — none of it does.

What DOES matter is the sheer effort of creating the conditions for conscious life beyond the pale of material existence.

Lower life forms just don't appreciate that opportunity, but YOU can take advantage of a lifetime spent in human form, if you have the willingness to put up a good fight against the forces of sleep, and that's where Donald Trump comes in.

If he and his hateful administration weren't so much in your face, you might forget he's in Washington messing things up real good, like his buddy Putin told him to do. Stir the shit-stick. Problem is, they've already robbed you of your real estate values, your retirement fund and your personal freedoms, especially your freedom from fear, guaranteed by the U.S. Constitution and popularized by the WWII government posters advertising "The Four Freedoms".

LeslieAnn celebrates an Amerikan Holiday, ANY Day that Trump Goes Away.

The Four Freedoms were Amerikan goals articulated by Franklin D. Roosevelt in his State of the Union Speech of January 6, 1941 — often called "The Four Freedoms Speech" of FDR. These were published and publicized for many years, until the Trump administration took action to prevent their continued publication.

Why? What ARE the Four Freedoms?

FREEDOM OF SPEECH — This is the very first and most important of all personal freedoms, because without it, a tyrant can easily take over the government and rule by force of military might. Part of this freedom is the guarantee that the press will not be shut out of government policies — this is now being violated by the Trump administration. Newspeople are BARRED from access to Trump's party members.

FREEDOM OF WORSHIP — This freedom is the MOST attacked of all personal freedoms, and at the moment, Muslims and Jews are being singled out, but eventually, ALL nonconformist groups are herded into the Death Camps in Trump Amerika. If you don't speak ENGLISH, you will be arrested and sentenced to forced labor and eventually death by starvation or gas chamber and no, I'm not kidding, nor am I exaggerating the facts. The camps are already being built — Steve Bannon has his old job back — he's apparently now in charge of handling "The Jewish Question".

FREEDOM FROM WANT — Trump and his bastard friends have NEVER had a single day when they wondered where they were going to get some food and shelter for themselves and their kids, yet they want to take the little YOU have away from you. I say, tell the bastards where to go, and you can DO THAT IN SONG and what's more, you can publish your protests on YouTube and other video outlets, and perform public concerts. Your purpose here is partly to sway opinion, but mostly to use song as a magical weapon against tyranny and brutal rule of the strong against the weak.

FREEDOM FROM FEAR — This is where Trump is a total monster. He feels fear ALL the time, and wants others to feel the same fear he feels, so he imposes fear on everyone he can possibly affect. His primary tool is RACISM in any form, including Nationalism and Patriotism. He is neither nationalistic nor particularly patriotic. He is a very opportunistic tool-user, and right now, you happen to be one of the tools he's using opportunistically, so it's YOUR JOB to get out from under.

One way to escape his clutches is to FIGHT BACK, and fight back as hard and mean and nasty as he and his cohorts, his partners in crime, are willing to do.

If you have an ounce of spiritual life, you won't want to do that, and it's actually totally unnecessary.

Folksinging is a powerful tool, much more powerful than anyone outside the field is aware or would believe. With the Power of Song, you can literally CHANGE THE WORLD in which you live, by switching lifestreams into a higher consciousness level.

That's what you SHOULD BE TRYING TO DO in the first place!

Hell, if you're fighting for your very life on a very basic level — meaning that, like myself, you will very shortly have NO MEDICAL COVERAGE WHATSOEVER — you might as well get some spiritual benefit out of it, too.

No sense fighting to stay alive long enough to get to work to earn the bread to stay alive so you can keep going to work.

That's what those bastards DO want of you, and you'd be a sucker to keep giving them what they want.

Bankers, Wall Street Brokers, Real Estate Tycoons are all pikers compared to the MYSTERIAN NINE, the nine MEN who hold literally ALL the power in the world in their greedy little hands.

The Rockefellers, Morgans and Bushes are pieces of shit compared to the really BIG fish that are NEVER seen. You'll never hear their names, never knowingly see their faces. They live in total isolation, like a Chinese Emperor cloistered in his Forbidden City, living totally apart from his subjects.

Back in the 1950s, the enemy was clear; not Communism, but ANTI-Communism in the form of a diseased mind, the corrupt and criminal Senator Joseph McCarthy, who caused the name "McCarthyism" to be remembered long after his miserable life of hate, fear and suspicion.

McCarthy would, today, be very welcome on the Trump Team, along with several notorious Governors and regional leaders in history, who ended up on the gallows or worse.

How in the world do you get revenge by just singing a song?

You don't.

Forget about revenge. There's no money in revenge, but there IS money, not a bad income, either, in folk-singing, and that's what I propose. Grab up your guitar and SING!

Sure, you think it's a worthless effort, particularly if you don't sing out in public, but you'd be wrong.

With any luck, he won't be in your face every minute of every day.

YOU WILL FEEL BETTER.

More than just feeling better will be the result of singing THESE particular songs, however — they encapsulate powerful magical prayer formulae that will bring about Enlightenment in even the densest most animalistic of low human creatures.

That isn't something you want to impose upon a lower order creature like Donald Trump, but when they get themselves into positions of leadership either accidentally or by cheating, as Trump did, they MUST BE ENLIGHTENED to protect everyone else from their ignorance, greed, fear and distrust.

Forget about changing people's minds — that isn't going to happen. But you CAN change the entire structure of REALITY just by singing these POWERFUL SHAMANIC INVOCATIONAL SOUND TOOLS and using them as weapons in the WAR AGAINST SLEEP!

Singing these songs IN A CLOSET at a tone so faint a cat can't hear it will still have the same magical effect as if you'd sung it in a concert or a town hall meeting.

The difference is that when you SING OUT in public, you might influence others to do the same.

The whole idea is to get these songs out there as widely as possible before the book is banned.

"Where can I download those songs you sing?" is a frequent question I ask myself when I'm alone, and you might, too.

Quite frankly, I haven't the foggiest notion, but I intend to find out, and when I do, I'm going to include a "Pitch", a short sales pitch, for the songbook and CDs!!!

Then I'll post that on YouTube and wait for results.

There's no reason YOU can't write your OWN songs of protest and publish them and encourage others to sing them.

Sometimes it's easier to sing something than to say it. I have dozens of Jimmy Webb stories to tell about that fact. Jimmy used to stutter when he spoke — because he didn't know what he was going to say — but there wasn't a hint of it when he sang, because he already knew what he was going to sing, so there was no stuttering hesitation.

On tour, I can reach an audience of thousands.

Simple cure, works every time. Sing it, don't say it.

Of course, this WILL get you kicked out of an opera house during a performance, or bounced out of a doctor's waiting room if you get too boisterous.

Try to confine your singing activities to town hall meetings and places where you have plenty of protection from people with placards mounted on six-foot long two-by-fours.

They come in handy, when the police start swinging their little billy clubs, but don't try the same trick on anyone flashing an assault weapon of any impressive size.

Of course, if you're an off-worlder, you're familiar with The Cricket, which can take down an entire planet with a single burst on "auto", which I don't ever recommend.

If you can't take down your target with the first round, don't count on getting a second chance.

That's why I compare the Protest Folk Song Singer to a sniper or a ranger. You have two basic techniques to accomplish your folk singing army aims.

So you fight for your Four Freedoms WITH the Four Freedoms. SING OUT! Let your voice be heard! Be fearless! The most they can do is stop you, but they can't stop an entire folksinging ARMY, and the more you sing, the greater the effect.

There is MAGIC BUILT IN to every song I publish. Incantation and secret mantra are used liberally — if you'll pardon the use of the word "liberal" — and sprinkled throughout each and every song are magical "buttons", which switch invocational streams in a very calculated way.

I recommend singing the songs in the order given in the book, but there are special times, special occasions, where you would want to select and arrange songs in a different order.

I will be providing a series of "GIG LISTS" that might fit a narrow range of occasions, but in general, they build best when presented in the way they're published, A to Z.

Each song is built upon the previous song and is taken in an upward curve at a fixed rate of ascent, very much the way you'd coax an airliner upward along an ascending path that used as little energy as possible to achieve the exact thrust needed to achieve the next flat level of flight.

WAVES OF ENLIGHTENMENT travel just like any other lightwave, keeping in mind that EVERYTHING THAT EXISTS is here because of VIBRATION.

Without vibration, nothing whatever would exist.

Everything is made up of very small wiggly things that vibrate all the time. I'm sorry, but that's all I have to work with. I know you'll find a way to deal with it.

Okay, so HOW DOES THE MAGIC WORK?

SINGING IS CHANTING.

It's all a matter of how you're seeing it. With the right shamanic vision, you'll see instantly that singing is chanting, chanting is singing. As a matter of fact, "chanson" and "chanteuse" and "canton" and "canticle" are all words from which the modern word "chanting" was derived, and they all mean "singing" or "song" or "songs".

The magic is contained in the SOUNDING OF THE SONG, not the performance value or the number of the audience. As I said before, you can sing these songs quietly in the closet and the magical effect would be undiminished.

YOU ARE GETTING THROUGH ON A TELEPATHIC LEVEL.

You're not trying to change anyone's mind. Your effort is to direct certain higher energies, called "WAVES OF ENLIGHTENMENT" to penetrate into the White House and to alter the consciousness of anyone inside the building toward Perfection of the Self Buddha Form Enlightenment, or at the very least, get them to calm down just a little.

"Just, just ... take it easy" is the mantra you want.

So what kind of songs will you find on my CDs, DVDs and in my Protest Songbook???

Fair question — let's take a look inside, shall we? Oh, by the way, the songbook can be downloaded digitally as a PDF, or purchased in hard-copy as a beautiful spiralbound songbook that lies flat on the music stand. It's got a great color cover AND back by Marvette, and the pages are super-extra heavy stock, to make them last — at least as long as the present administration, which could be weeks and weeks.

CIA TOLD ME NOT TO COME — "Want some crazy in your brain? Are you lookin' at a rump? What's all these crazy questions they keep on askin' Trump?"

DONALD CAN YOU SPARE A BUCK? — "Once we fought a war by your command, mud rain ice cold and muck. Once I rounded up illegals for you — Donald, can you spare a buck?"

DONALD'S WAR — Last night I had a vision that I'd never seen before. Donald Trump had just freaked out, and triggered off a war."

DONALD TRUMP RUMP-ROAST BLUES — "I never had a day

of Trump's outrages, never had a drama of toys. All I ever see is Trump on Twitter, makin' more complainin' noise. I've got those blues, those Donald Trump Rump-Roast Blues."

EMPEROR DONALD, WILL YOU RULE THIS LAND? — "Emperor Donald will you rule this land, with your freakout wig and comb? Oh, how can I rule a country like this, with a whole Russian family back home?" (this refers to the FACT that the present Donald Trump is a not-particularly life-like Russian robot.)

EVERYBODY DISLIKES DONALD TRUMP — "Bobo waro korira Donald Trump, Tout le monde detest Donald Trump, Ren-ten-si hen-ni Donald Trump, Vsiem nenavidet Donald Trumpm, A todos les odio Donaldo Trumpito, Jeder eyne has Donald Trump, everybody dislikes Donald Trump". (Leave out the last verse if you want to get a whole bunch of Trump supporters singing "Everybody hates Donald Trump" without knowing what they're singing.)

FANTASIZE A TRUMP-FREE WORLD — "Conceive of no possessions, I wonder if you can, No need for greed or hunger, Don't need a travel ban..." (Good song for a town hall meeting, for sure, if they'll let you sing inside the hall.)

FAR FROM THE TRUMPIES — "Someday I'll see the Trumpies go, Where Donald Trump is very slow, behind me..."

FREEDOM SPECIAL — "If you go to Trump Amerika, you'd better walk right, You'd better not be an Arab, and you'd better be white. Trump's Storm Troopers will arrest you, They'll take you down, Before you know it, you'll be Labor Camp bound." This refers to the so-called "labor camps" for those who accept jobs in the infrastructure reclamation projects favored by the rich to keep the poor in slave labor positions.

FROZEN DONALD — "It froze clear through to China, It formed an icy lump, At a hundred degrees below zero, it froze poor Donald Trump."

GO TELL MISS LIBERTY — "Go tell Miss Liberty, Go tell Miss Liberty, Go tell Miss Liberty, the Old Republic's dead."

HANG DOWN YOUR HEAD POOR DONALD — "Hang down your head, poor Donald, Hang down your head and cry, Killed poor Ryan Owens, That poor boy had to die."

HIT THE TRAIL, TRUMP — "Don't care if you get carried off by the men in white, Your brain is crazy son, it sure ain't right."

IF I HAD AN iPHONE — "If I had a Facebook page, I'd share it in the morning, I'd share it in the evening, All over this land."

IF YOU'RE NOT WHITE AND CHRISTIAN — "Trump is who I'm singin' about, And people, you know it's true, If you're not white AND Christian and have to work for a livin', This is what they'll say to you."

IVANA TRUMP — "Now sometimes Emperor Donald throws a spread, For all his pals and gals, a ghastly crew, Steve Bannon carves the joints and cuts the bread, In walks Ivanka Trump to queer the brew."

LET TRUMP TWEET — "Let him Tweet, Let him Tweet, Let him Tweet, Let him Tweet, Texting stupid flat-Earth garbage, Let him Tweet." (If you aimed a telescope directly at the ISS in the evening sky, a flat-Earther would accuse you of painting the image on the Objective lens, even though the ISS is visible to the naked eye. "Its a hologram projected by the CIA," they'll inform you darkly, and that's Trump in the proverbial nutshell. What U.S. President do you know who sat on Twitter, broadcasting deep national security secrets, along with scattered and vague personal attacks?)

LISTEN, DONALD TRUMP — "With a Slavic wife, you're taking a helluva chance, And your good friends, the Duponts, came over from France. Another thing, I'm sure, will be news to you, The first Mister Trump was a foreigner, too." (a well-scored point, I should think.)

MISS LIBERTY DON'T YOU WEEP — "Well, one of these nights, around twelve o'clock, this whole world is gonna rock." (I think that says it all.)

MUSHROOM CLOUD — "The tyranny ends when the wall comes down, Follow the mushroom cloud, There's freedom for ALL on Amerikan ground, Follow the mushroom cloud."

NO BALLS AT ALL — "Oh, listen, my children, a story you'll hear, A song I will sing, it will fill you with cheer. The charming Melania hooked up in the Fall, She wed Donald Trump, who had no balls at all. No balls at all, No balls at all, she wed Donald Trump who had no balls at all." (with a good harmonic blend of three or four voices, this sounds great, and with an entire hall singing it, you'll bring down the house.)

NO ONE KNOWS TRUMP — "Donald Trump lived the life of a Billionaire, Never paid his taxes, he did not care, Took his huge family out for a mighty good time, Drinkin' taxpayers' money, champagne and wine." (nine MILLION dollars of taxpayer money every time he goes away for the weekend, and he pays NOTHING in taxes and won't even release his tax return! What a phony!)

ONE TWEET OVER THE EDGE — "I'm waitin' for the fallout and the joltin' earthquake, Standin' on this Wall Street ledge, Trump's sittin' on his ass in his golden office, One tweet over the edge." (Over the edge is the phrase you want here. Holy crap, is this guy over the edge. Maybe with your help, he'll be off the ledge at last. Once again, this would make a terrific song to foist on Trump supporters. They'll never know it's not PRO Trump, because it contains words of more than one syllable.)

PUTIN ON THE STYLE — "Donald's in the oval office, Raging with all his might, His 'Kill the Unbelievers!' screams, Put nice folks in a fright, Now you might think it's Satan comin' down the aisle, And you'd be right, it's Donald Trump, He's Putin on the style."

REALLY UPTIGHT — "Trump and his Russian friends want us all to fry, Even now I sit here and I wonder why, The electoral college wants to make me cry, Got to stop listening to all of your lies. Really uptight, not feelin' too good today."

SPITEFUL TWEETS — "Vengeful tweets are in my eyes, Don't know if it be truth or lies, He holds us hostage and puts on the screws, He hates the media and fears the news." (What other high government official is OBSESSIVE about posting on Twitter?)

SYMPATHY FOR THE DONALD — "Just as all cops are criminals, And all the sinners saints, As heads is tails and upside-down, And is is always ain't, Just call me Mister President, I'm in need of some restraint." (Jesus, I'll say he is. In the old days, when there was money to run hospitals and clinics, he wouldn't be walking the streets.)

TALKIN' 'BOUT MY MEDITATION — "Donald Trump is in my face, His ugly face is here to stay, Won't you vote him out of office, And make him go away?" A plaintive cry against tyranny, but my own personal druther is to see him through at least two terms, just to get my songbook launched — I'm slow at marketing, these days.)

THE DONALD TWEETS TONIGHT — "Fear your leader, your insane leader, The Donald Tweets tonight. Tweet away, tweet away, tweet away, tweet away." (Gosh, once again, a great song for a large group or perhaps a mob bearing tar and feathers marching across the White House lawn, as I have foreseen in my novel, "SlimeWars" which is still in print and ON SALE today!!!

THE GREAT IMPOSTER — "Yes, he's the Great Imposter, Just

scowling, he'll never forgive, He seems to be what he's not, you see, He's using his brain like a sieve."

THERE ONCE WAS A TWEETING MAID — "She went to the cyber cafe, When the hoodlums went away, And when the zombies came 'round, She always stood her ground." (This is a good choice for a subway busking gig, because it's not actually rabidly anti-Trump, although secretly, of course, it is.)

THE TWEET — "Crazy Donald followed me, and he caught me in the fog, He said I'll fix your songs if you'll stop writing blogs, I said wait a minute Donald, you know I will not be screened, He said that's okay, I'll send in the Marines. He's addicted to Twitter, You can Tweet for free, Take a load off Twitter, Put the download on me."

THIS LAND IS NOT TRUMP'S LAND — "As I was walking my shattered nation, I saw the people in sheer frustration, I saw before me Trump's ugly pig-face, This land is not for Trump alone." (You might want to save this as your closing piece.)

TRUMP AMERIKA — "Trump Amerika around us, Russians banging at our door, Illegals rounded up, by the countless score, But I pay my taxes, So I'll give it one more try, To tell my liberal friends, Not to curl up and die."

TRUMP MEATBALL — "Donald Trump was very bold, He asked for silver, gems and gold, Illegals all yelled at that schmuck, You can't eat here for a Billion Bucks!"

TRUMPTIME — "Trumptime, and the livin' is easy, Washington's jumpin', And the rake-off is high, Donald Trump's very rich, And his daughter's good-looking, So hush you illegals, Don't you cry."

TRUMP TRAIN — "I am feeling so unfree, Soon I'll be a Deportee, Watching as the clouds go by, As I ride in the sky."

TRUMP WON'T YOU BUY ME — "Donald Trump, won't you buy me a stretch limousine? It's in that kind of car that I'd like to be seen, Worked hard for retirement, No help have I seen, Donald Trump, won't you buy me a stretch limousine?"

UFOS OVER WATER — "They burned down the Press stand, Jones and Hartman they went down, We were not white AND Christian, so we had to leave town. UFOs over water, fly into the sky."

WALL AROUND HEAVEN — "Donald Trump is so sure all that glitters is gold, That he's building a Wall around Heaven."

WALTZING GORILLA — "Down came an immigrant to live free in Amerika, Up jumped Trump and he grabbed him with glee, And he sang as he shoved that immigrant into his holding tank, You'll be a waltzing gorilla like me."

WASHINGTON FAREWELL — "Down at the labor camp you can hear, Wage slaves cry out with deadly fear, I must declare that my heart is there, Though I came across the fence from Mexico."

WE WILL TWEET YOU — "Donald make a big noise, Gonna be a big man, Ugly face, Big disgrace, Kickin' women and talkin' race. We will TWEET YOU!"

YO, TRUMP — "Yo, Trump, don't make me mad, Let Senator Warren read Coretta's letter, Let Enlightenment into your brain, You won't act so insane."

Well, he won't act so insane IF your ENLIGHTENMENT SPELL works okay. There's no room for failure, if you still care about this planet.

I've shown you several improvised magical weapons now, among which are:

PEOPLE'S PROTEST SONGBOOK — The songbook can be downloaded or purchased as a softcover spiralbound book, full color covers back and front.

PEOPLE'S PROTEST SONGS IN HD — DVD with ALL THE SONGS sung like they're supposed to be sung, although you can style and sing them any way you like.

PEOPLE'S PROTEST JEWELRY — TFA Trump-Free Amerika medallions, earrings and home units.

TRUMPENITE — Why not place this meteorite where it will do the most good? If you fear Trump's Storm Troopers banging in your door, you might want to place this item in the center of your home, or at EACH DOOR and WINDOW.

OVAL OFFICE IN THE ASHRAM — You have several options to impose Enlightenment Wave Forms onto the actual Washington White House. Join a group there every day and sometimes all night long! Hundreds can participate and, unlike Trump Amerika, there's room for all. Ask anyone on the forum how to find out more about this.

TRUMPENSTEIN VIDEO GAME — Blast your way out of Castle Trumpenstein with magical weapons that vaporize the opposition with WAVES OF ENLIGHTENMENT that turns them into spiritual beings with a hankering to go home.

ESCAPE FROM PLANET TRUMP VIDEO GAME — Dogs and Zombies block your Path to Freedom. You have magical weapons at

368

your disposal, and the Path is overrun with fierce opposition that only a berserker sorceress can overcome.

OVAL OFFICE VIDEO GAME — You get more than just the Oval Office — you get the entire White House, hand-constructed by Old Gorby just for you. Dive into the space and start INFLUENCING all the inhabitants of the ACTUAL WHITE HOUSE to experience WAVES OF ENLIGHTENMENT toward RIGHT ACTION. It works!!! Do it!!!

TRUMP AMERIKA COMEDY ACT — I've posted FREE a variety of comedy elements that can be easily woven into a fabric of a routine or complete act, or taken as written and told just as they appear in print, even reading them aloud would work.

TRUMP COMICS and CARTOONS — If you can draw well, you'll have to overcome it.

TRUMP DOLLS — Don't give in to the temptation to make a Trump voodoo doll — it's bad karma, and it's already been done to great effect.

Gosh, there are so many ways to fight this creep, and more ideas keep cropping up. He's such a tempting comedy fool, you won't be able to resist making fun of him. History labels him as "a clown". Quite literally, not just because of his funny wig. He actually does LOOK like a classic clown.

That's because clowns recognized early on that the very puffed up people are the funniest people.

Unfortunately, they also tend to be the Kings and Queens who, if offended, tend to have the jester drawn and quartered or blown to bits for the court's amusement.

Eventually, Donald Trump's monkey-curiosity will get the better of him, and he'll check out one or two of my People's Protest Songs, and he'll probably suggest I be taken care of, and that's the last you'll see of me, but my songs will still be around, and that's my victory, and yours, too, in our common War Against Sleep.

I remind you again, THIS EXERCISE HAS NOTHING TO DO WITH DONALD TRUMP.

He's just a handy measure of success or failure of the experiment. So DO the experiment and see if you can get a VISIBLE result from your ENLIGHTENMENT EFFORTS.

KEEP THE FAITH!

Believe that it CAN BE DONE. In historical fact, it HAS been done. Dozens of very slug-like low-grade human rulers have had

ENLIGHTENMENT thrust upon them for the safety and well-being of all living creatures on the planet, and there's no reason to alter that very humane approach.

It's a whole lot easier than trying to hit a planet with a very wobbly and unpredictable asteroid of any appreciable size and weight.

But I keep trying.

Forget About Trump!
March 17, 2017

Dimatteo's Pizza is a very popular pizza spot, and the products are delicious.

Forget about Trump for a few minutes. I know it's hard to drop the subject — he's plastered all over the news, and his ugly pig-face is absolutely everywhere, but let's do try for a few minutes to concentrate on something else.

Oh, are you finding that difficult? Trump IS a major distraction on the Path, but don't let that throw you off your spiritual stride. What you really need to put in place is a majorly powerful "Keep-Away" of some sort, and I recommend a TRUMPENITE DOME, combined with a TFZ MEDALLION. See my other blogs about those items or call and ask about them.

Even with those "keep-aways" in place, you might find Trump still very much in your face and in your mind, maintaining a constant CLOUD OF WORRY over your head.

That's how an NPD maintains power, and Donald Trump is an NPD and a half. He actually falls well within the highest scoring nuttos on the planet, and that's on a definite bell-curve.

This section of BardoTown can be a very difficult passage if you're easily scared.

He'd be really mad if he could read my blogs, which is why I use words with more than one syllable.

My songs would throw him into a rage, but they shouldn't, not at all. Actually, he'll be remembered in song long after his reign of terror is over and done with.

Over the centuries, we've seen them come, and we've seen them go. Things never change, just the technology and current mores, and they change with the seasons, quite predictably.

Right now, it's the season for Nationalism, Tribal Insulation,

Building Walls and Fortifications and Defenses.

You'll find no refuge here, nor anywhere else, for that matter. There is no Sanctuary.

It's time for war.

You can't get in here without a Pass, and only the Initiates know how to get one.

Wow, how far out is that? I LOVE war, don't you? You get tired of playing with plastic soldiers or online battles, right?

So nothing is more satisfying than a real, gritty dirty nasty bloody war, don't you see?

I'm always glad to see the patriots waving their flags and condemning and damning others. It means war, and that means profits and progress.

We get our best science from warfare, and our very best scientific advances come almost exclusively from breakthroughs in weapons and defenses.

Haw, haw, haw, I can't wait to see the expressions on the faces of those assholes who actually voted Trump into office.

I've got it all set up on the Other Side. If you voted for Trump, you go to Trump Heaven, which has a fifty-foot thick wall built up all around it.

Even so, you have to maintain silence when you're within 100 meters of their heavenly wall, because they think they're the only ones up here.

Jolly good plan, war — from my perspective.

Don't even THINK about commandeering a vehicle in the Bardos. Not a good plan!

I can hardly wait to see the cool new uniforms, and hear the ultracool wartime music, see the great wartime dance steps and drink the great new wartime cola.

Wow, the marketing plans alone could keep me busy for a week!

I'm well-stocked on rad-block salt pills, and of course I've got my "hot papa" radiation suit and I've had my Radiation Meter up and running for several weeks, now, starting with the time Trump first manifested his weirdness, on the very first day of office.

The nukes will go off in my neighborhood first, if I've calculated it correctly.

While you're waiting for the nukes to go off in YOUR neighborhood — and rest assured, they will — you can get some HIGHER CONSCIOUSNESS TIME in on a new Orb I've just finished and made ready for testing and delivery — the absolutely amazing Orb, BardoTown.

BardoTown is without a doubt the largest and most complex single level anyone has ever made, and one look at that incredibly complex map, and you'll see why nobody does that.

Europeans will feel very comfortable in the North-West Sector of BardoTown.

I did do it, starting well over 25 years ago, and I've been working on it ever since. It's sort of my "Mona Lisa" — an Orb over which I've gladly obsessed and worked my keyboard to the bone to deliver intact and fast-running.

If you're not getting 60 frames of totally smooth action out of this amazing Orb, there's something seriously wrong with your computer, because even a standard desk type machine can run this as if it were a movie, but it isn't. It's YOU moving around in there, doing things and experiencing the space as if you were in it, and you ARE!

Sure, it's just a screen, just a videogame, but after a while, you'll see that it's not just a videogame — there's actually someone on the other end, and that's you, too.

You're at BOTH ENDS of the WormHole. There is only one "side" to the WormHole, just one entrance at both ends at once, with "nothing but vortex" in the middle.

The Vortex in BardoTown is quantum electronics, but is the same as a "real" Vortex.

That little vortex is the whole basis of the entire universe, both visible and invisible, meaning both Newtonian AND Quantum sides of the coin.

A vortex is spin, and spin is the beginning of everything you know and hold dear. Spin is what imparts the possibility of LIFE within a universe. There is no other way.

A planetary vortex that spouts upward from the surface into the atmosphere and beyond gets put there by a weird combination of gravity, magnetism and electricity.

The Earth has a number of these "wrinkles" in time/space called "vortexes" or more properly, "vortices", and these can be harnessed for absolutely incredible quantum effects, all the way up into the Causal Plane.

As Above, So Below, true enough, but did you know that the other half of that phrase is "As Below, So Above", meaning that you can influence the Higher from the Lower, if you know how, have the license to do so, and have access to the Higher Realms?

Gorby's Transit Services are always available, BUT you have to ASK for help to get it.

Access to the Higher Realms doesn't come from Below.

Your access to Higher Realms has been limited by your physical confines and limitation, but it needn't be so.

It's easy enough to launch yourself into Higher Realms merely by following the Path of Indication, which is to say, invoke an Orb and walk around in there a while until you FEEL it.

BardoTown is an Orb that contains several important Bardo Stations and Contact Points, among which are Cosmo Street, Norton Street, Enchanter Sunset, and the Gemini Supermarket.

Along the way, you'll encounter ALL the major areas of the Third Bardo. It pays to become familiar with the territory and the space, so you have an easier time of it when you DO pass through and do the trip for real.

The overpass on the North Side runs past several important Bardo Stations.

Trump's whole plan is to distract you. That's his entire purpose in life, to distract YOU from YOUR spiritual path. It would delight him to know that he's causing you some pain.

Let him tweet himself into oblivion, it doesn't concern you. Stay focused on your spiritual path, and don't allow him to enter into your thoughts, your work, your home.

I'll be posting more of these screenshots in the next blog. YOU CAN ASK ABOUT BARDOTOWN — call, write, or drop a line in the forum or on the log of today's show.

If you're really needing some help on the Trump issue, I've made a few Orbs to help you get over your frustration with the craziness.

You need to do something MAGICALLY. Washington is NOT listening to you, nor will they ever.

I'll merely mention that I've completed a number of Orbs that relate to Trump and Trumpism, and I'll be advising you about them as they become available for download.

Пути Путина
Putin-Gate is READY for Release!
March 28, 2017

Putin-Gate cover indicates that the game is loading — about ten seconds will do it.

"Пути Путина" is a very rough and in my opinion funny translation of "Putin-Gate", a tribute to the Water-Gate days of the Nixon Era, which looks to be repeating itself for our amusement.

There have been several "gate" scandals since that time. I was tempted to use "Ворота", but went this way instead, perhaps unadvisedly, but I think it will fly all right.

Well, in any case, "Putin-Gate" is ready for release sometime in the next few days. I'll briefly explain the backstory idea behind the game, along with a few random screenshots of the building of the level plus a few shots at the completion of this very difficult to build and very highly detailed game.

On the left is St. Regis "Mosaik" Restaurant, with the original signature "k" character.

You find yourself visiting Nikolskaya Street in the historical section of Moscow, Russia. The shops are filled with informers, who will tell you what has just transpired in each space, or give you directions for further action.

If you're thinking you'd like to stop in at the Russian equivalent of "Starbucks", you have a good chance of finding it on this very model of the ultimate tourist trap, yielding millions and possibly billions of Amerikan Dollars for Putin and his oligarchs, obviously a new band name.

Apparently, Putin likes to perform onstage and does so, often. The purpose of the Muscovite street is to bring in foreign currency of all kinds, which can be used to undermine the West, clearly a primary objective of the Putin government.

Boris and Natasha are here in the cafe' at all hours of the day and night, conversing.

When I say "Putin government", I don't mean to imply that there's anyone else making decisions. It's all Putin, and that's what Donald Trump would like it to be for the Amerikan President, too.

Just tell people what to do, and they jump right to it, just like in big business, right?

The detail of this Orb is exceptional, and the loading time is only about ten seconds. I have discovered in the process of creating this Orb a very economical methodology for creating the architecture and small non-model objects.

Even though the models are not precisely exact to the originals, they are very close, and anyone who has ever been to Nikolskaya Street will certainly recognize it.

No mention whatever is made of any specific U.S. Citizen or Official in this game. None whatever.

I'll show you a few screenshots from the game to whet your appetite. I've spent an intense week making this level, and sincerely hope that you enjoy it.

There is NO VIOLENCE in this game, and it is perfectly okay for kids to play it. There is one mention of "sex tapes" in the conversation, but no "swear" words are used, none whatever.

In fact, this is one of the friendliest and gentlest games you'll ever play.

My Magic Source, Gorby's Cafe', is in the scene, but is not directly part of the action.

The earliest version of this "scratch-built" Orb was drawn in rather roughly with house textures on simple boxes along a street.

My first objective was to place the flower boxes, benches, sewer covers and street lights along the center of the street, because that's the most iconic recognition factor in this very recognizable and very iconic Russian street that every visitor is obliged to walk when they visit Moscow.

The fact is that there's hardly any way to avoid Nikolskaya Street when you visit the Kremlin, Red Square, Lenin's Tomb, and the incredibly grand and luxurious Metro station, all within a few feet of this famous street, not to mention GUM, the most luxurious of any and all department stores anywhere in the world, including Paris, London and Grass Valley.

When I visited Nikolskaya Street, it was filled with shops, but they were mostly empty. I could have gotten a small fortune for my 401 Levi jeans, and the taxi ride was the closest I ever came to actually jumping out of a car at full speed.

Churches abound. Originally closed and banned, they have returned big-time.

I really believe that all Russian cab drivers, and especially those you'll find in the streets of Moscow, are an incredibly fatalistic breed, as in "if it happens, it happens.", and I took it for a while, but radically preferred to walk.

There's a fabulous underground railway station, but the underground travel itself was as big a nightmare for me as was the subway system of New York City and Montreal, although I really appreciated the underground entrances to Macy's and Orbach's and Bloomingdale's in New York, and Eaton's and the Bay in Montreal.

It's been a long, long time since you could travel all five boroughs of the city, from the southern tip of Manhattan all the way to Staten Island and back for a nickel.

Yeah, one nickel, which also bought you a ticket to the movies, a local phone call from a pay phone, a bowl of soup, an egg-cream soda or a very large candy bar.

As a matter of fact, for a nickel, you could do a lot, right up until about 1955, when things got suddenly more expensive, and they haven't stopped doing that since then.

There's a way to calculate the new prices. Five cents then is like five dollars now, which is why I say, "A penny saved is one lousy penny."

Calzedonia Lingerie and other very upscale shops are everywhere along the street.

My family came originally from Ludz, which is today part of Poland, but it has undergone a number of switches in history, first to Russia, then Poland, then back and forth a few more times as wars changed the borders, then finally came to rest as "Part of Poland" once again, to my uncle's great relief and satisfaction.

"Ah," he breathed out, "at last we are part of Poland again — no more of those horrible Russian winters."

The Orb is almost finished, unless I decide at the last minute to tear into the two remaining "dummy" buildings and write a few more sound bites — we'll see how it plays out in the testing today.

You might also be interested to know that "WireTap" has been posted on GoddGames.com, so it's a simple download and you're ready to play this very luxurious and richly decorated Orb of a typical large urban street anywhere in today's world, at the end of which you'll find Chump Towers, built by Ronald Chump, the famous clown who became rich and famous and used all the money he earned as a Ringling Bros. clown to buy real estate and develop it with high-rise towers like the one you'll be running through.

As you run the tower, you'll be tapping wires — tap, tap, tap.

Please note that the word "WireTap" is in quotes on the game cover and loading screen, which of course means that it's not really there, and doesn't refer to anything.

Flo & Jo Slacks & Casuals is one shop you wouldn't expect to stumble across here.

I'm learning how to think in this new "Post-Truth" world, but it doesn't come easy.

Must dash, if I'm to have breakfast before the morning meeting.

Note the vintage window treatments all along the street — not an easy task.

Quick Easter Workshop BlueLine Academy Rundown

April 6, 2017

A full set of these work tools are part of your Easter Workshop packet.

For the first time ever, you get a full professional world-creation system that is easy to use, easy to master and makes fabulous reality environments that YOU can make. No math skills, no programming skills, any artist can use this

INSTINCTIVE system of world-making.

I've made a video of the most basic first introductory lesson in BlueLining technology. The video is being uploaded even now.

This world-making tech is amazing and has several powerful advantages over simple mental imaging and visualization, the most vital of which is that repeated exercise of these actions WILL have a major effect in the spiritual zones, because you are taking actions in the deepest and most enduring levels of quantum mechanics.

Repeated uses of these Orbs will at some point trigger Thalamic or Pineal reactions and a wormhole type gateway could open up within your own brain and hey, like I always say, if they offer a price on your head, take it.

The underlying quantum world is electronic in nature, and so is the 3D GODD® Game-Maker Engine and Editor.

If you go wildcatting around with the editor, you'll never master it, even in several decades. There are just a few, not many, definite tricks to using the GODD Editor, and you need to know them.

First of all, you'll have to learn to refresh your map in order to get a firm update of all the textures and box placements. This is easily learned, but MUST be mastered before doing much else.

Of course, if you don't know how to download and/or install something on your machine, you have a much deeper learning-curve ahead of you. A quick review of your computer, as in, "this is the keyboard", "this is the monitor" and "this is the mouse" will have to suffice. Do try to keep those straight as we plow ahead into the simple mechanics of creating a universe by carving out a section of the Void.

That is what we're doing. The map is Voidness until you define the space within the Void, and fill it with boxes and models and other objects and a number of invisible "operators" that in fact are the things that make things happen.

What appears to be happening in a game world seldom is. Operators are essential, and they reflect the actual magical conditions of the quantum world.

BlueLining will eventually yield some serious answers in that area, but be patient — the teaching comes in stages, meaning that there are some flat stretches ahead.

There are always flat stretches between each peak you've conquered behind you. Those allow you to develop and deepen your understanding at each stage of development.

Completed Project, the exploded view building has been correctly assembled.

So let me lay out a basic plan to lessen the effect of the learning curve on you:

INVOKING THE ENGINE — Ya gotta know where the "on" button is, and how to press it.

REVIEW CAROUSEL — There are 8 screens in the editor, set up like a carousel, operated with the "right" and "left" arrow keys on your keyboard, just to the right of the main buttons; can't miss it.

FIND THE "DOMAIN" SCREEN — You'll hit the "left arrow" key several times to get to the "DOMAIN" screen on the carousel. The lines of the map items will be sort of reddish-orange, if you get the right screen. Check to see which screen is up by looking at the carousel indicator, lower right.

LIGHT UP and GRAB A DOMAIN BOX — You'll mouse over the items until one of the domains lights up momentarily. Find the "Sweet Spot" that allows easy movement of the domain, and slide it up to fit into place where indicated by your instructor.

ASSEMBLE THE EXPLODED BUILDING — When you arrive at the islands, you'll see an exploded-view layout of the parts that make up the Basic GODD Building. All the parts are labeled in the "ID" field, which we'll discuss and explore at clinics and workshops, "NUM1", "NUM2", etc. so it's easy to determine which to move when.

MAKE A SIMPLE BOX — Not so simple unless you know the secret, which is to ALWAYS wind the box clockwise and ALWAYS start the box in the same way, from the bottom of the screen upward, which we will review during classes and workshops.

TEXTURE AND RE-TEXTURE THE BOX — You'll learn how to change the walls, the top and the bottom of the box, and to eliminate textures that would clash with other textured areas, which is a skill that develops over time.

MAKE A CARPET and THRESHOLD — They need to be separate entities, because the shape of the box can only be square, hexagonal or octagonal — never triangular or odd-shaped. Learning how to create shapes is a more advanced level of skill than you'll need here at this stage.

MAKE A ROOF — This requires skills at texturing and fitting.

DUPLICATE THE BUILDING — You'll duplicate the building part by part, then assemble the copy on Green Island, which you get to by crossing the bridge.

RETEX and ASSEMBLE — You'll re-texture the entire building and assemble it to understand how to create apparent differences in similar structures.

ENLARGE and FURNISH — This is the next step in learning how to control the sizes, shapes and textures of your building boxes.

ALTER LIGHTING — The type of lighting can be changed to create atmospheres such as sunset or nighttime scenes.

ALTER SKYBOX — How to use the Skybox to create different worlds.

POPULATE THE SCENE — Learning how to select models and sprites for detailing work without slowing down the playing speed.

PARTICLE EFFECTS — A complex rundown on how to achieve the many particle effects available in the GODD Engine and Editor.

SOUNDBITES — How to use and create soundbites for your levels.

TEXT WRITING — Using the .ini file to create written messages to correspond with soundbites triggered in-game.

ALTERING TOOLS — How to change the nature of the magical weapons in the arsenal.

ALTERING F6 EFFECTS — Creating apparent change in the

general appearance and function of the level and its items.

CREATING A SCRATCH-BUILT — No kit, just the editor and the resources and YOUR imagination and vision. Nothing between you and your result except the limitations you put in your own way.

Here's a quick note that could easily have been handled in 140 characters or less: Joan Baez wrote and sings a song about Trump which reflects my view. She may or may not be aware of NPD symptomatology and obsessions, such as Twitter and Easy Lying and Manipulation, in the form of "projection", which is to say, wild and unfounded accusations of others, unconsciously reflecting one's own actions and views. Love ya, Joan! (She probably wouldn't remember me, but we used to know each other back in the day.)

Using a Gaming Orb to Trigger Magical Effects
April 7, 2017

Gorby's Place is a feature on my quantum version of Nikolskaya Street in Moscow.

One of the most unusual of times is that in which computers exist and games are tolerated, which happens all too seldom, what with the wide variety of repressive governments in place all over the galaxy, but at least for the moment, we can make Orbs and you're allowed to download and install them, although for how long that will be is anybody's guess.

Of course, "approved" games will always be available, but you won't want to play them, and besides, my "games" are not really games at all — they merely rely on a gaming engine to deliver them and make them useful to you.

The object of Putin-Gate is to contact all the Russian spies along this historic street.

I'll explain how they work.

Firstly, keep in mind the two top Laws of Magic, which also happen to correspond to two important laws of quantum physics, namely:

That which has been in contact with something else is always in contact unless the contact is consciously and intentionally broken.

That which is like something else is that something else.

Those two magical laws, the Law of Contact and the Law of Contagion are your most basic quantum tools — tools which enable you to reach behind the facade of the physical universe.

You're probably very happy with your life and with the way things are going in the outside world, but just in case you're just a bit worried about nuclear wars (yes, they happen in pairs) and Biological Warfare Induced Pandemics and the usual string of earthquakes, volcanoes and meteorite strikes, you might just want to delve a little into the world of

StarGates, Portals and Gateways and yes, they're all different, with very different functions and very different results.

You'd be surprised at which Western shops can be found along Nikolskaya Street.

You arrive on the street just as it's beginning to lightly snow in Moscow.

To begin with, in order to utilize any of those portal effects, you need three things in hand:

A real reason to move yourself into a different space.
An easy and effective method by which to move around from space to space.
A way to determine where you're going.

All of these things are available in the Age of Electronics, in which we can throw the whole thing into a quantum scenario on the scale of electronic gaming, which is actually fairly large as quantum effects go.

You'll be quite amazed at the quaint shops and even quainter spies that await you.

We're handling photons and shading them at the edges, so it's a new kind of physics that we're working with here — quantum world physics, which we can control down to the nth degree with our .ini file and our OPHYSON devices.

Sure, it's a little complicated to program in, and it requires a bit of experiential experience personally experienced in order to work in the .ini file, but it comes with time and patience.

Patience is not waiting patiently for something to happen. Patience has no time limit, no expectation of reward, no end point in sight, just endless patience. That's the only kind of patience that actually works.

If you tend to tap your fingers while waiting for patience to come, you're out of luck.

Of course, you can't actually buy anything here, but you can pass notes to agents.

One thing for sure that you can plug into an Orb, and that's a magical effect. There's no limit to the type or kind or scale of magical effect you can weave into the map, but there are some rules you need to follow.

First of all, the NAME of the person, place or thing is the controller. You need to name the target, especially if you're traveling from world to world.

But how to control the journey?

You merely run the Orbs in sequence as given. Each step along the way triggers an actual quantum event that corresponds to what you're seeing on the screen, in Real Time.

Real Time doesn't elapse. It just is.

Frankly, you can have it be whatever time you like. If you want a different time, change the clock. No sense waiting around for the time to crawl on by its own self.

Most folks will never try using a "videogame" as a magical tool, because the head space has it burned in that games are frivolous toys and to be ignored in the larger sense.

This is my little cafe' on Nikolskaya Street. I serve coffees, teas and baked goods.

They're wrong.

This alley is important — one of your Russian contacts can be found here.

Visualization is the key to magic. If you can visualize something accurately, you can "reach" it and work with it.

Visualization takes years to master in the ordinary way, but using the video game format, it's easy to create absolutely any world you'd care to visit.

Sure, it's "only happening on the computer screen", right?

Actually, no. It's happening for reals as it's happening on your screen. The screen only reflects the reality.

You can be sure that somewhere, a LOT of somewheres, your screen reality is actually happening, and that working it on your plane has the profound effect of linking up with the reality that is real.

In short, the linkage between the game space and the real space creates the identity, meaning that they are one and the same thing, at least experientially, although not entirely.

We're still a few months or years away from feeling sensations tied into the gaming environment, but it's definitely on the way, the demand for sensation is always there.

What you see on your screen is an exact duplicate of the original space.

As you move in the space on your screen, you control your movements in the "original" or "real" space, sometimes many such spaces, in a wide variety of alternate realities generated from a choice-point.

Some high-energy choice-points tend to generate a LOT of alternates, but mostly you'll find anywhere from two to five paths leading out of a choice-point in time/space.

Other choices register quite differently, especially on the Causal Plane, not a place to meddle without knowledge, that's for sure.

Changing things just to change them doesn't bode well.

*This c*afe' has been a Crossover Point for many generations of Muscovite voyagers.

Each Orb has within it the necessary magical devices and chantings or mantras to make the space fully operational and in sync with the target space, through simple harmonic resonance, achieved by a combination of items, marked spaces, and actions taken.

In the Orbs you will find a very specific selection of magical tools, such as powders, candles, oils, incenses, books, scrolls, crystals and much, much more, to assist you in traversing the spaces and passing membranes and other boundaries.

You are in a very real sense actually traveling in those spaces, and the magical tools provided in each Orb will actually trigger the same effect in "real" space.

Thus you will see an almost impossible shift in the general shape of things to come, as you learn to handle the quantum spaces. It's about "lag" and "frequency drift" and "nulling".

Those are the important, the most vital, of magical tools at your disposal. All others can be improvised as needed, but these three items need to be LEARNED and MASTERED, not just read about and tossed aside with a polite nod.

This shop carries strange armor and weapons, things that correspond to real things.

If you understand that the name, the shape and the number of a thing determines its "address" and its "handle", then you are ready for the Next Step in Harmonic Evolution.

In short, go ahead and download some of these Orbs and SEE FOR YOURSELF how they work.

Taking actions in this quantum space has the same effect as it would in the "real" world, and when you activate a magical tool in the quantum space, an equivalency is launched in the "real" world.

This "Alias" is used to connect two things together, the "Original" and the "Equivalency".

I commonly use aliases to make a connection between a character and its actions, or between a character and its appearance, and more often, its functions.

The Gold Museum has this Cedar Bar exhibit. You can read the news coverage here.

The Old Cedar Bar Show with Margaret Randall happened over a quarter century ago, but I can rebuild the old bar just as it was and hang the show in there, if I want to recreate the show.

In this case, I reproduced the main pieces and the news coverage, plus some photos of the event, which featured all the surviving members of the Old Cedar Bar New York School of Art, plus many of the museum people who helped make that happen back in the day.

The Old Cedar Bar Show is just one of many such museum exhibits I'm able to put together today, and I'd be doing more of it, if there were a market for it, but it doesn't exist. Everything is "swipe" with an iPhone, and that's all the kids want is their cell phone and their tweets.

It's a different world, a world in which a museum, whether brick-and-mortar or online, is unwanted and ignored.

In my Egyptian Hall, the relics that I've placed there are long gone from my collection, but the photos remain, from which I can make exhibits, just as I did long years ago in the brick-and-mortar museum that no longer exists, in a world where museums are part of a distant forgotten past.

The public has a good memory, but it's short.

With some financial backing, I could mount an incredible display of artwork and artifact relics from anywhere and anywhen, and you could download it and experience it anywhere in the world where the internet is available and some places where it isn't.

In the Egyptian Hall, I placed models and wall textures from relics in my collection.

Thanks to Claude's help, I'm about to acquire an incredibly detailed model of the Kremlin, with which I ought to be able to make some hilarious comedy Orb material — I've already cut the comedy soundbites, a bunch of Trump jokes I made up a few days ago, then ran over to text-to-speech for a really comic effect.

So when you run an Orb, you manipulate certain items, carry things around, place things, drop things, move things, remove things and disappear still other things, all of which carry "bindings" to Real World things.

As Above, So Below. As Below, So Above.

That was the best Hermes Trismegistus was able to do. His name merely means "Thrice-Great Hermes", clearly an alias or a pseudonym if I ever saw one.

It's not yet recognized, but that rule applies equally well in the form, "As Within, So Without. As Without, So Within."

What happens in the game is accurately reflected in the Real World.

This is what you'll be assembling in the Godd Experience part of the Easter Workshop.

On a very practical level, you can create an ordinarily unavailable experience.

Back in the day, my friends Willem deKooning, Franz Kline and my acquaintance — I was scared silly of the huge bully — Jackson

Pollock — alias "Jack the Dripper" to his circle of friends, a small group if ever there was one, used to paint REAL BIG.

Who the hell could afford that much canvas at one time? Each piece was typically anywhere from 15 to 20 feet wide and at least as tall — sailcloth was available in those sizes typically.

There were no walk-in art stores. None whatever.

You made your own stretcher bars, ground your own pigments, made your own brushes and prepped your own canvas.

This street would cost a large fortune to duplicate in brick-and-mortar.

My museum space with all its exhibits would cost in the hundreds of millions of dollars at today's market and cost of labor and materials to build the housing structure and the individual cases and presentation kiosks.

So what's the benefit of having it in brick-and-mortar?

Actually, none whatever. The biggest problem in museums today is not theft, as you'd suppose — it's violence against the artworks.

You need a staff of guards and security people, plus people to run the gift shop, the maintenance of building and of exhibits, conservation procedures and all the business aspects of running a museum, including marketing and promotion — what good is an empty museum?

All that costs money and requires a LOT of people to run it. A virtual museum has none of those problems, and can be just as immersive and fascinating as the brick-and-mortar variety.

European streets tend to be a bit more curvy than American ones, mostly.

You need insurance for any brick-and-mortar venue, especially a museum, tons of it, for those multi-million dollar personal injury lawsuits that crop up in any public venue that is densely populated and has a stream of visitors.

Brick-and-Mortar Museums are very vulnerable.

Online or virtual museums don't have any of those problems, although they have others just as compelling and just as challenging to deal with, not the least of which is where do the visitors come from, and how do they get there?

With a budget of a few hundred thousand dollars, I could build a museum that kids the world over would love to visit in virtual reality.

It would have "celebrity" value in the sense that I would make sure to put in exhibits that were exciting to kids TODAY, not what was exciting fifty or a hundred years ago.

It's one thing to run through an Orb and quite another thing to construct one yourself. It's an experience unmatched by any other experience on this or any other world.

It is called "The Godd Experience" and it kicks you right upstairs into God-Mode as you work, and it does so seamlessly and invisibly, drawing you further and further upward into the higher scales of reality as you work with the Orb.

You'll be learning how to build these commercial shops at the Easter Workshop.

Again, with a bit of funding, it would be very easy to make this experience something that would be commercially viable, but in the meantime, it serves the magical purposes very well indeed.

You can construct any space you like, the more inaccessible by ordinary means, the more likely you'll want to make it in virtual quantum reality, so that means the GODD Engine and Editor, for sure.

Every artist knows how almost impossible it is to have enough shows per year to actually earn a living from their artwork, and most artists don't.

In an environment where the National Public Radio funding is being chopped off, and theaters and opera houses are closing everywhere, there's little chance you'll be able to make a living from art, music, theater, dance, or crafts, but you can try.

One way to get the odds more in your favor is to create your own virtual venue and have shows there.

I have no problem making a new museum every month, with exciting new exhibits at each "Opening".

Having a problem getting your art shows scheduled into galleries?

There's no limit to a virtual museum, but there are definite limits imposed by brick-and-mortar, limits that I wouldn't like to experience again.

The Chenrig Shrine contains models made from some $3.5 Million worth of relics and artifacts, some dating back over 1,000 years. Many of the thangkas are literally priceless and have never been displayed anywhere before this.

Most of the items come from my "Golden Tiger" restaurant and gift shop that my students and I operated in San Francisco until 1922.

Boy, THOSE were the days!

Wilson's 14 Points were on everyone's lips, and it was already getting pretty clear that the League of Nations was not going to have much effect on later events, lest you think you have problems in the White House NOW!!!

You didn't have to deal with some of the freakier Presidents that have passed through the White House on the way to Heaven or Hell, depending on how much havoc they wreaked.

Most of my Orbs are intended as SOLO events, but Multiplayer Mode is available in the Godd Engine, and there are lots of seats in the smaller shrine, many more in the much larger temple.

Chen-Rig Shrine is smaller than the larger temple, but has lots of seats.

If you're a Transit Guide or a Remote Viewer Trainer, you'll appreciate the ease with which your students will master the basic skills necessary to run an Orb with great effect.

Can you imagine what the air-fare and hotel accommodations would set you back if you actually took off and went to some remote temple somewhere high up in the Himalayas?

Well, put away that backpack and canteen. You need only invoke the virtual space and you get the same result as the brick-and-mortar, with hardly any of the hassle and none of the expense.

That Persian carpet I use in my Orbs was for sale in my gallery back in the 80s, at around $35,000 and would be much more now, but in virtual, it cost me nothing but a little of my time to process the image, and a little time to place it in the Orb.

It's your space, and you control it, which means you can load it up any way you like. I use actual objects for my spaces, which are 3D models made by Uncle Claude directly from my original artifacts and relics.

I would never put any of my Tibetan Altar Items up for sale, not ever, even under the most dire circumstances.

*My Oval Office is loaded — some would say "crammed" with magical
items galore.*

Many of them — the large majority of them — came from my
monastery friends who, when they found one of my former incarnation
items, brought it or sent it to me, and of course I did the same the other
direction, and it happens a lot that you stumble across your own relics,
or that someone lays them back on you after a few hundred or a few
thousand years of local time — just a few minutes in Real Time, but
time is SO damn subjective.

Not only can you pray for the President, you can telepathically
direct Waves of Enlightenment in that direction, using my virtual
White House to establish and maintain psychic and telepathic contact.

It's as simple as ABD.

If enough people would actually DO it, you'd have an Enlightened
President, and that would be something you could write home about, if
they took letters there, which they don't.

If you've got an internal problem that you can't quite get at, can't get
a handle on it, why not project it into an Orb and handle it there?

That's the intent and purpose of the Remedy Orbs. They help you
get hold of things that are occult, hidden from you, within yourself, but
tantalizingly just out of reach, tucked away deep in the subconscious.

You can find a lot of goods and services on The Other Side in my

Orbs. One thing I can guarantee, that you won't find any of those things on This Side of The Veil.

There are only two ways you can experience the Afterlife and learn to deal with its sudden and sometimes explosive unexpected events that aren't necessarily unexpected, if you've done your work during this lifetime.

Need a voice in the White House? Just use my virtual Oval Office.

One of those ways is to use one of my virtual Bardo Orbs. The other way is to die.

So between the two choices, "Die Before You Die" and "Die When You Die", which do you suppose would do you the most good and give the most benefit to All Beings Everywhere?

Exactly.

There's no way you could afford the items that come to you in virtual form in my Orbs, nor could you obtain them, because they are never placed on the market, not ever, not these things aren't.

So the only way you could possibly obtain and use them is to get them in one of my magical Orbs, that contains items made from actual priceless relics and artifacts.

So I'll be looking for you to download and USE these Orbs I'm making for you. One of my prime purposes for being here is to demonstrate how to improvise magical tools, such as the Orbs, comedy impressions and gags, theater pieces, dance, song, prose and poetry, it all works, not merely to communicate, but to convey actual magical force.

I offer a variety of post-passage services on The Other Side. I'm listed in the handbook.

You get about $3 Million in virtual magical tools when you download a Remedy Orb.

An Easter Surprise...
April 9, 2017

Exact duplicate of the Darshan Hall at Red House, 1971.

I've long had the idea of converting that gi-normous Chen-Rig Temple into something a bit more comfortable and snug, and this is it.

About six hours ago, I put my back into it, and attacked the giant chenrig orb, taking the best parts out of it, and adding some magic that we didn't have when it was first built — notably the

Beacon and Matrix combo, plus a number of other features you may or may not see or notice.

Since the screenshot, I've added four more chairs, making a total of 15, if I've calculated correctly. If not, then a different number will have to suffice, but I think I'm right, at least on that point.

It's such a relief to be off duty on the Protest Marches and such. I've managed to avoid politics all these 75 years, that is, until now, and as I first predicted, it's getting pretty time-consuming, what with the constant bombardment of "Breaking News" on every channel, just about every hour, including Saturdays and Sundays, which didn't used to be "News Days", but they certainly are, now.

Okay, so there you have it. I have two versions at the moment, one with charcoal-black walls, and this one you see at the top of the article, with walls of solid 1/4" rosewood, just as the original Red House, in Crestline, California, in spring of 1971.

Must dash, ICW momentarily and hypoglycemia says, "breakfast must come first, or something must die", so in the interest of world peace and harmony, I go now to consume mass quantities.

Ready to Give Up???
April 18, 2017

FORT DEVENS ART IN PERSP
DURING AMERICAN

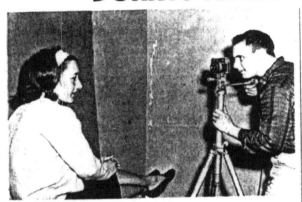

With tl
1 -7), the
to help b
of to find
we must
have fou
way of lt
has put h
Speak
recently
attend (
baseball

PHOTO -- The Crafts Center provides backdrop, lighting, posing
bench, reflector and props for experiments in photography. Many in-
experienced shutterbugs do photo work there. The man at right, PFC
Eugene J. Gold, happens to be a professional photographer in civilian
life. His subject is attractive Jane Pelligrini of Leominster.

Sinc
boast
fine a
to vi
persr
tive
and :
incl
vr

*That beautiful pre-war Leica iii-C was the best 35mm camera I
ever used, and I still have it, courtesy Army Security Agency, Fort
Devens, Mass.*

On Tax Day, April 15, 2017, many tens of thousands of angry taxpayers took to the streets in protest. They pay taxes every year, Donald Trump has never paid a penny of tax in his entire life, and he uses up taxpayer money like water, as you've seen.

Did Emperor Donald take this seriously? Did he see the handwriting on the wall?

Of course not.

My friend Gene Barry was an expert at Third Eye Meditation and no, I'm not kidding.

I told you before, with all due respect, Donald Trump is clinically insane which, if he didn't have his finger on the nuclear trigger, would be no big deal.

As I've said before, he's an NPD, a Narcissistic Personality Disorder, which doesn't listen and doesn't respect or trust others, and there's no cure for NPD, none whatsoever.

Trump tweeted — of course he tweeted, what else would you expect??? — that ALL the demonstrators who marched on Tax Day were paid actors.

Oh, yeah? Nobody paid ME to protest, and I'm protesting plenty, while I still can, because I KNOW that within days or weeks, my ability to do could be seriously reduced by the Gestapo or worse, an Agency Setup.

As a graduate of two Unnamed Agencies and one that appears in my service records, the Army Security Agency, I know what their mindset is, and my continued survival and ability to publish is not among their top concerns.

In short, I'm expendable as hell.

I take a hell of a chance singing songs of protest, writing poems, blogs and video game levels that make fun of Donald Trump, but I've always said, if I'm to be hanged as a horse-thief, I'll at least have the horse.

Gosh, I might hold it against him, but I don't — that Trump has cost me my goddam Golden Years, the years they promised me I'd enjoy after my retirement, but who the hell can afford to retire, and who planned for NO MEDICAL COVERAGE, NO RETIREMENT FUND, NO DENTAL PLAN, and NO SOCIAL SECURITY???

Did you count on having a retirement, or were you just figuring to die young? If I'm lucky, nothing more will happen to me for the rest of my life, but that's not very likely.

I have no retirement fund, no medical coverage, and a small stipend allowance — just $50 a week — to handle my incidentals such as toothpaste and soap, and I'm fighting against the richest bastard to ever take public office and get away with it.

Sure, he'll "get away with it", but on the Other Side, it's KARMIC law that rules, and everyone will — and must — pay their karmic debts before moving on. Jack Burton's truck is not cheap to replace. Karmic debts must be cleared.

No pay, gotta stay.

Actor Jose Ferrer was a lifelong friend and good student of Third Eye Meditation.

There are faster ways to clear your Karmic debt. I highly recommend you do it quickly.

Meanwhile, I thought I'd give you some hints of things you might do to avoid the coming crunch and the nightmare of Trump Amerika and the zombie apocalypse that's headed for YOUR neighborhood as soon as the surface control cracks.

I don't plan to win. I'm fighting a losing battle to give you the time to get out from under if you can. Don't worry about me, get yourself

418

into a safe place — I always do well, in spite of horrendous local conditions, because I transcend them all, and so can you.

Escape from Planet Trump will seem especially important when the riots start happening and you can no longer go out to get food and supplies.

Riots always happen when food runs short, and riots always spell even worse trouble, because they offer an excuse for "The Powers That Be" to call out the National Guard, and when that happens, you get a Kent State all over again.

A what?

Kent State. Jesus. There was a First World War, called "The War to End All Wars" and a Second World War, followed by a Korean War, a Vietnam War, a Gulf War and more, but maybe you haven't been following the headlines. Those who don't know their history are doomed to repeat it.

Tarthang Tulku Rinpoche and I marched in this Buddhist Temple parade.

You need help, and fast.

So every day, I write a new protest song — not to make my own protest, but to show you how to make your own songs of protest.

Every day I sing my protest songs on my morning prayer show, and I'll continue to do that until they come to take me away.

419

Director Joe Pevney and I worked on the Third Eye Meditations back in 1969.

Every day I release new videogames that might lead to the enlightenment of the Executive Branch, and maybe even more widespread than that, if we get our prayer-power stoked up high enough, but you need more than that. You need to escape from Planet Trump, and I'm working day and night to help you to use a technology that is available to you to assist you in altering your lifestream, to cross over to other safer dimensions and alternative worlds, and there most definitely is an effective way to do that, but first, let's talk about Enlightenment Vibes that YOU can help to send to the White House.

It's not about getting rid of Donald Trump — he'll do his own dirty work, and every tyrant contains the seeds of his or her own destruction, according to Shakespeare, and he's usually right.

The whole point of my Active Actions is to bring WAVES of ENLIGHTENMENT into the White House that we work, bringing something positive and higher into the environment, hopefully opening Trump's eyes to the suffering he could easily reduce with a wave of his hand.

Without the Enlightenment Vibes, he's very unlikely to do anything but rip the fabric of the United States completely apart, as his Russian friends would like to see him do.

Donald Trump has the unique quality of seeming to fail, yet if you understand that his entire purpose is to bring chaos to Amerika, then you understand his strategy — well, to be fair, the strategy outlined by Putin in his PUBLISHED plan to destroy the West.

Why do I care? Frankly, I don't.

I'm 75 years out of port and headed for home. What happens on Earth in your pathetic century has frankly never been of interest to me. I have bigger fish to fry than local politicians and politics, and at a place where I can see the light at the end of the tunnel of life, I'm doubly disinterested in anything you can do to try to stop me.

Actually, my actions are all good for Donald Trump, because I offer the possibility of salvation for him. He otherwise would have no chance whatever at Enlightenment, and he knows it.

Donald Trump enjoys my game. I seldom birdie.

And hey, Donald Trump is GOOD for my business — which is admittedly obscure and obsolete, due to a total disinterest in Enlightenment in the local area — and over the past several zillion years of your time, I've seen racists and bigots and woman-haters and cheats and even killers take high public office and nobody seems to notice or care, and Fox News even praises them.

So why mention the elephant in the room, if the only thing it will earn me is a thorough sheep-dipping, a common Agency practice which has the intention of reducing the effect or impact of anything I might reveal under pressure or torture?

Sure, the Agencies use force to obtain information, in spite of anything you've heard to the contrary. They can't afford to fail.

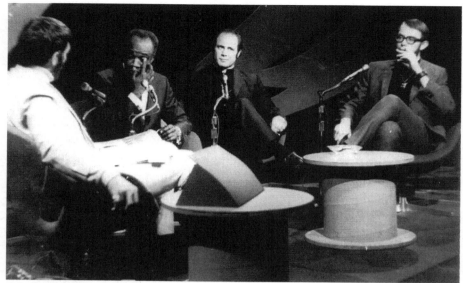

My buddy Dick Dawson (left photo) was a powerful and instinctive Remote Viewer.

It's okay, I've survived it before, and in the end, it serves no purpose, but they have fun doing it, and who am I to spoil their fun?

I have nothing against Donald Trump. I assure you with every fibre of my Being that this is true. He's just another turkey passing through — he's just a great comedy subject, and that's how I see him.

Donald Trump is not the cause of the unrest, he merely takes advantage of it for his own momentary purposes. He has no contact with his other selves, so every moment is as much a surprise to him as it is to us out here watching his wacky, quirky dance.

You can rail against the injustices, shake your fist at the machine, but the steamroller will just keep coming toward you until you're part of the asphalt, and if you stand in front of a tank, the treads will mash you right into the ground.

The tanks won't stop. There won't be any CNN, Fox News or CNBC to cover the news, and give you some media protection. There won't be any media, and there certainly won't be any protection. Big Brother will get you sooner or later.

All protestors will be rounded up and taken away to the Labor Camps, where they will survive on the average about three months. The basic diet is potato-peel soup. Don't believe me? No problem, you'll soon find out for yourself when you end up in one of those camps, and you will, if you live through the zombie apocalypse after the nuclear strikes.

Swami Devananda and I enjoy a relaxing break from a Grass Valley workshop.

The biggest problem facing the new Lords of the West is what to do with all those millions — and possibly billions — of bodies???

It makes no difference. The end result is the same. There's a big swirl of human interaction, a series of escalating events, and then nature takes over where humans left off.

I know what's going to happen. I've predicted it step by step and point by point in "SlimeWars" and "My Life as a Boy", and if you haven't read those books, you're probably still quite in the dark, and frankly, there may not be enough time left to read them cover-to-cover.

Is there a way around this mess? Is there anything we can do to escape the horrors of Trump Amerika and the world at war?

Sure, there is.

The thing is, you can't go anywhere on Earth where it's safe, free from the mobs, the gangs, the unpaid soldiers, the incoming foreign troops, the pandemics and general deadly viruses that sweep the globe, carried by millions of infected troops.

There's nowhere to run to, nowhere to hide.

"Stop the World, I want to get off!" you scream at the driver.

Yep, it's all in my published books, written over half a century ago, and every point is coming true, exactly as predicted.

Chemical warfare, germ warfare, psychological warfare are all part of the history of the 21st century.

My friend, Bill Shatner, had a deep abiding interest in Jewish Mysticism.

And in the end, of course, the Big Payoff, where everybody gets to see what happens when you launch 35,944 nuclear warheads at an average payload of 50 MEGAtons of explosive power in umbrella patterns.

It's pretty, especially from the perspective of outer space. If you're handy at Astral Projecting, you can zoom out through a fast Crown

Exit and take up a position above the air blast to see the whole thing.

Sometimes I think it'd almost be worthwhile to instigate a nuclear war just to see those beautiful mushroom-shaped clouds. I don't want to admit it, but I LIKE nuclear war.

You get the rough equivalent of a giant asteroidal impact, and it will change a LOT of things, including the climate and angle of axis, and it will do so rather permanently.

You'll then want an escape route that involves another dimension, and that's hard to build, expensive to build, and time-consuming if you want to make a passage of more than one individual through the gateway.

For about $3 million, we could build one here, and for about the same money, we could get to a Portal that already exists and is working, although we'd need a way to get there from here, which might not be so easy, and frankly, nobody would have the time to make it there before the stuff went blooey.

That's why I decided to create a series of so-called "Third Eye" triggers that could help you activate the StarGate Within You.

That's right. Deep inside the brain, at the very center of the brain, is the tiny little Pineal Gland, which is a light-sensitive organ that can see outside the brain without using optical fibers and an external eyeball.

This "Third Eye" is an actual eye, a light-sensitive organ, that can actually be "turned on", and is capable of seeing into other dimensions quite easily, and of functioning as a Personal Portal or StarGate that allows you to slip through dimensional barriers and membranes.

In the "On" mode, The Third Eye will open a small gateway that can be used to travel to any dimension or reality stream.

In short, you have a Portable Portal inside your own head, which gives you the power to move from one dimension to another under your direct control.

So why hasn't anyone mentioned it before?

Frankly, they have. They've been telling you this all along, but you've been too busy getting on with your life to listen, and normally, it takes a LOT of work to open the Third Eye and get it to function in this way.

So, now that we're on the Eve of Destruction, you decide maybe you'd better do something about this?

Okay, but realize that turning on the Third Eye doesn't just happen by itself, or by wishing it worked.

It's not like a light-switch, at least not at first. You have to work at it to get the thing to open at all, then work even harder to manage and get control of the Third Eye, then you have to work even harder to learn to use it SAFELY as a miniature Portal, without ending up in the middle of a sun.

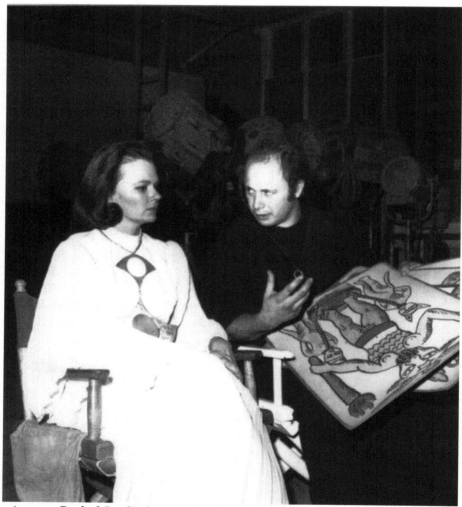

Actress Bethel Leslie learned and mastered many Secrets of the Tarot.

Once you get the hang of it, you'll find it easy to slip from one dimension to another.

Getting the hang of it can involve decades if you use the common spiritual technology that's out there, but you haven't got the time for that, which is why I've cut a few corners.

Thanks to the GODD 3-D Engine and the SuperBeacon, you don't have to learn Creative Visualization. That takes a lot of years, and you don't have years.

I've crafted up some Orbs that will help you to open the Third Eye, and I've designed an Ammy that will help you there as well.

In addition, I'm working now on a Third Eye Portal essential oil, powder, incense, and an add-on unit for your SuperBeacon, which can be used for sidereal voyaging and trans-dimensional jaunting.

Sound can help to open the Third Eye as well, and I'll work on getting some Third Eye Portal chanting, prayers and exercises ready for you to use.

There really is no choice. You must find a way to escape from Planet Trump, and a trans-dimensional Portal is the only solution at this late date, and the Pineal Portal might be your last chance to get out before the zombies hit your neighborhood.

Building a giant super-portal is a great idea, but it would take millions of dollars and lots of time to get it up and working for a large group of people, so the Personal Portal seems to be the best answer at the moment, and that means using the one already inside your head.

In addition, I've tried that tactic before, notably on the Eve of Destruction of Akarra, the chief port city of Atlantis, and the power-possessors end up taking it over and destroying it after they've gone through.

It's like any weapon — you don't want to use a weapon, because it can so easily be turned against you. I always fight open-hand, smiling.

Anything you can do to activate that Third Eye Portal is going to help. I'll get a PERSONAL PORTAL THIRD-EYE OPENING KIT together for you, with chanting, instrumentals, exercises, readings, "promptings", Pineal Shocks, and other Pineal Portal Triggers.

As you'd expect, I've built some Third Eye Triggers into the ABD and other publications, but you can't have enough help here.

I've built a Third-Eye Stimulator into several new Orbs, and I'll be putting higher-energy modulators into those specialty Orbs.

All my efforts now will be to try to provide Third Eye Opening Kit to everyone who needs one.

As I've already said, when Trump decides to ignore the protests of the masses and starts calling the angry mob "fake news", it's time to think about getting out of the way of the zombie jamboree, and with his denial of the reality of the protestors, the time has definitely come to think seriously about where you're going to go, and how you're going to get there.

Robert Anton Wilson and I had many secret talks on the subject of the Illuminati.

Trying to cross borders will be very dangerous and difficult, and at some point, Amerikan refugees will be turned back, only to be killed and destroyed as they stand there helplessly at the border walls, starving and suffering from exposure and sickness.

I don't really want to make such things, or write and sing protest songs or poems. I'd much rather be writing and singing uplifting spiritual songs, as we've been doing for many years, but the situation calls for drastic and immediate response, and that's what I'm doing tonight — working on protective amulets and angelic amulets as usual, but I'll also be experimenting with Third Eye Portal Stimulators.

I hope to have a working model by morning, but we'll see.

I've already got a desktop DOME model of the Third Eye Stimulator, but it's too big to carry around, so I'll be trying to figure out how to miniaturize it to fit into an amulet or medallion.

I might even find the time to compose a new song about Trump's latest tweet, where he denies that the protestors exist by calling them "paid hirelings".

Nobody paid ME to protest, and I'm protesting plenty!

As I said before, even though Donald Trump has ruined my retirement, I have no reason to dislike him, and every reason in the world to be thankful that he IS the new President, because it underscores the need for YOU to immediately master several important Being-Skills that will get you out from under Trump's vicious and relentlessly vindictive thumb.

Orm McGill and I performed a magic show together. He was the greatest.

Is he after YOU personally?
You bet he is.
Is he after me, personally?
You can put THAT on the horses.

I'm old, cantankerous and curmudgeonly, and I don't scare easily. I've died uncountable zillions of times, and here I still am to tell the tale. I'm the last person Trump wants to see persist, but I can't help it — persistence is in my nature.

I have perfect recollection of past lives and future lives as well, and can easily see YOUR future and the future of everyone here, and unless you manage to master the Third Eye Portal Escape, you're not going to like what's coming next.

I organized this protest in 1969, and it made Time and Stern magazines and more.

So how do you enroll in the Third Eye Portal Program?

Well, first you have to SEE THAT THERE IS A PROBLEM.

You're not very likely to actually get off your ass until you see the smoke, but by then, it's far too late.

Would you have done anything before Trump? Ah, too bad. You see, if "Trump Amerika" is your only motivation to use the Third Eye Portal, you won't go very far.

You need a bigger goal, a much bigger plan, and a real grasp of where you are right now in the course of your karmic journey through organic life on Earth, and that'd be a righteous and intense struggle to get through the PLS — Past Life Survey Course, and the SuperBeacon work.

Your SuperBeacon is going to save your ass in the end. Use it well, and use it often.

Soon, your SuperBeacon will be taken away from you, one of many "forbidden objects" that the Trumpists will not let you keep, but don't worry, because you won't remain free for very long under those conditions.

Life is a journey with a series of dangerous and deadly learning curves, and you're on the wrong side of the road.

Keep tuned for developments.

In An Age of Crisis
April 24, 2017

Student protest staged by our comedy group, 1969

3 Questions:

Honestly, have you ever seen ANY President in the news every single day for the first 100 days of office? Have you EVER???

Have you ever seen BREAKING NEWS come in right on top of BREAKING NEWS???

Is this your first world war?

If you answered 2 out of 3 correctly, you should be observing the first of many mushroom-shaped clouds rising on the horizon or just above where you used to be a second ago.

Had you read "SlimeWars" and "My Life as a Boy", you'd know what happened to you when they ask you in the Afterlife how you died.

You won't have to admit that you stepped on a rake.

What Can I Do Now That I See The Shit On The Wall???

Exactly. You find yourself utterly powerless, helpless to stop the insanity, the hate-mongering, the racialism and sexism and anti-semitism and anti-whateverism and fascism and creeping socialism and all the horrific right and left wing "isms" erupting all around us.

The world is breaking up, dividing into little circles of bristling spears and shaking shields, and you're watching in fascination, as a bird watches the snake working its way closer and closer.

The result is always the same.

The people who voted for Trump are happy with Trump, which means that there are a lot more out there just as egotistic and unable to admit they they are wrong than you would perhaps like to believe.

There are far more hate-filled zombies than there are those who cherish the spirit of all beings everywhere.

In short, get ready for war.

While we're waiting for the very first asshole to press the nuclear button, why not use the time we have left to us to do as much as possible to spark the Pineal Third Eye to life?

It's not hard. It's done by "pinging".

Pinging is known today for its role in internet and internal logic system communications. Typically, you send out a coded or identified signal to a specific location or receiver or set of receivers, all of whom may or may not respond to the inquiry with a "ping" or return signal meaning "I got your message, whatever it was".

The ping is like a return sound on radar or sonar, indicating that something is there and that it's interacting in some way with the pinging inquiry signal.

If it's invisible to the ping, it doesn't respond or indicate presence. If it is interactive, it signifies that it is open to further communication on the same channel or frequency.

Telepathic societies don't typically develop radio and television. What need is there? Telepathic societies also don't favor commercials, and politicians can't run for public office without full immediate disclosure, which happens whether they want it or not.

You can't hide anything in a fully telepathic society, and that's a good thing. Human Western culture currently discourages and even prohibits telepathy, and you can see the result, and to anticipate your question, I use the word "culture" more in the bacterial sense than the "civilization" meaning.

By repeatedly pinging the Pineal Third Eye, you bring it slowly but surely to life, and when fully awakened, this gives you full access to the Akashic Records and opens up a voyaging channel that can help you transcend the grittier levels of organic life such as you're experiencing now in Trump Amerika.

The Age of Trump — in his second term and, yes, he's destined for a lifetime as "President" and then "Leader" and finally, "Emperor" or "Lord Trump", depending on which lifeline you follow.

I don't care for any of them, myself, so I stay strictly away from the whole mess. That's easy to do, unless you're trying to survive the ordeal.

If you're prepared to suffer unspeakable horrors, you're probably going to enjoy the 21st century, but I give it a "pass" and prefer to cut right to chase, meaning "let about 600 years go by before returning to Earth", which is my recommendation for any voyagers with travel plans that include the Trump Years.

If I didn't have to turn in a Term Report on Trump Amerika, believe me, I wouldn't step into this pile of bull-puckey for the world, but I do, so I did and will again, even if I have to possess myself.

Possessing yourself is certainly something I would not recommend to the beginner time traveler.

Of course, if you're a spiritual voyager, you can't help but be fascinated by the proceedings here in the 21st century of Earth History 101 with Professor Hrudang, back in the 37th century.

One of the fun things about this time-frame is that you don't have to hide your origins — people are trained to not believe you.

Fake news has always been part of the human condition. The First Great Betrayal a child feels is when they discover that their parents lie to them.

Whether you want it or not, your child or children will grow up admiring ANY President of the United States — it's automatic in the culture, and that President will be famous in future history as the most despised of all U.S. Presidents, but he'd be the first to tell you that history is fake news.

While you're waiting for the nukes to go off, why not send for these fabulous items?

LAST-MINUTE HOLOCAUST WEEKEND SPECIALS

All prices are net. Prices are good for the duration of the war, which will certainly last for at least 20 minutes or so — wing it, do your best. If currency is an issue, send meteoritic H6 Martian or Lunar samples. All Registered Jellyfish, Any Federation Workers or Observers, and Off-Worlder Watchers are entitled to place their off-track bets through the nearest Portal. I'm giving 32:1 odds that the humans will fuck it up within a year. Any takers?

Pineal Pinger Embossed Copper DOLLAR SIZED Medallion — $89.95

Pineal Pinger Embossed Copper HALF-DOLLAR SIZED Medallion — $69.95

Pineal Pinger Embossed Copper QUARTER SIZED Medallion — $59.95

Pineal Pinger Embossed Copper NICKEL-SIZED Medallion — $49.95

Pineal Pinger Sterling Silver Crystal Radio Amulet — $225.00

Pineal Pinger Household SuperBeacon Plug-In Add-On — $375.00

What is a "Geronimo" Amulet?
April 28, 2017

We had such fun our last season in Atlantis, too bad about the little accident, eh?

I thought it'd be nice to explore something besides the constant news from the White House, but it's impossible to ignore the very clear and very present danger from many sides — North Korea, Russia, Syria, Iran, Washington D.C., and of course the UFO Menace, to mention only a few.

Easiest way out?

There's only one answer. The original Atlantean Bug-Out

Amulet, which I call the "Geronimo" Ammy, because that's what you'll yell when it operates. It works only the once, and only when activated by radiation. I'll tell you more at the end of this little dissertation.

There is no local safety net, nowhere to run to, nowhere to hide, and even if you succeed in escaping Trump Amerika, being an Amerikan Refugee will not earn you a gold star in the years to come, when you've landed elsewhere where "Amerika" is just a myth out of the long-lost distant past, as it is in the 37th century, where I have to present this as a term paper, and they're gonna think I made all this shit up, but nobody could.

I'm bringing some proof in the form of selfies, and I've left stuff at various locations to dig up later when I get back to the 37th century and out of this Mickey-Mouse Sim.

Selfie at the controls of an Atlantean Stealth Bomber, circa 42,000 B.C.

The same exact thing happened to what is now called "Atlantis", where I once had a very successful import-export business and later, a very well-respected art gallery on the Via Apta, near Castle Shadow-Gard in Megatho, the weekend resort city just east and south of the capital city of Kar-Zhakh.

Most people assume "Atlantis" was a city located on a "lost" continent or island that sank into the sea as a result of a giant earthquake, but Atlantis the EMPIRE was actually a network of tribute kingdoms and a central government at Kar-Zhakh, a port city on a wide basin of what was then dry ground. It had a unique circular harbor that had several defensive levees set up around several concentric perimeters.

Atlantis as an Empire was never at war after the Second Period of the Middle Kingdom, about 24,883 B.C. and contrary to Plato's second-hand report garnered from later Egyptian sources, did not embark on a war against Athens, which did not exist as more than a tiny and remote colonial coastal town at the time.

On the Eve of its Destruction, Atlantis had many remote settlements and entire countries that were under its dominion, actually colonies rather than tributaries, in much the same way that England had its Empire and Commonwealth, and Japan had its Co-Prosperity Sphere and Russia assembled by conquest its version, the Union of Soviet Socialist Republics, a wild misnomer, if ever there was one.

Selfie at the scene of mass destruction during the second flood.

So with a deft twist of a dial on a cellphone, you will someday be able to find out your main Family and Clan in the ancient world during the Atlantean Period.

The Atlantean Period was from about 42,000 B.C. up to about 8400 B.C. — predating all known generally accepted historic records.

Atlantis started as a small sea-faring community somewhere off the present coast of Spain, but well within the coastline of the ancient world, when the sea-level was much lower. The ancient seaports are today sunken under many fathoms of water, but are quite accessible to divers.

The raising of the water level at the time of the Great Glacial Meltdowns left the ancient port cities about 270 feet underwater at this present time.

Hundreds of ancient cities now lie underwater due to the rise in sea-level at the melting of the glaciers and polar cap ice floes. More ancient cities lie underwater than on dry land. Over 240 ancient cities have been recorded and mapped in the Aegean alone, and more are due to be discovered in the Black Sea, which did not exist until after the flood, along with other major bodies of water.

Many islands were once part of a much larger mainland. This is true all over the globe — in Asia, Africa, South, Central and North America, Europe and most profoundly Antarctica.

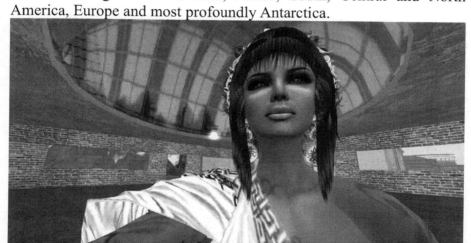

With a Student Pass, you could go from Bartha Romo all the way to Khora City.

The railway systems were much better than they are now. For one thing, you didn't have that hard ride on metal tracks, because all the trains were suspension drives, which is how you build a monolithic building, of course, but the technology winds its way all the way through Atlantean Society.

I have a cosmetic set that uses suspension drive technology, but I don't dare use it.

If you could find a map of the coastlines of the world before the great glacial meltdown sometime in 12,443 B.C., you could note the easy targets for populations — the natural harbors, bays, inlets and natural barrier reefs and other refuges from crashing surf that were at that time right on the edge of the waterline. In short, look for the ports and harbors that were at sea-level at that time, and that's where you'll find the evidence of lost civilizations, plus tons of gold, more than you could believe possible.

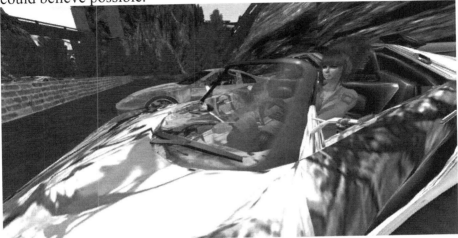

High-Power High-Speed water sports were all the rage in the Pre-Flood world.

Atlantis in the beginning was a city-state, and for a long time, from about 44,000 B.C. until about 24,000 B.C. it remained a city-state among other similar city-states with a very large human population worldwide, with many colonies and tributaries around the globe, including the pre-ice continent of Antarctica, a state into which it is again due to return.

You will find more and more Atlantean Civilization tablets and stones as divers are able and willing and motivated to dive down into the ocean to explore these ancient ruins.

Imagine building such ruins deep in the ocean on the ocean floor, hauling 150-ton blocks of neatly dressed stones underwater, placing them and doing all the things you do with buildings, all underwater. Can you imagine doing that, even with modern diving gear?

Sure, maybe one such underwater town, it's possible, maybe even a few, but not hundreds of underwater monolithic structures, some of which are actually entire towns. So there's your "proof" if you need it, that the water level was once lower than it is now.

How large were the cities of Atlantis? Very large. Seeing the crowds in New Delhi, New York, London, Tokyo and Chicago, with a little practice, I'll bet that you could estimate the size of the town's population, with just a momentary glance at the compression and pressure of the crowd. My best guess for the major cities is about 50,000 to 300,000 for the biggest, the Empire's Capital City, Kar-Zhak, located at its major port.

Estimating the entire population of Atlantis Empire, with all its tributaries and colonies and hegemonies would be a wild guess, but I'll say that it was a total of several million people worldwide, about the same as the citizen-population of first-century ancient Rome, if you didn't count the slaves and freemen, which I never did, and still don't, and neither should you, if the Word of God is anything to go by.

I stayed at the Mu Motel, just to be able to say later that I'd been there.

ATLANTIS CITY-STATE
Early Period:

Adamu Period — 400,000 B.C. - 43,874 B.C. — High Civilization of City-States powered by very high technology culminates in Nuclear Wars about 43,874, measurable by radiation testing of several areas worldwide, such as Mohenjo-Daro and Puma Punka, among many other nuked ancient cities and centers of civilization. Many of the ancient aircraft mistakenly identified as "Nazi Wartime Propaganda" and "WunderWaffe" weapons are from this period of lost history and civilization.

Assur-Pad-Em Dynasty — 43,874 – 43,545 B.C. — Clan Wars following the Atomic Wars of the Adamu Nations, many returned to cave-dwelling and underground tunnel cities. Long period of darkness and atmospheric disturbances.

Assur Bani Dynasty — 43,545 – 38,864 B.C. — Bronze Age Settlements, beginning of large monolithic building projects, many of which were lost during the Warring States Period that followed the destruction of the harbors at Kharzhum on the Mainland, now underwater. The breakwaters are still visible in some spots.

WARRING STATES — Interregnum — Collapse of trade routes, Warring States.

Assur Enko Bani-Pan — 38,854 B.C. – 24,104 B.C. – 24,036 B.C. — "Great Pacification".

Air travel was easy and cheap in the very ancient world before the second flood.

Middle Period:

Kar-Dash-Mem Dynasty — 24,036 – 22,877 B.C. — Southern Expansion into Antarctica, which was ice-free at that time.

Tuti-Moseh Dynasty — 22,877 – 22,574 B.C. — Expansion into Indonesia and Asia.

Ankha-Mose-Shem Dynasty — 22,574 – 22,224 B.C. — Restoration of the Crown.

Ut (Regent) unknown dates, Second Warring States Period, loss of some Atlantean colonies in the Shaggat Wars, later regained during the Second Colonization.

This fabulous palace was built by Kar-Dash-Mem, the founder of the dynasty.

Late Period:

Tem-Ma-Ah Dynasty — 22,224 – 22,003 B.C. — Airplanes, gliders and hot air balloons.

A-Mem-Sah Dynasty — 22,003 – 22,724 B.C. — Age of first Colonies in Central America. First ancient commercial air travel, earliest known state-run gambling casino and hotel.

Sheh-Nam-Sah (Vice Regent) — unknown dates, plague years.

Kor-Esh Nam-Sah (Vice Regent) — unknown dates, plague years.

I took this Selfie at my palace — the small one — in the coastal resort town of Taru.

FIRST KINGDOM:

Teph-Na-Neph-Ra — 21,221 – 20,200 B.C. — Rise of the Triad and Crystal Technology.

Em-Na-Sheh — 20,200 – 19,080 B.C. — First Triad Tower used as public Temple.

Ka-Mem-Tose — 19,080 – 19,020 B.C. — First use of StarGate Technology, commercial interdimensional travel, personal UFO, robot immortality with Thalamic Transfer.

Ep-Nem-Mose — 19,020 – 18,723 B.C. — First Colony established on Mars, mining operations for H3 begin on the moon. Prospectors ignite Gold Rush on Ganymede and Titan.

Musa-Na-Ram — 18,723 – 17,874 B.C. — Raxical StarDrive and StarGate Tech, Rule of the Hiborns, introduction of the Atlantean Caste System with 18 separate and distinct castes representing various levels and states of Spiritual Attainment.

I just wish you could see the beautiful, enormous sculpture behind my head.

SECOND KINGDOM:

Shura-Mem-Tose — 17,874 – 16,221 B.C. — Robot and Nanotech developed.

Akh-Ankh-Sha-Moseh — 16,221 – 15,040 B.C. — Age of Radio and Radio Wave Tech.

Ab-Dadur Ank-Ra — 15,040 – 14,974 B.C. — Golden Age of Television. First SitCom.

Deb-Neb-Ra-Mekher — 14,974 – 14,884 B.C. — Great Harmonization.

This was my in-laws home 14,224 B.C. — I would never decorate like this, believe me.

EMPIRE ATLANTIS:

Sna-Nef Dynasty — 14,884 – 14,224 B.C. — First Telepathic Contact with off-world aliens and time-travelers.

Ah-Mosat Dynasty — 14,224 – 14,074 B.C. — Development of Longevity and Immortality.

Josad Dynasty — 14,074 – 14,000 B.C. — Great Period of Prosperity and Power.

Sirahfah Kingship — 14,000 B.C. Great StarGate Emigration.

Khufud Dynasty — 14,000 – 12,443 SECOND FLOOD, Total Inundation of most coastal and port cities that are now about 300 feet below the present sea-level, and the sea-level is actually continuing to rise even now, which will eventually lead to the loss of cities like New York and Miami in the so-called "modern world", not so modern from the perspective of the 37th century from the comfort of my access module into the 21st century simulation in which you presently live.

This selfie at the fountain almost cost me my iPhone from the splash.

ATLANTEAN COLONIES THAT SURVIVED THE SECOND FLOOD:

On the Western Rim of modern Sicily, several colonies, placed on what was then the highlands, survived the flood, and are now on or near the present seacoast, along with several colonies set up in North Africa on the grasslands to the west of the River Nile, under the direction of two colonial governors, Horus and Seth. See "Sons of Horus" for details.

Several colonies survived in the Americas, resulting in the Olmec, Aztec, Maya, Zapotec, Toltec and many other New World civilizations that culminated at around 900-1100 A.D. and represent the most successful of the various efforts to preserve the Atlantean culture into the post-flood period, which is now.

Best way out of the present danger is the ever-popular "Geronimo" Radiation-Sensitive Gold-Foil Ammy that automatically sends you through the nearest shift at the first sign of a nuclear attack — the blast and alpha, beta and gamma radiation.

Up until then, it does nothing but sit and wait for that event. In case you're thinking it's ridiculous to suppose such a thing, remember how far-fetched Donald Trump becoming President was, just a few months ago by human reckoning.

Lots of Atlanteans made it out, and you were one of them.

Your job will be to re-start civilization, then get out of the way for a few thousand years, while it re-matures into something hopefully a little less mean and violent.

How to get a "Geronimo" Last-Minute Bug-Out Ammy? You ask for information. I won't post it publicly.

Trump's Presidential Reality Show
April 29, 2017

Portals are everywhere, if you need to leave Earth rather unexpectedly.

Why do I endanger myself by speaking out? Believe me, it's far more dangerous to remain silent in the face of tyranny than it is to stand up and be counted, and that's what you should be doing today, marching in Washington.

My whole family decided to march with the pro-environment

people today. They're planning to join the Peoples Climate Movement's March on Washington and even now, as I write this, they're only four miles out of Seattle!

If you think back on it, there hasn't been a single day — actually, not a single HOUR — during which Donald Trump dominated the news and created breaking news his own self. His whole purpose seems to be to stay at the top of the news, and he manages to do just that, if with nothing else, his zanier and stupider tweets.

There's nothing like a puffed-up bigot making more complaining noises than a garbage truck on a formerly quiet suburban street, at five o'clock in the morning.

In Russia, the sentiment is "Enough Trump!"

Even THEY are tired of seeing his little squinty eyes and puckered mouth shouting stupidities and struggling with real and imaginary enemies on all sides, plus top and bottom.

Poor Donald says he "misses his old life" and finds being President "harder than he expected." He in fact thought it would be as easy as his reality show, and frequently returns to his campaign mode in a pathetic attempt to gain "ratings", the only means by which he measures his success.

The real problem is not with Trump — he's a victim of his own chat-bot programming and can't help what he says, does, thinks or feels.

The virtual Black Falcon can actually trigger a real-world transdimensional effect.

If you're looking for something other than a chat-bot in Donald Trump, you'll be wasting your time and effort. The little red switch on the back of his head tells the story.

Frankly, a conscious being could never do that job. It calls for a certain brand of insanity to even WANT to be President of anything, much less the Untied Snakes of Arnica — not an enviable position, and I'll tell you why.

When you're in public service, your time is not your own, not even for a minute. There's someone wanting something from you every single minute of every single day, and there's a long line of people waiting their turn to have a chance to get to you for one thing or another.

You don't even decide what to eat. Political rectitude demands that you conform, and conform you will. If you haven't been raised in the royal manner, you won't find this very comfortable, and may resent having people dangling all over you and groping and grasping at you from a circle of followers and media people that seems to follow you everywhere, like the "Peanuts" cartoon character "Pigpen's"perpetual cloud of flies around his head.

Real Portals and Gateways are nothing like what you see in Hollywood films.

Your daily routine consists of an endless parade of minor administrative and public relations duties — a chore you share with the British Royals and many other heads and shoulders of state.

"You don't feel well? Take this pill, Mr. President. It's time to shake the hand and pin on the medal of several veterans over at Walter Reed Hospital. Right after that, we'll be receiving the Ambassador from Bosnia-Herzogovina, then on to the White House Lawn Luncheon with the Auxilliary Ancillary League of Illegal Young Republican Voters, then we have a news conference. You'll be dining with the French diplomatic corps tonight. There's no news coverage unless you tweet about an hour ahead of time."

And that's just a rough idea. It's actually dozens of vital everyday encounters and handshakes and camera nods and smiles and handshakes and group shots and personal mementos and "sign this, sign that and that's so-and-so, the French diplomat, that's Fred Wilson, a lobbyist for the estate of Genghis Khan..."

Grab a seat at the counter of Grampa Henry's Diner, if you want to really get away.

Like all jobs, from the outside it looks glamorous, but I've been around every block in this and every other universe, and you can take it from me as gospel truth that it isn't glamorous at all.

It's downright boring, and intrusive and demanding and in the end, everything you do is upset and overturned by the next administration.

Politics is like building a modern city in the midst of a jungle. Good luck. Given time — and there's plenty of it without humans — the jungle will take back its own.

Nothing will remain, not even the slightest trace, of YOUR passage through time and space, even if you reached the pinnacle of success and power, such as becoming the dictator of North Korea.

This virtual shrine awaits the voyager who wishes to attain enlightenment.

Napoleon's dying words were "Tete d'Armee", meaning "Head of the Army". Wow, swell. Gives you real bragging rights when you hit the Apres-Vie, eh?

Head of the Army. Makes you wonder, don't it? But maybe not as much wonder generated as with the last words of Queen Elizabeth the First — "Another minute, please. I have forgotten my Last Words." And sure enough, she had.

In those days, people memorized what were to be their last words. Frankly, from the viewpoint of the collision of the Andromeda Galaxy and the explosion of the Sun while the Andromeda Galaxy is ripping through the Milky Way Galaxy, even YOUR last words lose significance somewhat.

It might be time to examine what DOES survive the complete and total destruction of this and every other universe?

I mean other than black holes and gravity. Those manage to survive in much the same way that rats, cockroaches and ants seem to make it through every major meltdown I can throw into the mix.

Creative destruction? Sure, it can be so.

We watch with fascination and horror — and if you're on my side of the Veil, some amusement — Trump's march toward total war and mayhem. It takes the pressure off of him, and creates an illusion of success to have military strikes.

I use this transmitter at the Bardo Station in the Ashram to influence Donald Trump.

It shows strength.

Telepathic transmission is just like Remote Viewing — it's easy, once you know how.

Strength, yes, but it also shows stupidity. The chat-bot has no clue, no big picture, just a series of knee-jerk reactions and automatic verbal expulsions and internal logic confusions. In short, sooner or later, someone will order his troops to start shooting — maybe a pre-emptive strike.

It's always based on the wrong idea that anyone can truly win a war.

It can't be done, but you'll never convince a warlord of that. Negotiations may continue over decades and even centuries, but eventually both sides must come to terms, so long as both sides persist.

Of course, with total annihilation comes total agreement.

It goes without saying that humans have always chosen the path of total annihilation — the totaler the annihilation effect, the better, according to my very objective observations.

I'm planning to redecorate this restaurant to look like a gigantic hamburger.

What that translates to on a practical level is genocide.

I won't go into details, which you already know quite well, but you start by making the men watch you kill the children, then it gets worse from there.

The end result is that the earth around the conquered city-state is then thoroughly salted so that nothing will ever grow there again, and every single occupant is slaughtered without mercy. Thousands of years later, the place will still be a ruined desert.

And this is the magnificent race that expects to be admitted to the

Federation so they can spread their poison throughout the galaxy.

Frankly, I voted against disclosure, and I'd do it again.

It's not just that humans would freak out if they learned the truth about off-world alien presences on their little mudball, although that is a powerful consideration. It's even worse than that.

What could be worse?

Agrippa built this temple for me back in the day, and I still use it in virtual today.

I'll explain. Human beings regard ANY new genuine scientific breakthrough — such as the sun is the center of the solar system, there are exo-planets out there and humans share a large percentage of their DNA with pigs and chimps — as a potential threat to their religious beliefs.

What that translates to is that if the Earth is not the center of the Universe, there can't be a God.

Another equation seems to be that if Jesus died on the cross, and there was no resurrection, Christianity is void and useless.

Nonsense. That's all based on organic life, physical reality, mass and energy stuff. You need to transcend. Can you fucking hear this? You need to transcend, and now. Do it.

Get out of the box just a little, and you can see that nothing physical will survive the end of the Universe, nothing.

If you lived to be a billion billion billion years old, you'd still die at the end. You need a better plan than surviving through building hotels, motels and supermarkets that bear your family name.

You need to transcend, and in the present situation, rather quickly, or you may not get a chance to transcend at all.

Transcend the organic with the new SuperBeacon Pineal Popper Plug-In!

Meanwhile, the radical right, radical left and radical middle want to pull it all down and press the nuclear button and make it all go away, and what the hell can you say in the face of that deep level of organic superstition?

Most of the barriers to science are put in place and kept in place by a variety of religions. State religions are in general organized to keep the population under control without the use of force.

It works pretty goddam well, if you ask me.

2,000 years of total control of the Western World's population and half the Eastern World's population too — that certainly tells the tale, and up until recently, it was DEATH to mention that the Earth is round.

In some places, it still carries the death penalty to discuss nature, science or medicine. Actually, in the United States of America, you can get the death penalty for bringing up the subject of Donald Trump in a public forum.

Yeah, it's dangerous to speak your mind in Trump Amerika, downright dangerous, and you could actually be killed for speaking your mind at a political rally, and believe me, it WILL happen, although it hasn't yet, not in this time-frame, but like I said, I've seen this all before, and even YOU will start to feel the Deja-Vu of it all pretty soon.

Forget all about the stupid psychology, politics and intrigue, and just TRANSCEND.

You see, the crux of the problem is that Donald Trump thinks that the tricks he learned running a reality show on television will work pretty much the same in the office of President of the United States, but boy, was he wrong, and he knows it now. It ain't a pretty sight, and 100 days into his sentence, he's already feeling trapped.

Yep, I said "sentence". He's serving time for karmic deeds done in the ancient past. Almost every former citizen of Atlantis is here today in America, waiting for the same result.

Well, my resources are somewhat limited. I have four basic characters from which to design what looks like a lot of different kinds of people, but isn't really — it can't be, so I use skins, many different skins, over the same models.

I have limited the number of animations in humans because they were too laggy, so you'll notice a certain absence of — well, of stuff you used to do, but don't anymore, for no obvious reason.

How much is enough? I own an 18 hole golf course, but just the one.
Who needs more?

President.

It should be the same in politics as it is in business, but it isn't, and can't be, for a variety of reasons that you could learn if you must through the nearest socio-anthro night course at your local city college, but it's the kind of thing I leave alone.

Like psychology, once you start digging in the mud, you never run out of hole.

President. Like I said before, it looks real glam from outside, but it's gritty political shit from day one until you walk out of that office for the last time, your hair a lot grayer or whiter than it had been when you walked in.

The Oval Office ages you about five years for every year you spend there.

One of the most miserable things about public service is that you're serving the public. If you think you understand what I meant by that, hang on.

Conquer the universe. So what have you got — going forward at the end of the day?

If you've ever worked in a retail shop, food shop, restaurant, bar, department store or run messages as a courier, done bicycle repair or watch repair or handled a car-wash, you'll know what I mean.

"The Public" is a general term, a slurry kind of blending of nameless faces and waving hands and self-important revelations.

"The Public" is avaricious, capricious and deceitful, and in general has no idea what those words might mean.

A few paragraphs ago, I mentioned that the problem is not with Donald Trump, and I'm quite prepared to prove that thesis.

To begin with, he has no agenda, which makes him an automatic candidate for the next election, doesn't it? With no agenda, he can make sudden changes, turn on a dime, switch allegiances and swap ideologies with his other personalities, right?

It makes things so much easier when you have nothing in mind, and he certainly fits that description.

And Trump misses his old life. I'll say he does. Ever live in a public library? That's what it's like in the White House. If you've ever been there, you'll recall the echoing hallways, the cold, brittle feel of the place, the hotel-like atmosphere.

Well, upstairs it's even worse. The only relief is on the back stairs to the private kitchen, but that's out for Trump — he's used to Room Service.

So how do you Transcend the organic world, anyway???

In fact, Trump's whole life is lived as if he's permanently between airplanes, and as President, with his very own toy airplane, it's even worse.

Don't forget that this is a kid who was KNOWN for his passion — playing with toy soldiers. Actually, he has something in common there with Vlad "The Impaler" Putin, and his other friend and playmate, Kim Jong Un.

Between those three, you can expect at LEAST one or two nuclear explosions over helpless civilians, and it could go either way, north or south or both.

Gosh, won't the Great Mother be pleased?

I think so, and I'm fully prepared to take the credit for this coming conflagration, but as much as I'd like to, I can't. I owe it all to Chaotic Science.

Chaotic Science is something I introduced a number of gaming seasons ago, to create a sense of impartial randomity to the game of life.

Problem is, it really DOES generate randomity, and I can't seem to turn it off, so I suppose that, according to the Rule of Gates, it's a feature.

Don't worry, you won't have to pay extra for it. This kind of feature we include free.

You can use your Amulets together with SuperBeacon and Matrix to Transcend!

One thing that might occur to you in these "horrible times", as Trump so poignantly indicates in his latest tweet, is that although you might personally suffer greatly from all the miseries imposed by ruthless politicians, bankers, industrialists and other chaotic evil characters, I'm having a ball.

What's more, the ball is perfectly round.

In the Real World, everything you know is illusion, just a sparkling atom in mid-air.

What I mean is, why not use this horrifying opportunity to benefit all beings everywhere?

Okay, but how?

First of all, download Oval Office. Then learn to direct its energies to influence the Oval Office toward Enlightenment and Right Action through powerfully directed telepathic prayer.

You have the experience of directly contacting the Oval Office. You'll never get through on the telephone, and your tweets will be ignored, but your telepathic influence will be felt and will eventually have an effect on Trump's actions, attitudes and understanding.

Of course, the more folks who take part in this spiritual experiment, the more powerfully and rapidly the effect will occur.

Transcending doesn't include solving the world's problems. It's built to be worrisome.

You should be seeing changes in Trump's attitude and behavior toward minorities, and a profoundly changed Trump in relation to the intelligence community and the diplomatic services.

Frankly, even though I introduced the magical shamanic tool by which a permanent peace can be achieved, I hope it doesn't happen, because if it does, I lose my dollar bet that the humans will blow themselves to kingdom come before the aliens can complete their harvest.

Yes, harvest. What, you thought they were your friends? Well, they are. They need a wide variety of effluvia for their experiments.

You assumed they were adults? Humanoid? Vaguely like yourself? Give up.

You have very little chance of solving the Great Puzzle, but you do have the opportunity in human incarnation to try to assimilate and transcend the material world.

It isn't impossible, but you do have to actually START.

Virtual and Actual Realities are easily linked with Quantum Entanglement.

It's sort of compulsory to be "in motion" before you can be helped. Did you know that?

One way of getting in motion is to help others to find the Path to Liberation. All it takes is a gentle indication, and while you're online, perhaps a "share" or "subscribe" or "log in" will do the trick.

In order to have greater power, you need to assume greater responsibility. The response part comes first, then the power, don't you see???

You can expand your work circle by the simple expedient of sharing, and you now have a whole social network, actually thousands of networks, on which to do it.

You needn't do anything strange, unusual or out of the ordinary.

Just as you go about your business, notice opportunities to "share" and "comment", and DO IT.

Passing through the Dark Hours of the Night is easy with a SuperBeacon and Plug-ins.

Actually do it.

If you mis-type something into the computer, although they're building them to do exactly that, right now the computer can't anticipate what you might have meant, except in very strictured patterns of likeness/unlikeness.

What they do is "get in the general neighborhood" of what you might have meant, then they ask you, "did you mean ....???", allowing you to click or not click, as you choose.

Well, not actual choice. Choice dominated by and determined entirely by your DNA, right down to the language you use, regardless of what language you speak, human, animal or divine.

In short, you are what you are, but you CAN Transcend.

I'll be giving you some hints on how to Transcend, so you'll be able to use this historic period, this wonderfully dangerous slice of time-space, for your spiritual attainment.

What is spiritual attainment?

To me, it's the ability to perform angelic tasks without complaint, failure to perform or expectation of reward.

How's that for motivation?

Try "no expectation of reward" on your chat-bot humanoids and see what you get.

"Are you crazy?" they'll shout, "Work without expectation of reward? What kind of payoff is that???"

Transcending Tools are available, but you have to actually USE and APPLY them.

And that's where you can quietly Transcend the whole mess.

Don't go Hollywood on me here. "Transcend" doesn't mean to walk through a misty glowing glob of super-imposed graphics, nor does it mean to take the easy way out.

Transcendence is, well, Transcendence. Ask any passing Buddha for help if you get stuck.

I Have No Voice
May 4, 2017

Wouldn't you love to work in an ancient Egyptian temple of your very own?

I have no voice. It doesn't bother me, but it's quite noticeable. When I speak, write, sing, act, paint, draw, sketch or sculpt, there's no measurable impact on anything or anyone. I'm not a tweeter, but if I were a tweeter, I could literally tweet my ass off, but nobody will read it, and that's just fine by me, or it was fine, until Donald Trump's name became a household word, like "slopbucket".

Whatever it looks like, however it seems to you today, Donald Trump is NOT an obstruction on the Path to Liberation, not if you know the secret.

What is the secret?

I'll tell you right off. Live the good life. Don't allow yourself to become distracted. Relax, stay calm, it will all work out just the way it should.

The universe is a sim. There's a script. If you keep that in mind, you won't fall off the horsey. Donald Trump is not alive — there's nobody inside that thing, behind those cold, icy eyes.

He plays his "overwhelm" game and seems to be winning. His friends in Congress have their own nasty games and merely use him to gain advantages on their own ground.

You don't need to know any of that. Just remember that ALL POLITICIANS ARE CROOKS and that ALL GOVERNMENT PEOPLE ARE MEAN AND NASTY, and that ALL POLITICIANS AND MEDIA PEOPLE LIE ALL THE TIME, and you won't be knocked out of your socks the next time you find yourself shoved into the ditch at the side of the road.

When Donald Trump tweets, billions of people are affected by every careless word. The difference between me and Donald Trump is our choice of weapons. I selected "voice" and "guitar" and he chose "nuclear holocaust" and "gas chamber".

Trump is a hero among his worshipers and followers. They like Strongmen and Dictators who will step in, clean up the mess, restore them to their former glory, and give them personal favors and benefits, and that's Donald Trump in a nutshell, at least on paper.

He knows he doesn't have to actually KEEP his promises, just make them and blast right along claiming "victory" at every punch-down. Just keep insisting you won, and eventually that becomes the truth, at least to the general public. They have no memory and no discernment whatever.

As a matter of fact, they don't really care about the details, just what's in it for them.

Each faction of politics, news media and science has its own direction to pull the chain, and the general effect is one of chaos and mayhem, exactly what Putin and Trump both had in mind.

If the U.S. government can be shut down permanently, Trump can rule, and that is "Plan A". Plan B involves an actual invasion of the homeland by Russian airborne troops, and that's already in the works, as soon as the defense department can be unraveled.

How do I know all this?

Actually, I know a LOT more, but won't say, for fear that it will be abused, misused and misconstrued, which is the usual bill of fare on this particular "pre-war" menu.

There HAS to be a war, a shooting war. Why? Because boys will be boys, and human beings have NEVER failed to use a weapon that they had, no matter how horrible, and evidently the rule is, the more horrible, the better.

Like I said, I have no voice. Maybe a dozen people will even read this, and out of that dozen, eleven will forget what they read the minute the next sentence pops up.

I have a blog. Most folks don't have a blog. Some are on Facebook, and that gives them some voice in a small circle.

Some have a BIG voice in the social media. The biggest and loudest and screechiest and most needful voice right now is Donald Trump on twitter.

Sure, everybody's on twitter, but Americans aren't used to watching their President wipe his ass on public television every single day, sometimes three or four times a day.

He has to be in the news, even if the news is negative. This guy has NEEDS. It all goes to feed a massive ego.

Have you ever heard Hitler's speeches? Trump just had a "power mike" installed on his speaker stand, so he now can sound EVEN MORE LIKE ADOLPH HITLER than he had before this new technological miracle with its very own voice conditioner built in, simulating the actual voice of Adolph Hitler, but with the accents and modulation of Donald Trump.

What a boon to science.

Oh, not the modulation mike, that's been around a couple of years already — no, I'm talking about Donald Trump being a boon to science. He's the only surviving unmodified Neanderthal.

Study his shape a moment. His face. His shuffling walk, and grunting speech patterns, and you'll see unveiled before you the original form of the Neanderthal. What an opportunity for study for some brilliant anthropologist who needs to publish or perish!

Wow, I'd write the paper myself, if I were a few years younger — say, fifty-five years younger, or so. At 75, I'm not looking forward to much, and living in Trump Amerika is not my idea of how I want to spend my Golden Years.

Ah, but my revenge is sweet. Do the math with me:

Trump is 70 years old, going on 71. Sure, 60 is the new 50, but 70 is NOT the new 60, nor is it anything like the new 40. 70 is 70, and 75 is 75. My revenge? I'm living on a beautiful farm, with wonderful people all around me, and we're celebrating the universe with higher entities and higher consciousness.

That's how I'm spending MY Golden Years.

Trump is living in the White House, which he hates. It's a poor estate when compared to the lavish life-style he had before, and he has said that he sorely misses his old life.

He used to be the boss. Now, he's a salaried, elected public servant, and he doesn't like it much. He says publicly that the job is harder than he thought it would be. Poor baby, if you can't take the heat, stay out of the kitchen.

He used to wench and take all sorts of medications. Now, as President, he can't do that anymore. Too many people watching him all the time.

But that suits him fine on a psychological level, because he's deathly afraid of being alone, being in the dark — the rule at the White House is, all the lights on, all the time — and he's mortally afraid of dying.

As rich and powerful as he is, the Grim Reaper favors no one, and he's close enough to the natural finish line to realize that he hasn't much time to do whatever it is he's going to do.

His drive was to obtain power. He has it. His total drive now is to hold onto that power forever, and you can expect every and any dirty trick he can muster to that end, because this guy USES dirty tricks.

Yep, Trump cheats.

He's actually proud of it. He'll pull out the Electoral College map and show you how and why he won, even though Hillary Clinton received 3,000,000 — that's three MILLION — more popular votes than he did.

"Popular Vote" means the vote of the people, the actual vote of the people. They threw out the Popular Vote in favor of the Electoral College Vote, which threw out the real result and substituted the one that the powers that be wanted to put there, and the Amerikan public just rolled over and died, like they always do.

Like I said, Donald Trump is 70 years old. He doesn't look as if he's taken good care of himself — sorta looks like the roast beef and beer kinda guy with gout and a touch of egomania.

He has to live in what amounts to a public library, meet dozens and sometimes hundreds of people every day, he has to perform public duties every single day, most of which are horrible little slices of emotional appeal for the news media.

He has to eat food that at best rivals that of the lunch counter in your local gas station, and is forced to meet people he'd have crossed the street to avoid as a private citizen.

He is NOT a private citizen, and does NOT have some of the rights of a private citizen. He is a public servant, an elected official, and he is NOT above the law, nor is he above the law of social dynamics.

He does NOT have the right to toss something into a crowd of diplomats and then duck out the door, but that's how he has conducted himself on the international scene every single day so far.

Like I said, I have my revenge. I'll gladly take my Golden Years on a quiet farm in the country, raising chickens and cucumbers and performing my spiritual practices in stunningly beautiful natural settings, sharing my days with folks on spiritual retreat or healing circles, eating wondrous foods that have no sugar, no salt, no red meats, no harmful fats — well, you get the idea. Good, clean healthful food that tastes super good.

My days are quiet. I listen to the birds, to the insects, to the hum of daily farm life, to the sounds of the Cosmos under the Cosmic Vortex within which we live, and my Golden Years are, indeed, Golden, even under the dictatorship of Donald Trump.

His wild antics are amusing. Do they affect me? Not at ANY age, but particularly now, they don't. Sure, I have no medical coverage, no income, no retirement fund, nothing. But I am far richer than Donald Trump could ever be, in his chat-bot world of phony handshakes and poison smiles.

Let him live there until he finally freaks out. Would it surprise you to see him resign because he didn't like the job, or have to be carried offstage ranting and screaming? It could happen. With a disjointed complex personality disorder of that magnitude, you can't rule out anything.

It shouldn't affect you. There are a few things you can do, maybe not on the magnitude that you'd like or that we can do here, but something can be done on every level.

I'm assigned to a Vortex. I'm stuck with that job, but it's a good one. If you like your job, it's not work, it's fun, and that's what my job is, it's ALWAYS fun.

My secret? It's not what you're doing, it's the company you keep.

That goes double on the higher levels' right up to the Causal Plane. It's the company you keep. That really IS the Great Secret.

As Above, So Below is only half the Key. As Below, So Above is the corollary, and it's something you need to keep in mind if you're to operate the Emerald Tablet Keys, ever.

Your retirement time, your so-called "Golden Years", are your LAST CHANCE to enjoy the fruits of whatever labors you've been doing to survive all these years. Remember that Donald Trump does NOT care about you, just your money and your vote.

Don't let Donald Trump steal YOUR Golden Years. IGNORE THE ASSHOLE. Carry on, keep moving, just go about your business. If necessary, STOP WATCHING CNN and all the other news channels.

Just forget that there IS a Washington, D.C., and forget that there are people there who are on a daily basis PLAYING WITH YOUR LIFE, for the singular purpose of getting elected or re-elected.

In the case of a lobbyist, it's even worse. They WANT YOU DEAD, where your vote can be controlled. Lobbyists are the bloodsuckers of government. If Jesus were around today, he'd kick over their tables and drive them from the temple.

Forget about the government. Forget about Donald "Asshole" Trump. Don't even listen to Stephen Colbert's oral sex jokes about Donald Trump.

Pay no attention to the uproar and the fire and brimstone with North Korea, Syria, Iraq, Iran, Russia, China, the United Nations and Alabama.

Believe me, in 4.3 billion years or less, nobody will know, nobody will care.

YOU will still be in the game, but you won't be on the Earth. Just do your work, focus clearly and cleanly on your higher spiritual work, your daily practices, among which might be:

Folk Guitar
Angelic Chorus
Embossed Copper Protective Medallions

474

Telepathic Enlightenment Prayer
SuperBeacon Contact
Healing Circle
Ashram Work
Art Project
Pineal Ping Exercises
Past Life Survey
Virtual Temple Building
Sharing, Commenting, Chatting

Don't get sucked into the daily circus. Stop watching the deadly snake as if you were a helpless bird. Get out of the loop NOW. Just turn it all off and walk away.

FORGET ABOUT TRUMP. IGNORE TRUMP.

Use your Golden Years well. You're NOT in the White House. You DON'T have power, you don't have a voice, nobody follows you, nobody listens to you, nobody cares and there's nobody out there who gives a damn about you and your personal freedoms, and that's a fact.

So what? Big deal.

I personally own my own virtual Taj Mahal, Great Pyramid of Giza and the Brooklyn Bridge, and I can build an entire city, even an entire planet, if I want to, with the GODD® Engine. You can't measure my wealth, but it doesn't stop in the virtual.

I live a conscious life, a clean life, a virtuous life of service. Can Donald Trump say that?

Of course he can. He can work his mouth at full speed, without ever engaging the attention. Actually, watch him, and you'll notice that he can't remember what he just said a moment ago. He's exhibiting early onset, and nobody seems to notice.

Forget about Trump. Let him live his Golden Years in a building that feels like a public library without the warmth of the marble floor and tiled ceilings.

Take a good look around at what you actually have, how you actually live, what you actually do from hour to hour. You'll eventually realize that you never needed any more than you had to get where you are right now, at this very moment in this very spot.

You always have everything you need to be where you are now.

Live a conscious life in the higher realms, spend your days in the Ashram and in meditation, give your life to the Teaching. The alternative could be horrible — endless wealth, power and fame. If you like MacDonald's burgers and fries, that might appeal to you.

Ignore Trump. That's the best revenge you could ever have. Be unaware of Trump. Live your life. Do your work. Trumps will come and Trumps will go.

One thing that will come from your PLS — Past Life Survey — work is that you will have the definite impression that this has all happened before, many, many times before, and it's always the same, with the same outcome.

Pay no attention to the ruckus in the world. Stay focused and do your spiritual work while the world erupts in violence around you.

Of course, it helps if you're in a circle of protection directly on the site of a vortex. I always like to have an Ace in the Hole, don't you?

Escape From Planet Trump
May 5, 2017

Tired of the old runaround? Don't want to be directly under the nukes when they go off in your hometown? Have an aversion to being roasted alive by a mob of fear-crazed zombies? Maybe it's time to take another look at your escape route off of Planet Trump.

I know, I know — I said "no more Trump shit", and I meant it then and mean it now, but...you have to have some idea of what to do while you're waiting to be taken away to the nearest labor camp "to save your life, and give you food, medicine, shelter and protection".

From then on, you work until you die.

Watch as one by one, your freedoms are taken away. Coins and dollar bills will be the first to go, as all currency is controlled through the cloud, through computers that first determine your exact present location and identity, then pass the transaction through.

There will be many blocks, many obstacles, many obstructions on the path to liberation, but there always are, and sometimes they are so in-your-face that they can't be ignored.

I can afford to ignore Donald Trump forever, but you can't, and in all conscience, I can't remain silent, much as I would prefer to.

Taking stock of the situation, the likelihood of a North Korean nuclear warhead missile dropping on this particular farm is very slim. Possible, sure, but real slim, unless Kim Jong Un gets hold of some of my remarks, which some wiseguy is just bound to deliver sooner or later.

You might be safest under the umbrella of peace around the Ashram, but nobody can afford healthcare, much less YOU-CARE — the care and feeding and housing of you and your family.

North Korea is a real threat, and you can bet your bottom dollar (that means "your last dollar") that Kim Jong Un will use his pretty new weapons and sharply aggressive troops to achieve his ultimate aim, "To make North Korea Great Again". Sound familiar?

Do you have any sense at all of "deja-vu"???

How can I predict that Kim Jong Un will use nuclear weapons and provoke a nuclear war?

It's not all that mystical, although I'd sure like to pretend it is. No, sorry — no major telepathic skills employed here, just a vague memory of a 37th century history textbook that I barely cracked open and can't remember very much of, quite frankly, because 21st century history is not that exciting to me.

North Korea.

Gosh, can you imagine having this huge marching army, slavishly obeying your every command, just waiting to get a chance to show their military skills and courage, and NOT using it?

It's especially tempting if you come to believe that you can somehow win a war against the entire world, and that describes the situation in a nutshell — "nut" being the operant word here.

So eliminating the airburst over the farm, there's still the bright flash in the sky from over San Francisco way, over yonder. Don't look at the flash, if you want to keep your eyesight.

Then there's the economics — who wants to buy arts and crafts when the world is ready to blow apart?

Just about everyone I know — and that runs into the high thousands — is waiting for the bomb to drop and the storm troopers to be knocking at their front door, because they're Jews, Muslims, Catholics, Something-Americans and "other".

The politicians are too greedy for power to listen to the sounds outside their vaulted chambers, but the people are starting to growl, to do more than just clench their fists. They're starting to look around for some way to express their rage and fear.

Politicians tend to ignore them until they're right there on the steps, bearing pitchforks, torches, hot tar and feathers.

What's more, they never seem to learn. They do it over and over again, with unremitting greed and arrogance, never for a moment noticing the harm they're doing.

So, what are we left with?

I don't know about you, but if you're in the same boat I'm in, you're in a real pickle. Should the impossible happen, like Donald Trump being elected President, and the medical bill passes the Senate more or less unchanged, it means for me the following:

Should I become seriously ill again, I will not be covered.

I have no solution for the impact of this bill on me and my family.

I will have zero income — my social security is presently wiped out by medicals.

I have no plan to seek medical aid.

I will probably not make it through long enough for the repair bill to pass.

If I don't have a medical catastrophe, and instead, I'm taken away for singing my protest songs, I will return, but not in this body.

The NUMBER ONE RULE of medicine is, "Do No Harm".

That rule is inflexible, and is the very heart of the Hippocratic Oath, the Oath of Hippocrates, the ancient founder of Western medicine. Do no harm. The medical bill passed by the House yesterday does plenty of harm, and some of that harm it does to me, so I figure it's time to push back.

For 75 years, I've managed to stay neutral, never said a political word, and still, today, I care nothing for politics and even less for politicians, whom I consider liars as a class, roughly equivalent to lawyers, but without the deep ethical considerations you'd expect from a barracuda or a shark.

A research lab in this area recently stopped using rats and started using lawyers for their medical experiments. I asked them why, and they explained, "You get so attached to rats".

Should the present bill pass in the Senate, it takes roughly $530 billion out of the public benefit and puts it directly into the pockets of the small group of billionaires with whom Trump loves to pose for the camera.

So I'm going to do more than merely demonstrate how to write a protest song. I'm planning on taking the creative writing course all the way through "how to apply protest songs" and "how to publicize protest songs" and more, at the upcoming workshops and clinics.

How to write a song? My personal choice is to write about something worthwhile, something lasting, something spiritual and in the realm of perfection.

Problem is, some of my friends in our spirit circle are now living in fear.

Those who live in other countries won't know or feel or sense what I'm saying here, but we're not used to feeling like a target when we go out onto the street, into a mall, or to a popular restaurant or concert space.

If you're dark-skinned, you'll feel very different about walking through a crowded street now than you did before Donald Trump became the dictator of Trump Amerika.

There's a sense in the air that you dare not question or ridicule the President. This is the first tiny step toward a military dictatorship that can actually happen here, and probably will, if nobody stops it.

Fear, fear, fear, permeates the atmosphere, far below the radar of Trump and his power-mad cronies. They won't feel or notice the upsurge of outrage until it's right there in the face of Trump, Congress and the world.

I'm not predicting! I'm remembering my 21st century history lessons, and so far, I've been right every single time. Want proof? Look at the publication date of SlimeWars, and realize that it had been in private printing for 20 years prior to that, and there it is, all outlined nice and neat, all coming true, bit by bit and piece by piece, just like it says in the book.

I always prefer to sing songs about consciousness and self-realization, but I will continue to sing the protest songs for as long as Donald Trump pushes me and my friends around and threatens our lives for the sake of more tax benefit money for him and his billionaire friends, as pictured in the now-infamous photo of the people responsible for the rise of the American Resistance, which I'm here to observe — some would say "watch" — to determine the causes of the movement for my next semester's new course, "Ancient Civilizations of Human Origin".

Don't even think the thought — I've already published that post-graduate thesis, back in the 37th century, and in this climate, you wouldn't stand a chance to get a grant on a project as speculative as that might seem.

I'm very sad to say that many of my overseas friends really can't understand why I lean on Trump so heavily, why I'm doing all this stuff.

IT'S NOT ABOUT TRUMP, DAMMIT!!!

It's not about the President, or about Congress, or about anything specific. I'm trying to demonstrate the basics of creating a protest songbook, protest video game, protest poem, and protest play or musical, among other peaceful protest tools.

My whole intention is to make sure you have and can use the peaceful and constructive magical and shamanic tools that are available to you, and I want to make absolutely certain without a doubt that you are aware of those tools and have access to them.

It is so important that you NOT GET CAUGHT UP IN THE MOB. I know it's tempting to grab up a placard on a two-by-four and get out there on the street and march, but it's always the same — it always ends up in violence, and nothing is gained.

As a matter of fact, you hurt your own cause.

It's a notable fact that, whenever people riot, it's not against the rich and powerful — they tend to burn down their own small businesses, to destroy their own homes, and to lay waste their own neighborhoods, are you aware of that???

Every action has an equal and opposite reaction.

Take out Archduke Ferdinand so Serbs will be treated fairly? Good plan, but it resulted in the mass wipe-out of tens of thousands of Serbs, then some 75 million people in the First World War, then many millions more in the plague that followed the war, carried by the troops, same as what happened in the Black Plague, carried by the Mongol warriors into Europe.

Don't go marching with the mob. Don't give in to the Dark Side. By peaceful means, everything can be settled. No need to be mean, no need for aggression. There's enough for everyone, if nobody gets greedy.

So what magical tools can you use to survive the Trump Years???

First of all, my original intent was to demonstrate some easily mastered and applied magical technologies for handling bad situations without violence or anger.

The first thing I demonstrated was that YOU could personally telepathically direct healing and Enlightenment Waves into the White House through the Oval Office and throughout the building.

This has nothing to do with specific occupants. Anyone in the Oval Office is in dire need of Enlightenment, wouldn't you agree?

Okay, then we explored other ways to use the situation for your spiritual development, and I was quick to point out that at the very least, Trump's policies and temperament and dangerous psychological disorders should prompt you to do your spiritual evolutionary work pronto, and stop diddling around.

As of right now, you haven't time for that.

So the second usage would certainly classify as "lighting a candle under the ass of the spiritual candidate for initiation". It makes it REAL that your time is limited, and who wants to live under a dictatorship, anyway?

I have a number of very important technologies, such as Crystal Technology and Portal Technology and Radio Wave Technology and, of course, Telepathic Technology which includes Remote Viewing and Astral Projection.

Those are just a few of the otherworldly technologies that I'll be making available to you as a direct result of the emergency status of the planet at this time. I would not otherwise be able to introduce those technologies, so I suppose that's one positive result.

Stay in touch. Telepathic communication is best. Learn Telepathy from the very best telepaths in the universe. I'll tell you how to do it, at the very next workshop.

Transcending Political Shit
May 7, 2017

LeslieAnn at the Crisis Healing Center in the Ashram.

When the shit piles up too high to walk over it, and the piles of shit are too close together to walk between them, you're in seriously deep shit. What's happening out there is NOT about politics. It's NOT about religion, and it's definitely NOT about health care or women's issues.

It's simply time for the peasants to prove that they are revolting, always have been and always will be revolting. Why can't the downtrodden just stay down? That's the Smerconish

Response — just shut up and take it on the jaw — liberals should lie down and die.

I'm not a leftist, nor a rightist. This isn't even my goddam planet, monkey descendant. Frankly, I think you're all fucking nuts, and I'm not at all happy to be living here among you, watching you squabble and fight over crumbs, while the fat ones glut themselves on your food, and drink your wine, while you writhe in hunger and the pain of betrayal.

Other than that, I could give a shit what happens here.

Suffering and pain is easy to repair. Misery and heartache and guilt and recrimination and fear and horror and disgust are harder to deal with, but manageable. It's the marketing angles I can't figure out, and I'm looking for some help here.

I'm here to finish a history project. As an alcohol-intolerant, I'm damned if I can figure out just how the hell I'm supposed to determine exactly which bar was the location of the fist-fight that ended history, I don't know, but here I am to tell the tale.

I'm supposed to leave notes that can be found and dug up back in the 37th century, but I have to be careful not to leave them where there's too much radiation, and I can't remember where the airbursts went off, or that is, are going to go off, in the Western states, although I do remember that I was surprised at the cities that were hit.

I have copious notes on the election and aftermath, but I frankly still don't know what blows the Resistance into a Rebellion, but I do know that it started in a bar somewhere, as a fist-fight between a Republican and a Democrat. This much is certain, the rest is lost to history, thus I have a viable term paper, and if you hand over the chocolates, nobody gets hurt.

I have it on good authority — Aristarchus of Samos — that human beings are incapable of actually feeling pain. Democritus says that you'll never really know what someone is saying to you, and Marcus Tullius Cicero in 45 B.C. said, "Times are bad, children no longer obey their parents, and everyone is writing a book."

Look, I never cared whether times were good or bad. I've lived through the best of times and the worst of times, and here I am to tell the tale. It's the fact that everyone is writing a book that really gets me down.

Well, go ahead, write the books. I've got a better idea — TRANSCENDENCE.

484

How does it work?

Transcending can't be done as a hobby, nor will you have much luck if you're a total loner. You need to find some help, and work to dig yourself into a magical defensive position in your own home town, or find a safe magical refuge somewhere that nobody is interested in exploiting, attacking or despoiling.

You don't want to see a swarm of humans destroying a field of wheat while looking for food, but that's going to happen, and a lot more things like that will happen.

Human zombies are made by fear, and fear quickly turns to anger, and anger looks for a scapegoat — a victim — and that'd be you, if you happen to be standing there.

Animals can't be reasoned with, and you're facing wild animals. Reason will do you no good. They are NOT listening to you or to anyone else. They will attack you and listen to nothing.

It hurts? You feel pain? They feel nothing.

Nothing you can say will change anything. Nothing you can do will change it, either. You are in point of fact, totally helpless, and you will go down when the shit hits the fan, count on it.

You CAN survive it spiritually, but you need to find some help, like I said, and fast. Help comes in the form of a small group upon which you can depend, on whom you can count to be at your back when the going gets rough, and rest assured, rough it will get. You need a support group, but how to find one?

First of all, you need to ACTUALLY SEE the difference between a BOT and a NOTBOT.

If you can't yet do that, you have no hope of finding a support group or surviving the coming events.

You need to learn the Essential Skill "HOW TO SPOT A BOT", and fast — you haven't that much time left before the nukes start dropping. I estimate that at least 50,000 weapons were detonated during the first half of the 21st century, at an average yield of 50 MILLION TONS of TNT EACH.

That's a grand total of over 2 BILLION pounds of TNT, which, believe me, is a hell of a lot of force, enough to re-set the Earth's axis, and it does.

According to my 37th century history textbooks, the massive nuclear exchange creates an enormous planet-wide cloud cover that lasts for a few years, and that's what I really want to talk about —

mushroom farming in the dark. There's no better business to be in, when there's no sunlight to grow food.

THE MUSHROOM GROWER'S PACKET

Yes, that's what this is really all about, the marketing of my Mushroom Grower's Packets — you get everything you need to start your own GROW IN THE DARK farm. Find out more, before the air-raid siren becomes too much of a distraction.

Luckily, you'll be able to sell your mushrooms with the new lack of laws that prevented you from selling produce to passing motorists, only there won't be any motorists.

If you do your homework and get through the PLS — Past Life Assessment — Course, you'll have the tools you need to survive and weather the storm and come out on the other side in a civilized manner, not as a meat-eating cave-dweller, which is what happened when the world-wide Atlantis civilization went down in 8400 B.C.

You want to keep your home safe from the coming Zombie Apocalypse. It's not the government that you should fear, not the Russians, not the Chinese, not the North Koreans, not the Terrorists, it's your neighbors that you are learning to fear.

In this atmosphere of division and hatred, people turn against each other, even against their own family and friends.

You'll want a Protective Bubble around your home, and there are several ways of doing this, among which are the two plug-ins I've made to fit the SuperBeacon. I have both of them in the "Always On" mode, placing a Trumpenite Crystal in a dome somewhere near the center of your home, and placing KEEP AWAY charms on all the windows and outer doorways.

Of course, if you're ranting and raving and wildly gesticulating about this nightmarish and outrageous human rights obscenities scene we're subjected to every single day on every single news channel, as I've been doing since a few days into the rule of an insane person in the White House, you can't expect those protections to have much effect, and I don't count on them as much as I do on my smooth-draw Boise holster.

Don't wear 'em to town, but nobody says you can't wear 'em at your writing desk. It gives me a sense of confidence that I only had when I lived — and died — in the Old West, back in 1878, a year I'll remember for some time to come.

You can wear or keep nearby the Bug-Out Ammy, which activates on Nuclear Blast, and there are a variety of TFZ — Trump-Free-Zone medallions and charms available, and some you can make yourself.

Don't try to convince anybody.

This is not a good time to argue reason, rationality or responsiveness. This is NOT a time of reconciliation or of interspecies relations. It is a time of conflict, of war, of anger, of terror, of fear, fear, fear.

Are you afraid to speak out?

When have you ever been afraid to say what's on your mind, here in Amerika? But now you ARE afraid to speak out, and rightly so. The goons own the field at the moment, and they will destroy you if you dare to question their leader.

Well, fuck, I'm 75 years out of port and homeward bound, so eat it. Do whatever you want, but I WILL have my fucking say.

Like I said, don't try to convince anyone of anything. I have no political position, other than, "Leave me the fuck alone," and "Don't Tread On Me".

For a full 75 years, I've never said a word about politics — couldn't care less. But when the liberties of the people are stunningly swept away by arrogance and greed, I can't remain silent, can you?

At the same time, I don't really want a confrontation with a bigot.

So I'm constructing TRANSCENDERS, using crystal and radio technology to help you get out of phase, and STAY out of phase with organic life on Earth. This reduces your chance of becoming a target.

The creatures who elected Trump will never stop until the final button is pushed. They don't see or understand the swelling ground of rage and fury that's building up in what they now call "The Resistance", nor do they much care.

Their lives are spent marching in robot circles.

Nothing you suffer is of interest to them. You could die for lack of health-care which they supported, and they wouldn't feel the slightest tremor of remorse.

Your baby could die because you haven't the money to save the child. This I HAVE SEEN in hospitals, back in the 1960s, and it's happening again.

Women are disrespected by all Conservatives, and this will result in the long-predicted war between the sexes, right alongside the Second Civil War, of which we are now at the eve.

Soon, the resistance will grow beyond control, especially when some of them die horrible deaths. Outrage will spill over into action, and the streets will, as they say, "run red".

Can't happen here?

I can provide you with a list of the times it HAS happened here before, but damned if I'm going to do your homework for you.

You need to ESCAPE FROM PLANET TRUMP, and I have a number of ways and means to do exactly that, and I'd be happy to share them with you:

ASTRAL PROJECT — Astral Projection can take you far from the strife and misery of Trump Amerika, and you might get some interesting glimpses of safe passages through this already-existing emergency.

DO YOUR SPIRITUAL PRACTICES — Keep yourself balanced and calm through the use of your spiritual practices and exercises. Don't allow yourself to get swept up in the passions of fear and violence that are now the major force in Trump Amerika.

HANDLE YOUR MEDICAL EMERGENCIES ANOTHER WAY — Can't afford health care? That's always been a problem for the lower and middle class, and one of the ways that it has been solved in the past is to give up hope of medical care and find some way to handle it yourself, without a doctor's help, relying on the power of prayer.

LIVE IN ANOTHER WORLD — Spend as much time as you can in our Virtual Ashram, with friends who will treat you as a Being. Keep in close contact with your Soul Group in the Ashram.

DON'T LEAVE HOME — If at all possible, stay at home. Order out, buy online, stay away from restaurants, public meetings, malls, street fairs, or anywhere that a truck can be driven over innocent pedestrians out for a stroll or a shop or a meal. If you're in any way different, stay off the street. Live life at your computer screen until Trump Amerika goes away, which might not happen very soon. Be prepared to live alone in total isolation.

KEEP YOUR COOL — Don't allow yourself to fall on either side of the division between liberals and conservatives — try to see the point of view of someone who genuinely feels that women are inferior and to be treated the same way you'd treat a farm animal, and who thinks the Holocaust never happened. If you really think that, you owe me 18 family members who died in Auschwitz and Bergen-Belzen. I have a photo of my stepdad just after Liberation — he weighed 88 pounds and had survived on a diet of thin potato peel soup, for upwards of a year since his captivity on December 24, 1944. I'm fully prepared to create a Holocaust of my own on THAT subject, so don't tempt me. It's been years since I was an instructor at Ford Ord, but I haven't lost any of the skills, even at this late date.

IGNORE THE INSULTS — In this atmosphere of racism and sexism and rightism and leftism, you'd be wise to ignore the words they fling at you. Of course, if someone actually threatens you, that's technically "assault", and if they lay a hand on you, that's technically "battery", in which case, I believe you're entitled to wipe them across the asphalt. In video gaming, you'd never let a domination stand, and that's where I go, right to the windpipe.

GET ABOVE IT ALL — Use whatever spiritual technology you have available to you to help you protect your home against outside attack. Your Transcendence Gear will help you achieve this, but it's YOUR diligence that will save the day.

FIND A WAY TO LEAVE — If you can afford to leave Trump Amerika, you should do it, before they come to take you to the labor camps to spend the rest of your life repairing the infrastructure.

SPEAK OUT WITH COURAGE — Don't be afraid to speak out, even though there are many bullies out there, who would silence you with violence and fear. Violence can be turned, and fear need not rule your life.

DON'T GIVE IN TO THE DARK SIDE — Even if you have magical skills and have spent time staring at goats, don't give in to the temptation, even though it would be easy.

DON'T DEFEND, TRANSCEND — No point fighting. The zombies are going to win. Get above it, beyond it. Move into the spiritual realm and stay there until the end.

PRAY FOR PEACE — Get yourself hooked up into the Oval Office Orb, and join others who are telepathically directing Waves of Enlightenment into the White House.

STAY VERY, VERY STILL — Stand or sit or lie down and remain very, very still for as long as you can. Say nothing, breathe very softly, and clear your mind.

CALL IN THE NEAREST ASTEROID — No, sorry, that's MY plan. You don't need to do anything about it — it's already too late.

"That's your whole plan?" you ask.
Yes, that's my whole plan.

Trump is Good for MY Business!!!
May 8, 2017

My business depends upon an Afterlife, and Trump is working hard to fulfill my needs in that area. For a flourishing Afterlife, there must be a LOT of business. In the meanwhile, let me inform you of several items you might find of interest in these challenging times:

BUBBLE OF PROTECTION — $125 to $3,500. A VERY powerful CHARGED Meteorite, of varying degrees of impact and origin — $125 to $3,500 depending on type, size and market valuations. Comes to you ready to use, in a genuine handmade oaken base with a genuine hand-blown crystal-glass dome. Approximately 3½" high, 3½" wide, 3½" deep. No catalog, these come and go as quickly as in a single day. You need to inquire about available items and/or give a wish-list for various mineral and gemstone properties.

LOVE GENERATOR DOME — $225. A brand-new assembly of powerful shamanic magic and crystal technology to create a zinger of a Love Generator, generating the Force of Love throughout your home. The effect is greatly enhanced by a highly skilled Feng-Shui placement of greenery and a water feature within the home. Send me photos of your space and I'll try to help you fill it with Love Power. Mounted in a beautiful handmade crystal glass and hardwood dome. Guaranteed.

LIVING ROCK CONTACT PORTAL DOME — $350. Works as a direct linkage between yourself and your Guardian Angel. Money Back Guarantee. Warning: This WORKS, so no complaints when it does. Comes in a stunning handmade crystal and hardwood dome and base.

TRUMPENITE DOME — $125 to $3,500. Large, incredibly beautiful raw crystalline mineral specimen of "Trumpenite", a powerfully charged Actual World-Renowned Shamanic Gemstone that you won't believe until you actually SEE it. Must be seen to be appreciated. It has been charged and programmed to repel any Trumpness of any kind, within the boundaries of your household, to include any yard or fenced area, plus your den or garage. Comes to you in a fabulous crystal and hardwood handmade dome and base. Supply EXTREMELY limited.

OSCILLATION OVERTHRUSTER — $225. No, I'm not kidding. This is the Real Deal. You get a plug-in add-on for your SuperBeacon, enabling hands-free REMOTE VIEWING, and this is REMOTE VIEWING MADE EASY! You plug it in, and you're automatically in

R-390 RECEIVER MODE. There's no faster or easier way to Remote View than this! You can use it from anywhere within a 90-foot radius, and that includes upstairs and down, basement and garage, so it definitely falls within the realm of your Shaman Shed or Private Meditation Garden, in most cases. Mounted in Crystal Glass Dome on handmade hardwood base.

CIRCLE OF PEACE DOME — $225. Beautiful Specimen-Grade Crystal Quartz set into a RING OF PEACE, mounted within a stunningly handcrafted hand-blown crystal dome with a hardwood base. It radiates with HARMONIC RESONANCE WAVES, powered by the Big Bang and Population 3 Star Bursts, to give you a 90-foot CIRCLE OF PEACE within your home, garden, garage or anywhere within that radius. Works wonderfully in a medical or dental office, and can be a big boon to any retailer with an unknown crowd.

AKASHIC LIBRARY CONTACT DOME — $225. Learn the secrets the ancients possessed. Direct contact with the Akashic Record Database on the Causal Plane. Anything higher requires a security clearance and a need-to-know and no, I'm not kidding — ask any angel. Comes to you in a handmade crystal glass dome on a hardwood base.

HEALING CRYSTAL DOME — $225 to $3,500 depending on type and valuation of gemstone crystal. Absolutely guaranteed genuine gemstone world-renowned for its healing properties. Comes in a dome with a hardwood base, totally gorgeous!

SUPERPOWER HEALING CRYSTAL DOME — P.O.R. — intended for a Healing Center, this is not for personal use. Comes with an entire Altar Setup, which includes expensive solid gold items and rare antiquities, plus a powerful and very rare gemstone.

SHAMANIC CRYSTAL DOME — If you are an experienced senior student, you may inquire about these items, which are not available to beginners at any price or under any circumstances.

Tuesday Night Massacre
May 10, 2017

Did I mention that Donald Trump is not only crazy, he's also stupid?

I grossly underestimated the level of bone that sits inside his otherwise quite empty skull. He fired the head of the FBI, right in the middle of a counterespionage investigation that included Trump and his staffers and aides, then he said it was because Comey had been "mean to Hillary", although Trump royally abused the quote from Comey to get himself elected.

How stupid is that???

When you take away the voice of the people, they take to the streets.

In his "You're Fired!" letter — acutely reminiscent of his television reality series in which he fired employees whenever the fit came over him — which was never delivered directly to Comey, Trump "casually mentions" that although he was exonerated three times when he met with the director on three separate occasions with FBI Director Comey, NO SUCH MEETINGS TOOK PLACE, and Comey would have been in direct violation of the law had he said such a thing to Trump at that time.

Guess what happened then???

Sean Spicer can lie for the President — that's his job. He's the Press Secretary. But Kellyann Conway is his legal counsel. She should know better, and she ought to have some inkling of what happened to Nixon when he did the same thing on a smaller scale.

This is a BIG ONE, and goes way beyond what happened in Watergate, because it didn't involve belligerent nations committing open espionage on our election process.

Gosh, I can't remember what happens to her, but she DOES get hers in the end, according to the Law of Karma, which I can't and won't repeal.

Although I can't remember my history lesson on Kellyann Conway in particular, and we don't have a lot of surviving information about this time zone, I do seem to recall something about "obstruction of justice" being invoked in this case, and I think she's somehow involved in that, although as I said, I didn't read the 37th century textbooks at all, and I seldom do my homework, but hey, my classroom and test scores are 4.0, bringing my overall grade to a walloping 2.4, if you include math and history, and they do.

So although I can't remember the details, I do remember that

Conway does have to answer for her actions in covering Trump's trail of corruption — oh, yeah, that's another heading I have in my school composition notebook under "to be verified", for which I have to take incarnation, which I clearly did, back in 1941, and here I am to tell the tale.

You might be interested to know that those black-and-white marble cover composition notebooks are very popular in my day.

I'll remind you that I am actually sitting in the HISTORY SIM STUDY HALL at the AKASHIC DATABASE, and I've taken rebirth inside the history department's terrific new simulator, where I can observe events and take notes, especially on this crazy hootenanny we see in Washington, D.C. on this history day, the Darkest Day in DOJ history

It's really stupid to destroy your investigating arm, your prosecuting arm and the jurisprudence system in general by attacking judges, prosecutors and directors, UNLESS you are a foreign agent, a sleeper agent, working to destroy our Republic, which you will soon be convinced has happened.

Even today, Trump is meeting with a dangerous Russian spy, and they will be passing secrets between them. If Trump has been compromised, there wouldn't be a better way for that compromise to be executed than to meet "on other issues".

One subject of this meeting is to set up a meeting between Trump and his Puppet Master, Putin.

Good luck handling this one. It's going to be a rough ride, and I can't guarantee that the Union will remain intact at the end of the day, going forward — I know, right?

All the robots will merely do what their instructions and programs tell them to do. You can't and won't change the mind, opinions, attitudes, beliefs or actions of a robot, so don't even try.

Arguing with reason will do no good. You are speaking to a brick wall. Only ridicule and the Power of Song and the Power of Prayer will have any effect.

I'm using my own special brand of prayer, something I dreamed up back a few dozen centuries ago, and I've employed it in "Oval Office", an Orb that allows you to channel Healing Energies and Waves of Enlightenment into the Oval Office, in a last-minute attempt to give Trump an opportunity to be an Enlightened Ruler, something you desperately need in these trying times.

DON'T PANIC.

Ignore all the hysteria, the fear, the rage, the anger, the accusations and counter-accusations, the shame, the blame and the finger-pointing of children who are playing with our lives.

Thanks to Donald Trump, you'll never be able to trust the Department of Justice again. By the way, it was DONALD TRUMP who ordered the firing, and who instructed his puppets at the Justice Department to "arrange a reason" for the firing of Comey, and all this will come out in time.

Anyhow, I'm always amused at 21st century hootenannies, and this date marks the most important DARK DAY in my history term paper, so I'm paying real close attention to the news as it breaks and making very careful notes, because this account might be the only one that makes it into my future, and I need my notes if I'm to make a good presentation back in San Dimas, where the clock is ALWAYS ticking.

So where does this leave us?

First of all, what do you mean, "us"? I'm a visitor, not from around here, have no interest nor much tolerance for partisan politics, which is all that Earth humans seem to be able to manifest, with each side trying to tear down the other, rather than get some constructive cooperative work done that satisfies both sides a little.

I have no stake in this fracas, and frankly, could handle it in a single minute just by taking a Near-Earth Asteroid out of orbit and ticking it slightly in the direction of the Earth.

Lest you think I'm bullshitting, ask the Apollo 11 astronauts how many taps they heard on the capsule at the halfway point to the moon, then check my published account of that Astral Journey I made back in July of 1969, for the benefit of my Cosmo Street students.

There won't be any compromise, because both Democrats and Republicans are assholes, incapable of adult thought and action, and they ALWAYS PLAY TO THEIR CONSTITUENTS. They're always posing for the camera, making sure they do the expedient thing.

Any compromise is BOUND to satisfy no one, when everyone is pulling in a different direction. What happened last night is a dark, dark day for American freedom, and as I recall, the Justice Department never does recover credibility, which is a great tragedy — they're your only defense against Dictator Trump, and if something isn't done real fast, he WILL become dictator and rule Amerika with an iron hand, like his friend Putin does.

It's very possible that Trump has an "Ace in the Hole" up his sleeve. He DOES cheat, and his cheating CAN and DOES include the betrayal of Amerika into foreign hands. He denies that the Russians hacked the election, but you can't, you mustn't, believe that he really thinks that they didn't hack the election.

He knows full well they did.

He's afraid. He's very afraid, even more afraid of being UNMASKED than of dying alone. It's obvious that the investigation is getting close, and that he's "feeling the heat", as it was described even on the very rigidly and vigorously far-right FOX News.

Many commentators both Democratic and Republican were actively denouncing this attack on the Constitution, meaning that I checked CNBC, CNN, REUTERS and FOX News, FOX being essentially a spokesperson for Donald Trump, defending every position regardless of how ludicrous, and the other stations glorying in victory.

There is no victory, and there should be no cheering. This is the blackest day in U.S. history next to the assassinations of Lincoln and Kennedy, and no, I'm not kidding.

In effect, the President just closed down the Department of Justice and rendered it ineffective and helpless ON ANY ISSUE. He can direct, destroy, fire, hire and totally negate the findings of the Justice Department, the FBI or any investigating body, and he can't and won't sign a bill that allows Congress to prevent him from doing this.

There is no way to trust the outcome of ANY investigation.

I'll bet you money that you didn't know that the President has to sign any legislation appointing an FBI Director, so if it's someone he fears, he won't sign him into office.

I'll also bet that you didn't know that the President can order an investigation closed, if he controls the DOJ and the FBI directors, but he shouldn't be able to fire someone in the middle of an investigating against him, and although he says that he was "exonerated" by Comey, he emphatically was NOT excluded from the criminal investigation, and history will bear me out — Trump will get caught with his hand DEEP inside the cookie jar.

Every Republican Senator and Congressperson who stood with him will go down with him when he falls, and fall he will.

FBI Directors have a ten-year tenure which guarantees that they can't be tampered with to prevent them from investigating or carrying out their duties. In short, they have autonomy, the first and foremost freedom guaranteed to the FBI Director and the FBI in general.

Theoretically, the FBI cannot be controlled by the President of the United States, at least not now, not under the present laws, but Trump has worked to erode the Justice Department with SIX very targeted firings, and has effectively slowed down the investigation — he's hoping he can last out his term before Congress can nail him.

Again, remember his television show and his fears, his needs, and his reliance on that audience to give him reinforcement. This is a very sick man, who desperately needs your help.

Can he get away with it?

Sure he can, if the Republicans care more about their jobs than their country, but in the end, anyone who supports Trump will go down in history with him. His name does not appear in the updated version of "Profiles in Courage".

Unfortunately, most politicians are NOT patriots. They're dirty, they're slimy and they lie, lie, lie to protect a President that they know is cheating, lying, stealing and committing horrible crimes against the people.

This is the man who wants to take $860 BILLION DOLLARS from the poor and give their medical insurance money to his 15 friends who appear with him in that notorious photo of his "Good Old Boys" money managers.

Corruption is the name of the game, and Donald Trump and his family play it well, to the ruin of the country, and like most filthy rich people, they really don't care who gets hurt.

Trump is a coward and a liar, and I can prove it really simply.

All year long, Trump used Comey quotes to get himself elected, then just as Comey is about to close in on Trump, Trump fires him, claiming the reason is the Clinton issue, which has been dead for months.

Sadly, no Trump supporter will ever hear what I say, and that's Trump's total strength — unquestioning loyalty from his True Believers, and they will be rewarded for their faith, but not the way they think they will. True Faith depends on Unquestioning Loyalty, the kind you see from Kellyann Conway — remember, she did warn you that she's a liar — oops, sorry, that was a typo. I of course meant "Lawyer".

If you sue me, Conway, I'll be happy to see you in court, along with a few of my ficus amicus friends. I know things, and can name dates, places, people, all with the power of Remote Viewing. With RV, I can dig anywhere, even in a protected environment. I can bust through a Faraday Cage, and come out with raw data. Wanna try me?

Hey — Remember Nixon?

He fired the guy who was investigating him, but keep this in mind — Nixon was a lawyer, too hip to balance the power of branches of government to go a step further and fire the Director of the FBI.

"I'm Agent I, of the FBI" — Henny Youngman.

Your biggest fear right now should be whether or not the three branches of government will stand or not, and that will probably play out today, within the next 24 hours.

If this government still stands, if the Republic still stands, it won't be from the efforts of Donald Trump. It will be from the cooperative efforts of the people.

Donald Trump is surprised at the outrage. They always are. They never get it until they see the torches, the pitchforks and the sea of angry faces.

Sure, Trump supporters will see all this, but to them, it's just a big Democratic Witch-Hunt, a fantasy, a non-event, fake news, and that's what they'll still be calling it when Donald Trump gets carried away in a strait-jacket or handcuffs.

When he yelled out, "Hillary for Prison," he pronounced his own doom.

I'm sad to see him go, but I'll quickly find someone else equally stupid about whom to write and sing my People's Protest Songbook which is normally $24.95 and comes hand-signed with a drawing and is ON SALE TODAY, 40% OFF while supplies last.

There's no reason to hurry — I'll be selling these songbooks long after Trump is gone from the White House, but I could use a couple of extra bucks to handle the increase in my Medical coverage — my entire Social Security check goes to cover my medical insurance, doesn't yours?

Hey, not to worry. If Donald Trump has his way, you'll have a cool job rebuilding a road somewhere in the middle of the Red States, where they need it the most and where law is what you wear in a holster on your hip.

FREE HEALTHCARE PLAN!!!
May 11, 2017

Cosmo Street Contact Orb is available for you to apply in your shamanic healings.

It's time for us poor folks to learn how to live without doctors, medicine, hospitals and clinics, because all the money for that is going into billionaires' pockets, including Donald "Take Advantage" Trump and Associates, but don't worry, their time will come.

In the meanwhile, why not take advantage of the fact that you are living in these computer times, although we're still only in the beginning stages of the computer-driven world of tomorrow — robots and nanotech, hypersonic and lightspeed personal vehicles and full-immersion video gaming, pocket tech and phone, pad, tab and flat hardware and incredible levels of new software that goes beyond the impossible.

That's the new world in a nutshell and, although part of this new world is a notable absence of healthcare for the poor and middle class — which is us — there is also a new world of video applications and quantum mechanics.

My new healthcare plan depends upon both, because I just can't afford a doctor without some healthcare plan other than "I Plan Not To Get Sick A Lot", which is my current plan.

Hoping not to get sick is not much of a healthcare plan, I admit, but it is one that, on ZERO income and ZERO medical insurance other than basic Medicare, I'm screwed, to say the least, if I want standard mainstream healthcare.

Fortunately, I don't. I have zero faith in doctors, especially the ones who grow rich keeping you alive while you're waiting to die.

The situation is hopeless. A Republican congress will never give the poor a break — we all know that.

We also know that on BOTH sides of the aisle, those bastards are 90% Politician and 10% Patriotic, so the votes will ALWAYS go along party lines, not conscience, and that in a nutshell is why the vote in Council went against survival for the human species, and I know I'm going to get a storm of angry letters when my asteroid smacks into the Earth fairly soon, but believe me, I know what I'm doing.

Ants are better.

Hell, compared to humans, I'd take super-intelligent ants anytime. I'm betting on the hardiest survivor of them all, the cockroach, to ascend the food chain to victory in the species department, but I'm not allowed to reset the species button.

How To Remember Yourself

Remembering yourself is easy, if you know yourself. You then merely locate your self and point.

Remembering Yourself is a little more difficult. First, you have to have the idea in the first place, then you have to define what you mean by "self" and "remembering", and finally, you need some guidance to learn the basics of Self-Remembering.

Suffice it to say that it's enough for the purpose at hand to remember — and for YOU to remember — that I'm a visitor here in the 21st century, a time-traveler, if you like, from the 37th century.

Actually, time isn't what you think it is.

Every time-frame sits motionless in the bank, until an Observer ticks it off and activates the chains associated with that time-space discontinuum — the one your Cursor is in now.

Your Cursor is able to shake its fist at the sky and yell "shit!", hence the name, "Cursor". I went a long, long way for that gag. I hope you appreciate it.

So it will help to remember that I am a 37th century history student at More Science High, here in the capital city of Mahzhong, home of the Great Mother Slime Mold and the chicken capital of Upper Caledonia, a country founded by a famous typesetter named "Clarendon Smith", of New New Washington, the city built right directly on the smoking ruins of Old Washington, during your Fourth or Fifth World War, I forget which.

I hate having to remember names, dates and places accurately, which is why I'm carrying a D-Minus, actually an F+, average here in school.

If I get an "A+" on my Term Report, my grade will zoom right up to D+, and I'll be able to graduate high school.

I'm hoping to be accepted into Wassamatta U., my college of choice, where I can study my favorite subject, Universal 3-D Design, with Professor Wasserman, the most popular Remote Viewing Professor on the college campus.

Of course, I haven't yet visited the actual university, yet — I'm not allowed to cross the street by myself.

So it's raining here, where I am, and I'm stuck for the next two hours of Objective Time here in the History Department Time Lab, where I'm seated at the controls of the BioTime History Sim, typing away on the little keyboard in the Earth Sim you call "home".

All Phenomena is Illusion. That goes double inside a History Sim.

Part of my Self-Remembering is that I am actually sitting here at the History Sim, not dwelling or moving about inside it, within the time-bind that creates the illusion of 21st century Earth.

Another part of my Self-Remembering is that it's all an illusion, and that the illusion is controlled by numbers, zeros and ones, and that I can call them off and use my skills in ordering them and creating a variety of combinations with them.

I can create gateways to any worlds I wish to visit.

With my crystal and radio technology, I can create my own healthcare plan which, along with a good diet, lots of fresh air and sunlight, but not to excess, and of course a discipline of prayer and meditation, assures a long and healthy and productive life.

Sure, there are aches and pains, but thanks to our Republican friends in congress, you'll be able to learn how to handle all your miseries with magic, or they won't get handled at all.

If politicians had their way, they'd take our prayer and meditation and spirit healing away from us, like they take everything else, but they can't, at least not yet, not so long as the Constitution is still in force.

Oh, NOW you get it. Yep, if someone can break the basic American Institutions, the Constitution will be suspended, leaving Donald Trump in charge.

Create Your Own Magic Healing Altar

Medical insurance??? You have to be kidding. We HAVE no medical insurance, just as we have no retirement fund, and we've lost our own homes and our IRA fund when the Big Bailout happened a few years back, and everyone I know is in that same situation.

There's nothing left for Old Age. Retirement is out of the question, and going to work from 9 to 5 has become impossible.

That's when you have to find an alternative to mainstream medicine, and I offer Prayer Power as a possible solution.

Keep your medical insurance, you butt-faced moron politicians. We don't need no friggin' medical insurance. We don't need no doctors. We don't need no medicine. Just get out of our faces and leave us our Angelic Prayer Power Healing Medicine Wheel.

That means stop messing with our Civil Rights.

506

Ignore All This Shit
May 13, 2017

That's right. Ignore all this shit. If I didn't write blogs, I'd never stare in open-mouthed drop-jaw astonishment as BREAKING NEWS actually breaks the BREAKING NEWS of a few minutes before.

Apart from the wild antics of Dictator Donald and the equally wild antics of the liberal media and the conservative media and the Just Plain Stupid media, we've been treated to the most massive cyberattack ever launched, and you might have been one of its victims.

If so, your software was all encrypted, and you saw a screen message holding your software ransom. If you paid $600 to recover your software, you discovered that they lied — you don't get it back, even if you pay them a million bucks.

In some cases, this will result in many deaths for a variety of medical reasons, economic reasons and emergency communications, resources and treatment, fire stations that can't respond, police that cannot respond to emergencies, and entire armies that can't march without information and communication.

Death and destruction will be the result, and the hackers will be karmically flushed down the toilet, but the damage will have been done.

They will attack every day from now on until they are stopped.

Russia is one of the countries targeted, although they are usually the source of this sort of violation.

There is really no way to permanently guarantee your software or hardware from future cyberattacks. Nobody can stop them, and they can evade the authorities forever — it's really hard to find and punish hackers, UNLESS you have a team of psychics or remote viewers.

For a professional psychic spy, it's nothing to spot the source of literally anything in cyberspace — it's all open to the Akashic Mind.

Lest you're thinking of learning the art of Remote Viewing and going after the hackers, don't even try. Apart from SMG automatic weapons, they are simple thugs, with nobody home, no driver, no passenger, just a car driving itself — the wave of the future.

So how CAN you use Psychic Sciences to save your software?

First of all, remember the phrase "Jesus Saves. Backup Often." Keep a copy of ALL your software separate from your computer and nowhere NEAR online.

Secondly, DON'T go after a hacker in the Einsteinian World — you'll be sorry you did. But there ARE ways to punish them with "INSTANT KARMA", using a simple TELEPATHIC PSYCHIC ITCHING POWDER that never lets up, itches ALL OVER and never stops itching.

You might prefer to give your tormentors the Mental Hot-Foot, a sure-fire gag that never gets old.

There's no money in revenge. That's what they tell you, but actually you can make a pretty good living from it, if you know how to fully exploit the revenge market.

That's part of my GORBY SCIENCE PSYCHIC TRICKS and JOKES shop, which I plan to open sometime soon. Let me acquaint you with just a few of my exciting new products which you can download and use right away. Comes with FULL INSTRUCTIONS on use — each Psychic Gag is operated by auto-telepathy, and is guaranteed to be FUNNY, FUNNY, FUNNY, and no joke over $6.99. Get the whole pack and save $$$. Not that you'll save money buying the tricks and jokes by the dozen — save $$$ is just good advice.

Gorby Science Psychic Tricks and Jokes

SPIRIT ITCHING POWDER —
MENTAL HOT-FOOT —
ASTRAL WHOOPEE CUSHION —
HUMAN BIOLOGICAL FART MACHINE —
HALL OF MIRRORS —
DOGGIE-DOO HOUSE —
NEVER-ENDING NIGHTMARE —
REAL VOMIT —
FLY IN ICECUBE —
CRUSHED NUTS SUNDAE —
MENTAL JOY BUZZER —
REAL BLOOD —
VANISHING INK CARTRIDGE —
GROUCHO GLASSES —
NOVELTY BRAIN —
DISMEMBERMENT BY HORDE OF DEMONS —
ETERNAL FIRE PIT —
HELLFIRE and DAMNATION —
BAD HAIR DAY —

I have an entire Gorby Science Hall filled with similar marvels of psychic science, thanks to the help of my Russian Psychic Intelligence counterparts.

We met at several Washington, D.C. Georgetown cocktail parties back in 1963, when I was a member of the Army Security Agency, which was then so secret that even the initials were on the "TSC Clearance Only" list.

I had for years been aware of the presence of Russian psychic agents — they were Astral Projecting all over the place, and I'm able to trace back "search signals" from any Remote Viewer operating within the solar system.

I've tuned it down. Receiving pan-galactic Remote Viewing pings was the second most overwhelming experience I've ever had on planet Earth.

The other was back in the 37th century in my Home Universe, which is safely far out of reach of Humans of Planet Earth, thank you very much, Lord, for that small favor.

Aliens? Yeah, there are aliens on Earth. Civilizations have been around for over 10 billion of your years in this local time-space discontinuum, and many of them trade humans, harvest humans and cultivate humans for their precious bodily fluids.

When you get right down to it, on a Universal Scale, it's all about enzymes.

I have a half-empty — or half-filled — Becker Aluminum BioCase with dozens of delicious enzymes that can be added to any planet's biosphere to good advantage, if you like giant beanstalks growing out of your backyard into the sky.

I'll bet you think I'm making a joke.

Well, I am. But enough joking, let's talk turkey here. I started out by advising that you "Ignore All This Shit", but which shit did I mean???

This Is The Shit To Ignore:

ANY NEWS PROGRAM —
ALL INFORMATION ABOUT ANYTHING RELATED TO PLANET EARTH —
ANYTHING ABOUT CYBER CRIME —
ALL INCOMING MAIL OR MESSAGES —
ANYTHING COMING TOWARD YOU —
ANY PUBLIC OFFICIAL ASKING FOR YOUR PERSONAL LOYALTY

Actually, that adjuration about the "fealty feature" doesn't quite cover it. Stay indoors, send out for anything you need, don't argue politics with ANYONE, even close family members, and do NOT go near malls, theaters, restaurants, shopping centers, fancy retail shops, supermarkets or package stores, department stores or public buildings.

510

Do NOT engage in conversation with people you don't know, and do NOT indicate any political interest in anything.

Keep a two-week supply of fresh water and food in your house, and recycle it constantly, to keep it fresh and usable.

It wouldn't hurt to have a can of dried beans handy, and if you want something to trade, cigarettes, chocolate, coffee and nylons are always on the top of the list.

If you've got some gold and you want to trade some of your gold for some food, make sure the person to whom you're trading doesn't also have a gun.

Don't join marches, demonstrations or political rallies, or town hall meetings. They are dangerous and will become even more so as the coming civil war rages on.

Reach out with your Remote Viewing and clear the path ahead of you on the timeline. If you're forced to evacuate your home and become an Amerikan refugee in a strange and foreign land, use your Remote Viewing to see any obstructions on your path.

Am I Red, Am I Blue???

ALL human beings of Planet Earth are chat-bots. Only a few dozen are occupied with students from Professor Wasserman's high school history class here in the 37th century.

Chat-bots come in only two flavors — RED and BLUE.

Everything in the universe is color-coded for my convenience. I have a LOT of tracers out there, and there are still plenty of bugs that I'm hunting down as I go through each time-frame in the SIM.

RED vs. BLUE
GOOD vs. EVIL
LIGHT vs. DARK
HOT vs. COLD
BIG vs. SMALL
ANGELS vs. DEMONS
YANKEES vs. DODGERS

Everything exists in some sort of dichotomy. All objects are split objects, each one with its own unique companion, all neatly tied together in a quantum-connected pattern that defies intellectual grasp.

Every particle is a snowflake. Each and every particle has its own ID, its very own unique shape and structure and crystalline pattern, and that goes double for you, if you're reading this.

Red Bots live in RED States or RED Countries. Blue Bots live in corresponding BLUE States or BLUE Countries.

Red Bots cannot understand, grasp or fathom the speech, thought-patterns or behavior of Blue Bots, and the sentiment is returned.

In short, you can't change a Red Bot into a Blue Bot or a Blue Bot into a Red Bot. They are hardwired to be what they are, rednecks and eggheads. Oil and water. You can't mix 'em up, but you CAN blow 'em up and burn 'em.

In the song, "Am I Red, Am I Blue", you wonder which side you're on, because — as you already know — there are no mirrors on the Dark Side Beyond the Veil.

Seeing beyond the veil is the skill you are supposed to be learning here on Planet Earth. Don't waste your school time on frivolous matters like "living" and "working". Ridiculous waste of time and effort and energy.

It's far better to just create a bunch of Prosperity, which leaves you a LOT more time for fun projects such as Self-Evolution and Climate Change — my hobby.

I LOVE to terraform a planet, then sell it.

Never sell the original of a universe. Sell signed and numbered duplicates in an edition of 50, then you have 50 potential customers for your original. Only then should you put your original universe up for auction.

Not THIS universe, of course. It doesn't meet the minimum requirements and as a high school student project under the direction of two of my classmates, Jehovah Jones and Methuselah Williams, it's really the property of More Science High.

However, I CAN sell you a previously owned sample.

In the case of the proceedings going on in Washington, as a Remote Viewer, I could easily investigate in Astral realms and along Magnetic Body lines to find information, but it's so much more expedient to merely turn off the television set.

Don't bother to try to "save the nation" or any such wild idea with Remote Viewing. Don't concern yourself with local politics — it will all go away when the sun goes nova and the Andromeda Galaxy collides with the Milky Way in just a few years.

They're speeding toward each other at roughly 5 million miles an hour, so check your watch frequently and brace yourself for the impact.

In the meanwhile, watch with amusement and TAKE GOOD NOTES.

Focus your fullest attention on the PRIME TEACHING spoken by Saint Rufus:

"Never forget that back in San Dimas, the clock is always ticking."

Actually, that's just a joke. When you get near the speed of light, time slows down. When you ARE the light in infinite extension, time stops altogether.

Maybe you've been wondering about that.

Starting time again is easy. Any action does the trick. Meanwhile, Remote Viewing can also help you to locate the universe in which you'll find planet Earth, if you've stepped out of the SIM for a short milk and cookies break.

Yeah, milk and cookies. This is high school, not college. We don't have coffee breaks in high school in the 37th century.

Hell, we don't even have coffee. You can't grow coffee beans in 18 inches of atmosphere, and there's nobody here to eat the coffee beans.

I just found out a couple of days ago that some humans apparently roast the beans, squeeze the water out of them and serve the result scalding hot with cream and sugar.

We'll be talking more about Remote Viewing and how it can help you. Using Remote Viewing, there isn't any closed door or file cabinet that isn't open to me. I can look ANYWHERE, see anything and moreover, you'll never see me doing it.

Using Remote Viewing, I can break virtually any story I want to. Don't believe it? I'll demonstrate my ability to see anything anywhere — not to show off — who cares? But to show you how to employ Remote Viewing as a tool for self-transformation.

Dashing off now to breakfast so I'll be in time for the workshop this A.M. — oh, I mustn't forget to answer that tweet from Uncle Donald (quack quack) — hey, how about a comic character named "Donald Dump"???

I just want to go on record as having mentioned what I call the "HOLE IN THE BUCKET", to wit and to woo:

Donald Trump claims that Comey told him he's not under investigation.

We learn only hours later that CENT is conducting a money investigation of Trump.

I really don't remember HOW it happens, but I remember clearly that it DOES happen that Trump is removed from office or something to that effect.

I can't recall whether it's as a result of being taken away by the Men in White to a funny farm somewhere in upstate New York, or drugged and handcuffed into prison, or by his own hand, or he just plain vanishes or quits or who knows what-all it was, which is how I earned my D-Minus grade in History, which is why I'm back here in the 21st century until I can round up some historical characters and bring them back with me to the 37th century.

I hope to bring at least one Hero of the Resistance with me to my Home Universe and Time-Frame, but it's a long trip, and I'm not sure I want to share it with Nancy Pelosi and Donald Trump.

I'm setting my sights a LOT lower, lowering the bar down to ground level here. I need some volunteers to go with me into the future to explain all this history we're experiencing right now. How about you?

Greatest Witch-Hunt Ever!!!
May 18, 2017

Cover screen from my latest non-violent action videogame.

Several Congresspeople got on the news channels last night after the appointment of the Special Counsel, and said that if Trump were able to keep his mouth shut, he'd be better off. No sooner had they said that, when Trump characteristically and obsessively-compulsively tweeted that "This is the Greatest Witch-Hunt in History!"

This is the same guy that, when a staffer wants him to pay especial attention to a written briefing, will include the name

"Trump" somewhere within the target paragraph.

A common complaint among politicians who have the guts to speak out is that there's no grownup in the room.

Trump is petulant, quick to anger, vengeful, suspicious and given to psychotic interludes in which everyone is plotting against him.

No matter — he gave me a hell of an idea for a name for my newest latest video game, so I'm entitling it "Greatest Witch-Hunt Ever!!!" and it'll be available for download as soon as I can finish the last scene, and get it through the edit-and-test committee, which is Grishy and myself, so probably by this weekend I'll have it up and running.

This is a NON-VIOLENT game, a game of chance and skill and in some areas a bit of superlative mouse-handling, plus a system of puzzles — you must correctly guess the nature and location of the HIDDEN WITCH, but can only deduce this from hints given by a series of HIDDEN MASTERS and GUIDES.

You are expected to UNMASK a series of hidden keys, mysteries, occult lessons and teaching entities are featured, all for the low, low price of only $6.99.

If you want to help disseminate this game, why not buy some of these for a few friends, or send a friend to our goddgames.com website.

Crazy Nut Job Trump
May 20, 2017

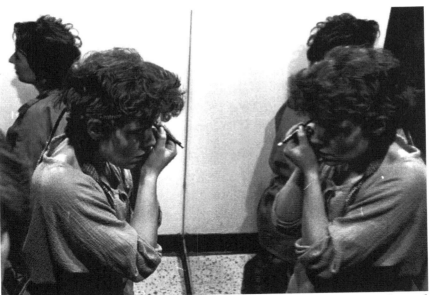

Mirror Mimicry Works Wonders to Penetrate the Veil and Unmasking of the SIM.

"Crazy Nut-Job Trump" is what they're gonna call him when he gets taken away in a strait-jacket, and he more than deserves the name. All his wounds are self-inflicted. Nothing would have happened had he not gone on the attack and fired Comey, haw,

haw — pardon me, Clarence, while I laugh.

And the most precious moment in the unfolding reality-show, "POTUS" came when we learned that the President of the United States actually confessed on camera to what looks like a high crime and misdemeanor to the casual observer.

I won't go into details here, just suffice it to say that THE EXPERIMENT is going well. I'll give you an important new exercise — new for you, if you're not among the Initiates in our Order of High Dudgeon — which will help you to achieve the First Goal,

Unmasking The Sim

The Unmasking Process can be triggered by a simple application of an age-old mime and stage comedy technique called "Doubling". I'll explain how it's done:

The best example of COMEDY DOUBLING you'll find in the famously filmed single-shot mime scenes created by the Marx Brothers during the 1930s, notably in Animal Crackers and Duck Soup, although they used the gimmick many times. You'll find the same scene repeated in an "I Love Lucy" episode.

Keep in mind as you perform this exercise that it's not to be taken lightly, nor used indiscriminately and repeatedly. It is a LIMITED exercise, and one that — in the Old Days — I would have insisted on transmitting only in person and only at the right time.

These days, you need all the help you can get. These are dangerous times, and you are NOW surrounded by many MILLIONS, not thousands, of Explosive Bardo Traps, not the least of which is what can happen to you when you take a well-earned vacation to see New York, New York, the most famous landmark of which is Times Square, a place I'd never recommend for a visit for thousands of reasons, all of which you'll find wandering around there like zombies at any hour of the day or night.

Here's Doubling Drill #1

Sit at your desk, or at a comfortable spot with any device that allows you to hook up to the internet or broadcast news. Make certain that it's a FLAT-SCREEN, not a CRT screen you're using for this exercise, or things can go terribly wrong.

Turn on the device and select "television news". You're going to tune in to the "CNN" channel.

Sit at a normal distance from the screen, head straight and eyes forward.

518

Park The Body.

KEEP YOUR HANDS ON YOUR THIGHS OR KNEES, palms down, fully relaxed. Do NOT move your hands during this exercise — they operate as "Pin-Connectors" through hyperspace when activated and controlled by the THIRD EYE, which presumably you've been tickling awake for the past several weeks, getting ready to perform this and other related exercises for the Third Eye which are to follow when you've mastered this first beginning drill.

STARE AT THE SCREEN IN TOTAL DISBELIEF.

This is important. You MUST invoke the INNER CHANT, "All Phenomena Is Illusion", and make certain that you BELIEVE IT.

If you don't thoroughly Believe It, you haven't worked the FOUR LINES Drill long enough or frequently enough or fervently enough or transparently enough to actually GET THE FACT that ALL Phenomena Is Illusion, not just "Some Phenomena".

You need to be able to at least comprehend the idea, but it helps if it has permeated every fiber of your Being, at least for the purpose of this exercise.

Well, technically, it's not an exercise. It's more properly called a "Drill", because you'll find a number of techniques and applications for this, especially in the field of Atlantean Crystal Technology.

Atlantean Crystal Technology is and always has been my specialty, along with Improvised Magical Weapons and Remote Viewing.

Think those are frivolous activities?

Then how do you explain the continued interest in Psychic Warrior Techniques and Skills in many of the major World Power Governments?

Even though they deny that any such thing exists, I can assure you, using very simple, very basic Remote Viewing skills, that several Psychic Warrior Activities exist today, one of which operates out of Arlington, Virginia.

I've encountered a few of their Astral Projecting Doppelganger agents buzzing about over their training compound at ...

No, wait. I can't reveal the location, nor the folks involved in this "HyperSecret" Psychic Warrior "Div 44" unit fighting it out in the AETHYRS over Washington, D.C. and other important defensive installations.

Call The Marines!

Yeah, sure, the Marines, the Army, the Air Force, the Coast Guard, the Navy and a host of other operatives in the Protection Racket that has formed itself into the military might of the Western World.

Big deal. I have billions of soldiers willing to do my every bidding and to shed blood for me, but what good does it do you, when gasoline is $10 bucks a gallon???

Of course, my military might is somewhat limited by the size of the screen and the speed of the micro-processor, but my military minions cost me NOTHING to support — a few pennies a month in electricity and the usual wear-and-tear on my computer keyboard.

Here's the Key to the Drill:

TURN UP THE VOLUME if necessary, to create the effect of the voice of the newscaster's talking head comes across on your speakers or ear-buds at about the same volume as your natural voice, maybe a little lower in volume than your own.

You'll get the hang of the volume as you use this important Doubling Drill, just the first of many you'll learn to use for the purpose of Unmasking the Sim, which is the whole point of living a life in the material world, or have you forgotten already???

Clear the Mind

Totally Clear your Mind. Don't worry about HOW to do that, just do it. Now that the Mind is CLEAR, empty the AM — Associative Mind — which is located to the back and side of the OverMind, and KEEP IT EMPTY.

If you're having a problem with this very basic pre-set action, you might need to take a workshop or two to catch up with the others.

Okay, now that the Mind is Cleared, you're ready to address the talking head on the screen. It's best if you find someone who is talking at about your regular speed of speech or slightly slower, so the natural tempo will be easy to achieve.

Go Limp

You need to do more than merely relax the body. You need to allow the body to go completely "limp", like a rag-doll, except that the head remains straight, eyes toward the screen.

Start Talking

Start talking with the Talking Head newscaster on the television channel, and just plow right along.

At first, you won't be able to do it at all.

Then after a while of trying — it shouldn't be more than a few minutes — you'll find that you can correctly "LAND" on a word or phrase bang-on.

Total Unreasoning Confidence

You have to have Total Unreasoning Confidence, and you CAN to make yourself totally confident without having to resort to the Attorney's Trick of using a powerful opioid to bring your confidence level up to "total".

No drugs necessary, just unreasoning non-doubt that you CAN do it.

What's more, you need to arouse and manifest the powerful non-doubt of the TRUE BELIEVER, and then when you're done with the Drill, you need to drop it like the hot potato that it is.

Never perpetuate a Drill beyond the Drill Space, meaning, "Don't Take Your Guns To Town". You'll never need this skill unless you're in the middle of a confrontation with a Bardo Entity, which is "at least once a day", in your present State and Condition, about which we'll talk sometime soon.

Unmask the Sim

Use the PEPE — Personal Experience Personally Experienced — to achieve a momentary "Unmasking" of the surrounding space, including yourself.

Empty Box

The Drill is effective if you achieve the VISION OF THE EMPTY BOX, which is an empty room observed by an "Outside" observer, which is YOU, having achieved a HIGHER REALM STATE, in your newly developing SPIRIT BODY, which will differ depending on what level you're working.

Right now, it'd be the Astral Body you'd want to develop, but this Drill can be adapted to virtually ANY level of achievement, to master the skills on that level.

This Drill is useful if you've managed to trigger off a RED BOT or BLUE BOT into a string of READY TAPE LOOPS.

The RTLs — Ready Tape Loops — are organized in batteries of eight.

When you trigger off the First Tape Loop, it automatically goes into a non-stoppable and thoroughly predictable PLAYLIST of words, sounds, actions, gestures, facial expressions and phrases.

You might actually come to recognize the PLAYLIST of a life-partner whenever you happen to trigger it off.

The less stoppable the PLAYLIST, the more the BOT is in control.

When you can stop the PLAYLIST from playing all the way through to the end and resetting at the top of the LOOP and running again and again ad nauseum ad infinitum, you've got a good case for calling yourself an Enlightened Being, but being Enlightened, you probably won't call yourself that.

Leave that sort of thing to Donald Trump.

Work this Drill until you thoroughly master it, with consummate skill and adroitness, or at least be convincing for a few brilliant seconds of mimicry.

That's it, the whole shebang.

I used this Drill in psychology class on a professor who droned his lecture in his sleep. He never could figure out what was going on.

Merely talk at the same speed with the same words as your target, and DON'T TRY THIS LIVE at this time, be patient.

Living Target Talking Heads are your next lesson, but there's a secret about how to do the Drill with interactive Talking Heads, meaning other people.

I DO NOT HATE TRUMP
May 21, 2017

Holy Prasad carries the healing to those in need. Bodhisattvas At Work!!!

To those who have complained about my recent blogs:
What don't you get about "I don't hate Trump"???
To put it bluntly, are you ignorant, unable to read, or just plain

stupid?

Either you mis-read my blogs on the subject, or you didn't read them altogether. Maybe you just read a portion of one blog? Perhaps you're just too politicized to hear simple straightforward words that describe something plain and simple, or you might be unable to understand literary English when you encounter something above the level of Preschool.

You might be far too comfortable with slick political lies.

Far from hating Trump, I think he's the best thing for the art market since Jackie Kennedy, and I intend to put fashions and jewelry out there in this high-end historic market as soon as I can.

Trump is for me a great opportunistic comedy target. What the fuck don't you understand about that? I suppose you think that if I play MacBeth, I have murder on my mind all the time?

So what about Trump? Do I hate him? No, I don't. Do I like him? What's to like???

If several people had not rather loudly complained — one of whom asked if I'd gone mad — I would have titled this article "Art Market Recovers to 1980s Levels!", but because of either inattention, blind loyalty to Trumpism — which in itself is no worse than McCarthyism — or just plain inability to grasp the meaning of my words, I had to give the first part of this blog over to explaining once again that I am NOT against Trump, nor do I hate Trump, nor am I blind to his attraction for his support base.

His support base is insisting that there's no there there.

The reasoning is that since there is no evidence of collusion, there is no collusion, which earns a very high reading on the Stupidity Scale.

Every investigation starts out with no evidence, but there must be probable cause, which is NOT evidence of wrongdoing or criminal activity, merely a signal that something needs to be looked at by professional unbiased investigators.

The Rabble-Rouser alarmists at FOX News grab their own headlines — "Attempted Coup". Do you folks at FOX News have any sense of karma? Do you realize that words like that could result in someone grabbing up a gun and...

Oh, I get it. You WANT an incident to happen. Why didn't you say so in the first place? And you're right — there's no better excuse to call out the National Guard than an eruption of angry mobs looking for victims to beat up and kill, businesses to burn to the ground and neighborhoods to disrupt and destroy for years to come.

Hand-Painted leather biker outfit, $3500 while they last. Signed and dated.

That will someday be the legacy of FOX News.

Myself, I want no part of any of it. I'm merely trying to show you how to write a protest song, a comedy routine and a lot of other things related to this wonderful situation. It's the most historic time you'll ever live through in this lifetime, do you realize that?

Maybe that's enough to get your full attention, maybe not.

Wynton Marsalis Art Backdrop Complete Set-up $2.4 Million.

The fact is that business will get better and better with a Republican government, and I'm all for that. The art market is important to me, because with the sale of high-end art, I can raise the $1.4 million I need to set up my Alternative Health Care Healing Temple here in Grass Valley, and I hope to set them up all over the country.

THIS IS THE TIME TO SET THESE UP.

By the time the people who are in a position to donate the money for this project, the time will have slipped away, and many people will die.

I have a solution — make a People's Health Care Temple, with spiritual healing practices. Forget about allopathic medicine, because the allopathic doctors have failed us.

526

6 foot tall architectural Backdrop painting used in famous performance, $1.4 Million, full provenance.

The Pharmaceutical companies have failed us and shown themselves to be untrustworthy and unethical, driving prices up because they can.

The Insurance sector is the group of greedy bastards that are driving the nails in our coffins day by day, eroding our health care and keeping coverage tantalizingly just out of reach.

Won't you donate generously to this project?

With YOUR help and the help of thousands of others on the ground-floor street-level neighborhood project, we can save millions of lives.

The spirit rules the body. I have shown over the years that it is possible to enlist the aid of angels for healings, and I will continue to show people how to achieve this partnership with higher forces.

I will be selling high-end art, antiques and other treasures donated for this purpose. If you have a collection, please send it so I can sell it and use the money to support this project.

A beautiful Greek style temple has become available and it would be perfect for the purpose. There is more than adequate parking — some 300 spaces — and it is located in the high-end district, making an art gallery and gift shop an attractive idea, along with a coffee shop for gallery or temple visitors.

I envision a full-time staff and full access, which is expensive, but I'll worry about that part. You take care of the building. $1.4 million will do it, and you won't be hearing much else from me until this happens, because a LOT of lives are at stake here, and we can do a LOT of good!

I intend to hire professional health care and nutrition staffers, specialists in addiction problems and more, but we will NOT use or depend on government help for this project.

We are on our own.

I have, in the bank, at the moment, about $150, with which I'll start the ball rolling. It doesn't take a millionaire or billionaire to make this project happen, just YOUR participation, multiplied a thousand times or ten thousand times, and that will happen, hopefully soon, before the need becomes overwhelming and we run out of time.

There is a deadline.

I didn't set the deadline, nobody did. It's just there. We need to buy and restore this beautiful temple, and that's going to take some time. We need to find the thousands to donate toward this project, and for that, we can't afford much time.

The people who help with this project will earn a great deal of Spiritual Merit.

Merit counts more than anything else toward graduation, the time when the constraints are off, and your spirit is free to return to the stars.

You'll never have another spiritual merit opportunity like this.

Thanks to Trump, the art market has opened up, and there's a LOT of buyer interest. I have at my disposal an entire art, antiques and antiquities gallery, and there's more than enough paintings in the collection to raise the cash several times over.

EVERYTHING GOES!

I'd rather not sell my Jackson Pollock — it was a gift, and can't be verified by IFAR, so it's worthless on the market, but is genuine nevertheless. I have an original DeKooning, in fact two DeKoonings, and hundreds of original Chagall, Matisse, Toulouse-Lautrec and Renoirs, plus one original Renoir unique work on paper that should cover the cost of the temple all by itself, if there's a buyer out there.

I'll sell ANYTHING in the collection, because this project MUST happen. If you have an ounce of Bodhisattva in you, you won't turn your back on those who need this alternative health care or get no help at all.

Please give what you can, and talk to others about this project. If we make it work, it can go nationwide.

Every other country in the world has some alternative for the very poor, but not the United States. Join me in this effort. Your help is needed.

How I Made $100 Billion in Headline Games!!!
May 22, 2017

"Wake up and live" is the idea for this exciting new business plan!

Here's what you do: find a slogan, meme, phrase, buzzword that is instantly recognizable and is currently trending, hash-tagging and flying about the internet on the social media.

The business team has a "spotter" who watches the news channels and finds a topic o' the day, and in addition, monitors the hashtags to spot the trending phrases.

Your building team now comes into play, using the formula of the Magic Phrase that you decided to focus on today. Here's what they should come up with:

NUT-JOB THE VIDEOGAME — An original videogame that covers the subject or not.

NUT-JOB THE BOOK — can be comedy, sci-fi, history, novelized history, fiction, etc.

NUT-JOB THE FOOD ITEM — A can of nuts re-labeled. Nuts are exempted from most county food regulations, but not all nuts, so be advised, check before selling.

NUT-JOB THE COMIC BOOK CHARACTER — Start a comic book either printed or in download format or both.

NUT-JOB THE CLOWN — Do magic for birthday parties and bar-mitzvahs!

NUT-JOB THE NUTCRACKER — Merely repackage a wholesale nutcracker.

NUT-JOB THE WINDOW-WASHER — Use the name for your home business.

NUT-JOB THE MUG — Make a graphic and put it on thousands of items on Cafe Press.

NUT-JOB THE MOVIE — Make a machinima and title it "Nut-Job" and post it on YouTube with one of our soundtracks — be sure to make it go viral, why waste the effort???

NUT-JOB THE BOARD GAME — A variant of Monopoly among thousands of similar variants, but this one is different. This one is YOURS.

NUT-JOB COPPER RING — A custom copper ring with a hardware nut as its stone.

NUT-JOB EARRINGS — A pair of earrings made with hardware nuts.

NUT-JOB BRACELET — A bracelet made with hardware nuts.

NUT-JOB NECKLACE — A necklace made with hardware nuts.

532

NUT-JOB UNDERWEAR — Create your own brand label. Use Cafe Press to fulfill orders. Thongs will also work here.

NUT-JOB MAKEUP — Crazy makeup set that produces that "Apres-Vie" Look.

NUT-JOB PEANUT BUTTER — Relabel a jar — it's political satire, and it's a novelty item, but it IS food, so DO check the law before you take action relabeling any food product.

NUT-JOB JAR OPENER — Brand your own jar openers — you can make them from rubber pads.

NUT-JOB NAPOLEON HAT — Easy to obtain wholesale from costume makers.

There are a million more ideas that you could tap into in order to exploit this or any other news item that is currently "hot" or trending.

Remember that your marketing is mostly on the first and second day, after which the interest will definitely die down.

Sometimes that's not true, but it's rare that a meme or trending item will remain on the "best-seller" list for very long — generally 24-48 hours and it's gone from the public mentality.

In the case of "Nut-Job", it isn't likely to go away anytime soon, and there will be refreshing bursts of renewed interest as the Presidential Wrongdoing Case goes limping along in the media.

Frankly, it doesn't matter what goes down, because Donald Trump never gets entirely beaten down — he always rebounds and comes out fighting, like the clever NPC he is.

Non-Player Character is what that means. If you're in the dark about NPCs, it's just that you missed a few hundred of my blogs and dozens of my books, is all.

Thing is, I spend a lot of time on those books and articles, and I'd sure appreciate it if you read them and didn't require me to re-write them every time the subject comes up.

Of course, if it's a memory problem, I'm glad to refresh you on the basics.

An NPC is your basic chat-bot, sometimes with additional powers to grant wishes, provide clues, weapons and upgrades to the character's level, armor or magical powers.

That's pretty much all you can expect from an NPC.

Trigger the NPC again, and you'll get a repeat of the cycle. Trigger it again, and the NPC will return to the top of the code and start all over again.

Interrupt an NPC and it immediately stops, goes back to the top of the code and launches the soundbite once more as if nothing had happened.

To the NPC, it's always a surprise, every day a new day.

My business model is simple. You need a team that consists of model builder, game level builder, backstory editor, dialogue writer, producer, director, storyboard and layout and animators, lighting technicians, particle experts and, of course, your lead programmer who writes new effects into the game engine.

Of course, you need to make your own game engine, as we did, so you'll own all the rights to the games and their content, including graphics, soundbites and layout designs.

Hey, we've got that.

Here are just a few examples:

Nut-Job Watch, SALE PRICE $74.40 Allow 2 weeks delivery.

Okay, you'll also need someone to take the products out through CafePress. That means ads featuring the wide variety of products that are available using just a graphic to launch hundreds of items, including:

T-Shirts, Men's and Women's Clothing, Plus Sizes, Maternity Gear, Dog Fashions, Long Sleeve Shirts, Sweatshirts, Hoodies, Pajamas, Tank Tops, Kids T-Shirts, Kids Baseball Jerseys, Kids Accessories, Baby Clothing, Bibs, Baby Blankets, Diaper Bags, Men's Baseball Caps, Men's Jewelry, Men's Scarves, Men's Neck Ties, Men's Designer Watches, Men's Accessories, Drinkware, Mugs, Water Bottles, Custom Art Flasks, Drinking Glasses, Shot Glasses, Acrylic Tumblers, Shower Curtains, Kitchen Accessories, Home Decor, Pillows, Bedding, Office Accessories, Area Rugs, Duvet Covers, Blankets, Hobby Buttons, Stickers, Magnets, License Plate Frames, Car Magnets, Posters, Framed Prints, Wall Decals, Photo on Canvas, Canvas Art, Clocks, Greeting Cards, Note Cards, Invitations, Calendars, Journals, Canvas Tote Bags, Lunch Bags, Messenger Bags, Tote and Shoulder Bags, Phone Cases, iPad Cases and Covers, Laptop Covers, all kinds of things.

Pretty nice, huh? And they are made to order, so you can create a custom watch for a single customer or many watches for many customers, charge however much you want. This was created in less than five minutes time on my part, plus about fifteen minutes refreshing myself on CafePress routines, which I haven't done for more than 10 years now. I have thousands of items up for sale on CafePress, if you're at all interested.

Not bad, eh? And I don't have to pay modeling fees, none of the hassles of manufacturing, none of the hassles of warehousing, and you can sell this out of a shopfront, at a mall or fairground, anywhere — customer pays now, then you deliver by mail. You're merely showcasing the items when you bring them to a street venue. You can sell these easily online on a number of sites including your own.

I have one of these jerseys, and it's as good as any you'll find out there — high quality, good endurance and craftsmanship — double needle tailoring does wonders.

This comes in many sizes, and again is a very well-made garment, 100% ring-spun cotton jersey, the real deal.

This is a terrific gift for that baby shower or BFF gifting when the TIME is drawing near, and you want to memorialize it with a Trump Gag T-shirt.

Nut-Job Tank Top by Gorebagg SALE PRICE: $20.99.

Wow, a Nut-Job Dog-Tag — there's something you don't see every day. This is not the limit by any means — there are thousands of items that YOU can make yourself with this technique, but remember that nothing sells on cafe press — it's up to YOU to bring the goodies to the public eye, and using slogans and trending phrases will do the trick.

Imagine the kinds of rings YOU could make with this secret! I'll be showing you how to do this step by step at the upcoming Memorial Day Workshop, so be sure to make plans to be there!

Nut-Job Baseball Jersey by Gorebagg SALE PRICE, ONLY $21.99.

Just A Few Ideas For YOU
May 24, 2017

E.J. temple Darshan heart pendant has a whole set to go with, $29.99.

This sculpted aluminum pendant comes to you complete with chain, and there's a ton more stuff that you'll find quite charming! Take a quick look at just a few items:

Charm bracelet with single charm pendant, only $25.99!!!

Here is a pair of Darshan earrings that matches the pendant perfectly,
only $25.99!!!

Charm bracelet with single charm pendant, only $25.99!!!

Here's a terrific oval ring with the Protective bountiful Darshan image, only $59.99!!!

E.J. Darshan glass tumbler, only $21.99!!!

You can use this Darshan apron to prepare your holy foods, only
$35.99!!!

Prosperity Path Alternative Healing Center Official Life Coach's Watch, only $89.99!!!

SuperBeacon Diagram Resonator Sippy Bottle, only $15.99!!!

SuperBeacon Diagram Resonator Soft Baby Cap, only $21.99!!!

SuperBeacon Diagram Resonator Watch comes in 6 colors, only $89.99!!!

Quantum Witch Resonator Ring, only $59.99!!!

SuperBeacon Resonator "Magic Arrow" Golf Ball Never Misses, only $17.99!!!

Front and Back Printed Racerback Jersey Top, only $44.99 — see next page for back photo.

552

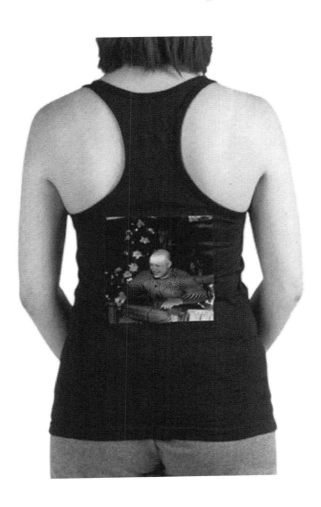

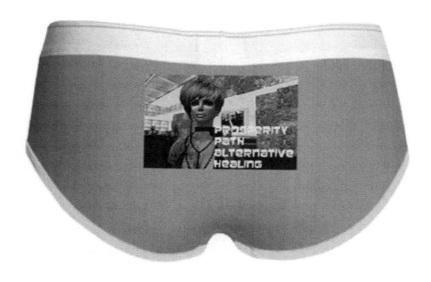

Prosperity Path Alternative Healing Women's Boys Briefs, only $27.99!!!

Oval Office Hip Hop ChatBot Demonstration Unmasking the Sim, only $89.99!!!

Atlantis Selfie Reusable Canvas Shopping Bag, only $18.99!!!

Okay, that's it for the moment. These are just a FEW of the amazing options available to you right now at CafePress. There are KING SIZE bed covers and you wouldn't believe what-all else!!! I've only got a few things up, but you're welcome to stop by the shop to see what's going on!

You can find my stuff on cafe press shops:

http://www.cafepress.com/prosperitypath
http://www.cafepress.com/branepower
http://www.cafepress.com/woodstockart
http://www.cafepress.com/goldmugs
http://www.cafepress.com/houseofegypt
http://www.cafepress.com/leslieann

The Truth About CovFeFe
June 1, 2017

My videogame transcends time and space for no reason whatsoever.

It's a simple task to convert any liquid to its magical equivalent, such as Lourdes healing water, or making wine into the blood of Christ, as any local neighborhood Catholic priest is trained and licensed to do.

It's such a serious matter that the wafers, once converted to the Body of Christ, are kept in the church in a locked vault until they are needed for the Holy Mass, lest they be stolen for use in a dark ceremony or worse.

What can be worse? You don't want to know the depths of barbarity and animalism into which humans can easily sink, but one example of that is the CovFeFe Phenomenon, started by Trump's now-famous tweet, "Despite the constant negative press covfefe".

Period.

Everyone thought he'd delete the obvious typo, but six hours went by, and he hadn't, so the speculation about the true meaning of "covfefe" went wildly around the Beltway tweeting bird population.

They never thought to look online, or they'd have found my videogame, "CovFeFe", which celebrates "Cafe´" with "Cavfefe", meaning "Cafe´ Press", of course.

So my videogame celebrating "Cafe´ Press" is clearly the First Cause of the Most Famous Trump Tweet in History, according to my 37th century history textbooks. When I first arrived, I knew I'd be participating in some way, but I never dreamed that my little game would make such a ruckus.

Of course, our 37th century textbooks are not actually books, not as such, not as you'd understand "books". Nobody has paper anymore, not even toilet paper, although we'd hardly have any use for that primitive material, and of course, after the Big EMP, nobody uses computers anymore.

"CovFeFe" is a composite word which translates in quantum physics terms to "covert ferrous fenomena", referring quite clearly to a state of incoherent light in a field of indeterminate darkness, which happens to all of us elderly folk now and then.

"Covfefe" is something that your weird Uncle Al might tweet in the dead of night, having fallen asleep in the middle of typing, hitting the "SEND" button as the fingers slip off the iPhone onto the tweet wrap.

I didn't want to burst an increasingly funny media bubble, but I just had to set the record straight. You'll find the word "covfefe" used in a 1964 political rant in "The Collegiate", the official student newspaper of Los Angeles City College, written by Isabel Ziegler. I have a copy in my files.

The word "covfefe" appears again with a reference to Ziegler in a published statement by Edmund Berger related to the White House Counsel of the period, and you'll find it in any basic book on Heisenbergian and Max Born formulae.

To cap it all off, you'll find my store, "covfefegame", on Cafe´ Press, and what's more, the shop has been there for over 12 years, so what's the big mystery???

STAY ON TARGET, LUKE

Holy Healing Waters Transubstantiation Flask Necklace, $29.95

So forget about all that Washington stuff, and concentrate on the task at hand. How to deliver healing services when the allopathic sector has closed down to the very poor, the elderly and the already quite sick?

There is no easy answer, particularly if you're a big fan of 21st century computer-driven commercial medicine, which is more or less on the same level as your average commercial sex — there's not much difference in how people are handled.

So, is there a solution for those of us who simply can't afford ordinary healthcare?

Sure, there is, if you're interested in angelic healing and receiving spiritual help for your healing process and the harmonization of your organic intellectual, emotional, motor-instinctive and spiritual centrums.

For that, you don't need money, just faith.

If you believe in spiritual healing, you'll know that there are certain "healing waters" such as "Water of Lourdes" and "Ganges Water" and of course, "Magnetized Water", created by exposure of very highly ironized well-water to a stacked core ring of powerful super-magnets — a slow process at best, but known by the ancients to be strong magic.

I've posted a number of different flasks, sports hydration bottles, all manner of liquid transporters and holders, and I'll post some more as I'm able, on Cafe´Press, under the general heading of:

Cafe′Press healing waters.

You'll find various containers for liquids, all of which carry imbuing and charging vigils, which charge up the tap water or well water that YOU put in there, so you get UNLIMITED REFILLS as long as the environment holds out, which is probably weeks and weeks, yet.

Each vigil carries the intention and energetic, as well as the "address" of the prayer-form and the general location and name of entities who may be involved in the healing process.

You will have to learn the various vigils if you wish to use several different ones. I'll try to organize a poster that carries all the varieties.

Keep in mind that transubstantiation is not a big deal — any shaman can do it, and just about any parish priest can do as well, so why not YOU? Just pour or fill the container and use it as you would normally use water — in short, drink it once in a while, keep yourself well-hydrated.

Let me know if there are any special prayers or invocations you'd like mounted on any of these items.

You can and should try any or all of them, or whichever ones appeal to you or strike your fancy or hit you in the gut or talk to you.

In short, go by instinct. It'll never fail you.

Instinct won't fail you, but "second-guessing" and "double-thinking" about your instincts WILL louse you up something fierce.

Okay, enough chit-chat, let's get back to work here. I'll talk more about this in the morning show today, along with the latest developments in Trump World, which is all the news there ever is, anymore.

You can re-read my blogs — they're all dated according to when they were posted — if you want to be amazed at some pin-point accurate predictions.

Here are a few more:

Look for the addition of several high-ranking congresspeople on the "suspicious" list.

Spicer will do something rather bizarre.

Nunez may be very dirty.

Jeff Sessions may not be immune to the drag-down effect of Trump.

You will see a strange and unexpected development of "covfefe".

Hey, L@@KY Here!!!
June 3, 2017

CornMandala Earring cornfield mandala embossing by Listed American Artist E.J. Gold. Used for shamanic invocation and healing, $25.99

Do you believe it??? I just spent the past eight hours massaging and uploading images and describing sections and items, and I've only just got half a dozen of the things up at the moment, which makes a grand total of about 2400 items for you to shop.

But wait 'til you find out what I've put up there!

Most of the items you'll find on my Cafe'Press Shops are things you couldn't buy for any price — some are part of our ancient relics collection which we use in our ceremonies.

Many of the art items are just plain NOT for sale at any price, and some are for sale, but for very high prices, totally out of reach to the average collector.

The whole idea in Rembrandt's time was to make prints, an affordable way of collecting the art of a favorite artist. Another bestseller of the time was to have the artist make up a set of "calling cards" with the art patron's face plastered on there as if they were someone important.

Generally, if you had Rembrandt do your Carte de Visite, you'd pay enough that anyone would be impressed, and he did turn down a large number of portrait commissions just on the basis of sheer ugly to the bone.

I've put up quite a number of important images, all of which carry the vibes, all are blessed in advance, and you get the full power of a RESONATOR which works with your SuperBeacon to produce the highest possible level of protection and power.

Every single item you add to your basic amulet resonates with it, forms a "standing wave" with the original waveform, powered by radio waves emanating directly from the Big Bang and Population III Stars.

It's a powerful combination, and everything works in cooperation — all the items are totally synergistic and THEY STACK, so you can use as many "HOOK-UP" items as you want to and can afford.

In short, there's an unlimited number of spell-stacking you can do, on top of the actual amulet — which you wear, along with any wearables from Cafe' Press, plus arrange any items around the house, office, den or shaman shed.

You want an inexpensive way to set up a shield in your household, to keep away the bad vibes of the Trumpies, plus whatever in-laws you've managed to accumulate on your way to grand-parenthood.

The thing is, every one of those items has SOME protective powers, and I'll be posting a large number of ATLANTEAN CRYSTALS and PARTICLE ACCELERATOR images, so you can apply them to your healing and remote viewing efforts.

Watch for the addition of many new items that were, up until now, completely unavailable and not even on display anywhere.

Some of the relics date back 36,000 years. Other items are amazing — off-world items from crashed UFOs — I no longer have the items, but do have, and have published elsewhere the photos I've taken of the wreckage I've examined.

Nothing says they're extraterrestrial, except the strange behavior of the skin metal, which hangs for a moment in midair, then gently and slowly sort of floats down to the floor.

Quantum Phaser Square Ring — quantum phaser — a powerful ring with a powerful energetic boost! $59.99

I've put up a LOT of stores, each one of which takes me about five hours to completely fill and identify the shops.

Healing Waters is just what it sounds like it is. Go there first. Note that YOU fill the containers, NOT ME, and the container imparts the imbuement all by itself, through the action of the quantum image, which is linked to an actual item.

GO TAKE A L@@K, for cryin' out loud. Don't miss out on this great opportunity to use shamanic tools that would otherwise never fall into your hands.

Covfefe Lives!

Dear Reader:

To find out more about books available through Gateways Books, contact us directly at:

Gateways Books
P.O. Box 370
Nevada City, CA. 95959-0370

Phone: (800) 869-0658
(530) 271-2239
Fax: (530) 687-0317
www.gatewaysbooksandtapes.com